YUGOSLAVISM

DEJAN DJOKIĆ

editor

Yugoslavism

Histories of a Failed Idea
1918–1992

The University of Wisconsin Press

First published in the United Kingdom by
C. Hurst & Co. (Publishers) Ltd, London
© Dejan Djokic, 2003
All rights reserved.

The University of Wisconsin Press
1930 Monroe Street, 3rd floor
Madison, Wisconsin 53711-2059
uwpress.wisc.edu

3 Henrietta Street
London WC2E 8LU, England
eurospanbookstore.com

Printed in the United States of America

Library of Congress Cataloging-in-Publication data
Yugoslavism: histories of a failed idea, 1918–1992/edited by Dejan Djokić
p. cm.
Includes bibliographical references and index.
ISBN 0-299-18610-5 (cloth: alk. paper)
ISBN 0-299-18614-8 (pbk.: alk. paper)
1. Yugoslavia—History. I. Djokić, Dejan.
DR1282. Y845   2003
949.7103—dc21   2002075665

ISBN-13: 978-0-299-18614-2 (pbk: alk. paper)

PREFACE AND ACKNOWLEDGEMENTS

The idea for a book of this kind probably first occurred to me when I began teaching a course on Yugoslavia's history at School of Slavonic and East European Studies (SSEES), University College London in 1998–9, together with Dr Peter Siani-Davies. It was thanks to the faith that Peter and Prof. David Kirby (Head of the Department of History at SSEES) showed in me that I became involved in the course as much more than an average teaching assistant. Lecturing on 'The Rise and Fall of Yugoslavia' gave me the immense pleasure of working with several generations of talented and, most important, curious students. They have often asked me if in my opinion King Alexander was a genuine Yugoslav or a Greater Serbian in disguise, if Stjepan Radić was a separatist or a true Yugoslav, if Tito could have been both an internationalist and a Yugoslav nationalist, and if Slobodan Milošević was really a Serbian nationalist or just a conservative Communist apparatchik. Were Croats always anti-Yugoslav and Serbs pro-Yugoslav? Could Albanians ever be Yugoslavs? I realised that it was not always easy to answer these and similar questions, especially when there is not enough literature in English (or in any of the languages of the former Yugoslavia) that would help students and scholars alike to provide answers to them.

But the opportunity to edit this book came somewhat unexpectedly. It was thanks to Michael Dwyer of Hurst & Co., the publishers, who was bold enough to approach a young and unknown historian, still in the process of writing his PhD dissertation, and offer him a contract pretty much on the basis of an article published in the *Times Higher Education Supplement* (my indirect thanks therefore to David Jobbins, who commissioned that article) in May 1999 during the NATO bombing of Yugoslavia.[1]

[1] Dejan Djokić, 'Individualism becomes the first casualty of war', *Times Higher Education Supplement*, 7 May 1999.

My thanks go to all the contributors to this volume for their hard work and for seriously considering all the suggestions and instructions from someone who is their junior not only in age but as a scholar and for more or less abiding by the timetable. But I thank especially Prof. Stevan K. Pavlowitch, who provided moral support and encouragement, and who read parts of the manuscript, including my own chapter, selflessly offering his expert advice and critical comments. I am also grateful to Dr Wendy Bracewell and Dr Peter Siani-Davies, my PhD mentors, who to my great amazement remain patient, supportive and, above all, good friends despite my work on this book taking too much of the time I should have devoted to writing the thesis. Peter's part has already been acknowledged, while Wendy's unparalleled understanding of Yugoslav national ideologies has helped and influenced me more over the last few years than she probably realises. My warmest thanks are also due to those authors who for various reasons could not take part in the writing of this book, but who encouraged me simply by considering their participation. They are, in alphabetical order: Prof. Ivo Banac, Mr Dušan Djordjević, Prof. Marco Dogo, Dr James Gow, Dr Miroslav Hadžić Prof. Robert Hayden, Prof. Marko Krševan, Prof. Predrag Matvejević, Prof. Paul Mojzes, Dr Branka Prpa, Prof. Žarko Puhovski, Prof. Paul Shoup, Dr Simon Trew, Prof. Stefan Troebst and Dr Mark Wheeler. I would also like to thank an anonymous reader for her/his expert comments.

More authors in the book are from Serbia than from any other ex-Yugoslav region, but this is not because of editorial bias: before approaching potential contributors I had in mind themes, not names. Of course, it would be dishonest to claim that I did not try to have as many of the former Yugoslav nations represented in the volume as possible (although I hoped that the authors would write as scholars rather than as their nations' ambassadors). Another reason for this over-representation lies in the fact that there are more historians working on the history of the Yugoslav state in Serbia than anywhere else in the former Yugoslavia. My regret is that there are not more authors whose assessment of Yugoslavia and Yugoslavism could have been more critical. With them included, this book would undoubtedly have been more complete.

I am grateful to Dr Ivan Vejvoda of the Belgrade office of the Open Society Institute for providing financial help which covered the cost of translating some of the chapters into English. I should also express my sincere thanks to Dr Nebojša Popov for allowing me to reproduce the two texts on UJDI, originally published in *Republika* (Belgrade), of which he is the editor, and to Dr Marko Ivanović and Petar Ladjević, who gave the permission for 'The Design for a Democratic Alternative: Final Text' to be reproduced.

My greatest regret is that Vane Ivanović (1913–99), a rare Yugo-slav and a democrat, is no longer among us, for I would have been proud to show him this book, not only because discussions with him made me understand the idea of Yugoslav unity much better than most books I have read. If I had been the sole author of the present volume, it would have been dedicated to his memory. Thus, only those sections of the book I have personally written can be dedicated to this great man.

The acknowledgement pages are usually a good place to thank those emotionally connected to the author/editor. I therefore take this opportunity to thank my family, especially my mother, for their absolute support and encouragement. As for women, I should prob-ably mention a certain C., because without the inspiration she pro-vided many things would not have been the same, including this book (although without her the book would probably have been finished earlier). My final regret is that she is no longer my muse, but it is perhaps only fitting to acknowledge her in a book dealing with a 'failed idea'.

While all those mentioned above by name, position, relation or initial, but above all the contributors, should be credited for the book's merits, I accept responsibility for its shortcomings.

London, November 2002 DEJAN DJOKIĆ

CONTENTS

Part IV. INTELLECTUALS

Part V. ALTERNATIVES

MAPS

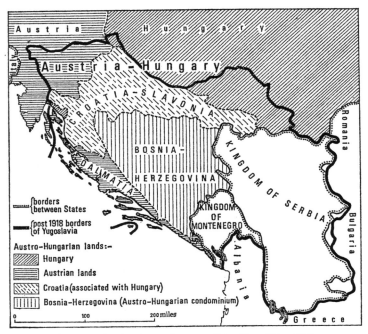

The Yugoslav lands on the eve of the First World War.

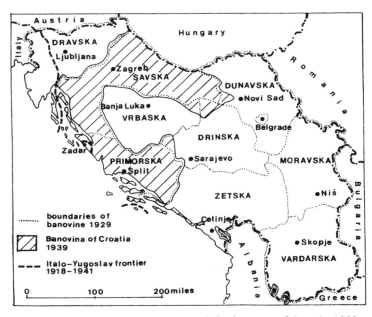

The *banovine* of Yugoslavia, 1929, and the *banovina* of Croatia, 1939.

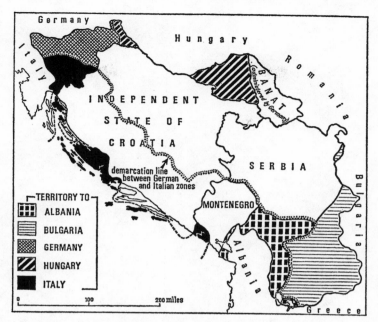

The territory of Yugoslavia during the Second World War.

The federated units of Yugoslavia after 1945.

INTRODUCTION

YUGOSLAVISM: HISTORIES, MYTHS, CONCEPTS

Dejan Djokić

In all the former Yugoslav republics the year 2002 was the tenth anniversary either of their international recognition as independent states or of the beginning of the war and imposition of international sanctions, or…both. However, the present volume, though completed and published in the 'anniversary' year, is not meant to commemorate anything. This is not only because ten years ago began a period most former Yugoslavs would rather forget. Nor is it because '[s]cholarly research and anniversaries [...] are not usually comfortable bedfellows', because it is 'in the nature of research that it rarely comes to fruition in time to be published on an appropriate anniversary', as the editor of another collection of essays written on a different but almost equally contentious subject observed.[1] This book is primarily concerned with Yugoslavia's life and not so much its tragic death, with what happened before rather than during the country's break-up and its aftermath, although the chapters by Aleksa Djilas, Jasna Dragović-Soso, Ramadan Marmullaku and Aleksandar Pavković address Yugoslavia's disintegration, while most other chapters do so implicitly. After all, the volume's contributors have inevitably written through the spectacles of the present, with a safe 'knowledge' that they were writing not just about a 'failed idea' but also about a failed state.

To say that literature dealing with the collapse of Yugoslavia is vast is not an overstatement. In English alone there are hundreds, if

[1] Paul Preston, 'Introduction' in Paul Preston and Ann L. Mackenzie (eds), *The Republic Besieged: Civil War in Spain, 1936–1939*, Edinburgh University Press, 1996, p. v.

1

not thousands, of scholarly and less scholarly monographs, edited books, articles, travelogues, diaries, memoirs and all kinds of accounts of the Yugoslav 'Balkan' wars, written by academics and non-academics alike (which is not to say that academics write 'academic' works *per se* and non-academics do not), by journalists-turned-historians and historians-turned-journalists, and by 'professional' and 'emotional' propagandists (the latter usually connected to ex-Yugoslavia through a spouse, a lover or, less commonly, a friend).[2]

Now that a united Yugoslavia has officially been consigned to history, together with its almost equally short-lived contemporary, the Twentieth Century, it seemed to the editor of this book that it was the right time for historians and other scholars to (re)visit it. The book's main aim is to explore the history of the Yugoslav idea, or Yugoslavism, *during* Yugoslavia's existence between its creation in 1918 and its dissolution in the early 1990s. It is a collection of twenty-one essays divided into five thematic sections: 'Context',

[2] John Lampe provides an excellent brief overview of the 1990s in 'Ethnic wars and successor states, 1991–1999', the last chapter in the second edition of his *Yugoslavia as History: Twice There Was a Country*, Cambridge University Press, 2000. Aleksandar Pavković's *The Fragmentation of Yugoslavia: Nationalism and War in the Balkans*, 2nd edn, London, 2000, is particularly good on the national ideologies and the way they were used by former-Yugoslav political and intellectual élites to legitimise the 'wars of liberation'. Steven L. Burg and Paul S. Shoup's *The War in Bosnia-Herzegovina: Ethnic Conflict and International Intervention*, Armonk, NY, 1999, offers the best analysis of Bosnia's tragedy, and Tim Judah's *Kosovo: War and Revenge*, Yale University Press, 2000, does the same for Kosovo. Perhaps the two most thorough general accounts of the disintegration of Yugoslavia are Lenard J. Cohen's *Broken Bonds: Yugoslavia's Disintegration and Balkan Politics in Transition*, 2nd edn, Boulder, CO, 1995, and Susan L. Woodward's *The Balkan Tragedy: Chaos and Dissolution after the Cold War*, Washington, DC, 1995, while Laura Silber and Alan Little's *The Death of Yugoslavia*, revised edn, London, 1997, is unrivalled for its documentary value, and Misha Glenny's *The Fall of Yugoslavia: The Third Balkan War*, 3rd edn, 1996, is the best account written by a journalist who was actually there. For detailed, useful and inevitably outdated reviews of the literature in English dealing with the break-up of Yugoslavia see James Gow, 'After the Flood: Literature on the Context, Causes and Course of the Yugoslav Wars—Reflections and Refractions', *Slavonic and East European Review*, vol. 75, no. 3, 1997, pp. 446–84; Sarah Kent, 'Writing the Yugoslav Wars: English Language Books on Bosnia (1992–1996) and the Challenge of Analysing Contemporary History', *American Historical Review*, vol. 102, no. 4, 1997, pp. 1085–1114; and Gale Stokes, John Lampe and Dennison Rusinow, with Julie Mostov, 'Instant History: Understanding the Wars of Yugoslav Succession', *Slavic Review*, vol. 55, no. 1, 1996, pp. 136–60.

'Nations', 'Leaders and Institutions', 'Intellectuals' and 'Alternatives'. Written both by established and younger scholars from Western countries and the region, as well as former and current politicians, *Yugoslavism* offers a unique perspective on Yugoslavia's political, social, diplomatic and economic history, and provides a background to the wars of the 1990s and (early?) 2000s.

There were of course difficulties presented by a (relative) lack of temporal and emotional distance. As will become clear to the reader, not all contributors managed to distance themselves equally from their own prejudices. Perhaps this would have been inevitable even if nearly half the contributors had not personally experienced the disintegration of Yugoslavia and the consequent wars, and others had not also been closely involved, personally and/or professionally, with the region, including the book's editor. In addition to being a secondary source of scholarly standard, this book thus might in time also provide a useful insight into the state of the academic community in the former Yugoslavia and the West only ten years after Yugoslavia's collapse. If the past, distant or recent, is the historian's 'Other', then the former-Yugoslavia represented the 'Other' to the contributors of the present volume. But the volume's title, *Yugoslavism*, is not meant merely to echo that of Edward Said's classic work[3]—it above all suggests that stereotypical conceptions about Yugoslavia cannot not be easily avoided, even in a volume of this kind.

This book also does not venture much into the history of Yugoslavism before the creation of Yugoslavia in 1918, with the obvious and necessary exception of Dennison Rusinow's introductory chapter and Ljubinka Trgovčević's contribution. Introductory sections of all chapters in Part II and Dejan Djokić's chapter in Part III also offer brief accounts of Yugoslavism before Yugoslavia. History of the Yugoslav idea before Yugoslavia's unification has been the subject of a number of works, the most useful of which are cited by Rusinow (although this is not to suggest that there is no need for further study of the origins of Yugoslavism). However, very few

---

[3] Edward Said, *Orientalism: Western Conceptions of the Orient*, London, 1978. However, I am not suggesting that Yugoslavism was a product of cultural imperialism or that it was invented from outside, as in the case of Said's 'Orient'. Which is not to say that external stereotypes and misunderstandings of Yugoslavia and Yugoslavism have never existed—they have and they do, as is suggested by Aleksa Djilas in his chapter.

scholars have looked at Yugoslavism *during* the entire existence of
the Yugoslav state (1918–92)[4], and it is here that this book aims
to fill a significant gap. Its overall contention is that Yugoslavism
was a fluid concept, understood differently at different times by different Yugoslav nations, leaders and social groups. There was no
single definition of who and what was (or was not) 'Yugoslav', and
this perhaps indirectly contributed to the ultimate failure of the
Yugoslav idea and with it the Yugoslav state.

The idea of Yugoslav unity, originally based on the notion of
Serbo-Croat linguistic unity propounded by Croat 'Illyrianists' in
the 1830s, was almost a century old when the Kingdom of Serbs,
Croats and Slovenes (in 1929 renamed Yugoslavia) was created in
1918. Dennison Rusinow provides a concise overview of its history,
arguing that before 1918 Yugoslavism was 'a more complex, convoluted, and as an ideological-political movement by itself less important factor than in the portrait of an evolving but essentially single-
minded idea…that is painted in most Yugophil and Yugo-nostalgic
historiography.' Yet, as Rusinow rightly points out, the Yugoslav
idea, just like the Yugoslav state, was not an 'artificial' idea, as is now
fashionably claimed—certainly it was not less 'natural' than other

---

[4] With the exception of Andrew B. Wachtel's study of cultural Yugoslavism in
both inter-war and post-1945 Yugoslavia, *Making a Nation, Breaking a Nation:
Literature and Cultural Politics in Yugoslavia*, Stanford, CA, 1998. Ivo Banac in *The
National Question in Yugoslavia: Origins, History, Politics*, 4th edn, Ithaca, NY, 1994,
and Paul S. Shoup in *Communism and the Yugoslav National Question*, New York,
1968, deal with Yugoslavism in the formative years of the first and second
Yugoslavias, respectively, while Aleksa Djilas provides an account of the Yugoslav
Communists' changing attitudes to the national question in the inter-war, war
and immediate post-war periods in his *The Contested Country: Yugoslav Unity and
the Communist Revolution, 1919–1953*, 3rd edn, Cambridge, MA, 1996. In addition to the work of Banac, Dimitrije Djordjević's edited volume *The Creation of
Yugoslavia, 1914–1918*, Santa Barbara, CA, 1980, and Ivo J. Lederer, *Yugoslavia
at the Paris Peace Conference: A Study in Frontier-Making*, New Haven, CT, and Lon-
don, 1963, also examine Yugoslavia's formation. Lampe's general history of
Yugoslavia built on several well-known predecessors, most notably Stevan
K. Pavlowitch's *Yugoslavia*, London, 1971, and *The Improbable Survivor: Yugoslavia
and its Problems, 1918–1988*, London, 1988, Fred Singleton's *A Short History of the
Yugoslav Peoples*, Cambridge University Press, 1985, and Wayne S. Vucinich (ed.),
Contemporary Yugoslavia: Twenty Years of Socialist Experiment, Berkeley, CA, 1969.
Two welcome recent additions to the existing literature on Yugoslavia's history
have been John Allcock's all-encompassing *Explaining Yugoslavia*, London, 2000,
and Leslie Benson's useful *Yugoslavia: A Concise History*, London, 2001.

national(ist) ideologies, including the Serbian and Croatian ones. By the time of Yugoslavia's creation there emerged two strands of Yugoslavism: 'integral Yugoslavism', which recognised no differences between the Yugoslav 'tribes' (at that time Serbs, Croats and Slovenes) or superseded any differences between them which might have existed, and Yugoslavism which, in Rusinow's words, 'acknowledged and approved enduring separate nationhoods and sought federal and other devices for a multi-national state of related peoples with shared interests and aspirations.'

Despite the strong appeal of the Yugoslav idea(s) at the beginning of the twentieth century, not many Yugoslavs and non-Yugoslavs imagined that there would be a unified Yugoslav state by the end of the First World War, as is argued by both Kosta St. Pavlowitch and Ljubinka Trgovčević. The Serbian wartime government and the Habsburg South Slav leaders both desired a unified state, but the two sides had (in the words of Kosta Pavlowitch) at times 'used Yugoslavism as an extension of their own aspirations, and both had expected to carry out unification on their own terms, within the framework of their own historical agendas'. Particularly illuminating, especially in the light of popular claims to the contrary, is Pavlowitch's contention that although Yugoslav unification had come somewhat unexpectedly to everyone, at the end it was the only option acceptable to all and there was no real alternative: neither a 'Greater Serbia' nor a mini, Croat-dominated 'Habsburg Yugoslavia' was really possible. Yet Yugoslavia was created by Yugoslavs themselves and not by the Great Powers, who had waited several months before recognising the act of unification of 1 December 1918, as Andrej Mitrović reminds us in his chapter dealing with the Paris Peace Conference and international diplomacy *vis-à-vis* the Yugoslav question during the First World War and its immediate aftermath. Mitrović dismantles popular myths related to the role of the then 'international community' in the creation of the Kingdom of Serbs, Croats and Slovenes.

Unlike their political leaders, the South Slav intellectuals were not interested in a domination of one centre over another—the argument shared by Trgovčević and Andrew B. Wachtel. Trgovčević's chapter fills a hitherto existing gap in English literature regarding the attitude of Serbian intelligentsia towards the unification of Yugoslavia: as she clearly shows, there were several pro-Yugoslav groups among prominent Serb intellectuals, including the federalists and republicans—the two political concepts usually associated within the former-Yugoslav framework exclusively with Croats (and Slovenes). Wachtel's parallel examination of the Yugoslavism of the two great Bosnian- and Catholic-born Yugoslav 'prophets', the sculptor Ivan Meštrović and writer Ivo Andrić, is equally illuminating and offers a unique insight into (interwar) Yugoslavism.

Different Yugoslav nations had different experiences in Yugoslavia and consequently different views of their life in it. Throughout the nineteenth century the Serbs showed little interest in the Yugoslav ideas of 'Illyrianists' and their successors, since they had their own 'liberation and unification' to carry out. The unification of Serbia and Montenegro, the only two South Slav states to achieve independence before the creation of Yugoslavia, was considered in Belgrade and Cetinje ahead of the unification of all Yugoslavs, even though the Montenegrin Prince Bishop and poet Peter II (better known as Njegoš) in the 1840s and Serbian Prince Michael Obrenović in the 1860s were among early advocates of a South Slav cooperation, as Stevan K. Pavlowitch shows in his chapter. The Serbs eventually came to accept the Yugoslav state, and played a major role in the creation of both Yugoslavias. Pavlowitch takes an overview of the modern history of Serbia, Montenegro, and Yugoslavia, tracing all the main developments in this complex inter-relationship which remains relevant while Serbia and Montenegro constitute the Federal Republic of Yugoslavia—a union that faces a highly uncertain future.

Although the development of Croatism and Yugoslavism cannot be easily separated since they went hand in hand, the Croats grew increasingly disillusioned with the Serb-dominated Yugoslav kingdom which, as Tihomir Cipek argues, stripped Croatia of state symbols it had managed to preserve during centuries of Hungarian and Austrian rule. The Croats had more reasons to accept the Communists' Yugoslavia, in which Croatia was one of the six socialist republics, but the renewed Serbian nationalism of Slobodan Milošević, in Cipek's view, finally forced it to leave Yugoslavia and seek integration into West European institutions.

The Slovenes, which besides the Serbs and Croats was the only Yugoslav group to have developed its national identity before Yugoslavia, accepted the Yugoslav unification as well as the unitarist

Yugoslavism with great enthusiasm, as Mitja Velikonja shows. He argues that the modern identity of Slovenes cannot be understood without an analysis of Slovenia's 'Yugoslav century', and concludes that the Slovenes played an integral part in the creation, development and ultimate dissolution of the Yugoslav state.

Although there is little evidence that Bosnian Muslims were interested in the Yugoslav idea, which was essentially the idea of Christian, Serb-Croat-Slovene unity, they became enthusiastic supporters of the common Yugoslav state once it had been created, as Xavier Bougarel convincingly argues. Throughout the period, the Muslim Slavs of Bosnia-Herzegovina accepted Yugoslavism and Yugoslavia as the best protection against both Serbian and Croatian nationalist claims—a trend abandoned only in the early 1990s by the Party of Democratic Action (SDA) led by Alija Izetbegović, the first president of independent Bosnia. In Bougarel's view, the SDA decision to risk and even sacrifice Bosnia's territorial unity in exchange for independence for its Muslim community had tragic consequences for both the Muslims and Bosnia as a whole.

Yugoslav Macedonians and Albanians were incorporated into the Kingdom of Serbs, Croats and Slovenes as part of the pre-existing independent Serbian kingdom. Macedonians were considered 'Southern Serbs' throughout the interwar period, and Albanians—predominantly Muslim non-Slavs—remained second-class citizens during much of Yugoslavia's existence. However, as Hugh Poulton shows, at the time of Yugoslavia's dissolution, the Macedonians reluctantly left and the Slovenians were held against their will in what remained of Yugoslavia (Serbia-Montenegro), and in the newly independent Macedonia. Although both experienced 'national affirmation' in Tito's Yugoslavia, the Macedonians, as South Slavs, were given their own socialist republic, while the large Albanian minority in Serbia could not achieve more than a high degree of autonomy for Kosovo—and in Macedonia, where Albanians today form around one third of the population, not even that.

Various versions of the 'integral' (unitarist-centralist) and anti-centralist Yugoslavisms—the two main strands of Yugoslavism, which according to Rusinow had emerged even before the creation of Yugoslavia—would clash both in the 'first' and 'second' Yugoslavias, as the chapters by Dejan Djokić and Dejan Jović respectively show. While Djokić examines the Yugoslavism of the interwar period, particularly the 'integral' Yugoslavism of King Alexander, and Jović concentrates on Tito and Kardelj's different concepts of 'socialist' Yugoslavism, they both argue that political contests in the two Yugoslavias more often than not ignored ethnic boundaries. In other words, it would be too simplistic to reduce Yugoslavia's seemingly perennial crises to the Serbo-Croat or any other inter-ethnic conflict.

Could more emphasis on an economic union have created a viable state-building rationale for Yugoslavia? Would economic integration have succeeded where attempts to impose from above ethnic and ideological unity in the Kingdom and the Socialist Republic, respectively, failed? John R. Lampe believes that despite numerous problems in integrating diverse and differently developed economies, after the destruction of the two World Wars, there was a genuine promise of economic integration which could have created a more viable Yugoslav state.

Radmila Radić offers a valuable overview of the interrelationship of Yugoslavia's three main religious groups, Orthodox Christians, Roman Catholics and Sunni Muslims with each other and with the state. She argues that the three religious communities never established a genuine mutual cooperation during the existence of Yugoslavia, and suggests that this was perhaps an important factor behind the country's ultimate failure. If the religious groups were usually seen by Yugoslav governments as potentially destructive factors, the army of both Yugoslavias was regarded, on the other hand, as the best guarantor of the country's unity. Mile Bjelajac provides a detailed account of the attempts to make the army in both Yugoslavias truly Yugoslav. He also examines Draža Mihailović's 'Yugoslav Army in the Homeland' (better known as the Četniks), in fact a diverse guerrilla movement and a successor of the (royal) Yugoslav army.

Yugoslavism, like all national ideologies, was created and ultimately also destroyed by intellectuals. The already mentioned contributions by Trgovčević and Wachtel are complemented in Part IV of the book with chapters by Aleksandar Pavković and Jasna Dragović-Soso. Pavković analyses three main variants of (utopian) Yugoslavism among Serb intellectuals in late- and post-socialist Yugoslavia, as exemplified by the writer Dobrica Ćosić's 'Yugoslav federalism',

Yugoslavism as 'a community of languages' as once propagated by the historian Milorad Ekmečić, and Yugoslavism as 'a federation of regions' as formulated by a group of pro-Yugoslav intellectuals gathered around a project led by Boris Vukobrat in the early 1990s. Jasna Dragović-Soso analyses the decisive crisis of the 1980s, particularly the Kosovo issue and the Serb-Slovene conflict, through the collapse of the Yugoslav Writers' Union. The end of the Writers' Union, which ceased to exist in 1989, was clearly linked to the end of Yugoslavia. It failed to create 'a genuine alternative to Yugoslavia's moribund communist system and negotiate a democratic, compromise solution to the country's complex "national question"' thus, as Dragović-Soso argues, setting 'a precedent for the disintegration of the common state'.

Not that there were no alternatives to the attempts to solve Yugoslavia's national question made in the post-1945 period. Desimir Tošić, himself a founding member of the Democratic Alternative, writes of the alternative Yugoslavism of this group of pro-Yugoslav émigré democrats, which was equally critical of the official Yugoslavism of the interwar period and of the Communists' national policies, as well as of the nationalist Serb and Croat diasporas. Tošić's introductory piece on the Democratic Alternative is followed by the text of the group's final proposal of 1982, 'The Design for a Democratic Alternative: Final Text'. If the Democratic Alternative offered an alternative from abroad, the Association for Yugoslav Democratic Initiative (UJDI) founded in 1989 by former-Yugoslavia's anti-nationalist intellectual élite, did so from within the country. 'Introductory Remarks' by Branko Horvat, the President of the Council of the UJDI, as well as a 'Manifesto for a Yugoslav Democratic Initiative', are published for the first time in English.

The book ends with two personal essays. Ramadan Marmullaku offers an account of Kosovo Albanians' experience in Yugoslavia, which to some extent goes together with Hugh Poulton's contribution: he argues that despite being, for the most part, *de facto* second-class citizens, most Kosovo Albanians did accept the Yugoslav state during the short period in the 1970s and early 1980s when they enjoyed full political and cultural autonomy within Serbia and Yugoslavia. He also draws on his personal experience as a Yugoslav diplomat to offer some hitherto unknown or little-known details from Kosovo and Yugoslavia's post-1945 history.

With his 'Funeral Oration for Yugoslavia' Aleksa Djilas provides erudite and thought-provoking afterword. He laments Yugoslavia and is not reluctant to state that his 'Yugonostalgia is improving all the time', yearning not so much for what Yugoslavia was 'but even more so for what it might have been.' Djilas is critical of the West's often hypocritical, biased or superficial attitudes to the former Yugoslavia and its successor states, but he does not free the Yugoslavs themselves of their responsibility for the destruction of the common state:

Let us hope that the time is not far away when many 'former Yugoslavs' will realize that the civil war we fought was against ourselves and our future. Than we can transform the South Slav peace into something more than the absence of war: open borders for visitors and goods, economic cooperation, cultural exchanges, respect for differences and an end to denial of similarities, common search for historical truth, solidarity and common voice on regional and European issues. In this way we will both build a monument to Yugoslavia and raise it from the dead.

Part I. CONTEXT

THE YUGOSLAV IDEA BEFORE YUGOSLAVIA[1]

Dennison Rusinow

Historians are almost as inclined as social scientists to interpretations based on the logic of *post hoc, propter hoc*: what happens has its causes, which can be discovered and analyzed, and becomes to some degree the 'inevitable' consequence of these causes. Thus there is a tendency in studies of and following the second death of Yugoslavia, and with it the second death of the Yugoslav idea, to regard these as the ultimately inevitable consequences of the 'artificiality' of the Yugoslav state and Yugoslavism (presumably in contrast to the 'naturalness' of a nation-state and nationalist ideologies?). Yugoslavia was a doomed creation—in the words of a kind of litany I heard frequently in Slovenia in 1989 and often in Croatia and Serbia by the following year, 'a seventy-year-old mistake that should finally be rectified.'[2]

Conversely, historiography in the lifetime of both Yugoslavias correspondingly tended to view Yugoslavia as a viable (if always problematic) proposition,[3] Yugoslav unity as 'the best solution' and even 'the most natural possibility,'[4] and the Yugoslav idea as a powerful

---

[1] Portions of this introductory essay have been adapted from Dennison Rusinow, 'The Yugoslav Peoples' in Peter Sugar (ed.), *Eastern European Nationalism in the Twentieth Century*, Washington, DC, 1995, pp. 305–411.

[2] Originally cited in Dennison Rusinow, 'To Be or Not to Be? Yugoslavia as Hamlet', *Field Staff Reports*, 1990–91/No. 18, p. 3.

[3] Thus both the title and text of Stevan K. Pavlowitch's *The Improbable Survivor— Yugoslavia and Its Problems: 1918–1988*, Columbus, OH, 1988, implicitly assumed that Yugoslavia would somehow and improbably continue to exist in some form.

[4] Gale Stokes, 'Yugoslavism in the 1860s?' in *Southeastern Europe*, I, 2 (1974), p. 126, quoting Vasilije Krestić, *Hrvatsko-ugarska nagodba 1868. godine*, Belgrade, 1969, p. 334, to make the same point.

explanatory factor in its creation and maintenance that merits serious (and approving?) study for that reason. Yugoslavia happened (twice), the Yugoslav idea preceded it (as 'brotherhood and unity' on the second occasion), *ergo*...

The Yugoslav idea, as 'Illyrianism' and then 'Yugoslavism', was indeed a century old when it was realized in the first Yugoslavia (which is how people even then usually referred to what was formally the Kingdom of Serbs, Croats, and Slovenes until 1929). It was indeed also a significant factor (cause?) in the creation and maintenance of two Yugoslavias. However, recent and critical studies[5] suggest that it was a more complex, convoluted, and as an ideological-political movement by itself less important factor than in the portrait of an evolving but essentially single-minded idea, grabbing a widening circle of South Slav minds and energies, that is painted in most Yugophil and currently Yugo-nostalgic historiography.

This does not mean that the Yugoslav idea does not merit the serious examination it has received and is again receiving in this volume—or that it and Yugoslavia were not a Good Idea and 'the best solution' to the problems raised by confrontation between the ethno-religious and linguistic mosaic and the national aspirations of the South Slavs in 'the age of nationalism'. Especially if this last may be a valid judgment, and arguably applicable to other parts of the world, why the Yugoslav idea 'failed' is an important question. The search for answers must logically begin with the history of 'Yugoslavism before Yugoslavia.'[6]

The core Yugoslav idea, first formulated in the 1830s by the 'Illyrianist awakeners' (mostly Croats, with Ljudevit Gaj as their chief ideologist), held that the South (*Jugo-*) Slavs, having the same origin and speaking variants of basically the same language, are actually or potentially a single people or nation and consequently endowed with a 'natural right' to independence and unity in a state of their own. In the century before the creation of the first Yugoslavia this core idea would appear in a variety of forms, guises, and combinations with other state- and nation-building ideas in various times and places. In the end its most important contribution to the

[5] Including mostly English-language sources cited and quoted in this essay.
[6] The subtitle of Lenard Cohen's concise and useful summary of the subject in his *Broken Bonds: The Disintegration of Yugoslavia*, Boulder, CO, 1993, pp. 4–12.

eventual creation of a multi-national Yugoslav state was primarily and ironically the result of its appropriation and adaptation into originally and philosophically competitive national ideas and nationalist programs that happened to be more in tune with the times and with pre-existing 'popular proto-national'[7] Croat, Serb, and Slovene communal identities.

In an influential study published in 1968, the Czech historian Miroslav Hroch identified three stages of modern national integration among eastern Europe's 'small' peoples. First a group of 'awakened' intellectuals (like the Illyrianists) starts studying their language, culture, and history as evidence of their historic credentials and worth as a distinct nation. Then these ideas are transmitted and propagated by 'patriots' (carriers of national ideologies) and the nationalist movements and parties they create. In the third stage these last become mass movements and parties.[8] As Ivo Banac notes, 'Hroch's sequence aptly sums up the course of national revivals among the South Slavs.'[9] This is certainly true of the Serbs, Croats, and Slovenes. However, Yugoslavism in its 'pure' form—what I have called 'the core idea', from Illyrianism through and beyond its revival and elaboration by Josip Juraj Strossmayer and Franjo Rački—never progressed beyond a feeble approximation of the second stage.[10]

Yugoslavism's active proponents, at least until the early twentieth century, were few in number and almost entirely Croats drawn from a very small social stratum. The Illyrianists of the 1830s and 1840s were exclusively members of 'the intellectual class' (clergy, officials, soldiers, artists, and students), wealthier merchants, and members of the lower nobility. In the first Austrian census in 1857, when

---

[7] The term and concept are from Eric Hobsbawm, *Nations and Nationalism Since 1780*, Cambridge, 1990, chapter 2, entitled 'Popular Proto-nationalism.'

[8] Miroslav Hroch, *Die Vorkaempfer der nationalen Bewegung bei den kleinen Voelkern Europas. Eine vergleichende Analyse zur gesellschaftlichen Schichtung der patriotischen Gruppen*, Prague, 1968, pp. 24–5.

[9] Ivo Banac, *The National Question in Yugoslavia*, Ithaca, NY, 1984, p. 29.

[10] Dimitrije Djordjević, 'Yugoslavism: Some Aspects and Comment', *Southeastern Europe*, I, 2 (1974), p. 14, speaks of Croatian, Serbian, Bulgarian, and other 'national *movements*' but calls Yugoslavism 'an *ideology*' and 'a rational solution based on ethnic similarities,' adding that '[t]he difference between the two phenomena is obvious.' (Italics added).

Strossmayer and Rački's revival of Yugoslavism was appealing to
the same groups, all of these together (including many or even a
preponderance of Germans, Magyars, and Jews in most of them)
constituted less than two percent of the population of Civil
Croatia. By 1910 the 'intellectual classes', still the principal pool for
the core Yugoslav idea's recruits and sympathizers, had grown to
approximately 16,000 persons, but this was still barely one percent
of Croatia-Slavonia's total population.[11]

Until they were well into Hroch's second stage, Serb, Croat, and
Slovene nationalists (his 'awakened intellectuals' and 'patriots') and
their programs were also reaching and recruiting from the same
narrow social strata as their Yugoslavist competitors. However,
and importantly, most Slavic members of these strata already knew
that they were Serbs, Croats, or Slovenes. Moreover, a growing
number of members of other classes, including peasants and workers, were learning—especially through expanding networks of primary schools—that they too were Serbs, Croats, or Slovenes. All of
these were therefore already possessed or were acquiring an ethno-
religious or ethno-linguistic identity and 'proto-national' consciousness that distinguished 'we' from 'they.' Such people were or became
(especially if they also became literate) readier recruits to a corresponding national consciousness and to movements or parties with
national(ist) programs than to a broader and more abstract Yugoslav
consciousness and program.

This line of argument finds support in Arnold Suppan's explanation of how Ante Starčević's Croatian-nationalist Party of Right
could grow from so few adherents that it is better termed a 'sect' in
the 1860s into a 'mass movement' (along with its proliferating and
sometimes more nationalist-exclusivist offspring) by the end of the
century. Unlike Strossmayer and Rački's People's Party, with its

---

[11] Arnold Suppan's numbers and analysis in his 'Comments,' in *Austrian History
Yearbook*, vols 15–16 (1979–80), pp. 34–5, on Mirjana Gross, 'Croatian National-
Integrational Ideologies from the End of Illyrism to the Creation of Yugoslavia,'
ibid., pp. 3–33. Cf. Banac's analysis of the 217 members [sic!] of *Matica Ilirska*
(the Illyrianists' cultural and patriotic organization) at its apogee ca. 1840:
approximately 27 per cent were administers and public servants, 22 per cent
were clerics, 18 per cent belonged to the free professions (mostly lawyers), 14 per
cent were craftsmen and merchants, 7 per cent were teachers, and 11 per cent
identified themselves only by their noble titles; no students, peasants, or workers.

dependence on 'the liberal bourgeoisie, the 'middle-class intelligentsia,' [and] the liberal Catholic clergy,' the Party of Right was supported 'by the petite bourgeoisie, primarily by small-scale retailers and tradesmen.' Not only were this social stratum's size and growth rate larger than those of the People's Party's recruitment pool:

Moreover, after the 1890s the economic conditions of wider sections of merchants, tradesmen, and peasants who farmed on a large scale had improved substantially; consequently, the intellectuals who advocated integrational ideologies now were able to attract larger groups of supporters. However, this was also increasingly true of the ideologies that sought to push national integration 'from the bottom,' especially the ideologies of the Peasant Party formulated by Ante Radić and of the Social Democrats. In 1910 approximately 250,000 Croatian peasants and 350,000 family members, laborers, and domestic servants engaged in occupations in agriculture and forestry, as well as 100,000 Croatian workers, day laborers, and menials lived in Croatia-Slavonia. These figures alone indicate that if both of these classes increased their participation in political life the national integration of the Croats could be realized only if the peasants and the workers were included in the national movements. The relative social significance of the ideologies developed among the Croats during the last decade before the First World War (the 'new course,' Josip Frank's Party, Mile Starčević's Party, etc.), therefore, ought to be reexamined from this perspective.[12]

The circumstances confronting Miroslav Hroch's 'awakened' (proto-nationalist?) intellectuals among the Slovenes, and therefore their initial goals, were in important respects different and more difficult than those confronting their Croat and Serb counterparts. Until the second half of the 19th century the Slovenes were almost entirely a rural and illiterate peasantry speaking a number of mutually almost incomprehensible dialects and living in Habsburg-ruled lands where the literate upper and urban classes were German or Italian, or germanized and italianized, and the language of administration and education also was German or Italian. Moreover, these lands were several in number: Carniola, Gorizia, the Austrian Kustenland, parts of Styria and Carinthia (all quasi-autonomous in the decentralized Austrian system) and Hungarian Prekomurje. Although the

[12] Ibid., pp. 35–6.

Slovenes lacked the 'state tradition' of Serbs and Croats, they did have a strong tradition of defending and cultivating their language and culture against a millennium of alien rule and assimilative pressures.

In this combination of circumstances, the primary focus of several generations of Slovene 'awakeners' was first the development and dissemination of a standardized Slovene literary language and then its acceptance as a language of education and administration (and thereby a vehicle for rural–urban and upward social mobility) wherever Slovenes were a majority or significant minority. Their geopolitical fragmentation provided an increasingly important secondary focus expressed in demands or hopes for an administrative re-organization that would bring most of them under a single Austrian province based on their Carniola heartland and Ljubljana as its capital. As a cultural and later increasingly political movement on behalf of a small Slavic people living almost entirely in the Austrian half of what became the Dual Monarchy after 1867, Slovene proto-nationalists tended to feel a closer kinship and to seek support from Austria's other Slavs, in particular the Czechs, or even the Russians, rather than among their fellow South Slavs. Until very late in the day their political élites of all parties looked to Vienna for solutions and were Austro-Slav or at most 'Trialist' rather than Yugo-Slav in their orientation and goals. By then, and the principal accomplishment of their 'awakeners', the Slovenes were almost all literate and nationally conscious as Slovenes.[13]

In Serbia the comparative advantages enjoyed by Serb national(ist) programs and parties included but went beyond those deriving from Serbian equivalents of the role of social structure, the spread of literacy, and other factors also in play in Croatia. The Serbians[14] possessed an expanding autonomous principality and later fully independent kingdom after the first quarter of the 19th century. Unlike the Croats, Slovenes, and Habsburg Serbs, their state and their 'national awakening' developed together. Both drew inspiration and

---

[13] The standard and thoroughly researched work on the subject is Carol Rogel, *The Slovenes and Yugoslavism, 1890–1914*, Boulder, CO, 1977.

[14] It is often and here particularly useful to distinguish between 'Serbians' (*Srbijanci*), the Serbs of Serbia, and 'Serbs' (*Srbi*) for members of that nation or people more generally and wherever.

legitimacy from pre-existing 'popular proto-nationalism' vested in communal memories of and identification with medieval Serb statehood and grandeur,[15] transmitted to successive generations through epic poems and the institution, art, and liturgy of their sometimes autocephalous Serbian Orthodox Church.

Enjoying the protection of a state of their own, which was a mono-ethnic Serb nation-state until the addition of Kosovo and large parts of Macedonia and the Sandžak in 1912–13, the Serbians had no reason to fear for their survival as a people, a culture, and a nation—again unlike the Croats, Slovenes, and Serb communities outside Serbia. On the other hand, they also had no experience of competitive co-existence in a multi-cultural environment. By seeking from the outset to include other Serbs (and putative Serbs) who remained outside their initially diminutive state, they were irredentists before the term was invented for an identical Italian national program (which Serbian political élites later saw as a model and legitimation for their own aspiration to unite all Serbs in a single state). In any case, Serbian nationalists and nationalism were basically outward-looking, expansionist, and self-confident. Until late in the day they tended to view the Yugoslav idea as basically irrelevant or, especially as espoused by Strossmayer and Rački (both Roman Catholic priests as well as Croatian patriots), as a disguise for Greater Croatian nationalism and a new variation on Roman Catholicism's historic *Drang nach Osten* into the schismatic Orthodox world.[16] The only exception in the nineteenth century was a brief period in the 1860s, when Strossmayer and Serbian Foreign Minister Ilija Garašanin agreed, in the context of Serbian Prince Michael Obrenović's plans for a coalition against the Ottoman Empire, to work for 'a Yugoslav state independent from both Austria and the Ottoman Empire.'[17] With the failure Michael's plans and his assassination, the agreement broke down in less than two years. Garašanin passed into history more famous for his *Načertanije* (Proposal) of 1844, actually published only in 1906, which proposed a 'Greater Serbia' encompassing all regions with a large Serb population.

---

[15] This much also applied to the Croats but not to the Slovenes, whose nationalists had a hard time finding an historically dubious *Slovene* state in their history.

[16] Rusinow in Sugar, op. cit., p. 357.

[17] Stokes, op. cit., pp. 129–35.

'Exclusivist' or 'integral nationalist' versions of Croat and Serb nationalist ideologies and programs thus tended to be more attractive to more politically and nationally conscious Croats and Serbians (but not necessarily Serbs in Croatia and Bosnia) than the core Yugoslav idea *per se*. At the same time, however, other considerations were pushing Croatian, Serbian, and also Slovene political élites toward cooperation, with implications for their attitudes to Yugoslavist ideas. As Dimitrije Djordjević puts it:

> The appraisal of their national interests in different historic periods moved the Yugoslavs to accommodate their separate nationalisms to Yugoslavism but also pushed them to return to their specific national identities… Historical experience showed the Slovenes and Croats, for example, that they needed the support of the Balkan South Slav—primarily Serbian— hinterland in their respective confrontations with Vienna and Budapest to secure greater recognition of their own national and political individualities…On the other hand, Serbian attempts to safeguard the Morava valley and to unite all the Serbs could be realized only through support obtained from the Habsburg Yugoslavs. The Serbs were [also] geographically so dispersed that their unification imposed the necessity of joining with other Yugoslavs. Only if they were bound together would the Serbs and Croats be able to secure their national territories: the Serbs in the Vojvodina, the Croats in Dalmatia, and both of them in Bosnia-Herzegovina.[18]

The response to these 'national interest' reasons and other pressures to 'accommodate' separate nationalisms to Yugoslavism varied over time and by party and place. The two most significant responses, measured in terms of the political and historic importance of the parties that espoused them, produced ideologies that flatly contradicted Strossmayer/Rački's and other Yugoslavists' insistence that the Yugoslav idea allowed for the continued existence and inclusion of separate Croat, Serb, Slovene, and other 'tribal' or even 'national' identities and interests.[19] But even these appropriated and adapted

[18] Djordjević, op. cit., p. 193.
[19] 'According to most Yugoslavist ideologues, the "spiritual" community of South Slavs could be achieved only by retaining the separate *names* of Croats, Serbs, Slovenes, and Bulgarians while at the same time harmoniously intermingling their traditions and respecting their respective *equality* and *individuality* by nurturing their "tribal" characteristics' (Gross, op. cit., p. 12, emphasis added).

(or perverted) aspects of the Yugoslav idea that supported their interest in claiming the largest possible territory for 'their' nation. Others, like the significantly temporary cooperation between Stross-mayer and Garašanin which Gale Stokes queries as 'Yugoslavism in the 1860s?',[20] sought to accommodate versions of Yugoslavism that envisioned the continued validity of separate 'tribal' or 'national' cultures.

The language question, and how it was answered, enveloped all of these issues and interests for both Yugoslavist and integral nation-alist ideologies.[21] All of them implicitly accepted nineteenth cen-tury definitions of the nation that focused on a distinctive language as the primary and even necessary criterion of nationhood. This was not a problem for the Slovenes. Almost everyone agreed with them that they had a language of their own, although initially in a variety of dialects that required 'standardization' to become a national literary language. It was a problem for Serbs, Croats, and later Slavic Muslims, all of whom (along with the Montenegrins) spoke dialects and wrote in variants of what could be considered a single language—although usually called 'Serbian' by Serbs and 'Croatian' by Croats.[22] The issue was complicated by the fact that those who felt in some measure that they were Croats spoke and wrote in three quite distinct dialects: čakavian, kajkavian, and štokavian, the last of which was also spoken by almost all Serbs. Nationalist ideologues could deal with this problem in one of two ways. If what these people spoke was in fact or could be developed into a single language, they were or should be one nation. If they (or their nationally conscious élites) 'knew' they were separate nations, then they must be speaking separate languages.[23]

[20] Stokes, op. cit.
[21] Rusinow in Sugar, op. cit., pp. 363–4; cf. Banac, op. cit., Part I, passim.
[22] Or simply 'naški' ('ours') by all of the above, thus avoiding the issue!
[23] The issue carried over into the second Yugoslavia, when a régime-sponsored agreement, signed in Novi Sad in 1954 and defining a common language with two variants (Serbo-Croatian or Croato-Serbian but also known as Serbian or Croatian) was repudiated in a 'Declaration on the Croatian language' endorsed by all important Croatian cultural organizations in 1967. Serb intellectuals responded with a 'Proposal for Discussion' arguing that in this case Serb children in Croatia should be educated in their own Serb language. Paul Shoup, *Commu-nism and the Yugoslav National Question*, New York, 1968, pp. 195 and 215, describes the incident and the uproar it produced.

Both Serb and Croat integral nationalists sought to cope with this problem in a variety of ways. One was to define the other(s) out of existence. This could be done by asserting that a religious difference had been misconstrued as a national distinction. Accordingly, Croats were 'really' Roman Catholic Serbs, or Serbs were 'really' Orthodox Croats, and Slavic Muslims were either Islamicized Croats or Islamicized Serbs. Focusing on language, and asserting or devising a common language, produced similar but not identical conclusions. If that common language was 'Serbian,' in a variant (štokavian) also spoken by most Croats, that would re-define štokavian-speaking Croats as Serbs. This was the task the great Serb linguistic nationalist Vuk Karadžić set for himself. If the same supposedly common language was 'Croatian,' then Serbs were also Croats. If they were not wanted as Croats—the view at times of Starčević and other Serbophobe members of his Party of Right and its progeny[24]—they were to be excluded from membership in what Starčević called 'the Croatian political people' because they used another alphabet (Cyrillic), practiced another religion (Orthodox Christianity), or were culturally simply too different (primitive and violent).

The Illyrianists had also argued that the South Slavs spoke variants of basically the same language, and that this as well as their supposed common descent from the ancient Illyrians made them actually or potentially a single people. In practicing what they preached, the Illyrianists' probably most lasting contribution came from their choice and successful promotion of the štokavian dialect, precisely because it was also spoken by almost all Serbs, as the Croatian literary language—although *they* called it Illyrian. (This choice represented a deliberate sacrifice to the cause of South Slav unity, as Gaj repeatedly pointed out, since he and most Illyrianists spoke and wrote in kajkavian, the dialect of the Croatian heartland around Zagreb and of a large and distinguished part of prior Croatian literature. Some of them urged the Slovenes, whose own language was close to kajkavian, to make the same sacrifice for the same reason by adopting štokavian as their literary language.[25]) They thereby inadvertently (along with Vuk Karadžić quite deliberately for the Serbs)

---

[24] At other times Starčević and the Party of Right 'formulated the concept that the Slovenes *and Serbs* were actually Croats' (Gross, op. cit., p. 8, emphasis added).

[25] Gross, op. cit., p. 10.

prepared the ground for those later language-based claims by Serb and Croat integral nationalists that Croats were Roman Catholic Serbs or Serbs were Orthodox Croats.

But were all of these efforts to assert or devise a common language and thus a single people, whatever the intentions and goals of their advocates, in effect and simultaneously as much Yugoslav-integrational as Croat- and Serb-integrational? Were they thus as conducive to arousing and disseminating Yugoslav as Croat and Serb identity and consciousness? Mirjana Gross, whose research on South Slav ideologies extends over decades, thinks that they were, at least among the South Slavs of the Habsburg Empire and especially the Croats. She also thinks that these efforts became part of a pattern of ideological evolution that gradually intermingled and interconnected initially contradictory and competitive Yugoslavist and nationalist ideologies.[26]

Surveying the pre-1914 history of both Yugoslavist and especially Croatian 'national-integrational' ideologies in the context of political and social developments in and beyond the Habsburg Empire that shaped and altered them, Gross finds that in the late nineteenth century

> both [Yugoslavist and Croatian national-integrational] ideologies underwent a fundamental metamorphosis and branched out into several ideological variants. Rački's ideology was no longer found adequate, but it inspired the concepts of the Progressive Youth, the 'new course,' and the Yugoslav nationalist [sic] youth, as well as those of the peasant and socialist workers' movements. The 'Frankist' ideology, named after Dr. Josip Frank, and subsequently its clerical variant, sprang from the ruins of Starčević's and Kvaternik's ideology, and later Starčević's tradition was reconstituted in a different form.[27]

A number of considerations, including the political imperative of countering the appeal and propaganda of competing ideologies, explain these often bewildering mutations and permutations. Two seem to have been of particular importance. One was 'the appraisal of their national interests in different historic periods' noted by Dimitrije Djordjević. The second arose from these movements'

[26] Ibid., passim.
[27] Ibid., pp. 4–5.

search for ways to achieve vertical and horizontal penetration beyond the narrow class spectrum and one or a few narrow geographic regions in which all were initially trapped (except late arrivals like the Radić brothers' Peasant Party and the social democrats). In the final analysis, according to Gross,

'Yugoslavism' and 'Croatianism' cannot be clearly delineated. There is a form of 'Croatianism' that excludes 'Yugoslavism.' I have used the not very auspicious term of 'exclusive' to denote this type. With only a few exceptions, 'Yugoslavism,' however, included 'Croatianism,' because the Yugoslav ideology was a Croatian national integrational ideology. That is to say, it mobilized different social classes for political, cultural, and economic activities that furthered the integrational process in and the modernization of the Croatian nation. [At the same time, Yugoslavism was also supranational.] On the other hand, we can also say that 'Croatianism' included 'Yugoslavism,' e.g. [in some of its political activities and programs]...Until the 1880s the boundary between 'exclusive Croatianism' and 'Yugoslavism' was clearly defined. After that parties with a 'Yugoslav' and a Party of Right tradition were able to coalesce or unite with each other and a larger number of persons could go over from 'exclusive Croatianism' to 'Yugoslavism' and vice versa.[28]

It has already been noted, and is generally accepted, that the Yugoslav idea tended to encounter disinterest or opposition among Serbians and their political élites (except for that brief Garašanin-Strossmayer courtship in the 1860s) until developments in the early twentieth century and during the First World War encouraged them to pay more serious attention to how it could further Serbian national and territorial goals. This was not the case with the more complex story of the Serbs of the Habsburg Empire (after 1878 *de facto* and after 1908 *de jure* including Bosnia-Herzegovina). These Serbs lived as dispersed rural and later also urban minorities, except where they constituted local majorities in the Habsburg Military Frontier (Vojna Krajina) and Vojvodina. In this multi-ethnic, multi-confessional environment the Habsburg Serbs, like their Croat and in Bosnia also Slavic Muslim neighbors, were experiencing Austrian and Hungarian variants of the empire's increasingly dominant national question, sometimes competitive and sometimes cooperative

---

[28] Ibid., p. 43 (in Gross' response to Suppan's 'Comments' on her article).

coexistence with members of other nationalities, and the challenge of both Croat nationalist and Yugoslavist ideologies and programs. The reactions of those whose views we know something about—as usual in that period meaning people with secondary or higher education—were varied, in contrast to the single-minded irredentism of Serbian nationalism until the First World War. All but the first of these reactions were more Yugoslavist than integral Serb nationalist.

Many Habsburg Serbs were increasingly drawn toward Serbia as their 'Piedmont', but in two quite different understandings of what this meant. The first looked forward to a Greater Serbia in which all Serbs, but in principle only Serbs, would ultimately be included. This goal was identical to that of the dominant pre-war current in Serbian nationalism. It either ignored the existence of the Croats and others among whom the Habsburg Serbs lived, or it defined these others out of existence (in ways already discussed). The second looked to Serbia as the core, by virtue of population and its 'state-creating' role as well as Serb kinship, of a united state of Serbs, Croats, and Slovenes as separate and in principle equal peoples. This was nearly identical to the Strossmayer-Rački variant of Yugoslavism and its successors. The only difference was in the special role and status these Serbs assigned to Serbia as the Yugoslav Piedmont, but a growing number of Yugoslavist Croats and Slovenes were adopting the same view by the early twentieth century. Including Serbia in a unified South Slav state implied either the dismemberment of the Habsburg Empire or Serbia's inclusion in it. Shying away from either of these prospects (and with the second usually even less attractive to Serbs than to most but not all Yugoslavist Croats and Slovenes), some Habsburg Serbs were attracted to either or both of two less radical, largely compatible, and generally Yugoslavist solutions. The first and more limited was binational Serbo-Croat political collaboration against common enemies (which could be partly different in different regions) and in pursuit of common interests. This tendency produced the Croat-Serb Coalition, founded by a group of like-minded Croat and Serb political leaders in 1905 and the dominant party in Croatia for the next ten years. The second, which was also at times the most popular variant of the Yugoslav idea among Croats and Slovenes, was Yugoslavia as an autonomous South Slav entity within the Habsburg Empire ('trialism' in place of Austro-Hungarian 'dualism').

Many politically conscious and active Habsburg Serbs and the movements and parties they joined vacillated frenetically among several or all of these aims; others simply never decided or vaguely tried to combine them. One of these last was Young Bosnia (*Mlada Bosna*), whose adherents included Bosnian Serbs, Croats, and Muslims. Whether Young Bosnia, and particularly Gavrilo Princip (a Bosnian Serb whose five co-conspirators in Sarajevo on 28 June 1914 'represented' Bosnia's Serbs, Croats, and Slavic Muslims), should be described as Yugoslavist or Greater Serbian in their motivation and goal is still a matter of dispute and may never be known with certainty—perhaps because they did not know.[29]

The status of national consciousness, national(ist) projects, and attitudes to the Yugoslav idea among the Serbs, Croats, and Slovenes in the last years before the First World War can be roughly summarized as follows:[30]

The *Serbians* possessed a widespread but not yet ubiquitous national consciousness armed with a clear and fundamentally irredentist national program in two substantively identical variants: Greater-Serbianism and a Yugoslavism in which the concept of Yugoslavia was hardly distinguishable from the first variant's vision of Greater Serbia. (The principal difference was territorial: Serbian Yugoslavism included but Greater Serbianism usually excluded Slovenia and kajkavian-speaking Croatia around Zagreb.)

The *Croats* and *diaspora Serbs* of Croatia and Bosnia-Herzegovina possessed a similarly widespread national consciousness, which was less prevalent in isolated and usually illiterate rural environments, and a greater variety of national programs and corresponding political parties than the Serbians. Some of these envisioned Croat-Serb cooperation in some kind of Habsburg or independent entity, sometimes limited to the 'triune kingdom' (Croatia, Slavonia, and Dalmatia) plus Istria and sometimes including (with the Slovenes)

---

[29] For the most persuasive argument that most of them were basically if often vaguely or confusedly Yugoslav nationalists, see Drago Ljubibratić, *Gavrilo Princip*, Sarajevo, 1959, and *Vladimir Gaćinović*, Sarajevo, 1961.

[30] Rusinow in Sugar, op. cit., pp. 270–1. The national and social programs of the other South Slavs who would also be included in Yugoslavia (Macedonians, Montenegrins, and Slavic Muslims) were still under construction, limited to few members of these groups, and usually ambivalent and/or changeable. They are not considered here but are summarized in ibid., pp. 365–70.

all Habsburg South Slavs. Others envisioned an exclusivist Greater Croatia or Greater Serbia. Still others, including most leaders of Croatian Peasant and Social-democratic parties and some youth movements, fully embraced the core Yugoslav idea in its currently prevalent form in Croatia and Slovenia: a federal South Slav state with their own federal units and full equality for Serbs, Croats, and Slovenes as separate nations, 'tribes' or 'names'.

The *Slovenes* had achieved nearly universal literacy and national consciousness, except where the language and culture of primary education was not Slovene, as in Carinthia. However, until those last years the national aspirations of most Slovenes were still primarily cultural or culturo-political, and conceived in an (Austrian) Habsburg framework. This was now changing. By the eve of the First World War a growing number of primarily younger Slovenes, despairing of any hope of realizing their aims within the Habsburg Empire, were turning to Yugoslavism even in its own 'integralist' form, which demanded the melting of Slovene, Croat, and Serb identities into a single Yugoslav identity and nation. A manifesto issued by a group of young Slovene intellectuals in 1913 put it in classic 'integral Yugoslav' terms previously seldom encountered in Slovenia:

As it is a fact that we Slovenes, Croats and Serbs constitute a compact linguistic and ethnic group with similar economic conditions, and so indissolubly linked by common fate on a common territory that no one of the three can aspire to a separate future, and in consideration of the fact that among the Slovenes, Croats, and Serbs, the Jugoslav thought is even today strongly developed, we have extended our national sentiments beyond our frontier to the Croats and Serbs...By this we all become members of one united Jugo-slav nation.[31]

By the early twentieth century, on the evidence and arguments briefly summarized here, Yugoslavism had been assimilated, adopted, and co-opted by a range of Serb, Croat, and even Slovene national ideologies and programs that were originally and philosophically its competitors and denials. It was also gaining some momentum of its

[31] Edward Woodhouse, *Italy and the Yugoslavs*, Boston, 1920, p. 68, as cited by Cohen, op. cit., p. 10.

own in the last years before the war that incidentally created the conditions necessary for Yugoslavia's creation (especially international support and the collapse of the Habsburg Empire). In the end, but most importantly as a result of its incorporation into those other ideologies and programs (always to their own ends) Yugoslavism indeed became the focus and fulcrum around which both Yugoslavias were founded and sought their legitimacy.

The central problem and weakness of Yugoslavism was that this proliferation and adaptation of the Yugoslav idea left as its legacy a variety of fatefully contradictory comprehensions of Yugoslavism and Yugoslavia. For most Serbs the Yugoslav idea and Yugoslavia meant either Greater Serbia by another name or at least an expedient and effective way to include and protect all Serbs in a single state (but only if Serbs played a major or hegemonic role in that state?). For many Slovenes and Croats their primary meaning and function was protection against Italian, Austro-German, or Magyar domination and cultural challenges (but only if the identity and autonomy of each Yugoslav nation was protected by equality in managing their joint state). Even Yugoslavists *per se* were of two minds and two kinds. The first, exemplified by the Slovene manifesto quoted above, has been called 'integral Yugoslavism' or 'Yugoslavist unitarism.' It either denied the separate nationhoods of Slovenes, Croats, and Serbs alike, or sought to supersede these by positing the existence or potential (now called 'nation-building') of a single Yugoslav nation subdivided into historically formed 'tribes' or merely 'names.' The second acknowledged and approved enduring separate nationhoods and sought federal and other devices for a multi-national state of related peoples with shared interests and aspirations. The adherents of each of these conceptions tended to represent the respective national interests and prejudices and nationalist programs that had been articulated and developed by the movements and parties that had assimilated and adapted aspects of Yugoslavism to serve precisely those interests and prejudices.

These were the rocks on which Yugoslavia and the Yugoslav idea eventually foundered.

THE FIRST WORLD WAR AND THE UNIFICATION OF YUGOSLAVIA

Kosta St. Pavlowitch

Few at the outbreak of the First World War would have imagined the manner of Yugoslav unification as it took place in the dying days of the conflict in 1918. The Kingdom of Serbs, Croats and Slovenes proclaimed in Belgrade on 1 December 1918 was born of a breathless precipitation of events in the last weeks of the war, which left its participants scrambling around for solutions that would safeguard their interests in a shattered political landscape.

Clearly the idea of unification did not come out of the blue in 1918. It had been laid down as a war aim by the Serbian government from 1914, its cause defended in Allied capitals with the help of émigrés from Austria-Hungary. Until the very end, however, the balance of probability was against its realisation, and when it did take place it was driven by events in a way as unexpected as it would be decisive for the balance of power that would shape the first Yugoslavia.

Yugoslavism—the idea of an overriding South Slav national unity that could encompass established political identities—has often been decried as a figment of ethnological imagination. The Croatian opposition politician Ivo Frank dismissed it in the summer of 1917 as a 'nebulous, mystical, insatiable hold-all concept',[1] a response in part nourished by its supporters' use of arguments burdened with academic concepts of anthropological and linguistic unity. Yet if the concept had not also had some political grounding, both in the

---

[1] Bogdan Krizman, *Hrvatska u prvom svijetskom ratu. Hrvatsko-srpski politički odnosi*, Zagreb, 1989, p. 137. Frank belonged to the nationalist Croatian Party of Rights, a minority party in the Croatian diet, the *Sabor.*

Habsburg lands and in Serbia, it would not have developed into the reality that emerged at the end of the war.

In fact, the language of unification was commonplace in the pre-war politics of both Belgrade and Zagreb, with each seeing itself as a nucleus for national integration. Serbia had the advantage of its own independent state, recognised since 1878, and continuously expanding from its first insurrection against the Ottomans in 1804.

That growth was driven both by the existence of many Serbs still living beyond Serbia's borders and by the sense that a small state would be weak and subject to preying larger neighbours. It also coincided with a growing awareness of the linguistic unity of South Slav populations in Austria-Hungary. Whether these were seen in Belgrade as Slav Catholics who were basically Serb but did not know it, or in a more genuine Yugoslav vision, sympathy and aid for Southern Slav aspirations became a crucial element of Belgrade's policy towards the Dual Monarchy, where there were still large Serbian populations awaiting liberation.

Within the Monarchy, however, it was Zagreb that saw itself as the centre of unification. Squeezed between Austria and Hungary, Croatia was divided into its historic core of Croatia-Slavonia, which answered to Hungary, though with a considerable measure of executive autonomy, and Dalmatia, which was part of Austria. There was also an important Croat minority in Bosnia, annexed from the Ottoman Empire and under direct rule from Vienna in 1908. The theme of unification of historic Croatian lands was therefore a *leitmotiv* of Zagreb politics, in the hope that a unified Croatia would have the clout to stand up to Vienna and Budapest. To boost its case, however, Croatia needed to draw into this vision its fellow South Slavs, who could transform those historic territories into a homogeneous national whole from Bosnia all the way up to Slovenia.

The fact that the concept of some kind of broader unity existed in both Zagreb and Belgrade prepared the ground for the creation of Yugoslavia when the circumstances demanded it in 1918. However, both nationalisms had used Yugoslavism as an extension of their own aspirations, and both had expected to carry out unification on their own terms, within the framework of their own historical agendas. It was easy enough to note the similarities of linguistic or ethnographical patterns, far more difficult to take stock of the implications of uniting two distinct political traditions, both of which expected to be the dominating factor in the process.

From the outbreak of the First World War in July 1914, Serbia began to consider the possibility of territorial aggrandizement that would go beyond Serb-inhabited territories in Austria–Hungary. When a committee of experts was tasked with drawing up Serbian war aims, it came up with a programme for a Yugoslav state that would include Croatia-Slavonia, Slovenia, Vojvodina, Bosnia–Herzegovina, and Dalmatia. From Niš in southern Serbia, where the government had withdrawn, the National Assembly in December officially proclaimed 'the struggle for the liberation and unification of all our brothers, Serbs, Croats and Slovenes, who are still not free'.[2]

The war posed a threat to the very survival of the country. 'Serbia must die' was the clarion call among the hawks in Vienna. By staking a claim to all the South Slav lands in Austria–Hungary, the Serbian government of Nikola Pašić responded in kind. It was a bold 'winner-take-all' approach that sought to secure Serbia's future in the new order that would emerge after the war, while undermining South Slav loyalty to the Habsburg dynasty.

That loyalty, however, remained firm. The assassination of Archduke Francis Ferdinand by a young South Slav revolutionary, Gavrilo Princip, in Sarajevo on 28 June, aroused genuine revulsion and anti-Serb feelings across the Dual Monarchy, feelings the authorities did their best to fan. A session of the Croatian diet, the *Sabor*, called to adopt a statement of condolences, had to be suspended because of the relentless barrage against Serb deputies and their Croatian partners in the governing Croat-Serb Coalition. Attacks were reported against Serb properties across Croatia and especially in Bosnia, where military rule was imposed and often brutally enforced against the Serb population by Croat and Muslim volunteers recruited into 'defensive anti-bandit' units.

The Serbs themselves, however, mostly kept a low profile and there was little sign of the insurrection that the authorities feared. Austria-Hungary's mobilisation proceeded smoothly, and the bulk of forces sent into action on the Serbian front was in fact drawn

[2] Ferdo Šišić, *Dokumenti o postanku Kraljevine Srba, Hrvata i Slovenaca 1914–1919*, Zagreb, 1920, p. 10.

from South Slav areas of the Habsburg Monarchy, with more than 50 per cent of some of its divisions made up of Croats and up to 25 per cent of Serbs.

On the political front, life in Croatia—where the Croat-Serb Coalition remained in power—continued along well-trodden lines into the war, dominated as before by the quest for the affirmation of Croatian State rights and the desire to renegotiate the troubled relationship with Hungary. In fact, Croatia hoped that its loyal performance in the war would strengthen its hand in that struggle, its sacrifices perhaps rewarded by the national unification it had long sought.

The war was after all going well for the Central Powers. After initial successes, Serbia had by 1915 been overwhelmed by a combined German-Austrian-Bulgarian offensive, its army and government only surviving by an epic winter retreat through Albania before finding safe haven on the Greek island of Corfu in early 1916.

If there was any way that Yugoslavia was going to be achieved— on Serbia's terms rather than as a confederal unit within a reorganised Habsburg empire—it was going to have to be with the help of the Entente. That was how Serbia had seen it from the beginning, and from 1914 it had set about trying to sell the idea in somewhat sceptical allied capitals. To this end, it enlisted the help of the Yugoslav Committee, a group of South Slav personalities from Austria-Hungary (mostly from the Croat-Serb Coalition), who had gone abroad at the outbreak of war.[3]

It would be an uphill task. Awareness of the Yugoslav issue was almost nil outside the Balkans, and, while the Entente was willing to reward its ally Serbia, it had little time for the aspirations of Croats and Slovenes fighting with its enemies. In April 1915, a Serbian delegation to Petrograd received a blunt rebuff from Russian Foreign Minister Sergeï Sazonov when it sought to raise the South Slav issue: 'As for the Croats and the Slovenes, I have nothing to say. They are fighting against us. I would not give my approval for the Russian people to fight even half a day to free the Slovenes.'[4]

---

[3] The Yugoslav Committee operated from London between 1915 and 1918 under the chairmanship of the Croat Ante Trumbić, a lawyer from Split in Dalmatia.

[4] Michael Boro Petrovich, 'Russia's Role in the Creation of the Yugoslav State', in Dimitrije Djordjević, *The Creation of Yugoslavia 1914–1918*, Santa Barbara, CA, and Oxford, 1980, pp. 73–94, p. 76.

Indeed, far from committing themselves to the Yugoslav idea, the Entente Powers were busy promising South Slav territories in Austria-Hungary (and even Serbia) to potential allies. Thus in the spring of 1915 they sought, in vain, to lure still neutral Bulgaria with Serbian land in Macedonia, while the following year they promised Romania the Hungarian territory of Banat, which Serbia wanted for itself. Of greatest significance, however, were promises made to Italy in the Treaty of London, signed on 26 April 1915. In exchange for joining the war on the allied side, Italy extracted the promise of vast swathes of Austro-Hungarian territory in Slovenia and Dalmatia.

Italy's claim to these lands was to tilt the already unbalanced relationship between Serbia and the (majority Dalmatian) Yugoslav Committee. As émigrés from an enemy power, the members of the Committee stood little chance of convincing the allied powers that those lands should go to them rather than to fellow ally Italy. Without Serbia, their homeland ran the risk of simply switching from one foreign dominion to another.

Above all, moreover, Yugoslav unification presupposed a dismantling of Austria-Hungary that the Allies were not willing to consider until the very end of the war. They preferred to see the Dual Monarchy maintained, shorn of the various territories promised to its neighbours, but remaining as a counterweight to Germany.

Things were not looking good for the advocates of South Slav unification. The Serbian government had the restoration of its own state to think about, let alone the creation of a new one that might bring it into conflict with its Allies. As for the Yugoslav Committee, its position was precarious: it had no mandate to represent the South Slavs of Austria-Hungary, who continued to profess their loyalty to the Habsburg dynasty, its territorial aspirations were irreconcilable with those of allied Italy, and its relations with the Serbian government were fraught, the two sides differing in their vision of unification.

By 1917, however, the balance began to tip: this was the year in which the United States joined the war and Russia, shaken by revolution, dropped out. Both Russia's new leaders and American President Woodrow Wilson spoke a new language, that of self-determination and national liberation, and both undermined the very foundations of the Austro-Hungarian Monarchy. Within that monarchy, moreover, the accession to the throne of a new emperor, Charles I, after the death in November 1916 of Emperor Franz Joseph, seemed to provide the opportunity for a long-overdue political reorganisation.

In fact, from early February 1917, the outspoken leader of the opposition Croatian People's Peasant Party, Stjepan Radić, berated the Habsburg authorities for not paying sufficient attention to the national problem. Pointing out that the Yugoslav Committee was active in promoting South Slav interests among the allies, Radić told the *Sabor* 'It is in all our interests... that the dynasty be aware of our feelings, our thoughts and our aspirations, at least to the same degree of awareness that exists among our enemies abroad.'[5]

However, it was in Vienna, not Zagreb, that those aspirations would for the first time be formulated officially within the Monarchy. Reconvening after the lifting of emergency measures in force since the outbreak of the war, Yugoslav deputies in the Austrian parliament, the *Reichsrat*, had organised themselves into a Yugoslav Parliamentary Group,[6] following the example of their Polish and Czech colleagues. On 30 May, they demanded, 'on the basis of the principle of nationality and of the historical rights of the Croatian State, the unification of all those territories in the Monarchy inhabited by Croats, Slovenes and Serbs into an independent and democratic state, free from domination by any foreign nation, under the sceptre of the dynasty of Habsburg and Lorraine.'[7]

The declaration had a tremendous impact: the following week in the *Sabor*, Ante Pavelić,[8] the leader of Starčević's Party of Right,[9] welcomed it in the warmest terms, citing the democratic spirit awakened across Europe by the 'great and enlightened Russia', and echoing its appeal for unification into a separate state entity.[10]

---

[5] 8 Feb. 1917. Krizman, *Hrvatska u prvom svijetskom ratu*, op. cit., pp. 107–8.

[6] The 'Yugoslav Club' was made up of 23 Slovenes, 12 Croats and 2 Serbs, under the chairmanship of the Slovenian clerical leader Anton Korošec.

[7] Šišić, op. cit., p. 94.

[8] No relation to the Second World War Ustaša leader of the same name.

[9] Starčević's Party of Right was the second largest party in the *Sabor*. Defending a Croatian national agenda, it nevertheless evolved into one of the leading advocates of South Slav unity in Croatia.

[10] 5 June 1917. Krizman, *Hrvatska u prvom svijetskom ratu*, op. cit., p. 109.

The significance of the May Declaration, moreover, lay not only in the fact that it spelled out the demand for unification, but that it was inspired by Slovene deputies, calling into question a loyalty that had always been taken for granted in Vienna, and removing the issue of unification from the Croatian framework in which it had so far been formulated, taking it into a broader 'Yugoslav' domain.

For the Serbian government in Corfu, however, it posed a dilemma: with the Entente exploring the possibility of a separate peace with Austria–Hungary and a coherent Yugoslav movement emerging within the Monarchy, there was a serious risk of a Habsburg solution to the South Slav question that would leave Serbia empty-handed. The Yugoslav Committee also found itself in a predicament: it claimed to speak for the South Slavs of Austria–Hungary, yet here they were speaking quite openly for themselves. It therefore became essential for the Serbian government and the Yugoslav Committee to draw up a programme of complete unification that would regain the initiative. It took them more than a month to do so, gathered in Corfu from 15 June to 20 July 1917. For the first time, Serb and Croat politicians confronted their radically differing conceptions of unification in an attempt to reach consensus on the internal arrangements of a future state. Mostly, they spoke at cross-purposes, the Croats insisting on issues that were the bread and butter of Zagreb politics: local autonomies, legal institutions, federalism, and above all Croatian State Right—the continuity of state sovereignty surrendered to Hungary in 1102 yet in theory at least maintained till the present day. To the Serbs, these were arcane legalistic subterfuges—'remnants of the struggle against the enemy (Austria–Hungary)'[11]—that would weaken the unified state. They could not understand their relevance in the face of what they saw as the simpler, modern concepts of universal suffrage and parliamentary democracy, concepts that for the Croats, however, would merely enshrine politically the numerical advantage of the Serbs in a unified state.

The resulting Corfu Declaration glossed over the issue, referring constitutional arrangements to a Constituent Assembly that would adopt them by an unspecified qualified majority. It did, however,

---

[11] Pašić, 26 June 1917. Djordje Stanković, *Nikola Pašić i jugoslovensko pitanje*, Belgrade, 1985, vol. 1, p. 219.

commit Serbia to an all-or-nothing solution of the Yugoslav question: 'Our people lays down as an indivisible whole the issue of its
liberation from Austria-Hungary and its unification with Serbia
and Montenegro into a single state.'[12] That state would be a constitutional, democratic and parliamentary monarchy under the reign-
ing Serbian Karadjordjević dynasty. In creating the new state,
Serbia would abandon its flag and its name, and would guarantee
the freedom and equality of worship and national symbols.

At first sight, the May and Corfu declarations may have seemed
mutually exclusive, the former insisting on Croatian state rights and
pledging loyalty to the Habsburg dynasty, while the latter sought
unification around the existing Serbian state under the Karadjordjević
dynasty. Yet both were born of the principle of self-determination
and both accepted the dissolution of existing national identities into
a broader South Slav state, whatever form it might take. They also
ensured that the issue of unification was set firmly on the agenda,
among the Allies and in Austria-Hungary itself, where both declarations received widespread press coverage.

The Allies, however, were still not convinced, continuing to sound
out Austria-Hungary with the offer of a separate peace, hoping to
detach it from Germany rather than dismember it in favour of its
constituent parts. Yet Austria-Hungary remained oblivious to the
offers and paralysed in the face of its unfolding crisis; and while
Russia's February Revolution had acted as a catalyst for democratic
and national demands in the Dual Monarchy, its October Bolshevik
Revolution would set an altogether more dangerous precedent.

In February, a mutiny at the Kotor naval base in southern Dalmatia
allied a call for immediate peace with social and national demands
into an explosive mix. The mutiny was suppressed, but it sounded a
warning. The peace of Brest-Litovsk, signed with the new Soviet
authorities on 3 March, posed another problem, as up to half a million former prisoners of war began streaming back to Austria-
Hungary from Russia, not only war-weary, but inspired at first hand
by the Bolshevik revolution. Large numbers simply dissolved into
the countryside in armed bands, known as the 'green cadre'. In

---

[12] During the negotiations, Pašić had pointedly reminded Trumbić that Serbia's
first priority was to liberate the Serbs, 'then the Croats and the Slovenes'. Ibid.
p. 224.

Bosnia, many swelled the ranks of Serbian guerrilla groups; in Croatia their aims were less politically defined, but they still posed a mounting public order problem.

With the disintegration of central authority, local authorities—so-called 'National Councils'—sprang up to fill the vacuum, gradually establishing a parallel administration. When their representatives[13] gathered in Zagreb in March to discuss ways of co-ordinating their action, they issued a declaration demanding unification that for the first time made no mention of the Habsburg Monarchy. The movement had gathered a momentum of its own. On 2 July, a 'National Organisation of Serbs, Croats and Slovenes of Dalmatia' was proclaimed in Split, soon followed by a similar body in Istria. A month later, the Yugoslav Club in Ljubljana proclaimed the National Council (*Narodni Svet*) for Slovenia, Istria and Dalmatia, declaring its intention of joining up with like-minded forces in Croatia-Slavonia to form a 'universal Yugoslav committee'.

By the time the Habsburg authorities began to wake up to the problem it was too late. Austrian efforts to reform the structures of the Dual Monarchy came up against Hungarian resistance to any kind of change, making it impossible to reach any remotely acceptable solution. In a last ditch-effort to make the Hungarian understand how critical the situation was, the Emperor ordered the veteran Hungarian politician Count István Tisza on a fact-finding mission to the south of the Monarchy. The mission was an unmitigated disaster: wherever Tisza went, he was confronted with hostility and pro-Yugoslav sentiments, and shocked at the disorder and erosion of loyalty. Yet his only reaction was a defiant retreat onto existing positions: 'Hungary remains strong and will deal with its enemies!' he told his host General Stjepan Sarkotić as he left Sarajevo on 23 September.[14] If there had been any lingering doubts among his various Yugoslav interlocutors, they now knew for certain they could expect nothing from Austria-Hungary.

While Tisza was on his ill-fated mission, an allied offensive spearheaded by Serbian and French forces burst through the Macedonia

---

[13] They included parties from Slovenia, Istria, Dalmatia and Bosnia (both Serb and Croat), as well as Starčević's Party of Rights. The Croat-Serb Coalition kept away, as did Radić's Peasant Party.
[14] Krizman, *Hrvatska u prvom svijetskom ratu*, op. cit., p. 261.

front, forcing Bulgaria out of the war and carving north through occupied Serbia. Austro-Hungarian defences crumbled, desertions increased and fleeing soldiers began heading back into Bosnia and Croatia, many joining the 'green cadre' and adding further to the sense of chronic insecurity. Galvanised by the pressure of circumstances, South Slav parliamentarians met again in Zagreb in early October. This time they were joined by the governing Croat-Serb Coalition, and on 8 October established the National Council of Slovenes, Croats and Serbs (*Narodno Vijeće SHS*), a de facto government for all the Yugoslav lands of the Monarchy. The Council appointed the Slovene Anton Korošec as president, with Pavelić, a Croat, and Svetozar Pribićević, the Serb leader of the Croat-Serb Coalition, as vice-presidents.

Faced with the growing vacuum of power and reports of spiralling anarchy, the National Council realised the need for a formal assumption of power and dispatched the *ban* (governor) of Croatia to Vienna to sound out Emperor Charles I on how he might react to such a development. 'Do as you please,' was his reply.[15] *Ban* Antun Mihalović duly summoned the *Sabor,* which on October 29 unanimously declared the dissolution of all links with the Habsburg Monarchy and proclaimed 'the sovereign national State of the Slovenes, Croats and Serbs over the whole ethnographic territory of that nation.'[16]

The celebrations that marked the event belied the precarious situation in which the new state found itself. On 3 November, the Entente signed an armistice with Austria-Hungary, allowing allied forces to occupy areas up to a line that coincided with the territories promised to Italy under the Treaty of London. The new 'Slovene-Croat-Serb State' was neither recognised by the Allies (and was therefore still strictly speaking enemy territory), nor did it have properly delineated frontiers. It was therefore essential to establish contact with the Serbian government as quickly as possible to work towards a unification that would save Yugoslav lands from Italian claims and give them a seat on the victors' side at the future peace conference.

---

[15] Ibid, p. 299.
[16] Šišić, op. cit., pp. 189–210.

Serbia suddenly found itself in an unexpected position: it had expected either to be granted Yugoslav lands as spoils of war at a peace conference or to liberate them during a military campaign. Now those lands had liberated themselves, almost by default, and Serbia found itself faced with interlocutors who had altogether more legitimacy than the émigrés of the Yugoslav Committee.

The two sides, led respectively by Pašić and Korošec and joined by the Yugoslav Committee and the Serbian opposition, met in Geneva almost immediately, from 6 to 9 November, in an effort to thrash out a declaration of intent that they could present to the Allies ahead of formal unification. The resulting agreement proclaimed that intent, but it also delivered a stinging blow to Serbia's vision of unification. Under pressure not only from Korošec and Trumbić but also from his own opposition, Pašić backed down on his insistence that Serbia be the sole representative of Yugoslav interests until a peace conference, recognising the National Council as the legitimate government of the South Slav lands of the former Austro-Hungary. The accord also agreed to set up transitional dualistic arrangements very much along the Habsburg model favoured by the Croats and Slovenes, with existing institutions remaining in place until a Constituent Assembly, and a joint transitional government whose ministers would swear loyalty to their respective heads of state. The future form of the state was left open, without even a commitment to whether it would be a monarchy or a republic.

The agreement, however, was stillborn. The Serbian government in Corfu, under acting premier Stojan Protić, refused to ratify it and resigned, with the support of the Regent Alexander. In Zagreb too it was rejected, under pressure from the Croat-Serb Coalition, whose leader Pribićević argued the delegation in Geneva had no mandate to carry out binding negotiations.

Events in Geneva had given a misleading impression of the National Council's strength. In fact, the new state faced a threat of disintegration as real as that which had just dismembered Austria-Hungary. To the West, Italian forces began taking over the lands that had been promised to them, entering Trieste and Rijeka (Fiume), before moving down the Dalmatian coast to Zadar, Pula and Šibenik. To the south and east, law and order were breaking down fast. A flood of reports began coming in to Zagreb from all over the

Kosta St. Pavlowitch

country, suggesting the country was on the verge of anarchy. In Osijek, armed peasants were reported to be looting the town, while the mayor of one town in Slavonia told the authorities he could not set up a military tribunal to deal with the situation because it would have had to hang the whole locality. In Bosnia, Serbs turned on Muslims in a violent revolt that combined national and social revenge against Ottoman feudatories.

The National Council's problem was that it had no armed force. Attempts to assemble one from soldiers of the old Austro-Hungarian army were a total failure, with most adding to the chaos rather than controlling it. Instead, the politicians had to turn to Serbian soldiers returning from captivity, who agreed to set up a force in Ljubljana as a deterrent to the approaching Italians, and dispatch another to Zagreb. It soon became clear that the Serbian army was the only force capable of both forestalling Italian ambitions and restoring order. In fact, some local authorities appealed directly to the Serbian high command for help. On 10 November the National Council in Sarajevo informed Zagreb that it had invited Serbian forces into Bosnia. To the northeast, local authorities in Zemun and Pančevo across the Danube from Belgrade, and Osijek in Slavonia, did likewise.

In many ways, the leaders of the National Council in Zagreb were ill prepared for the task at hand. Many were lawyers steeped in the legalistic politics of life in the Dual Monarchy, elected by restricted suffrage and out of touch with the situation on the ground. Their insistence on proper legal frameworks and their belief that all would be sorted out on Wilsonian principles at a future Peace Conference appears naïve compared to the hard-nosed realpolitik practised by Serbia's leaders, who had a fine-tuned understanding of allied power politics, and enjoyed active support within the National Council from pro-unification forces co-ordinated by Pribićević.

Thus when the National Council sent a delegation to the Serbian High Command on 8 November to ask Serbia to put forces at the Council's disposal as far as the Osijek–Šamac line, Pribićević took one of its members, Laza Popović, aside and told him to insist the Serbian army should go as far west as possible. 'That means as far as Zagreb!' said Popović. 'Of course: at least as far as Zagreb,' replied Pribićević.[17]

[17] Krizman, *Hrvatska u prvom svijetskom ratu*, op. cit., p. 323.

Serbia understood that unification was going to take place on the ground, and worked the situation to its advantage. On 16 November, Momčilo Ninčić, the first Serbian minister back in liberated Belgrade, wrote to Pribićević: 'It seems to me that the majority of Croats in Croatia will accept the idea of an inseparable and indivisible state of the Serbs, Croats and Slovenes under the Karadjordjević dynasty only if it is tangibly proved to them that, unless they quickly and sincerely accept that idea, all the Serbs will go over to Serbia without hesitation.'[18] To this end, the Serbian authorities were involved in direct negotiations with local National Councils to encourage them to bypass the National Council in Zagreb and proclaim instant unification with Serbia.[19]

However, the pressure was not only coming from Serbia. In Dalmatia, the Italian threat provided a potent reminder of the international isolation of the new state. Dalmatia had always been at the forefront of the struggle for Yugoslavia, and showed increasing impatience with what it saw as the procrastination of the Zagreb authorities. On 16 November, the Dalmatian National Council in Split submitted an ultimatum to Zagreb: decide on unification within five days, or we shall do it alone. Three days later, the National Council of Bosnia-Herzegovina announced it would do the same.

The central committee of the National Council duly met on 23 November to decide its course of action, as events gathered momentum: on the next day, Srem declared its unification with Serbia; and on the day after, it was the turn of Novi Sad, Banat, Bačka and Baranja; the following day it would be Montenegro. Finally the committee agreed a set of guidelines for its delegates to take to Belgrade, demanding the creation of a Council of State that would include representatives from the National Council, the Yugoslav Committee and the legislatures of Serbia and Montenegro. The Council would act as a provisional government pending the election of a Constituent Assembly, which would decide on the form of the unified state by a majority of two-thirds.

---

[18] Ivo Banac, *The National Question in Yugoslavia: Origins, History, Politics,* Ithaca, NY, 1984, p. 135.

[19] A similar process was going on in Montenegro, culminating in a meeting on 26 Nov. 1918 of the Grand National Assembly in Podgorica, which deposed the Petrović dynasty and proclaimed unification with Serbia.

The delegation arrived in Belgrade on 28 November and entered talks with Serbian government representatives. Within the next two days, dozens more localities were sending in announcements of unification with Serbia, while the Dalmatian authorities warned in a telegram that allied commanders were insisting on the urgency of immediate unification as the only way to grant international status to the Yugoslavs of former Austria-Hungary.

These were the circumstances in which the final address to the Regent was drawn up. The pressure was decisive, convincing a reluctant Pavelić to abandon his insistence on the inviolability of historic borders, rights and autonomies, as well as on the two-thirds majority required to ratify the constitution. Pribićević's line won the day, arguing that the act of unification was all that mattered, while the details could be put off to a later date. The address read to the Regent on 1 December by Pavelić, in the name of the National Council of Slovenes, Croats and Serbs, therefore professed an unconditional desire for unification, leaving further arrangements to the Constituent Assembly. In his reply, Prince Alexander proclaimed 'the unification of Serbia with the lands of the independent State of Slovenes, Croats and Serbs into a united Kingdom of Serbs, Croats and Slovenes.'[20]

'It could not have been otherwise,' one of the National Council's representatives, Mate Drinković, wrote the next day to Trumbić.[21] The combination of international and internal pressures left the National Council with no choice but to declare unconditional unification with Serbia. With an ever-shrinking anarchic territory under its control, the Council was hardly in a position to play hard to get with a Serbia that held the two trump cards—armed force and a victor's seat at the international conference table.

The Serbian government knew this was the case and played the situation to its advantage, driven by a growing mistrust of Croatian intentions: 'In Belgrade, we increasingly have the impression that some Croatian circles have a plan to separate Serbia and Montenegro from our other territories in order to create, instead of a unified Yugoslavia in which they fear Serbian domination, a purely Austrian combination.'[22]

[20] Šišić, op. cit., pp. 280–3.

[21] Krizman, *Raspad Austro-Ugarske i stvaranje Jugoslovenske države*, Zagreb, 1977, p. 239.

[22] Ninčić to Pribićević, 28 Nov. 1918. Milorad Ekmečić, *Stvaranje Jugoslavije 1790–1918*, 2 vols, vol. 2, Belgrade, 1989, p. 811.

However, Serbia too had little choice but to seek an arrangement with the National Council. Had it set aside the Yugoslav option in favour of a Greater Serbia, it would have had difficulty justifying to the allies the full extent of its territorial claims, thus leaving its national integration incomplete, with many Serbs still living as minorities in Italy, Hungary or a rump Croatia. Neither would it have altogether avoided the national problems that were to plague Yugoslavia, adding large Croatian, Muslim and Hungarian minorities to the Albanian and still nationally undefined Macedonian populations Serbia had taken on after the Balkan wars.

By December 1918, most of the populations involved (inasmuch as they had any political consciousness) appeared to support the creation of some sort of Yugoslavia—though how they understood that common state varied wildly. Most ordinary Serbs would undoubtedly have backed it as an extension of Serbia, as the culmination of their national struggle. In the Yugoslav lands of Austria-Hungary, the perception was obviously different: nevertheless, the estimates available[23] suggest a majority in favour of unification, with a strong 'Yugo-sceptic' vein in the Croatian heartland.

Of those in positions of influence, however, few realised that a unified state required them to sublimate existing national preoccupations if it was to have any chance of succeeding. Serbian politicians took it for granted that, while they had sacrificed flag and name to the common state, it would otherwise be pretty much business as usual. Most Croatian politicians, on the other hand, still hoped the relationship with Serbia would be an improved version of the autonomy they enjoyed within Austria-Hungary. Both were mistaken, yet what they did share in 1918 was a realisation that the only way their respective national programmes could be achieved was in co-operation with the other. The only other solutions were mutual elimination or exchanges of population, solutions that would be left to later generations.

---

[23] In August 1918, the governor of Bosnia, General Sarkotić, estimated that Dalmatia was 100 per cent behind unification, as were 60 per cent of the populations in Bosnia-Herzegovina and Croatia-Slavonia. This tallies with Serbian reports from Zagreb back to Belgrade in November, which nevertheless warned of a strong Republican and Croatian nationalist tendency in Croatia proper.

THE YUGOSLAV QUESTION, THE FIRST WORLD WAR AND THE PEACE CONFERENCE, 1914–20

Andrej Mitrović

Several weeks before the outbreak of hostilities, in an official Austro-Hungarian memorandum of 2 July 1914 submitted to the German government, the assassination of the Habsburg archduke in Sarajevo was interpreted as a result of the Serbian policy aimed at 'unification of all South Slavs under the Serbian flag'.[1] The ultimatum to Serbia of 23 July 1914 contained the following phrase: 'a subversive movement aimed at detaching parts of the territory belonging to the Austro-Hungarian monarchy'.[2] The Joint Ministerial Council, at its meeting of 7 July, argued for 'a radical solution [of the 'Serbian question'] by military intervention'.[3] On 19 July it concluded that strategic border alterations, at Serbia's expense and in favour of 'other states', were necessary.[4]

After receiving the declaration of war from Vienna on 28 July 1914, the Serbian government responded by formulating the programme of Yugoslav unification. Perhaps because the unification of South Slavs in an independent state had to be carried out at the

[1] 'Auf die Vereinigung aller Südslawen unter serbischer Flagge' in L. Bittner and H. Ueberberger (eds), *Oesterreich-Ungarns Aussenpolitik (OeUAP)*, vol. VIII, Vienna, 1930, p. 251.

[2] 'Un mouvement subversif dont le but est de détacher de la Monarchie austro-hongroise certaines parties de son territoire', ibid., pp. 515–17. Vladimir Dedijer and Života Anić, (eds), *Dokumenti o spoljnoj politici Kraljevine Srbije 1903–1914*, vol. VII-2, Belgrade, 1980, pp. 628–31.

[3] 'Eine radikale Lösung im Wege militärischen Eingreifens', in M. Komjathy (ed.) *Protokolle des Gemeinsamen Ministerrates der Osterreich-ungarischen Monarchie 1914–1918* (hereafter *Protokolle*), ed. Budapest, 1966, pp. 141–50.

[4] Ibid., pp. 150–4.

expense of Austria-Hungary, Belgrade waited for nearly four and a half months before it publicly declared the unification and liberation of all Serbs, Croats and Slovenes as its main war aim. However, already on 29 July, in a Manifest issued by Prince Regent Alexander of Serbia, the Habsburgs were criticized for their ungratefulness to both Serbs and Croats', for their 'sacrifices for the Empire'. In a speech given to the Serbian army on 4 August he talked about 'millions of our brothers…from Bosnia and Herzegovina, from Banat and Bačka, from Croatia, Slavonia, Srem, and from our coast […] Dalmatia', indicating that Serbia looked beyond its borders and beyond merely unifying with just Serbs from outside Serbia.[5] Although there is no strong evidence in Serbian official documents that the Belgrade government was very Yugoslav-minded, according to a reliable source, Nikola Pašić, the then Serbian Prime Minister, stated in a private conversation that in the case of a favourable outcome of the war, north-western borders of a new state would run 'along the Klagenfurt-Marburg-Szeged line'.[6] According to what a representative of the Serbian Foreign Minister told the Russian envoy in Belgrade, Pašić said on 25 August 1914, 'this time it [the 'Yugoslav question'] should be solved […] by unification of all South Slavs', for 'if a lasting peace is to be achieved […] Serbs and Croats and Slovenes should be united to be one', in a strong state, which can 'only be Serbia with Croats and Slovenes'.[7]

Systematic and complex preparations for a 'Yugoslav Programme' were carried out between August and November and were revised in early December 1914. Serbia's leading politicians and intellectuals took part in these preparations. Serbian envoys with the Entente Powers received instructions from their government on 4 September 1914 that the future state should be composed of 'Serbia with Bosnia, Herzegovina, Vojvodina, Croatia, Istria and Slovenia'.[8] On 22 September they were sent a set of 'gudelines for action and conversation about [the Serbian government's] aspirations … should the

---

[5] Ferdo Šišić, *Dokumenti o postanku Kraljevine Srba, Hrvata i Slovenaca, 1914–1918*, Zagreb, 1920, pp. 2–3, 5–6.

[6] Panta M. Draškić, *Moji memoari*, Belgrade, 1990, p. 87.

[7] Arhiv Jugoslavije Belgrade (Archives of Yugoslavia, hereafter AJ), Papers of Jovan M. Jovanović, 80–54–492–3, Diary of Jovan M. Jovanović, minute of 12/25 Aug. 1914.

[8] Milorad Ekmečić, *Ratni ciljevi Srbije 1914*, Belgrade, 1973, p. 87.

issue [of its war aims] be raised'. Future borders were also mentioned: starting from the east, going westwards in a semicircle, the projected borders encompassed the towns of Bela Crkva, Vršac, Timişoara, Subotica, Baja, the region of Baranja and the city of Osijek; they ran along the Drava and Mura rivers all the way to Leibnitz, encompassing the Kranjska region and descending down to Istria.[9] Contacts with Croatian émigré leaders were soon established in Italy, where the first steps towards the establishment of the Yugoslav Committee were made. The Committee moved its headquarters to London in the spring of 1915 and remained there until the end of the war.

Towards the end of 1914, the Serbian government finally publicly announced its 'Yugoslav' Declaration, which was presented to the National Assembly, convened in Niš on 7 December. The Declaration stated that the government placed all its efforts 'into the service of the great cause of the Serbian state and the Serbo-Croatian and Slovenian tribe' and stressed that its 'only task is to ensure successful end of this great war which at the time when it started became also a fight for liberation and unification of all our unliberated brothers Serbs, Croats and Slovenes'.[10]

Just over four years later, in January 1919, representatives of a country named the Kingdom of Serbs, Croats and Slovenes [hereafter KSCS] appeared at the Peace Conference held in Paris.[11] Because officially the KSCS was not among the winners (nor among the losers, for that matter), as it was only just created, the question arose whether it should be entitled to take part in the Conference. To complicate things even further, the KSCS was not an entirely new

[9] AJ–80–7–441.

[10] Šišić, op. cit., p. 10.

[11] For the history of the Paris Peace Conference see H.W.V. Temperley, *A History of the Peace Conference of Paris*, 4 vols, London, 1920–4. For an account of the Yugoslav delegation at the Conference see Andrej Mitrović, *Jugoslavija na Konferenciji mira 1919–1920*, Belgrade, 1969, and 'The 1919–1920 Peace Conference in Paris and the Yugoslav State: An Historical Evaluation' in Dimitrije Djordjević (ed.), *The Creation of Yugoslavia 1914–1918*, Santa Barbara, CA, 1980, pp. 207–17. See also Ivo J. Lederer, *Yugoslavia at the Paris Conference: a Study in Frontiermaking*, New Haven, CT, 1963.

country, either. The KSCS delegation included representatives of two allied states. One was Serbia, the only country which took part in the war from its first to its last day (from 28 July 1914, when Austria–Hungary declared war on Serbia, until 11 November 1918, the day of the final truce, when, following orders from the commander of the Allied Eastern Army, the Serbian Army blocked the remaining German troops in Romania). The other was Montenegro, whose army capitulated in 1916, but whose government did not sign a separate peace with Austria–Hungary. However, the KSCS delegation also included former citizens of Austria–Hungary, the defeated enemy.

The Conference accepted the delegation, but only under its official name: 'The Delegation of the Kingdom of Serbia'. This did not prevent the KSCS delegates to argue for the right to self-determination of its 'people of three tribes and three names' and to insist on using the full name of the country (rather than just the Kingdom of Serbia) in both verbal and written communication.[12] Therefore, the delegation's first goal was to secure the recognition of its country by the Peace Conference (which then ammounted to international recognition), and then make sure to get as favourable borders as possible. A delicate issue of war reparations—with Serbia due to receive payments and former Austro-Hungarian provinces, now parts of the KSCS, expected to pay, was after a while entrusted to a special Reparations Commission.[13]

Although the new Kingdom was not yet recognized, the presence of its delegation at the Peace Conference was tolerated. At the plenary session in the Hall of Mirrors of the Versailles Palace it had three representatives—less than Britain, France and the US, which had five representatives each, but more than any other country except Belgium, which also had three delegates. (This was in recognition of the contribution of Serbia and Belgium to the Allied victory).

The Provisional Government in Belgrade and the Delegation at the Peace Conference were the two main political bodies of the young Yugoslav Kingdom. Both formed on 20 December 1918,

[12] For instance, the delegation used for all correspondence paper headed 'The Kingdom of Serbs, Croats and Slovenes'.
[13] Mitrović, *Jugoslavija na Konferenciji mira*, p. viii.

they were by their composition unquestionably representative of
the new state's 'historical provinces', all three major religions (Eastern Orthodox, Roman Catholic and Sunni Muslim), and main
political parties. The Government included the most prominent
South Slav politicians, with the notable exception of Nikola Pašić,
the Serbian wartime Prime Minister, whose nomination for Prime
Minister was not accepted by Prince-Regent Alexander. Pašić was
instead head of the seven-member delegation, which included
three representatives from Serbia (in the autumn 1919, one of them
was replaced by a representative of Montenegro, who was in the
meantime the head of the Montenegrin Section within the Delegation) and four representatives of former Austro-Hungarian provinces: two Croats, including Ante Trumbić, the new country's
Minister of Foreign Affairs and during the war the president of the
Yugoslav Committee. Slovenes were separately organized within
the Delegation and had their own Secretariat. Professional sections
of the Delegation also had a mixed composition.[14]

The 'mixed' composition of the KSCS delegation was not well
received among all the Entente Powers, because some of its members were citizens of defeated enemy countries. The Italian delegation particularly objected to the participation of Ivan Žolger, a
Minister without portfolio in the last Austrian government, but
now a fourth ranked official of the Yugoslav delegation. The American delegation suggested that Žolger be withdrawn, but the KSCS
delegates refused to do so, particularly as Slovenian ministers in the
Provisional Government in Belgrade strongly objected to the
American proposal.[15] Official Montenegro, which capitulated mili-
tarily, but did not sign a separate peace, looked for its place at the
Conference in vain.[16]

---

[14] The original seven members of the KSCS delegation were: Nikola Pašić (Serb),
President of the Delegation; Ante Trumbić (Croat), Foreign Minister in the Pro-
visional Government and its sole representative in the Delegation; Milenko
Vesnić (Serb); Ivan Žolger (Slovene); Mateja Bošković (Serb); Josip Smodlaka
(Croat); and Otokar Ribarž (Slovene).

[15] Dittmar Dahlmann, 'Gewiner oder Verlierer? Die Bedeutung der Pariser
Friedensverträge für Jugoslawien und Ungarn' in Gerd Krumeich (ed.), *Versailles
1919: Ziele-Wirkungen-Wahrnehmung*, Cologne, 2001, pp. 193–201, p. 196.

[16] For more on Montenegro in this period see Novica Rakočević, *Crna Gora u
Prvom svjetskom ratu, 1914–1918*, Cetinje, 1969; Gavro Perazić, *Nestanak crnogorske*

Although only the Serbs were unquestionably treated as an allied nation, the situation with them was not straightforward either. A number of Habsburg Serbs fought for the Empire against the Entente countries, including Serbia. The Entente governments were aware of this since early stages of the war. For instance, the French minister to Serbia reported in mid-October 1914 that 'many Slavs, [including] Serbs and Croats' fought for the Habsburg Monarchy, while the Russian envoy in late January 1915 observed that Serbia will have the problem of unifying with other Serbs, since the war separated Serbs of the Kingdom from those of the Dual Monarchy.[17] During the three years of Austro-Hungarian occupation of Serbia (1915–18), the enemy troops, in addition to dominant Austrian and Hungarian, also included Bosnian, Croatian, Slovenian and Serb units. A gendarmerie battalion from Bosnia, mostly consisting of Muslim Slavs, was brought on several occasions to crush the Serbian resistance, while major Austro-Hungarian 'cleansing' campaigns were undertaken under the command of a Croat and a Serb lieutenant colonels.[18] In the regions of Toplica, Jablanica and Kopaonik a spontaneous uprising broke out in late February 1917, but was crushed a month later, when according to Austro-Hungarian estimates some 25,000 Serbs were killed.[19] Serbian Austrophiles, although small in number, offered to Vienna to make the new National Assembly, to overthrow the King and the government-in-exile and join the Dual Monarchy as a third unit. On the other hand, a number of Slovenes, Croats and particularly Serbs, joined Serbian and Russian armies, forming volunteer units.

A complex pattern emerged throughout the territory of the future Yugoslav state, although in Croatia, both the ruling Croat-Serb Coalition and the main opposition parties were pro-Yugoslav

države u Prvom svetskom ratu, Belgrade, 1988; and Dragoljub Živojinović, *Crna Gora u borbi za opstanak 1914–1922*, Belgrade, 1996.

[17] Ministère des affaires étrangères, Archives, Paris (MAE), Guerre 1914–1918, Serbie, vol. 370, p. 20, Nisch 14 oct. 1914, no. 20; *Mezhdunarodnye otnosheniia v epokhu imperializma. Dokumenty iz arkhivov tsarskogo i vremennogo pravitelstv 1878–1917. gg.*, Moscow, 1935, p. 112.

[18] See Andrej Mitrović, *Ustaničke borbe u Srbiji 1916–1918*, Belgrade, 1987, passim and *Srbija u Prvom svetskom ratu*, Belgrade, 1984, pp. 390–93.

[19] Haus-, Hof- und Staatsarchiv, Vienna (hereafter HHStA), PA I, K. 976, Nr. 11/P., Nish, 11 July 1917.

and there was a similar situation in Slovenia. There, the leader of the Slovenian clericals, Ivan Šušterčič, supported the Habsburg Empire, but his brother Admiral Vjekoslav Šušterčič, joined the Yugoslav volunteers and was later a member of the Military Mission within the KSCS delegation at the Peace Conference in Paris.[20] The leading representative of the Slovenian youth movement *Preporodovci* (Revivalists), Agostin Jenko, was killed as a Serbian volunteer at the battle of the Cer Mountain in August 1914, his friend Vladislav Fabjančič was wounded, while another Slovene volunteer, Dragotin Gustinčič, was a prominent advocate of merging the Slovene language with the Serbo-Croat. Meanwhile, the Montenegrin Prince Mirko offered the strategic mountain Lovćen to the Austrians and advised from Vienna his father, King Nicholas, who was in France, to conclude a separate peace with the Empire.[21] While the Committee for the National Unification operated in exile, inside Montenegro guerrilla resistance groups operated throughout the Austrian occupation.[22]

The politics of secret treaties

Hardly an area of the future Yugoslav state remained outside numerous secret plans on the post-war division of the region. In all cases, the belligerent parties followed their short-term goals—to acquire an ally and to win the war.[23] Opposed to this was the Serbian programme (basically identical to the subsequently presented program of the Yugoslav movement in Austria-Hungary), which was not a product of any secret diplomacy, but stated the view of the Serbian government and its experts concerning the Serb-Croat-

[20] Janko Pleterski, *Dr. Ivan Šušterčič 1863–1925*, Ljubljana, 1998, pp. 430–86. Ivan Šušterčič later became a supporter of the Yugoslav union and argued that Alexander Karadjordjević should become a Tsar of a large Yugoslav Empire which would also include Bulgaria. For his brother, Admiral Šušterčič, see Mitrović, *Jugoslavija na Konferenciji mira*, pp. 213, 215.

[21] HHStA, PA I, K. 964, 13 Dec. 1917 and 16 Jan. 1918.

[22] Rakočević, op. cit., esp. pp. 278–80, 348–49, 373–455.

[23] See Jacques de Launay, *Secrets diplomatiques 1914–1918*, Brussels, 1963; and W.W. Gottlieb, *Studies in Secret Diplomacy during the First World War*, London, 1957.

Slovene territory: that this territory should be politically united in an independent state.

The Entente Powers secured Italy's entry into the war on their side by the secret Treaty of London signed on 26 April 1915. Italy was promised Trieste, Gorizia, Gradisca, the whole of Istria and of the historic Dalmatia, with its capital Zara (Zadar). Serbia and Montenegro were to be awarded the coast south of the Italian Dalmatia, including Split and Dubrovnik, as well as parts of the present-day Montenegrin coast. To reassure Italy, this area was also to be demilitarized. Croatia would be left just with the Volosko bay and its coast.[24] In exchange for the territory in Dalmatia, as well as the whole of Bosnia-Herzegovina, Srem, Bačka and perhaps Slavonia, Serbia was expected to give up a considerable part of Vardar Macedonia, which was offered to Bulgaria, if the latter joined the Entente bloc.[25] The Slovenes, clearly out of the focus of European diplomacy, seemed destined to be left to Austria, although Serbia raised the question of their status throughout the war.

When at the end of 1917 Vienna began, in secrecy, to negotiate a separate peace,[26] the Entente Powers saw the possible agreement as an opportunity to weaken considerably Germany, compensate to some extent the loss of Russia (which, led by the Bolsheviks, opted for a separate peace) or at least undermine the internal confidence among the Central Powers.[27] The meeting between the Austro-Hungarian diplomat, Count Mensdorff, and Britain's General Smuts in December 1917 in Geneva was interpreted by the British side as an opportunity to eliminate 'new worries for the future of Europe' by turning Austria-Hungary into a 'counter-balance to Germany

---

[24] See *I documenti diplomatici italiani*; Quinta serie, vol. III, Rome, 1985, pp. 369–73; Mario Toscano, *Il Patto di Londra*, Rome, 1934; Milan Marjanović, *Londonski ugovor*, Zagreb, 1960.

[25] Public Record Office (PRO), London, FO 371/2265/1814, The British Minister's Report from Nish, Confidential, 31 Aug. 1915.

[26] Prince Sixte de Bourbon, *L'Offre de paix séparée de l'Autriche (5 décembre 1916–12 octobre 1917)*, Paris, 1920; Ingeborg Meckling, *Die Aussenpolitik des Grafen Czernin*, Munich, 1969; David Stevenson, *The First World War and International Politics*, Oxford, 1988.

[27] Stevenson, op. cit.; V.H. Rothwell, *British War Aims and Peace Diplomacy 1914–1918*, Oxford, 1971; Robert A. Kann, *Die Sixtusaffäre und die geheimen Friedensverhandlungen Österreich-Ungarns im Ersten Weltkrieg*, Vienna, 1966.

instead of Russia'. Smuts, who obviously focused on the rearrangement of the Monarchy by giving wide autonomies to its peoples, believed that Austria–Hungary would preserve its territorial integrity, and even become attractive for the neighbouring countries. It appears that this was a reference to Serbia, because Smuts saw it 'closely connected' with the Habsburg Monarchy after the war. Such a Serbia would include Bosnia–Herzegovina and possibly Montenegro, but would lose most of Macedonia to Bulgaria. The creation of a Yugoslav state, 'independent, but in lose alliance with the Monarchy', was not ruled out by the British either.[28] Serbia had little say in these calculations, and its plans and aims were often ignored.

With the United States entering the war in April 1917 everything changed, not only in terms of military balance. The US proclaimed that it was fighting a war for democracy (instead of a war for territories) and publicly refused to recognize secret treaties. This complicated the situation within the Entente bloc, but strengthened the position of Serbia and the Habsburg South Slavs.

Serbia did not pose so much an external as it posed an internal threat to Austria–Hungary. Soon after the war began, and increasingly after 1917, it was clear that the idea of Yugoslav unity had strong support within the Monarchy. This explains the creation of an 'internal front'—arrests and internment, persecution and pogroms of the Empire's South Slavs, particularly in Bosnia–Herzegovina.[29] There seemed to be no other solution for the Yugoslav question, but to incorporate Serbia and form a third, South Slav unit within the Empire. However, the trialistic solution was strongly rejected by the Hungarians, who already feared Slav predominance in what they regarded as historic Hungarian lands. Internal instability of the Empire, combined with its powerlessness in terms of foreign policy, where Germany was increasingly taking an upper hand, all contributed to Austria–Hungary's eventual collapse.

[28] HHStA, P.A. I, K. 963, Materials of Mensdorff's Mission; PRO, FO 800/2864, Materials of the Smuts Mission with Report of General Smuts Mission, Geneva, 18–19 Dec. 1917; Andrej Mitrović, 'Tajni razgovori Mensdorf-Smats i jugoslovensko pitanje', *Istorijski časopis* (Belgrade), vol. XXIV, 1977, pp. 235–61.

[29] Pero Slijepčević *et al.* (eds), *Napor Bosne i Hercegovine za oslobodjenje i ujedinjenje*, Sarajevo, 1929, pp. 221–3; Ferdinand Hauptmann, *Die Österreichisch-ungarische Herrschaft in Bosnien und der Herzegovina 1878–1918*, Graz, 1983.

As regards Serbia only one thing was certain in Vienna and Budapest: that it must be permanently destroyed. How to achieve this was not clear. Part of the solution was perhaps to offer Bulgaria large chunks of Serbian territory—indeed, this was the main proviso of a secret treaty between the Central Powers and Bulgaria signed in Sofia in September 1915, by which the latter was promised 59 per cent of Serbia's territory if it joined the former.[30] The Hungarian leadership was opposed to the annexation, although it had plans to incorporate Belgrade, parts of north-western Serbia, and of eastern Serbia, an area rich in copper and silver.[31] However, once Serbia was occupied, it was the German Empire which exploited most of its mineral resources.[32] In fact, Germany's interests and aims were often drastically different from Austria-Hungary's, not only in relation to the Balkans.[33]

Vienna's ultimate aim was 'the final supremacy in the Balkans... by way of a permanent settlement of borders', as well as by establishing a protectorate over Albania, to which territories of Serbia and Montenegro with ethnic Albanian population would be annexed (and, if necessary, also by awarding Greece with smaller parts of southern Albania).[34] Rump Serbia, reduced to a relatively small mountainous region with the population of around 1,5

---

[30] Andrej Mitrović, 'Tajni ugovor izmedju Centralnih sila i Bugarske od 6. septembra 1915.', *Medjunarodni problemi* (Belgrade), no. 3–4, 1978, pp. 47–65.

[31] See for instance Fritz Fellner, 'Die Mission Hoyos', in Vasa Čubrilović (ed.), *Velike sile i Srbija pred Prvi svetski rat*, Belgrade, 1976, pp. 387–419; 'Zwischen Kriegsbegeisterung und Resignation (Jaener 1915)', *Archiv der Universitaet Graz*, Bd IV, pp. 153–62; Georg Schmid, 'Der Ballhausplatz 1848–1918' *Österreichische Osthefte*, Jahrgang 23 (1981), pp. 18–33; Wolfdieter Bihl, 'Zu den österreichischungarischen Kriegszielen 1914', *Jahrbücher für Geschichte Osteuropas*, Band 16 (1968), pp. 505–30; Andrej Mitrović, 'Die Balkanpläne der Ballhausplatz-Bürokratie im Ersten Weltkrieg (1914–1916)' in Ferenc Glatz and Ralph Melville (eds), *Gesellschaft, Politik und Verwaltung in der Habsburgermonarchie 1830–1918*, Stuttgart, 1987, pp. 343–71.

[32] Andrej Mitrović, 'Balkanski ratni cilj nemačkog vojnog vodjstva i privredna bogatstva Srbije 1917–1918' in *Glas SANU*, Odeljenje istorijskih nauka, vol. 8, Belgrade, 1993, pp. 171–207; Gary W. Shanafelt, *The Secret Enemy: Austria-Hungary and the German Alliance 1914–1918*, New York, 1985.

[33] See Mitrović, ibid.

[34] As it was elaborated at a governmental meeting of 7 Jan. 1916, soon after the occupation of Serbia. *Protokolle*, p. 354.

million would be politically and economically completely dependent on the Empire, which is why it was believed in Vienna that 'the Draconian measures must be used'.[35]

As already indicated, because of its leading role among the South Slavs, Serbia represented both an internal and external threat to the survival of Austria-Hungary. In the aftermath of the May 1917 Declaration, issued by the political leadership of the Habsburg South Slavs, which called for unification of all South Slav lands as a separate unit within the Monarchy, the Habsburg government concluded that 'the development and solution of the Yugoslav question is the vital issue for the survival and future of the Monarchy.'[36] In the conditions of eroding power, an increasing number of military deserters (the so-called 'green cadre') and imminent revolutions inspired by nationalism, social democracy and communism, the number of proposals and hence of alternatives for dealing with the crisis grew in Vienna and Budapest.[37] Most plans envisaged Slovenia remaining part of Austria and emphasized the importance of making sure that Serbs do not constitute a majority in any of newly-founded regions, although some plans provided for the unification of rump Serbia and Montenegro.[38]

At the session of the Crown Council, held on 30 May 1918, the Yugoslav question, the only item on the agenda, was described by the Emperor as 'a matter of utmost importance' (*von allergrößter Wichtigkeit*), and that urgent action was necessary to avoid exposure 'to gravest threats' (*den ärgsten Gefahren*). Opposing annexationist proposals of the military leadership and aware of the imperative to end the war, the Habsburg Foreign Minister warned that one must not 'wage war one day longer because of the annexation of Serbia and Montenegro', which 'must not be obstacles to peace'.[39]

[35] Ibid.
[36] Felix Hoeglinger, *Ministarpräsident Heinrich Graf Clam Martinc*, Graz, 1964, pp. 210–13.
[37] See Richard Georg Plaschka *et al., Innere Front*, vols I–II, Vienna, 1974; Bernard Stulli, 'Prilozi gradji za historiju jugoslavenskog pitanja 1918. godine', *Arhivski vjesnik*, no. 2, Zagreb, 1959, pp. 279–335; Mark Cornwall (ed.), *The Last Years of Austria-Hungary*, Exeter, 1990; Janusz Zaranowski, *November 1918*, Warsaw, 1982.
[38] 'Zapisnik zasjedanja', Sarajevo, 13–14 May 1918, in Stulli, op. cit., pp. 281–305; *Protokolle*, pp. 661–9.
[39] *Protokolle*, pp. 661–9.

However, the victory of the Entente armies, the Serbian one among them, led to the collapse of the Empire and to the creation of a large South Slav state, with Serbia at its core. Plans for annihilation of Serbia and Montenegro, as well as those for internal reorganization of Austria-Hungary, remained in archives.

The aftermath

The end of the war brought about the resolution of the Yugoslav question. Austria-Hungary disintegrated, its last Emperor abdicated, and six new states were founded fully or partly on its territory. One of them was the Kingdom of Serbs, Croats and Slovenes, proclaimed on 1 December 1918. The most significant legacy of the Great War was that the right to national self-determination had won, at least in theory, over the principle of historic rights. Yet, the Entente powers never officially accepted Serbia's 'Niš Declaration' of December 1914. Only after the US entered the war did the Yugoslav liberation and unification come to be seen in a more positive light.[40]

The legacy of secret treaties survived the war and affected the relations between the winning powers at the Peace Conference.[41] Italy, which had the status of a great power and accordingly a seat in the Supreme Council of the Conference, insisted that terms of the London Treaty be respected.[42] Great Britain and France looked for a compromise solution, while the US rejected secret treaties as undemocratic, promising instead just and more lasting solutions based on self-determination of the peoples.[43]

What was the Yugoslav Delegation's position vis-à-vis the London Treaty? It clearly rejected it, claiming not only Serbia's share of eastern Adriatic, but Italian, too, as the population of northern Dalmatia, Istria and Trieste was predominantly South Slav. The

[40] Bogdan Krizman, 'Predsjednik Wilson i jadransko pitanje do primirja s Austro-Ugarskom 1918', *Anali Jadranskog instituta JAZU*, Zagreb, vol. 2, pp. 81–116; V. Mamatey, *The United States and East Central Europe 1914–1918*, Princeton, NJ, 1957. Ubavka Ostojić-Fejić, *Sjedinjene Američke Države i Srbija 1914–1918*, Belgrade, 1994.
[41] Stevenson, op. cit., pp. 281–93.
[42] René Albrecht Carrie, *Italy at the Paris Peace Conference*, New York, 1938; Paolo Alatri, *Nitti, D'Annunzio e la questione adriatica*, Milan, 1959.
[43] Lorens Gelfand, *The Inquiry: American preparation for peace 1917–1919*, Yale, 1963.

KSCS delegates argued that Serbia had fought bravely on the Entente side, sustaining enormous casualties. It had declared war on Germany on 6 August 1914, after Germany had declared war on Russia and France. And the delegation of the KSCS, appearing before the representatives of the Great Powers on 18 February 1919, used its strongest argument: that Serbia had fought for the rights to equality and self-determination of peoples. Its delegates argued convincingly that such a just struggle was above all treaties, whether they were secret or public. Since the US particularly disputed the London Treaty, the Yugoslav requests and resistance made the American interference possible.[44] France and Great Britain remained passive, while Italy, unwillingly, backed down and both directly and indirectly made contacts with the KSCS delegation after its official recognition, seeking a compromise solution.[45] All this made the Treaty of London unfeasible, and the problem of the Italian-Yugoslav border unsolvable for the Peace Conference.[46]

It became clear that the recognition of the young Yugoslav state was not going to face major obstacles when an invitation to the 'Serbian delegation' for the first plenary session of the Peace Conference was answered with an information that the session would be attended by the representatives of 'The Kingdom of Serbs, Croats and Slovenes'. On this occasion, the Yugoslav Delegation subsequently explained that 'all members of this mission out of solidarity represent their common interests' (*tous les membres de cette Mission représentent solidairement les intérêts communs*).[47] Greece was the first country to recognize the new state (26 January 1919), followed by Norway (29 January) and Switzerland (26 February). At the meeting of the representatives of France, the US, Great Britain and Italy

---

[44] See *Zapisnici sa sednica Delegacije Kraljevine SHS na Mirovnoj konferenciji u Parizu 1919–20*, p. 53; *Papers Relating to the Foreign Relations of the United States: The Paris Peace Conference 1919*, vol. IV, Washington, DC, 1943, pp. 44–53.

[45] Andrej Mitrović, 'Tajni kontakti Nitijeve vlade sa jugoslovenskom delegacijom 1919. godine', *Zbornik Filozofskog Fakulteta u Beogradu* (Belgrade), vol. VIII-1, 1964, pp. 753–72.

[46] The problem was solved by the treaties of Rapallo (13 Nov. 1920) and Rome (27 Jan. 1924). See Bogdan Krizman, *Vanjska politika jugoslavenske države 1918– 1941*, Zagreb, 1975, pp. 29, 43.

[47] MAE, Conférence de la Paix 1919–1920, a letter of the Delegation dated 20 Feb. 1919.

(which took place on 12 January 1919), when Czechoslovakia and Poland were recognized, the recognition of the Yugoslav state was postponed until the Peace Conference. Apart from the obvious explanation for the postponement, the Italian resistance, there was another reason. The allies wanted to wait a little and see how stable the new country and its government would be.[48] A Serbian diplomat reported from London on 27 December 1918 that the British position depended on whether 'the present situation [in the KSCS] is going to be stabilized'.[49] French documents reveal that before recognizing it, France wanted to see if the new state could survive.[50] That is why a Yugoslav representative in Paris recommended to his government that it was necessary 'to work hard to maintain the new situation at home'.[51] Armed Albanian bands revolted against the Yugoslav authorities, there were armed clashes in Montenegro, between the supporters and opponents of the exiled King Nicholas,[52] and there was unrest in Croatia. But Washington believed that there was no reason to wait and on 7 February 1919 it officially recognized the Belgrade government as the first Great Power to do so. In March the Americans even attempted in vain to encourage their European allies to follow their example.[53] In the Supreme Council the question of recognition was raised on 26 April and the decision to recognize *le Royaume des Serbes, Croates et Slovènes* was passed on 29 April by accepting the credentials of the Yugoslav delegates.[54] The arrival of the German delegation almost certainly speeded up the decision, as the Allies feared the Germans might try to dispute the credibility of some of

[48] Arhiva Jugoslavenskog odbora, Ostavština Ante Trumbića, Arhiv Historijskog instituta HAZU (Zagreb), no. 45/72.
[49] Miladin Milošević, 'Kraljevstvo Srba, Hrvata i Slovenaca. Prvi naziv jugoslovenske države', *Arhiv* (Belgrade), vol. I, no. 1, 2000, pp. 97–111, pp. 102–3.
[50] MAE, Conférence de la Paix 1919–1920, vol. 30.
[51] AJ, Parisko poslanstvo, f. 1, Izveštaj od 3/16. januara 1919.
[52] For two sides of the argument see Jovan Bojović, *Podgorička skupština 1918*, Gornji Milanovac, 1989 and Dimitrije Dimo Vujović, *Podgorička skupština 1918*, Zagreb, 1989.
[53] Milošević, op. cit., pp. 102–3.
[54] MAE, Conférence de la Paix 1919–1920, vol. 30., coded, to the representative missions in Belgrade, Rome and London, 1 May, 1919.

the participants at the Peace Conference.[55] Britain finally recognized the KSCS on 2 June 1919, and France did so three days later.

That was the international *début* of the new state, born from the hardships brought about by First World War. At the Peace Conference it asserted itself as a member of the democratic world. Out of four peace treaties it signed in the suburbs of Paris, the one in Versailles, signed on 28 June 1919, was considered the most important as it was the new country's first international treaty. The treaties of Saint-Germain (10 September 1919), Neuilly (with Bulgaria on 27 November 1919) and Trianon (4 June 1920) settled most of its borders. Yugoslavia existed for some seventy years. Yet, after its collapse during the last decade of the last century, there still remain a number of myths about the nature of the Yugoslav unification, the role of international diplomacy and the Paris Peace Conference. The collapse of both Yugoslavias and the civil wars of the 1940s and 1990s have only fuelled speculations that Yugoslavia was an artificial creation, created by the Great Powers, imposed on non-Serbs by Serbs or vice versa. It is hoped that this chapter has contributed, at least in part, to the dismantling of such myths.

---

[55] *Les délibérations du conseil des quatre*, I, Notes de l'officier interprète Paul Mantoux, Paris, 1955, pp. 385, 411.

Part II. NATIONS

SERBIA, MONTENEGRO AND YUGOSLAVIA

Stevan K. Pavlowitch

Serbia had existed as an autonomous principality within the Ottoman Empire since 1830. Like all the young Balkan states, it had
conceptualized nationality into a territory. Its nationalism was born
of opposition to imperial rule. Its rulers wanted to strengthen the
state, so as to be able to expand and gather kindred populations.

They first envisaged the inclusion of Bosnia, Herzegovina and
parts of Albania to secure the route to a maritime outlet, in order to
escape a takeover by other Powers when the Ottoman Empire collapsed. They hoped for unity with Montenegro, whose prince-
bishops had, in their humble way, set up the first Serbian polity in
modern times. The greatest of them, the poet Peter II, even used to
be regarded as a precursor of the Yugoslav idea. Montenegro was
one of those areas where the Ottoman conquest was never completed; its inhabitants had come to believe they were the only survivors of medieval Serbia.

It was in the Austrian Empire, however, that the revolutionary
events of 1848 saw something like a popular South Slav movement.
Its promoters came from a youthful intellectual élite in Croatia.
Their aim was to regroup the Habsburg dominions into ethnic
units, and they needed a broader base to extend Croatia's claims.
They used the classical name of the Illyrians (as Napoleon had
done) before settling for 'Yugoslavs'—Southern Slavs. Although
they had adherents among educated urban Habsburg Serbs, their
movement did not really catch on among Serbs. The memories and
myths of medieval Serbia were too strong among the Habsburgs'
Orthodox South Slavs. In Belgrade there was little need for the
Illyrian-Yugoslav vision, and a reluctance to give up a name upheld
by Serbia's rising statehood.

57

When the 'Illyrian' General Jelačić was appointed *ban* or crown representative in Croatia by the Austrian emperor in 1848, he told the diet—'We are all one people; we have left behind both Serbs and Croats', and Peter II of Montenegro hailed him as the saviour of the South Slavs. Jelačić's Serb and Croat soldiers fought together alongside imperial forces to crush Hungary's intransigent nationalist revolutionaries, after which centralized government from Vienna was restored over all alike.

In the 1860s contacts between Prince Michael Obrenović's government in Serbia and Croatian nationalists were frequent. Plans were made for a 'Yugoslav' union, federation or confederation around Serbia, to encompass one nation with three religious faiths. The area ranged from Carniola, southern Styria and Carinthia, to northern Albania, Bulgaria and Thrace.

These were amateurish and unrealistic plans. Keeping up the mystique of South Slav unity inspired by the Italian Risorgimento as the ultimate outcome, interlocutors in Belgrade and Zagreb used it as an auxiliary to promote their nearer separate aims—that of uniting Serbian (primarily Ottoman) and Croatian (primarily Habsburg) lands respectively, as circumstances permitted. The reorganization of the Austrian empire in 1867 and the death of Prince Michael in 1868 brought the scheming to an end. By transferring Bosnia and Herzegovina to Austria-Hungary, the Treaty of Berlin in 1878 put an end to the illusion that all Serbs could be united in an independent Serbia, or that Bosnia could be a bridge between Serbia and Croatia for a future Yugoslavia.

Michael Obrenović's Serbia may have perceived itself as a potential Piedmont, but there was also Montenegro which had since been consolidated and secularized. Its last ruler, Prince, later King, Nicholas was supportive of the common Serbian cause, but nurtured his own dynastic and territorial objectives. Montenegro's increased sense of its historic identity did not lessen the feeling that it was the bastion of Serbdom.

Since no dissolution of the Habsburg Monarchy could be foreseen, the search for a Yugoslav unifying framework could do no more than provide support for separate efforts. Questioned, challenged, revised and altered, the Yugoslav idea offered national rights based on ethnicity and language in lieu of acquired or historic rights. It was at the root of Austria-Hungary's distrust of Serbia.

Only in the decade preceding the First World War, under King Peter Karadjordjević, did Serbia once again become attractive to Serbs and other Southern Slavs still under Ottoman and Habsburg rule. In Belgrade the attraction felt outside Serbia for the kingdom's modernization could easily be confused with a desire to unite with Serbia. The officers who had brought about the change of dynasty in 1903 had formed a secret society commonly known as the Black Hand, to organize nationalist propaganda boosted by the action of armed bands in the 'unredeemed Serbian provinces', listed as Bosnia, Herzegovina, Montenegro, 'Old Serbia' (Kosovo), Macedonia, Croatia, Slavonia, Srem, Vojvodina and Dalmatia.

It was not until the Balkan Wars of 1912–13 that Serbia was strong enough, in conjunction with its Balkan partners, to defeat the Ottoman Empire. Its victories brought in the long neglected and disparate populations of Macedonia and Kosovo, many with no clear national consciousness, others inimically disposed. Yet the victories had not only enhanced the prestige of its military; they had inspired the Serbs in Austria-Hungary, and once again more Croats and Slovenes, to think of a new Yugoslav state as an alternative in the nearer rather than the remoter future. Serbia's Radical government and Prime Minister Pašić began to talk of a possible future union, and to explore ways of cooperating with the coalition of parties that controlled the diet of Croatia.

In Montenegro's case enlargement proved an even greater strain that for Serbia. The small kingdom could not support its population. Expatriates and the educated youth viewed Serbia as superior in every aspect. When a common border was established, many demanded immediate unification. Negotiations were indeed opened with Belgrade, but the complete loss of identity was as difficult to envisage as the survival of a second and economically non-viable Serbian kingdom. The dilemma made the third option of a larger Yugoslavia attractive to sections of opinion.

In Croatia the young in both the Croatian majority and the Serbian minority were demanding reforms, until the opposition parties and the Serbian ethnic parties merged into the Croat-Serb Coalition that won the elections to the diet of Croatia in 1906. Ethnic Serbs offered their willingness to respect Croatia's historic rights and to contribute to the struggle for the unification of Croatia's historic lands, in exchange for a full acknowledgement of their equal partnership. On the eve of the First World War, there was a strong feeling of South Slav solidarity within the Habsburg Monarchy, but the strongest political groupings worked within the constitution, and openly anti-Habsburg aspirations were limited to a fringe.

In Serbia, there had been ambivalence between a narrowly Serbian identity, expressed in striving for a greater Serbia, and a hazier Yugoslav identity, with Serbia as the potential Piedmont of South Slav unification. In 1914 before the outbreak of war, there were no plans and no popular movement for the creation of a Yugoslav state in any near future. The government was preparing to go to the polls, to strengthen its hand in imposing control over an army whose influential Black Hand officers thought in the simpler terms of the Serbian question.

When Austria-Hungary decided to go for a quick military operation to destroy Serbia, the Pašić government understood that the outcome of the war would bring great changes, for better or for worse, to the country's position. It decided to supersede the possible resolution through war of the 'Serbian question' by posing the 'Yugoslav question', albeit within the parameter of liberating kith and kin from foreign rule. The Niš Declaration of December 1914 asserted that Serbia was fighting for the liberation and unification of all Serbs, Croats and Slovenes.

In late 1915, however, Serbia was struck down by the full weight of a German-Austrian-Bulgarian offensive. Its territory was occupied. Its decimated army rescued by Allied shipping after retreating through Albania. Its exiled government survived on foreign soil. Montenegro was even worse off. Negotiations on union had pointed to a German-type arrangement, with King Nicholas's kingdom retaining its identity. The Montenegrin monarch, who had expressed his solidarity in defence of 'our Serbian nation', also went into exile, where he was increasingly sidelined, by Montenegrin exiles and by the Serbian government.

Neither the Serbian government nor the leaders of the Habsburg Southern Slavs knew what was going to be the outcome of the war. Both sides aimed at ensuring what could be obtained, while keeping contact with and through the exiled South Slav personalities from Austria-Hungary gathered in the Yugoslav Committee who propagated the aim of a Yugoslav state. In total uncertainty about the future, the Serbian government concentrated on union with Montenegro. As one after another of the leading Montenegrins in exile abandoned their king, a one-time prime minister formed a Committee for National Unification with the backing of the Serbian government.

Serbian politicians and members of the Yugoslav Committee realized that it was essential to present a programme of unification at a time when the Allies were seriously thinking of a separate peace with Austria-Hungary. In Corfu in 1917, they issued a declaration which set out the basic principles on which the new state would be founded. It was a compromise that glossed over the differences. Over all the lands on which the Yugoslav nation of the Serbs, Croats and Slovenes lived, there would be an independent state known as the Kingdom of the Serbs, Croats and Slovenes, under the Karadjordjević dynasty. Its constitution would be drawn up by a constituent assembly elected after peace had been restored, and adopted by a 'qualified majority'.

Nobody had anticipated the rapid collapse of the Habsburg Monarchy which started in September 1918. The spontaneous appearance of local autonomous forces compromised Serbia's rôle as liberator and unifier. A National Council of elected members of various representative bodies set up a State of the Slovenes, Croats and Serbs over the whole ethnographic territory of that nation in Austria-Hungary. The pace of the unification process with Serbia and Montenegro quickened. Various local councils pushed for immediate unification with a Serbian government that had just returned to liberated Belgrade. Token detachments of Serbian troops were asked to appear, to prevent the deterioration of order, or to anticipate the arrival of Italian troops.

Meanwhile in liberated Montenegro, the Committee for National Unification took over. Amidst public demonstrations in favour of immediate unification, it organized elections for an assembly to decide on the future of the state. On 26 November, the gathering proclaimed the deposition of King Nicholas and his house, and union with Serbia in a wider fatherland of the Serbs, Croats and Slovenes. The decision satisfied a majority, generally urban, more educated and young. It left a minority to nurse their wounded pride at the way in which Montenegro's rôle had been brushed aside. With Italian support, a rebellion was stirred up in the area around the capital which quickly collapsed as the partisans of total union set upon the autonomists.

The day before the proclamation of Montenegro's union with Serbia, the National Council in Zagreb had taken the decision to unite the Yugoslav territories of the former Austro-Hungarian monarchy with Serbia and Montenegro. A delegation was sent to Belgrade to invite Serbia's regent, Crown Prince Alexander, to proclaim the union and assume the regency of the new state, which he did on 1 December 1918.

In spite of pushes here and there, Serbia had not controlled the process of unification. Pašić wanted to ensure that Serbia retained the advantage of its status in bringing about unification; he was not out to impose Serbia's rule over a united Yugoslavia. The problem was that he, and many others in Serbia, did not really understand the difference between Serbia and Yugoslavia.

Pre-war Serbia represented 35 per cent of the territory of Yugoslavia, and Serbs (half of them from the old Kingdom) 39–40 per cent of the population. The Belgrade government was confident that it could control the non-South-Slav minorities, such as Albanians, Germans and Magyars. Macedonians, deemed to be Serbs, would be assimilated, but there was no question of turning other South Slavs into Serbs. All that Serbian politicians wanted, those from Serbia and those from other provinces, was to ensure that all Serbs were gathered in one state, and they realized that this could only be done in a united state of the Serbs, Croats and Slovenes.

Serbia had come out of the Great War with huge losses, and great prestige. For many of the survivors, that alone seemed to justify that its existing state structures should be the heart of the new Yugoslav body. The Constituent Assembly eventually adopted the constitutional draft presented by the government dominated by the two largest, and Serb-based, parties—the Radicals and the Democrats. The essentials of Serbia's 1903 constitution were kept, adapted and updated.

Although voted by a majority of 223 out of the full total of 419 members, the Constitution of 1921 was unacceptable to, or disapproved by, many others, notably the Croat voters massed behind the Croatian Peasant Party. 161 deputies had stayed away. The boycotting Croatian bloc thought of Yugoslavia as an improved South Slav version of Austria-Hungary where Croatia would be Serbia's Hungary, while the government acted as if Yugoslavia was just an extended Serbia that took in Croats and Slovenes as well. Cabinets concentrated too much effort on surviving through unstable parliamentary coalitions, allowing the royal prerogative to be pushed well beyond the spirit of the Constitution.

Formally monarch since the death of King Peter I in 1921, Alexander was an authoritarian. He had had excellent if ill-informed intentions towards the creation of a united state to which non-Serbs could feel as loyal as Serbs. He was still carried by a sincere if nebulous Yugoslavism when in 1929 he invalidated the constitution, and took it upon himself to organize institutions that would better correspond to the country's needs, at a moment when it seemed that parliamentary government had broken down. It was he who officially adopted the designation 'Kingdom of Yugoslavia'.

A weary public opinion was initially willing to give King Alexander a chance, but different sections had differing expectations. His 'Yugoslavicizing' dictatorship was quickly perceived by most Croats as a more efficient way of implementing the Serbian style of centralism, if not hegemony. The king granted a new Constitution in 1931 which made him 'guardian of the unity of the nation and of the integrity of the state'. In 1934, he was assassinated by the Ustašas, a fascist-inspired separatist Croatian group, sheltered by Italy and Hungary.

Alexander's Constitution survived under the regency of Prince Paul, exercised on behalf of the boy King Peter II. The ideology of one-nation Yugoslavism was tacitly abandoned. As the 1930s proceeded, the Serbian-based opposition parties and the Croatian Peasant Party came together to work out a transition to a new constitutional structure which would satisfy a majority within each of the three acknowledged national communities. The process was derailed by Prince Paul's determination to settle quickly with the Croats and formally within the Constitution of 1931. The

'Agreement', as it is generally referred to, reached between the regency and the Croatian Peasant Party leader Maček in 1939 set up a self-governing Province of Croatia within Yugoslavia, over Croatia, Slavonia, Dalmatia and additional districts from Bosnia and Hezegovina. It put an end to the united opposition.

Serbian opinion felt frustrated. It had generally considered that the 'Serbian question'—that of their community's integration—had been solved by the mere fact that all Serbs were in Yugoslavia. There no longer was a Serbia, and it was no longer even clear in people's minds what Serbia was, geographically or historically. Montenegrins felt that they were Serbs even when they were dissatisfied with the complete loss of their separate political identity.

Notwithstanding the Comintern's view of satisfied and hegemonic Serbs lording over Yugoslavia, there were dissatisfied Serbs by the late 1930s, and most of them were not Communists. Founded in 1937 as a think tank to work for the integration of Serbian culture within Yugoslavia, the Serbian Cultural Club became the centre of opposition to the Agreement, a pressure group to define and defend Serbian interests in Yugoslavia, and the most vocal expression of the Serbian intelligentsia's loss of faith in pan-Yugoslav nationalism.

The Comintern was right to the extent that Serbs had on the whole been satisfied with the general framework of the Yugoslav state. There had been no Serbian national or majority party, or indeed any explicitly 'Serbian' political party. Divided into regions and parties, far from seeing themselves as a domineering element, they had rather fancied themselves to be the ultimate defenders of Yugoslavia, for which they had given up their identity.

When Hitler decided in 1941 to destroy the 'Versailles construct', Yugoslavia collapsed and was partitioned. King and government left for exile in London. The Serbs were singled out as the defeated enemy to be punished collectively. The Ustašas were allowed to proclaim their Independent State of Croatia over a territory that stretched across Bosnia and Herzegovina to the gates of Belgrade. They launched massive operations of ethnic cleansing to eradicate the 1.9 million Serbs of their Croatian state.

Not surprisingly, there were Serbs who turned against what they saw as the mistaken experiment that Yugoslavia had been.

Paradoxically, it was pro-German collaborators who expressed the most extreme pan-Serbian vision. Resistance was on the whole Serb-based. General Mihailović, elevated by the government in exile as head of the Yugoslav resistance, was a loyal officer who stressed the legitimist Yugoslav nature of his movement, which was in fact almost entirely Serbian, based in Serbia, with little or no attraction to non-Serbs. The Communist Party leader Tito, on the other hand, was a genuine internationalist. Both Mihailović and Tito eventually wanted to restore Yugoslavia as a federation, but the Communists set up their programme on totally new foundations. They too were a Serb-based movement, but based on Serbs outside Serbia, and they were able to attract non-Serbs.

The outcome of the Second World War led again to a united Yugoslavia. The Yugoslav Communist leaders had followed the twists and turns of the Comintern, and endorsed a federation on the principle of nationality under centralized Party control. They had denounced 'greater-Serbian hegemony'. They did not want a Serbia that dwarfed the other federated units. Satisfaction had to be given to those who felt dominated or humiliated by Serbia. At the same time, they utilized a structure to acquire and hold on to power that was largely manned by the Serbs of Croatia and Bosnia. The Constitution of 1946 enshrined Yugoslavia's new structure as 'a community of nations equal in rights who, on the basis of the right of self-determination, including the right of secession, have expressed their will to live together in a federative state'.

Montenegro recovered its historical identity, thus going against the age-old tendency for unification with Serbia. Its inhabitants were henceforth encouraged to think of themselves as Montenegrins. By the time of the first post-war census in 1948, when the rubric 'nationality' was introduced, 426,000 defined themselves as Montenegrins (of whom 342,000 in Montenegro). The Communists of Montenegro had won a particularly bitter civil war in their home territory. They had also contributed substantially to winning the multifaceted civil war throughout Yugoslavia. The status of republic was thus also a reward. Every republic and city ended up by having a town whose name was preceded by the predicate 'Tito's' (the Titoist Yugoslav counterpart to the English *Regis*), to mark some association with the leader; in Montenegro's case the very capital city of the republic was renamed Titograd.

Macedonia was set up a separate republic for the Macedonian nation, ending the Serbian fiction of 'Southern Serbia' for the benefit of more ambitious Balkan plans. Two autonomous provinces were carved out of the Republic of Serbia, in border areas with mixed Yugoslav and non-Yugoslav populations–Vojvodina where Serbs were now in a majority, and Kosovo where Albanians were in a majority.

The position of Serbs in the Communist federation was a complex one. The Bosnian Serbs had formed the core of Tito's partisan army. With the Serbs of Croatia and the partisans of Montenegro, they provided much of the executive and military personnel of the régime. Serbs made up over half the Party membership in the 1950s (over 60 per cent if Montenegrins are included). At the same time Serbia felt in part conquered and occupied by western Serbs and Montenegrins who had come to Belgrade to man the administration, the army and the police. Serbia was the only republic to have autonomous provinces within its territory. Tito did not forget that his strongest opponents had been the somewhat disorganized, yet also anti-fascist, movement that looked up to Mihailović and the pre-war political parties.

When decentralization started to become more of a reality from the late 1950s, it was felt in Serbia that everything which expressed its pride and tradition had been clipped back, in order to satisfy others, but the republican apparatus was too close to the central power nucleus on which it modelled itself to provide real leadership. The only way that the leadership dealt with the problem of relations between nationalities was to draw more ideology out of Yugoslavia's peculiar position as a Communist country wedged between rival blocs.

As continued devolution encouraged association of nationality with territory, there emerged a strand in Serbia's intellectual dissidence that began to criticize the Communist solution to the national question. Some of Serbia's Communists, worried that the unity of the Yugoslav working class was being undermined by bureaucratic republican nationalism, found common ground with those who feared increasing discrimination against Serbs and Montenegrins outside their respective republics. Communists and former Communists who had sacrificed their Serbian identity for the sake of socialist Yugoslavia, saw the régime's capitulation to particularist aspirations as a negation of the ideal they had fought for. Having once embraced Yugoslavism as a solution to the Serbian national question, they began confusedly to disentangle their Serbianism from their Yugoslavism.

The Serbian malaise was increased by the Constitution of 1974. Yugoslavia was turned into an eight-unit confederation of party-states, with the provinces equal to the republics in all but name. Tito and the army were left as the ultimate guardians of the union. With Yugoslavia reduced to an ideological construct, whose contents had all but evaporated, Serbian nationalism began to resemble an opposition to the régime, as Croatian nationalism had done before the Second World War.

Serbia's position was illogical in that its autonomous provinces could veto decisions at the level of the republic of which they were formally part, but that the republican authority in Belgrade could not do the same for Kosovo and Vojvodina. Serbia had effectively been reduced to 'inner Serbia'. The proposals put forward by Serbia's leadership after Tito's death in 1980, initially meant to avoid selective or incorrect interpretations of the Constitution, met with hostility from those who argued that they were a deviation from 'Tito's path'. They were also not in tune with a political discourse in Serbia itself that was turning to the nation rather than to the republic as the real political factor. Tendencies began to pull in opposite directions, as Serbia at one end tried to tighten up the federation again, and Slovenia at the other tried to loosen it even further.

Serbia's leaders used the explosion of ethnic Albanian feeling in Kosovo in 1981 to bolster the need for changes in the constitutional relations between the republic and its provinces. They argued that a weak Serbia fuelled its nationalism, which was no good for Yugoslavia. A link had been established between Kosovo and Serbia's status. The problem of relations between the decreasing Serbian minority in the province, and its increasing Albanian majority turned into that of relations between Serbs and all the other nationalities.

By 1985 there was a widespread sense in Yugoslavia that Communism had failed. Belgrade had benefited from the latitude accorded to non-conforming intellectuals by Serbia's leadership in search of a broader-based legitimacy. They were the vanguard of a pan-Yugoslav civil rights movement, and they put forward political demands that amounted to a radical critique of the Communist system. Fusing democracy and nationalism, they moved from protecting individual human rights to lamenting the fate of their nation.

When Milošević in 1987 began to assume control of Serbia's ruling Party, he moved adroitly to the nationalist side. He defended the interests of Serbia, allowed an unprecedented degree of liberalization of Serbia's cultural scene, and most of the one-time critical intelligentsia put democracy on hold. Milošević's seduction of the intellectuals was one of his many ways of legitimizing his authority.

He had something to offer to most people. He had his supporters in Montenegro. Many of Serbia's Communists had come from there, or, like Milošević himself, been born in Serbia of Montenegro-born parents. Elsewhere, leaders rather liked him, or did not seem to mind as he completed his assumption of control over Serbia. Having absorbed most of the opposition potential there, he spoke of the need to re-centralize authority, first in Serbia, then in the federation. In 1988 mass rallies organized through the Party apparatus laid the groundwork for replacing the faceless leaderships of the provinces and of the sister republic of Montenegro.

Milošević's ambition to appear as a new Tito, not only in Serbia but in the whole of Yugoslavia, was impossible under existing arrangements. He needed a radical overhaul, which he attempted to do by obtaining half the necessary votes in the federal presidency, then an extraordinary Party congress. Through his control of the Party machinery in the whole of Serbia and in Montenegro, and with help from elsewhere, he could count on a sizeable majority at the Fourteenth Congress that assembled in Belgrade in January 1990.

His plans seemed to be working at the congress, until the Slovenes walked out, and the Croats obtained an adjournment. Thereafter Yugoslavia disintegrated as the first competitive elections were held in all the republics. The threat of dissolution posed the question of Serbs outside Serbia. What rights to self-determination the constitution acknowledged was vested in nations and not in republics. The possibility of secession by republics gave Serbian nationalists a basis for the claim to redraw borders. Milošević's renamed Socialist (ex-Communist) Party of Serbia obtained a majority of seats on a minority of votes when multiparty elections were at last held in Serbia, but not before a new constitution had been adopted which drastically reduced the authority delegated to the provinces, and Kosovo's institutions had been suspended.

Milošević talked of Yugoslavia at the same time as he asserted 'Serbia's right to statehood' (the reunification of the provinces). The implication was that, if Yugoslavia could not be turned back to what it had been under Tito in earlier times, he would fashion another one, perhaps one shorn of those who did not want to remain in it, but one that would continue to encompass all Serbs.

Other nationalisms had preceded the Serbian reaction, which, when it came, was destructive because it was not contained within one republic, and because it was hysterical. In defending Yugoslavia as they saw it—the only state in which all Serbs were gathered—the leadership of Serbia under Milošević and Serbian nationalists throughout Yugoslavia in fact gave the final blow to that state.

Milošević really wanted to exert power over as much territory as he could–initially the whole of Yugoslavia, then as much of it as he could salvage. Eventually he could only create a new state with the two remaining republics. Montenegro had voted almost unanimously to continue to live as a sovereign republic in Yugoslavia, equal to all the other republics who wished to do so. The idea of unity between Serbia and Montenegro had run parallel to the broader Yugoslav idea, and the two states had actually united a few days before the fuller unification with the Habsburg South Slav territories. Milošević's new 'rump Yugoslavia' was called the Federal Republic of Yugoslavia, dropping the adjective 'socialist'.

Montenegro had seen an increasingly bitter struggle within its ruling party. By mid-1997, Milošević's henchmen there, President Bulatović and his prime minister Djukanović, had split over control of Party structures and sources of patronage. When they both stood for president, Djukanović, who had acquired the image of a modernizer, just about managed to win on a second ballot. The smaller republic thereafter was no longer considered a mere adjunct to Milošević's Serbia. It declared its neutrality in the 'Atlantico-Serbian war' over Kosovo, and demanded a re-negotiation of the federation, if not outright separation, but it was dangerously divided 50–50.

Finally, when in July 2000 Milošević amended the federal constitution to enable the president and the upper house to be chosen by direct elections, Montenegro refused to recognize the changes, and boycotted the September elections that finally toppled Milošević.

Yugoslavia, South Slavia, was never the state of all of the Southern Slavs, for it never encompassed the Bulgars. It now only has the Serbs of Serbia (including some 800,000 refugees from elsewhere), the Montenegrins (are they still Serbs? are they still even Yugoslavs?) and the minorities. Kosovo, although still formally under Yugoslav sovereignty, is in fact under an international protectorate and occupation, as much under Yugoslav sovereignty as Bosnia-Herzegovina or Cyprus remained Ottoman while they were ruled respectively by Austria-Hungary and Great Britain. After the secession of all of Yugoslavia's republics but two, and after four Yugoslav wars, what is to become of the Federal Republic of Yugoslavia, the rump of what was once the fuller Yugoslavia?

THE CROATS AND YUGOSLAVISM[1]

Tihomir Cipek

This chapter attempts to illustrate the ideology of Croatian political élites and their relation to the concept of Yugoslavism. I begin by looking at the construction of the Croat national identity, which went parallel with the development of the Yugoslav idea. The Croatian variant of Yugoslavism envisaged the fulfilment of Croats' quests for statehood within a wider South Slav framework. On the other hand, the ideology of the Croat Party of Right rejected any notion of Yugoslavia. I also look at the role of the Croats in the formation of the Kingdom of Serbs, Croats and Slovenes in 1918, as well as at the political system in the interwar Yugoslav state. I argue that the Croat experience in the first Yugoslavia influenced decisively Croats' perceptions of the common South Slav state. The fact that the political will was expressed at relatively free and democratic elections enables us to take a more reliable look at Croatian perceptions of Yugoslavia in the interwar period. In the final section of this chapter, I look at the Croat experience in Yugoslavia after the Second World War. Socialist Yugoslavia was a federation in which the Croats had their own federal unit, the Socialist Republic of Croatia. Since the post-1945 system did not allow an expression of political will at elections, it is more difficult to define Croat perceptions of second Yugoslavia. However, an attempt is made to trace main developments relating to history of Croatia within Yugoslavia during the period 1945–91.

[1] This work was written while I was a visiting Humboldt scholar at Goettingen University (Germany). My deepest thanks therefore go to the Humboldt Foundation and Goettingen University for providing me with such a stimulating academic environment.

The Yugoslav idea was initially developed by a group of Croat intellectuals in the 1830s. The Illyrians, as they were commonly known, used popular myths and legends in order to construct Croatian history, which they saw as an integral part of a wider South Slav history. They argued that Croats and Serbs (and sometimes also Slovenes and even Bulgarians) were in fact one, Illyrian nation. The word 'Illyrian' was used as a neutral term and was eventually replaced by another, more appropriate one: Yugoslav (South Slav). The Illyrian movement was initially primarily a cultural movement, but eventually it grew into a political party. It had two dimensions: Croatiansm—integration of all Croatian provinces, divided within the Habsburg Empire—and Yugoslavism—gathering of all South Slavs into one commonwealth, inside or outside the Empire. Both ideas were inspired by the need for unity in face of the growing threat of Magyarization and Germanization. By 1948 the Illyrian movement achieved its first goal, i.e. the integration of the Croatian national identity, but it failed in its second, wider aim. One of the reasons for the failure was that it met with little response among non-Croats, both Serbs and Slovenes, but also because for a Yugoslav unification to be realised, both the Austrian and Ottoman Empires had to collapse first.

Yugoslavism as a political concept was developed in the 1860s by two Croatian Catholic priests: Josip Juraj Strossmayer (1815–1905) and Franjo Rački (1828–94). Their Yugoslavism reflected the desire of the majority of the Croatian political élite to unite Croatian provinces within the Habsburg monarchy. It was also a consequence of the fear of the German *Drang nach Osten*. Strossmayer and Rački believed that Croats can only resist the Germanization, as well as Magyarization, if they united with other South Slav peoples, particularly the Serbs.

Just like the Illyrianism, the ideology of Strossmayer and Rački's Yugoslavism was based on cultural and linguistic unity of Croats and Serbs. The Yugoslavists were also 'encouraged' by Herder's well known assertion that the Slavs were a 'nation of the future', whose mission would be to 'regenerate' the western world. Rački, the principal Yugoslav ideologist, believed in creating a unified education system which would develop a uniform national language, 'essential for a spiritual bond' between the South Slavs. This 'spiritual bond' between the Slovenes, Croats, Serbs, and Bulgarians was to be achieved by uniting their individual traditions, while respecting their particularities.

The Serbo-Croat unity was to be at the heart of a future Yugoslavia. Rački based his theory on the thesis that the Serbs and Croats were, originally, one nation with two names, separated by different histories, state traditions and cultures. Yugoslavism, therefore, essentially aimed to integrate several identities into a new, single one. However, the Croatian 'Triune Kingdom' first needed to be united itself, and gain autonomy within the Habsburg Monarchy. Croatia would then gather all other South Slavs within the Monarchy. In the next stage, Croatia would join Serbia and other South Slavs in a (con)federative union. Strossmayer and Rački also hoped that the Yugoslav union would bring about a religious unification between the Catholic and Orthodox Church. They believed that there was no salvation of the humanity without the unification of all Christians. They hoped their Yugoslavist plans would be acceptable for Serbia as well, but that was not the case. The Serbian principality, which had by 1878 achieved full independence from the Ottoman Empire, had as its main priority the unification with other Serbs, still living under foreign rule.

Strossmayer and Rački's Yugoslavist ideas, politically implemented by the People's Party (the new name for the old Illyrian Party), were accepted by the educated population and the clergy, but fell on deaf ears among the majority peasant population and a small bourgeoisie. Ante Starčević and Eugen Kvaternik, leaders of the Croatian Party of [State] Right, strongly opposed Yugoslavism, favouring instead the idea of an independent Croatia. In their opinion, the Croats were the only 'political' nation on the territory of 'Greater Croatia', which would incorporate territories populated by Serbs and Slovenes, as well as the old Croatian Kingdom.

Yet, the Yugoslav idea survived among Croats, and gradually became more accepted by Serbs, especially those living alongside Croats in the Habsburg Empire. The Croat-Serb Coalition won the elections for the *Sabor* in 1906 and remained the main political force until the Yugoslav unification in 1918.

Debates about the unification demonstrated that there existed significant differences between Serbs and Croats in understanding of

the term Yugoslavism. Most Serbs favoured a centralist and unitarist
government, while most Croats envisaged a (con)federation. Advocates of the Croatian variant of Yugoslavism had hoped that the
political union would propel Croatia's economic and cultural
development, and gradually, Croatia's political development, too.
The Corfu Declaration of July 1917, signed between the Yugoslav
Committee (the representatives of pro-Yugoslav émigrés from
Austria-Hungary) and the government of the Kingdom of Serbia,
was meant to ensure that all key decisions would be decided by the
majority vote in a future constituent assembly. Croatian members
of the Yugoslav Committee, led by Ante Trumbić, considered the
Corfu Declaration the guarantee for a consensus about the government system. They could not have known that after the unification
in December 1918, the Serbian political élite would ignore the
Declaration, bribe some non-Serbs, and in 1921 enact a highly
centralizing Constitution by only a relative majority.

There were Croats who opposed the way the unification was
carried out. Stjepan Radić, leader of the then still small Croatian
People's Peasant Party viewed Yugoslavism as a harmony of separate
national interests of Slovenes, Croats, Serbs, and Bulgarians. He
believed that Croatia should enter the union only as a separate subject. Radić questioned the popular legitimacy of the members of
the pro-unificationist Croatian élite. He called for a referendum, so
that 'ordinary' people could decide whether they wanted a union
or not, and if yes, what kind of a union.

Yet, Radić stayed in minority. Most Croat leaders wanted the
unification with Serbia to take place as soon as possible, mainly
because of the fear of Italy's ambitions in Dalmatia and also because
of the fear of social upheavals. They considered the union to be a
Croatian national interest, especially as otherwise there was the danger of parts of Croatia joining in a Greater Serbia, and other parts
going to Italy. The Croat leaders, however, saw the future union as a
federation. Unfortunately, their ideas were not shared by the Serbian political élite, which, as already indicated, preferred a centralist
and Serb-dominated state. By entering the new Yugoslav state,
Croatia had lost all the state elements and symbols it had preserved
for centuries while part of Austria-Hungary.

The leading role in the political life of the new state was taken by Prince Regent, later King, Alexander Karadjordjević. He regarded the new state as essentially an expanded Serbia, not a union of equal components. He was given great powers by the Constitution, but in practice his powers were even greater. Every political party, especially the Serbian ones, had factions loyal to the King, and he practically formed and dismissed governments. He also had a complete control over the army, gendarmerie, and the secret police.

The main obstacle to creating a stable political system during the interwar period was the 'Croatian question'. Centralism and negation of Croats' national particularities provoked resistance of Croatian public and the majority of Croatian élite.[2] With the purpose of finding a solution to the Croatian national question, a number of political options were formed among the Croats during the formative period of the new Kingdom.

Federalist-minded Yugoslav unitarists. Croatian members of the Croat-Serb Coalition and liberal intellectuals, who believed that the Yugoslav nation can be formed gradually, but only in a federation, which would allow 'tribal' differences. They played a major role in the unification process. They had gathered around the Croatian Union, a newly formed political party descending from the pro-Yugoslav wing of Starčević' Party of Rights.

The Croatian Union stood for liberal ideas, including Yugoslavism. However, disappointed by the King's policies, they eventually joined the opposition led by Stjepan Radić. They were part of the Croatian élite that accepted the political and economic aspects of liberalism. They emphasized individual interest and principally believed in the free market. However, it turned out that the idea of free market and liberal values did not bring them many votes. The Croat voters turned the Croatian Union into a minor party by overwhelmingly rejecting its ideas.

Confederalists. They recognized the national particularities within the Kingdom of Serbs, Croats and Slovenes, favoured Croatia's

---

[2] See Ivo Banac, *The National Question in Yugoslavia: Origins, History, Politics*, Ithaca, NY, and London, 1984.

independence, but approved of the union with other South Slavs. They gathered around the Croatian Republican Peasant Party (HRSS; later HSS), led by the charismatic Stjepan Radić. The HSS political program included both national and social issues, and it was by far the strongest Croatian interwar party. During the period, it grew into a national movement. The HSS ideology favoured a 'third way', a political system that was between capitalism and socialism. It was the so-called 'agrarianism'. Radić worshiped the peasantry as the supreme class. His party desired a confederative union between the South Slavs, whereby Croatia would play a prominent role.

Following a brief spell in the government (1925–7), Radić joined forces with Svetozar Pribićević, leader of the Serbs from the former Habsburg territories, to form the opposition Peasant-Democratic Coalition—in fact a united Serbo-Croat opposition bloc. His career and life came to a tragic end in the summer of 1928, when he was shot, together with another three HSS deputies, in the Belgrade parliament by a member of the [Serb] National Radical Party.

Uncompromising Croatian nationalists—the Frankists.   The Frankists favoured Croatia's independence outside the Yugoslav Kingdom They descended from the anti-Yugoslav wing of Starčević's old party, and were before the war led by Josip Frank (hence Frankists). Ante Pavelić, a leading Frankist, later formed the Ustaša organisation and was the leader of the Independent State of Croatia (1941–5).

The True Right Party strayed from Starčević's ideas ever since Josip Frank came to its head, and then turned to the corporative ideology of the Karl Lueger's Social Christians. However, the Frankists largely ignored Social Christian principles, turning instead to extreme nationalism. While loyalist to the Habsburg monarchy, after 1918 they called for Croatia's right to independence and breaking off all relations with the Belgrade régime. Lack of social program and an extreme nationalist rhetoric did not bring them much popularity among the Croats, and the Frankists remained a rather marginal party.

Along with these parties there was also the Communist Party. Initially, the Communists favoured the unification along the lines of centralism and unitarism, but soon began to argue for the recognition of national differences and federalization of the country.

Following the Moscow anti-Versailles line, the Yugoslav Communists called for the dissolution of Yugoslavia soon after its unification, and for the establishment of a number of Soviet Socialist Republics on its territory. After they carried out the assassination of the Interior Minister, the Communists were banned in 1921, and almost disappeared by the mid-1920s. Only in the late 1930s will they be reorganised, under the leadership of Josip Broz Tito, but by this time their line would be once again pro-Yugoslav.[3]

The parliamentary system came to an end in January 1929, when King Alexander dissolved the parliament and banned all political parties. His measures were apparently designed to bring stability to the country following the crisis which culminated with Radić's murder, but instead the royal dictatorship further radicalized the Croatian opinion. The Frankists, who up until 1929 participated in political life, went into exile and turned to terrorism. They found 'Ustaša—the Croatian Revolutionary Organisation', led by Ante Pavelić. The Ustašas argued that the violence of the régime must be met with violence, since the parliamentary opposition proved inefficient. The Ustaša organisation modelled itself on the Irish Republican Army (IRA) and cooperated with the Internal Macedonian Revolutionary Organisation (VMRO). The Ustašas blamed the régime for the assasination of Radić, whom they described as the 'Croatian Gandhi'. They argued that the murder of Radić demonstrated the fallacy of a peaceful resistance, and that it was time to reach for weapons. They seemed to had forgotten that Radić had them thrown out of the opposition coalition back in 1922 for their radical nationalism. The Ustaša ideology, influenced by the Italian fascism and German Nazism, was based on anti-Serbianism, anti-Communism, anti-Semitism and anti-Masonry.[4]

Before Germany and Italy brought them to power, the Ustašas did not have much popular support inside Croatia. Throughout the 1930s they organised several terrorist actions, but apart from the assassination of King Alexander in 1934, Ustaša activities did not

---

[3] See Gordana Vlajčić, *Jugoslavenska revolucija i nacionalno pitanje 1919–1927*, Zagreb, 1984.

[4] Bogdan Krizman, *Pavelić i ustaše*, Zagreb, 1978, p. 118.

pose serious threat to the Yugoslav interwar state. However, the overall disappointment with the Yugoslav experience made many Croats welcome an independent Croatia. Even the creation of an autonomous Croatia in August 1939, which was negotiated between Vladko Maček, Radić's successor as the HSS leader, and the Yugoslav government and the Crown, could not immediately erase memories of years of Croat disatisfaction with Yugoslavia. The 1939 Agreement was perhaps the first step towards solving the Yugoslav national question. Many Serbs, but also Slovenes and Bosnia's Muslims demanded their own *banovinas*. The federalisation of Yugoslavia, which seemed inevitable after 1939, was interrupted by the Second World War.

In April 1941 Yugoslavia was occupied and partitioned between Germany, Italy and their allies from within and outside the country. Croatia, expanded to include whole of Bosnia-Herzegovina and parts of Vojvodina, was proclaimed an independent state under the government of Ante Pavelić's Ustašas. Many Croats, however, soon turned against the new régime, which committed mass crimes against the Serbs, Jews, Roma, and left-wing Croats. The majority, however, offered only a passive resistance, including Maček. The HSS leader spent the war in house arrest (and was even sent briefly to the Jasenovac concentration camp). With the HSS virtually neutralised, and the Ustašas increasingly unpopular, Croats came to support the resistance movement organized by the Communist Party of Yugoslavia and led by its General Secretary, Josip Broz Tito.

The Communist victory resulted in liberation of Yugoslavia and its re-establishment in 1945. Croatia, now including formerly Italian parts of Dalmatia and Istria, became a socialist republic of the Communist-governed Yugoslav federation. Since many Croats took part in the Communist resistance movement, the new political union enjoyed a far greater legitimacy among them than the Karadjordjević monarchy. Surviving Ustašas, including Pavelić, who found refuge abroad, as well as members of their families who remained in the country, opposed Tito's régime, but they never posed a serious threat to the country's unity.

It seemed as if the Communists had found a recipe for dealing with national disputes and for creating social equality. However, the 'legitimacy' of the new system was based on the fact that freedom was replaced by security. The Communists abolished private ownership and other liberal freedoms, but provided 'safety' in return. People were not obliged to take personal responsibilities. The state, or the Communist Party, was to take care of everything.[5]

Post-1945 Yugoslavia was a federation of six republics: Slovenia, Croatia, Bosnia-Herzegovina, Serbia, Montenegro and Macedonia. However, the country was a strongly centralized, one-party state. All decisions were made by Tito and his Party leadership, based in the state capital, Belgrade. A new type of community was being created—the Communist community of 'new people'. The slogan 'brotherhood and unity' was most convenient for this purpose. The 'brotherhood' referred to the community of nations living in the socialist Yugoslavia. It certainly encouraged tolerance between the peoples. The 'unity' referred to the unity of the working class. The country's unity was to be ensured by the Communist Party. Furthermore, the Communists used the slogan 'Factories to the workers, land to the peasants', thus appealing to egalitarian ideas already rooted in people's minds.

The Communist centralism suited the Serbs, who believed it was the best way of protecting their own interests. The state unitarism prompted the resistance of the majority among the Croatian cultural élite. Croatian-minded intellectuals opposed the Novi Sad Agreement of 1954, whereby Serb and Croat linguists re-confirmed that Croatian and Serbian was a single language, called Serbo-Croatian or Croato-Serbian. The language had two variants, Serbian and Croatian, and both were declared equal. But in the central state institutions the Serbian variant was more frequently used, so the Serbian seemed to have been 'more equal'. Those who opposed the cultural unitarism, decided to speak in public. The Matica Hrvatska and the Croatian Society of Authors, two respectable institutions headed by leading Croat intellectuals, issued in 1967 a 'Declaration on the Name and Importance of the Croatian Standard Language'. The Declaration was supported by sixteen academic and cultural institutions in Croatia. It claimed that the Croatian language was

---

[5] Ivan Prpić, 'Kriza legitimnosti komunističkih poredaka', Politička misao (Zagreb), vol. XXVIII, no. 3, 1991, pp. 153–69.

placed in an unequal position because the government apparatus used Serbian as the 'language of the state'. They demanded 'respect' of the Croatian language, and equality of *four* standard languages: Croatian, Serbian, Slovene, and Macedonian.[6]

The line between culture and politics in the former Yugoslavia was a very thin one. The Declaration talked of the Croatian sovereignty achieved in the Second World War and of 'inalienable right of every people to name their language after themselves.'

The Declaration was denounced by the Communist Party, but its ideas were accepted by most Croats. The protest against cultural unitarism coincided with the Croatian Communist leadership's calls for reforms within the federation. The Croat reform-minded Communists argued for the introduction of some elements of market-oriented economy, and for more freedom in public life in general. After the break-up of the conservative centralist faction in the Communist Party, led by Aleksandar Ranković, in the mid-1960s, there was a general tendency for reforms throughout Yugoslavia.

Major opponents of reforms were centralist hardliners in the federal government, but also some members the League of Communists of Croatia (SKH). The centralists and anti-reformists accused the reformers of nationalism and separatism. At its 10th Session in 1970, the Central Committee of the SKH (CK SKH), stated that unitarist and centralist forces were the main obstacle to the reforms, but that the CK SKH would continue to carry them out regardless. The conclusions made at the Session received support of the Croatian public, but encouraged the dogmatics to attack again. Tito initially sided with the reformists, appointing a Constitutional commission to reform the federation. The Commission, presided over by Edvard Kardelj, suggested that the federation should be in charge of foreign affairs, common defense and market, while preserving unity of the political system. The sovereignty was to be transferred to the republics, which were styled as 'states', while Serbia's provinces of Vojvodina and Kosovo were to gain much greater autonomy. The proposal for the parity-representation of the republics in the federal institutions (the assembly, federal government, presidency) was welcomed by the Croatian Communists and by

---

[6] Dušan Bilandžić, *Hrvatska moderna povijest*, Zagreb, 1999, p. 516.

Croatian public in general. They believed that it satisfied Croatia's ambitions for a greater autonomy within the federation. After all, that was the essence of the Croats' Yugoslavism.

In the late 1960s and early 1970s the Croats' national enthusiasm had grown, and the Croat public now expected Croatia's position within the federation to change to its advantage. The debate brought out into light the old ideological divisions within the Croatian élite. Radical nationalists and Ustaša nostalgists, talked about Croatian historic rights, but were still in a small minority. Majority of Croats supported a looser Yugoslav federation, and a 'softer' variant of socialism. The opposition to the party—because it could not exist outside the party—was formed within it. The non-party opposition which favoured liberal and democratic values was completely marginalized.

The 'Mass movement' (*Maspok*), initiated by the CK SKH and *Matica Hrvatska*, and also known as the 'Croatian Spring', was supported by students, too. Student leaders wanted everything, and they wanted it right now. Their most radical demand was an independent Croatia, outside of Yugoslavia. Students' actions and demands gave Tito a good excuse to dismis the Croat Party 'liberal' leadership, led by Savka Dabčević-Kučar and Miko Tripalo, and to take reprisals against student leaders and intellectuals in the *Matica Hrvatska*.

Tito and a number of party officials loyal to him initially supported reforms, but when they realized these posed a threat to their power and to the government system, decided against them. To make things even more absurd, after carrying out purges in all six republics, the Yugoslav Communist leadership returned to the reformist line. The result was a new Constitution of February 1974. The Constitution made Yugoslavia a *de facto* confederation. The republics were described as states which had volutarily entered the union, while the two Serbian provinces became virtually equal to the republics.

The new Constitution and a relatively high standard of living reduced tensions in Croatia, although there were still some who saw Yugoslavia as the 'Croatian people's prison'. However, it were now the Serbs who began to question their position within the common state. They argued that the 1974 Constitution fragmented Serbia because the provinces of Vojvodina and Kosovo *de facto* became republics within a republic. Already in the late 1970s the Serbian Communists argued for the revision of the Constitution. Leaderships of the two provinces resisted these attempts. The conflict was temporarily halted by Tito, who disapproved of any changes to the Constitution. But after Tito's death in 1980, the conflict erupted again, this time in a more violent form.

In the 1980s Yugoslavia was struck by its most serious crisis thus far. Serbian nationalist intellectuals, who in the mid-1980s drew a Memorandum (of the Serbian Academy of Arts and Sciences), heavily criticised Communist Yugoslavia, accusing it of anti-Serbian bias. They blamed the Communists of conspiring with the Vatican to break-up Serbia and Yugoslavia. They wished Yugoslavia to be re-centralised, and possibly to be once again dominated by Serbs. The Kosovo Albanian nationalism, which demanded the status of a republic for Kosovo and thus its separation from Serbia, (more radical Albanians wanted Kosovo to leave Yugoslavia altogether and join Albania) fuelled Serbian nationalism. A state of emergency was declared in Kosovo in 1981 and the Albanian movement neutralised, but only for the time being.

The Yugoslav system's identity crisis was enhanced by an economic crisis. Yugoslavia's foreign debt rose to US$ 20 billion in 1980, while inflation reached 45 per cent in 1981. Short supplies of many products increased the country's inability to pay for necessary imports, above all oil, technical equipment and raw-materials. There was a shortage of consumer goods, such as coffee, sugar, cooking oil, washing detergents, and there were electricity cuts. To save on petrol, the government ordered that private cars could only be driven every other day. The government introduced the so-called 'stabilization programme', which brought in long ques, but no ultimate answer to the crisis—Yugoslavia's ailing economy could not be easily revitalised.

In the midst of this overall crisis, Slobodan Milošević came to power in Serbia. He used the Greater-Serbian propaganda, under the cover of Yugoslavism, and manipulatively won the support of a majority of Serbs accross Yugoslavia. The more the Serbian public favoured a return to centralism, the more the Croats turned to the idea of an independent Croatia. The political élites and the peoples of Slovenia and Croatia stood against Milošević's policies of centralism and Serb domination. The Croats, whose Yugoslavism based on equality clearly failed, gradually turned to complete independence from Yugoslavia and integration into Western European institutions.

SLOVENIA'S YUGOSLAV CENTURY

Mitja Velikonja

'If they did not know yet, they should now realize that we are not only Slovenes, still less only Austrians, but a limb of a great family living from the Julian Alps to the Aegean.' (Ivan Cankar, 1913)

The modern Slovenian identity cannot be understood without an analysis of Slovenia's 'Yugoslav century'. Slovenes, together with Serbs and Croats, the three 'tribes' of one, Yugoslav nation, formed the Kingdom of Serbs, Croats and Slovenes (in 1929 renamed Yugoslavia) after the First World War. In the aftermath of the Cold War, as Yugoslavia was disintegrating, the Slovenes emerged as a separate nation, with their own state. In this chapter I trace this evolution, but first I provide a historical background to the development of the Slovene national ideology before the creation of Yugoslavia in 1918.

Slovenes' national ideologies before 1918

The first Slovene national programme, the so-called 'United Slovenia', inspired by the events of 1848, called for a political and administrative unification of all Slovene lands within the Habsburg Empire and for the right of public use of Slovene language in schools and administration. During the next few decades, as a reaction to the threat of Germanization, the idea of collaboration and even political unification of South Slavs living under Habsburgs—Slovenes, Croats, and Serbs—slowly began to emerge among the Slovene intellectual élite.

The Illyrian idea—an idea of South Slav ethnic and lingustic unity—had reached the Slovene lands in the 1830s, soon after it was first formulated by a group of Croat intellectuals led by Ljudevit Gaj. Because Illyrianism denied a separate Slovene (as well as any other South Slav) identity, it was accepted only by a small number of Slovene intellectuals, such as Stanko Vraz and Matija Majar-Ziljski, but was rejected by many others, including the greatest Slovene poet France Prešeren. Ideas of complete cultural and linguistic unification of South Slavs reappeared in the late nineteenth century in the form of neo-Illyrianism. According to some intellectuals—for instance, the theologian Aleš Ušeničnik, Liberal Fran Ilešič and Social-Democrat Etbin Kristan—the Slovenes should, during the process of political and national unification with other South Slavs, adopt the Serbo-Croat language. The Slovene neo-Illyrianists believed that linguistic and cultural unification was inseparable from political unification. But this view was opposed by other leading Slovene intellectuals, including Henrik Tuma, Ivan Cankar and Bishop Anton Bonaventura Jeglič, who advocated a political unification with Serbs and Croats which would preserve separate Slovene language and culture.

Faced with a harsh choice of becoming 'either Russians or Prussians'[1], the Slovenes turned to the idea of Austro-Slavism. All three Slovene political groupings—the Clericals (full name: the Slovene People's Party—SLS), Liberals and Social-Democrats, saw Slovenia politically and/or culturally united with other South Slavs within the borders of a reformed Habsburg Monarchy.[2] Advocates of political unification preferred trialistic reorganization (even federalization) and democratization of the Empire, as was favoured by the heir to the Habsburg throne, Archduke Francis Ferdinand.

In the 1890s, both the Liberals and Clericals argued for the unification of the Slovene lands with Croat and other Habsburg South Slav lands in a separate state, but under the Habsburg dynasty.[3] The

[1] Ivan Prijatelj, *Slovenska kulturnopolitična in slovstvena zgodovina 1848–1895*, vol. 4, Ljubljana, 1961, p. 94.

[2] Ervin Dolenc, 'The Slovene Question: A Change of View on the Yugoslav Community', paper presented at the workshop 'Ideology and Historiography: The Making of Identity in Yugoslav Historiography', Florence, 8–9 May 2000, pp. 1–2.

[3] Predominantly on the basis of the Croat historic state right idea. See Janko Pleterski, 'Slovenačke političke stranke u prvom svetskom ratu i jugoslovensko pitanje', *Sveske Trećeg programa*, Belgrade, 1973, pp. 129–47, p. 132.

Social-Democrats also believed that the Empire had a future only as a federation of its emancipated nationalities. They urged the unification, within the Empire, of all South Slavs, whom they regarded as one nation artifically partitioned by different cultures, languages, religions and states. Although loyal to the Habsburg state, the Social-Democrats supported the idea of a Balkan (con)federation, consisting of all four South Slav nations: Slovenes, Croats, Serbs and Bulgarians. The only group that was openly anti-Austrian (and therefore operated semi-illegally) prior to the First World War was the *Preporod* (Revival), formed in 1912 by a group of young pro-Yugoslav revolutionaries. The Revivalists established close links with other similar Yugoslav revolutionary groups, notably the Young Bosnia, and called for the unification of all South Slavs into an independent state. Some of them fought as volunteers in the Serbian army during the First World War.

Serbia's growing prestige following the May coup of 1903, prompted Janez Krek, a pro-Yugoslav SLS leader and a Catholic priest, to brand the Serbs 'our Neapolitans', making a clear and then common parallel between the Italian and Yugoslav unificationist movements.[4] Yet, even the most pro-Yugoslav among the Slovenes were aware of differences which existed between the South Slavs. In his famous lecture, 'The Slovenes and Yugoslavs', given in Ljubljana in April 1913, the poet Ivan Cankar, while calling for a South Slav unification, noted cultural differences between the Slovenes, Croats and Serbs.[5]

During the war, several Slovene émigrés joined the Yugoslav Committee, initiated in late 1914 by a group of exiled Habsburg South Slav intellectuals and politicians. Those who stayed behind remained loyal the Empire, in spite (or because?) of an increasingly autocratic Austrian war régime. Croat, Serb and Slovene deputies in the Vienna parliament formed a parliamentary group, the 'Yugoslav Club', under the leadership of Anton Korošec, also the SLS leader. The 'Yugoslav Club' issued a declaration in May 1917, calling for the unification of all Habsburg South Slav territories into an autonomous unit, but within the Empire.

[4] *Slovenska kronika XX stoletja*, vol. 1, Ljubljana, 1996, p. 131.
[5] The lecture earned him a huge applause from the audience, but also a trouble with authorities and a week in prison.

The Slovene political parties began to prepare for the eventual collapse of the Habsburg Monarchy by establishing the National Council of Slovenia (*Narodni svet*) in August 1918. On 6 October 1918, the National Council (*Narodno vijeće*) of Habsburg South Slavs was formed in Zagreb (headed by Korošec) and on 29 October the State of Slovenes, Croats and Serbs was proclaimed. The unification between the Habsburg South Slavs and Serbia, which had just united with Montenegro, was proclaimed in Belgrade on 1 December 1918.

Slovenes in the Kingdom of the South Slavs

'In His wise providence, God gathered us within one body in a truly miraculous way. The great day has begun, and in the heavens a sign appeared with the inscription S.H.S. [Serbs, Croats, Slovenes]. My people, you will conquer in that sign. Croats, Serbs, Slovenes! It is God's will that you remain indissolubly united forever. Providence has assigned to you a great purpose. Your salvation and your future is only in your unity.' (Bishop Anton Mahnič, November 1920[6])

Despite the 'degradation' to a 'tribe' of a larger, Yugoslav nation, and although many Slovenes remained outside the borders of the Kingdom of Serbs, Croats and Slovenes—in Austria and Italy—the Slovenes enthusiastically supported the creation of the new state. There were three main reasons for this. Firstly, the Yugoslav state offered guarantees against Italy and Austria, and possibilities for national emancipation and cultural and economic development. Secondly, many Slovenes saw Yugoslavia as the fulfilment of a century old idea of unification with other South Slavs. Thirdly, the oppressive Habsburg war régime made sure that hardly anybody felt sorry for the dissolution of the Monarchy. The Slovene enthusiasm for Yugoslavia was somewhat marred by the fact that a large number of Slovenes (as well as Croats) remained outside the borders of the new state. The Rapallo Treaty of November 1920 settled the border dispute between Italy and the Kingdom of Serbs, Croats and Slovenes, but it left some 350,000 Slovenes and Croats to Italy.[7]

---

[6] Cited in Ivo Banac, *The National Question in Yugoslavia: Origins, History, Politics*, 4th edn, Ithaca, NY, 1994, p. 411.

[7] Pro-Yugoslav Slovene and Croatian nationalists from Italy created in 1924 an illegal organization TIGR (acronym for Trieste, Istria, Gorizia, Rijeka), which

Well organized and coherent, under Korošec's pragmatic and charismatic leadership, the Clericals were the strongest Slovene interwar party. Except in the 1920 elections, when it received a relative majority, the SLS always won with an absolute majority in Slovene-populated areas of the Kingdom.[8] Korošec was the leading interwar Yugoslav politician; member of several cabinets in the 1920s and 1930s, he was also the only non-Serb prime minister during the interwar period. His party initially stood for a federal Yugoslavia, in which the Slovenes would gain sufficient political autonomy, but eventually the SLS would officially accept the state centralism.

The SLS was the only political party which officially supported King Alexander's dictatorship introduced in 1929. Although Korošec fell out with the King in 1931 and issued the famous 'Ljubljana points' in 1932, demanding greater autonomy for Slovenes within Yugoslavia and the country's democratisation, he was, alongside Milan Stojadinović, leader of the largest faction of the [Serbian] National Radical Party and Mehmed Spaho, the Bosnian Muslim leader, one of the founders of the governing Yugoslav Radical Union (JRZ) in 1935. While his supporters argue that Korošec's political shifts benefited the Slovenes, his critics tend to emphasize his political opportunism, pragmatism and close links with the Roman Catholic Church in Slovenia (which, by the way, was overall pro-Yugoslav). What seems clear, however, is that to Korošec even the worst Yugoslavia was for Slovenes a far better solution than no Yugoslavia at all.[9]

The Slovene Liberals (divided into several smaller parties and fractions) enthusiastically advocated national unitarism and were—with a few exceptions—against federalism. Some of their leaders argued for a full linguistic and cultural synthesis with Serbs and Croats, which is why their critics often accused them of being anti-Slovene. In Slovene-populated parts of the new Kingdom the

---

fought for the annexation to Yugoslavia of South Slav populated Italian territories. TIGR had contacts with Yugoslavia's nationalist organizations, especially with ORJUNA.

[8] In the last interwar elections of Dec. 1938, the SLS, as part of the Yugoslav Radical Union (JRZ), won as much as 78.7 per cent of Slovene votes.

[9] Ruda Jurčec, *Skozi luči in sence*, III, Buenos Aires, 1969, p. 293.

Liberals commanded between almost 30 per cent of the vote (in the 1920 elections) and 14–15 per cent (in 1923 and in 1925; 21 per cent in 1927), but neither the party nor its most eminent leaders, such as Albert Kramer, exerted anywhere near as much influence on interwar Yugoslav politics as did Korošec and the SLS.[10]

The Social Democrats—from December 1921 divided into several factions—advocated unitarism and centralism, while defending workers' rights and principles of social democracy. One of the factions, led by Zvonimir Bernot, opted for federalism. The Communists initially called for a Soviet-type Slovene republic of peasants and workers and for the dissolution of Yugoslavia, in their view an artificial product of the Versailles treaty. Although the third largest Yugoslav party in the 1920 elections, the Communist Party of Yugoslavia (KPJ) almost disappeared by the mid-1920s. The Communist Party of Slovenia was formed as a branch of the KPJ in April 1937, but by this time the party line was pro-Yugoslav. The Slovene Party aimed at solving the Slovene national question by revolution, within the borders of Yugoslavia.

The Slovenes generally rejected integral Yugoslavism[11], but neither the major Slovene political parties nor Slovene intellectuals were anti-Yugoslav. The Slovenes accepted the new state, and were at the same time eager to preserve their distinct language and culture. This was, for instance, the argument of an important and controversial essay by the literary critic Josip Vidmar, published in Ljubljana in 1932.[12] In the new state the Slovenes were indeed able to set up their own education and cultural institutions: the Ljubljana University was founded as early as July 1919[13], the Slovene radio in 1928, and the Slovene Academy of Arts and Sciences in 1938.[14]

---

[10] For more on the Slovene Libarals see Jurij Perovšek, *Liberalizem in vprašanje slovenstva—Nacionalna politika liberalnega tabora v letih 1918–1929*, Ljubljana, 1996.

[11] Notable exceptions were the Liberals and intellectuals such as the poet Oton Župančič, who argued for linguistic unitarism.

[12] Josip Vidmar, *Kulturni problem slovenstva*, Ljubljana, 1932.

[13] The first Slovene secondary school was allowed by Austrian authorities only in 1904. It was a private school.

[14] Literacy in Slovene lands was 91.1 per cent, while in rest of the country it was just over 40 per cent in 1921. Ten years later it reached 95 per cent, while in the rest of the country the level of literacy grew to 47 per cent.

The Slovene economic development in the interwar period was also significant. Slovenia (like most of Croatia and Vojvodina) was among economically less developed regions of the Habsburg Empire. However, after 1918 it became economically the most developed part of the new state. Yugoslavia offered excellent market opportunities for Slovene products. Despite a centralised economic policy and the loss of direct connection with the port of Trieste (which went to Italy), the level of industrialization in Slovenia grew rapidly. For instance, while in 1918 there were 270 industrial and mining plants employing 40,000 workers, in 1941 the number grew to 520 plants with over 100,000 workers. The Slovenes, only 8 per cent of the Yugoslav population, contributed 26 per cent of whole industrial production of the state in the late 1930s.[15] Slovene peasants were protected by well organized net of cooperatives. Although Slovenia, like the rest of Yugoslavia and Europe, was hit by the world economic crisis in the 1930s, it may be argued that overall, the Slovene economy did quite well during the interwar years.

Between Hitler, Mussolini, Horthy and Tito: Slovenes in the Second World War

'The nation will write its sentence by itself.' (Popular Slovene Partisan slogan[16])

The Belgrade *coup d'état* of 27 March 1941, which brought down the government that signed the Tripartite Pact two days previously, was welcomed in Slovenia, where demonstrations against the former government had been held in Ljubljana and Celje. After Yugoslavia's defeat in the short April war, the Slovene territory was

---

[15] Slovenia was particularly highly represented in paper industry (43 per cent of the whole Yugoslav production), metalurgy and textile industry (both 38 per cent of the Yugoslav total), machine industry (32 per cent), electrical and timber industry (both 30 per cent). On the eve of the Second World War the national income per capita in the Dravska *banovina* was 4,000 dinars, while an average income in Yugoslavia as a whole was 2,800 dinars. *Zgodovina Slovencev*, Ljubljana, 1979, p. 705, pp. 694–6.

[16] The slogan was borrowed from Cankar's drama 'The Servants' (1910).

divided between Germany (the central part), Italy (the Ljubljana province) and Hungary (Prekmurje). The ultimate aim of the occupiers was a complete annihilation of Slovenes as a nation, although life under the Italian occupation was more bearable. The SLS was left without the leadership. Fran Kulovec—another priest, who took over the party following Korošec's death in 1940—was killed on the first day of the war, in the German bombardment of Belgrade, while the SLS ministers in the government fled to London, with the King and rest of the government.

The main Slovene resistance group, the Liberation Front (*Osvobodilna fronta—OF*), was established already on 26 April 1941, as a coalition of four major groups—the Communists, the Christian Socialists, members of the *Sokol* athletic organisation and liberal intelligentsia.[17] The OF fought for the right of the Slovene nation to self-determination, liberation and unification, who would then form a unit in a post-war federal Yugoslavia. Its activities extended from propaganda, collecting of information, material and arms to sabotages, liquidations and guerrilla fighting. The OF enjoyed the support of a majority of Slovenes.[18] The Communists took complete control over the OF only in March 1943, and the parallel process of Socialist revolution in liberated areas—which was until then implicit—became obvious.

Other Slovene political parties and groups issued statements and programmes similar to that of the OF, foreseeing united Slovenia as part of a federal Yugoslav monarchy, but they did not form any efficient resistance to the occupiers—some even collaborated with them.[19] Some politicians and members of the Catholic clergy

---

[17] The Communists were led by Boris Kidrič and Edvard Kardelj; the Christian Socialists by Edvard Kocbek and Tone Fajfar, while the most notable member of the intelligenstia to join the OF was Josip Vidmar.

[18] James Gow and Cathie Carmichael, *Slovenia and the Slovenes*, London, 2000, p. 44.

[19] The most important were: 'National-political programme' of leaders of SLS and Liberals Natlačen and Kramer of Sept. 1941; the émigré Yugoslav minister Miha Krek's 'National programme', London, Oct. 1942; 'The London Points' issued by Slovene émigré politicians of the London-based Yugoslav government-in-exile, London, Nov. 1941; Memorandum issued by the *Slovenska zaveza*, the Ljubljana Province, Spring 1942; The 'National Proclamation' by the National

(headed by the conservative bishop Gregorij Rožman) in the Province of Ljubljana accepted integration of that part of Slovenia into the Italian Kingdom. Because of their pro-Fascist inclinations and fears of a Communist revolution, they helped form in 1942 'The Voluntary Anti-Communist Militia', which was placed under the Italian military command. The Militia was completely defeated by the Partisans after the Italian capitulation in September 1943. The tragic fratricidal bloodshed thus began. 'The Home Guards' (*Domobranci*) fought against the Partisans from Autumn 1943 to May 1945. While its pro-Nazi leadership saw Slovenia as part of Hitler's New Europe, most of the ranks enlisted because of their anti-Communism; they believed in the Allied victory in the war. Anyhow, the *Domobranci* remained loyal to Germany until the end of the war, despite Tito declaring amnesty for collaborators twice in 1944 (in August and November). There was also a small number of Slovenian Četniks under Draža Mihailović's command.

Slovenia was liberated by well organized and equipped Slovene partisans, with the help of partisan units from other parts of Yugoslavia.[20] Total civilian and military losses among the Slovenes are estimated at around 70,000–80,000—including the victims of the victorious Partisans in the war's immediate aftermath.[21] Like in the rest of Yugoslavia, non-Communist opposition was supressed, often brutally. Victory in the Second World War brought the Slovene Littoral to Yugoslavia, although parts of Slovene ethnic territory remained in Italy. Borders with Hungary and Austria—despite the fact that Partisans liberated also parts of Carinthia—remained the same.[22]

Committee for Slovenia, consisting of Clericals and Liberals, Oct. 1944; a memorandum issued by the self-proclaimed 'Slovene Parliament', in the German-occupied Ljubljana, 3 May 1945. For details see Bojan Godeša, 'Slovenci in jugoslovanska skupnost v letih 1941 do 1945' in Božo Repe, Dušan Nećak, Jože Prinčič (eds), *Slovenci in Makedonci v Jugoslaviji*, Ljubljana and Skopje, 1999, pp. 71–85.

[20] And only in some eastern parts of Slovenia by the Red Army.

[21] *Ilustrirana zgodovina Slovencev*, Ljubljana, 1999, p. 347.

[22] Estimates of the number of Slovenes living outside Slovenia today are as follows: 60,000–80,000 in Italy, 20,000–40,000 in Austria, 22,000 in Croatia (according to the 1991 census) and 4,500 in Hungary.

Second Attempt: The Slovenes in Socialist Yugoslavia

'Slovenia—the land of my dreams,
Slovenia—the promised land...'
(*Buldožer*, the Slovene rock band[23])

Even if we take into account the sarcasm of the authors of the above lyrics, Slovenia—now one of six Yugoslav Socialist Republics, with its own constitution, legislative parliament, government, police and with the constitutionally guaranteed right to self-determination and secession—was seen by many Slovenes and non-Slovenes as a promised land within the post-war Yugoslavia. The economic development of Slovenia continued, and it was gradually turning from a predominantly agrarian into a predominantly industrial society.[24] It remained the most developed Yugoslav republic, with large employment opportunities and relatively high standard of living. In 1958, the GDP per capita in Slovenia was $400, while Yugoslavia's average was $220.[25]

But the growth of Slovene economy was not as rapid as it could have been, because of the economic centralization, substantial (and often non-productively used) financial help to underdeveloped parts of Yugoslavia, orientation of Tito's Yugoslavia toward the Third World (instead the West), adaptation to the economies of less developed Yugoslav republics and high federal taxes.[26] On the other

---

[23] 'Slovenija', LP *Nevino srce* ('Innocent heart', 1983; lyrics in Serbo-Croat).

[24] The share of rural population in 1900 was 73.2 per cent, in 1921 66 per cent, in 1940 55 per cent, in 1953 41 per cent, in 1961 31 per cent, in 1981 9.4 per cent and in 1991 only 6 per cent.

[25] *Zgodovina*, op. cit., p. 905. From the 1960s we can speak of further 'liberalization' of Slovene economy which had beneficial effects on all aspects of social life. By the mid-1960s, the GDP in Slovenia reached $1,000 per capita (*Slovenska kronika XX stoletja*, II, Ljubljana, 1996, p. 275). In 1960, Slovenia's GDP was 80 per cent higher than the Yugoslav average, and in 1989 100 per cent higher (*Ilustrirana zgodovina*, op. cit., p. 387).

[26] For example with only 8.3 per cent of the population, Slovenia contributed in the late 1970s with 16.5 per cent of the Yugoslav GDP and 20 per cent of total Yugoslav exports. Jože Pirjevec, *Jugoslavija 1918–1992*, Koper, 1995, pp. 355–6. See also Viktor Meier, *Zakaj je razpadla Jugoslavija*, Ljubljana, 1996, p. 92. Slovene economy covered between 17 and 20 per cent of federal costs, Pirjevec, op. cit., p. 292. Slovenia contributed substantial part of its GDP to federal funds: eg. 54 per cent only between 1947 and 1952. *Slovenska kronika XX stoletja*, II, 1996, p. 145.

hand, these handicaps were compensated by a large Yugoslav market, inexpensive raw materials and cheap labour, which all assured considerable profits for Slovene enterprises. Slovene politicians, especially Boris Kidrič (until his early death in 1953), Boris Kraigher in the 1960s and Sergej Kraigher in the early 1980s, were among creators of necessary, but ultimately not very effective economic reforms in Yugoslavia.

Slovene Communists were unquestionably pro-Yugoslav, although they often represented Slovene national interests within the federal state. They rejected 'integral' or 'assimilative' Yugoslavism, which would lead to the formation of a single Yugoslav nation.[27] They preferred Yugoslavism which would guarantee that every Yugoslav nation preserves its national identity in a voluntary union.[28] Two almost diametrically opposed models were advocated by Aleksandar Ranković on the one side and by Edvard Kardelj on the other. Ranković and Kardelj, a Serb and a Slovene, respectively, were two of Tito's closest allies (the third, Milovan Djilas, had been purged in the mid-1950s, for his criticism of the Communist 'New Class'). Their conflict was perceived as a Serb-Slovene conflict, with the former advocating a continued centralisation, and the latter de-centralisation. The conflict spilled out of the top Party leadership in the early 1960s, and was epitomised by the debate between the Serbian writer Dobrica Ćosić and the Slovene philosopher Dušan Pirjevec, although it is possible that Serbia's and Slovenia's party leaderships were behind the debate.[29]

The 'Slovene argument' prevailed, as the highly de-centralised 1974 Constitution demonstrated. But, the fall of Stane Kavčič's 'liberal' government in 1972 (which coincided with purges in other republics, particularly Serbia and Croatia) was a lost chance for the

---

[27] See for example Kardelj's new introduction to the 1957 edition of his *The Development of the Slovene National Question*, Ljubljana, pp. L-LXVI.

[28] During the whole postwar period, Slovene critics of Yugoslav integralism were criticised as 'egoists', 'traitors', 'separatists', 'destroyers of Socialist Yugoslavia', etc.

[29] Aleš Gabrič, *Socialistična kulturna revolucija*, Ljubljana, 1995, pp. 345–53; Jelena Milojković-Djurić, 'Approaches to National Identities: Ćosić's and Pirjevec's Debate on Ideological and Literary Issues', *East European Quarterly*, vol. 30, no. 1, spring 1996, pp. 63–73; Dimitrij Rupel, *Slovenski intelektualci*, Ljubljana, 1989, pp. 98–116.

liberalization of Slovene (and Yugoslav) society.[30] The Slovenes also complained of being underrepresented in key federal institutions, particularly the army. In 1970, they made up 5 per cent of the Yugoslav officer corps (6 per cent army generals were Slovenes), but in 1990 only 2 per cent of the Yugoslav army officers were Slovenes.[31]

Towards independence

'*Burek*[32]? *Nein Danke!*' (graffito in Ljubljana, late 1980s)

In the 1980s Slovenia had a more liberal Communist leadership than other Yugoslav republics, but in spite (or because?) of this first elements of an opposition movement began to emerge. The youth branch of the party and independent-minded intellectuals started to openly criticise the régime. A number of alternative groups—the 'punks', 'ecologists', 'pacifists', 'feminists', 'homosexuals'—and media (Radio Student, the journals *Mladina* and *Nova revija*) were tolerated by an increasingly reform-minded faction within the Slovene Party. The population at large responded well to the growth of the opposition to the régime (which was slowly turning into opposition to Yugoslavia), and it did not help that there was also a widespread belief that Slovenia was being economically exploited by other, less rich, republics.[33]

Aspirations for the democratisation of Slovenia in the late 1980s were coupled, under threats of a renewed centralisation, with aspirations for a complete national emancipation. At first it was believed

---

[30] It followed two other conflicts which concerned two important issues: relationship between the republics and federation (the so-called 'Road Affair' of the summer 1969) and between 'liberals' and 'conservatives' within the League of Communists of Slovenia ('The Affair of the 25 delegates' of May 1971).

[31] Pirjevec, op. cit., p. 336.

[32] *Burek* is a pastry containing cheese, minced meat or spinach, popular throughout the Balkans, and is associated with the region's Ottoman heritage. In this context the rejection of *burek* was meant to symbolise the rejection of Yugoslavia, emphasising Slovenia's differentiation from the other Yugoslav republics, in particular Serbia and Bosnia.

[33] In the late 1980s, Slovenia, with 8 per cent of the whole population, produced 22 per cent of Yugoslavia's public revenues, 30 per cent of the export to countries with hard currencies, and 25 per cent of Yugoslavia's export in general. Meier, op. cit., p. 171.

these were possible within a Yugoslav confederation or an asymmetrical federation, but calls for a complete independence soon prevailed. The civil society's democratic initiative was taken over by new political forces that were oriented also towards the national independence. In my opinion this was the turning point: instead of becoming the avantgarde for political democratization of Yugoslavia as a whole, leading political forces in Slovenia decided to build their own democratic nation-state. Intellectuals around the *Nova revija* magazine published in February 1987 a special issue under the title 'Contributions to the Slovene national programme'. It critically discussed the situation of Slovenia in Yugoslavia, demanding a higher level of sovereignty for the northern republic. The group around the *Nova revija* came under attack from authorities in both Slovenia and other republics.

Loss of legitimacy of the Communists in the late 1980s coincided with the rise of nationalism in Slobodan Milošević's Serbia. Tensions between the federal army and Slovenia grew, as was illustrated by the 'Trial of the Four' in the Spring of 1988.[34]

Slovenia's Communists—led since May 1986 by the moderate Milan Kučan—approved gradual changes of the political system, under the slogan 'descent from the power'. The 1989 'May Declaration' of opposition parties demanded independence for Slovenia, but Kučan's Communists still insisted on the preservation of Yugoslavia, although they called for fundamental transformation of the federation. As for the public, it still seemed relatively divided in 1989: according to a public opinion survey, 46.7 per cent of Slovenes were for a debate on whether Slovenia should secede from Yugoslavia and 28 per cent were against any debate on the issue.[35]

But it seemed already too late to save Yugoslavia. A verbal war between Serbian and pro-Yugoslav media on one side and Slovene on the other culminated when Slovenia supported Albanian claims in Kosovo. The clearest signs of the collapse of the federation came in September 1989 when the Slovene Assembly adopted constitutional amendments according to which the federal legislation is not

[34] Trial at Military Court in Ljubljana provoked mass demonstration of Slovenes. A public opinion survey showed that 86.2 per cent of respondents perceived the trial, conducted in Serbo-Croat, as 'a restriction of Slovenia's sovereignty'. Janko Prunk, *Slovenski narodni programi*, Ljubljana, 1986, p. 331.
[35] Ibid.

valid in Slovenia if it is contrary to its Constitution. On 1 December 1989 (the birthday of the first Yugoslavia), Slovene authorities banned the so-called 'Meeting of the Truth' in Ljubljana, which was to be held by Kosovo Serbs, and supported by Milošević. Serbia responded by introducing an economic blockade on Slovenian goods. Yugoslavia seemed finished in January 1990, when the Slovene delegation walked out of the Fourteenth and the last Congress of the League of Communists of Yugoslavia.

The first post-war democratic elections in Slovenia were held in April 1990. The Democratic Opposition of Slovenia (DEMOS) coalition won with 55 per cent of the vote, enough to enable it to create a government. Kučan, however, remained the president of the republic. The new Slovene government accelerated preparations for Slovenia's independence, by now supported by an overwhelming majority of Slovenes. At a referendum held in December 1990, 88.2 per cent voted for independence (the turnout was 93.2 per cent). Slovenia formally declared independence on 25 June 1991. The 'ten-day war' between the Yugoslav army and Slovene troops of June–July 1991, was followed by an internationally brokered agreement which effectively sealed Slovenia's independence. The federal army left by October 1991 and a new Slovene Constitution was promulgated in December the same year. International recognition followed, and on 22 May 1992 Slovenia became a member of the UN.

Epilogue: Contemporary Slovene views of the 'Yugoslav century'

'Slovenia to Slovenes!' (Slogan of the extreme right-wing Slovene National Party [1992])

'If you don't realize what you've lost, then you've lost nothing.' (Aleš Debeljak, the Slovenian writer[36])

Slovenia is today a stable democracy and, relatively, a fast developing country. In 1999 its GDP was $20.01 billion (1999), or $10,802 *per capita*, while the inflation rate was 8 per cent.[37] Average monthly salaries reached over 1,000 DEM in September 2000. The ambitious economic re-direction towards western markets succeeded (although,

[36] Aleš Debeljak, *Twilight of the Idols*, New York, 1994, p. 54.
[37] In 1989 it was $10.92 billion or $5,463 *per capita* ($3,336 in 1985).

it was helped by the fact that already in the early 1980s one third
of all Yugoslav export goods that went to the West were from
Slovenia). Today, Slovenia exports two thirds of its products to the
EU countries, and only about 15 per cent to the other former-
Yugoslav republics. Slovenia is rapidly approaching the inclusion in
the EU and NATO.[38] Transition—social, political and economic—
has been relatively smooth and non-traumatic thus far, although
the country faces several serious problems such as the unemployment and the decline of industrial production,[39] restructuring of the
economy, deepening of social differences, rise of manifested and
'hidden' national exclusiveness and complex State-Church relations.

Before and in the aftermath of the independence, anti-Yugoslavism
and even radical Slovene nationalism emerged. The Slovene nationalism is essentially based on the nation's linguistic and cultural unique-
ness vis-à-vis other South Slavs, rather than on myths of a glorious
past and lost mediaeval kingdoms. Extreme nationalists argue that
Slovenes are superior to other Yugoslavs, who are often depicted as
'Byzantine', 'barbarian', 'southerners' and 'Balkanites'. To them,
Yugoslavia was a result either of the 'Karadjordjević or Tito conspiracy', 'Great-Serbian expansionism', or the 'Communist terror'.[40]
Theories about Slovenes' non-South Slav origins also appeared in
the 1980s and 1990s. According to them, Slovenes descend from the
ancient Wends—allegedly a proto-Slavonic tribe which inhabited
Central Europe in the twelfth century BC, eventually spreading across
Europe. Therefore, the Slovenes are not only an autochthonous Central European nation, but are not related to Serbs and Croats, either,
who settled in the Balkans in the sixth and seventh centuries AD.[41]

---

[38] A public opinion survey carried out in 1988 showed that 84.9 per cent of
respondents were completely or mostly for inclusion of Yugoslavia in the EC
(Prunk, op. cit., p. 345); ten years later, in the independent Slovenia, only 56.2
per cent said they supported Slovenia joining the EU. Niko Toš (ed.), *Vrednote v
prehodu*, vol. 2, Ljubljana, 1999, p. 858.

[39] The unemployment in Aug. 2000 was 11.7 per cent. The industrial production
in 2000 was still 20 per cent below the production rate in 1986.

[40] See for example an analysis of hate-speech in newspaper columns in Tonči
Kuzmanić, *Hate-Speech in Slovenia*, Ljubljana, 1999. Other Yogoslavs' stereotypes
about Slovenes include: 'cold', 'selfish', 'stingy', 'Austrian lackeys and even
'homosexuals'.

[41] See Matej Bor, Joško Šavli and Ivan Tomažič, *Veneti, naši davni predniki*, Vienna
and Maribor, 1989; and Joško Šavli, *Slovenska država Karantanija*, Koper and
Vienna, 1990.

After a decade of independence, however, the Slovenes are coming to more balanced view(s) of their Yugoslav experience. Public opinion surveys show moderate views in regard to the former-Yugoslavia. In 1998 47.8 per cent of Slovenes had mixed (both positive and negative) memories of the former state, 36.9 per cent mostly positive and only 5.4 per cent had mostly negative memories.[42] Most Slovenes see Yugoslavia as a 'finished chapter' in their history, but 'Yugo-nostalgia', mostly cultural, is very common.

In my view, both Yugoslavias played a key role in the development and formation of the modern Slovenian national identity, just like the Slovenes played an important part in history of Yugoslavism(s) and Yugoslav state(s). As the authors of a recent western study on Slovenia argue, 'Slovene self-governance within that South Slav framework was therefore vital to the existence of the common state. Ironically, the Yugoslav framework was also vital for the growth of Slovene statehood and ultimate self-governance.'[43] Whether Slovenia would be better or worse off without its 'Yugoslav century' are mere speculations. Yugoslavia was neither a 'fate', nor the 'best' or the 'worst' solution—it was a result of complex historical processes in which the Slovenes played an integral part.

[42] In 1995, the figures were 50.4 per cent, 34.1 per cent and 6.8 per cent, respectively *Vrednote*, op. cit., pp. 871, 565. Interestingly, Tito's historical role was judged as positive and very positive by as many as 83.6 per cent of respondents in 1995 and 84.3 per cent in 1998, while that of Kardelj was seen as a positive one only by 45.1 per cent in 1995 and 47.8 per cent in 1998, *Vrednote*, op. cit., pp. 563, 564, 870, 871. Surprisingly perhaps, in 1998 as many as 88.2 per cent of respondents said that the quality of life in Yugoslavia was good or very good (88.1 per cent in 1995), and only 5.5 per cent and 7 per cent, respectively, as bad and very bad, *Vrednote*, op. cit., pp. 565, 872.

[43] Gow and Carmichael, op. cit., pp. 25–6.

BOSNIAN MUSLIMS AND
THE YUGOSLAV IDEA

Xavier Bougarel

Perhaps not unusually for Bosnia–Herzegovina, relationship between the Bosnian Muslims and Yugoslavism can be summarized by a paradox: Bosnian Muslims hardly contributed to the formulation of the Yugoslav idea, but they had probably been the last among the Yugoslav nations who sincerely held onto it. In 1990, this belated Yugoslavism of the Bosnian Muslim community led the Yugoslav Prime Minister Ante Marković to launch his pro–Yugoslav Alliance of the Reformist Forces of Yugoslavia in Bosnia–Herzegovina, in a last attempt to oppose the growing nationalism with a Yugoslav project. Yet, despite opinion polls predicting a victory for the Reformists, the nationalist parties won the Bosnian general elections of 18 November 1990, and about 70 per cent of Bosnian Muslims voted for the Party of Democratic Action (SDA). At that time, the position of the SDA leaders vis-à-vis the Yugoslav idea was still ambiguous, with the party president Alija Izetbegović declaring that 'Yugoslavia is not our love, but it is in our interest'.[1]

Attitude of Bosnian Muslims towards the Yugoslav idea has often been misunderstood, and their motives sometimes reduced by outside observers to simple political opportunism. Beyond tactical manoeuvring, it is nevertheless possible to discern some genuine identity cleavages and strategic dilemmas, some slow changes and violent ruptures. In order to identify such phenomena, it is first necessary to analyze the attitude of the Bosnian Muslim community and its main representatives towards the first and the second Yugoslavia. It is then

---

[1] Statement made at a SDA meeting in Bihać on 10 Feb. 1991. See *Oslobodjenje*, Sarajevo, 12 Feb. 1991.

important to take a closer look at the stance of the SDA leaders during the dissolution of thé Yugoslav state, in order to establish whether they were for or against the preservation of Yugoslavia, and whether their actions represented continuity or discontinuity in relation to the Bosnian Muslim élites of the interwar and communist periods.

First Yugoslavia: a refuge or a threat for the Bosnian Muslims?

Before the First World War, the Bosnian Muslims did not seem to be attracted by the Yugoslav idea. Only a few individuals, often belonging to the nascent Muslim intelligentsia or educated youth, participated in movements that can be considered as pro-Yugoslav, such as the secret organisation Young Bosnia (*Mlada Bosna*).[2] After the Congress of Berlin of 1878, Bosnian Muslim leaders had very quickly pledged allegiance to the new Austro-Hungarian authorities, concentrating on defending the religious identity and institutions of their community and, to this end, entering into shifting tactical alliances with both Serb and Croat political groups. This structuring of the Bosnian Muslim community into a kind of a post-Ottoman Muslim *millet*, a non-sovereign religious community renouncing any nationalist project of its own, is illustrated by the emergence of the community name 'Muslims' at the end of the nineteenth century, and by the achievement of the religious and cultural autonomy in 1909.[3] At the same time, the strong desire of the tiny Muslim intelligentsia to be integrated into European political and cultural modernity, and its rejection of religious divisions inherited from the Ottoman Empire, led it to support the idea of *bošnjaštvo* (Bosnianism) launched by the Habsburg Governor Benjámin Kállay.[4] The Muslim secular intelligentsia was divided into pro-Croat and pro-Serb factions, which both equally rejected the

[2] For more on the Young Bosnia see Vladimir Dedijer, *The Road to Sarajevo*, London, 1966.
[3] See Nusret Šehić, *Autonomni pokret Muslimana za vrijeme austrougarske uprave u Bosni i Hercegovini*, Sarajevo, 1980; Robert Donia, *Islam under the Double Eagle: The Muslims of Bosnia and Herzegovina 1878–1914*, New York, 1981.
[4] See Tomislav Kraljačić, *Kallajev režim u Bosni i Hercegovini (1882–1903)*, Sarajevo, 1987.

name 'Muslims', preferring to declare themselves Croats or Serbs 'of Islamic faith'.[5] The absence of Bosnian Muslims from the Yugoslav Committee, or their small number within the provisional institutions set up following the Yugoslav unification in 1918, can be explained as much by their own attitude as by the scant attention paid to them by other South Slavs. The hardships of the immediate post-war period (the land reform, anti-Muslim riots and resumption of emigration to Turkey) led the Bosnian Muslim élites to reproduce political strategies elaborated during the Austro-Hungarian period. In June 1921, the Yugoslav Muslim Organisation (JMO) exchanged its support for the centralising Constitution of the new Kingdom of Serbs, Croats and Slovenes, for the preservation of old Bosnian borders within the new administrative division of the country, the maintenance of the autonomy of Islamic religious institutions, and guarantees of financial compensation for properties affected by the land reform. Thereafter, the JMO oscillated between governments led by the National Radical Party (NRS) or by the Democratic Party (DS)—the two Serb-dominated parties—and opposition coalitions led by the Croatian Peasant Party (HSS).[6]

Allegiance to central power and frequent shifting between Serb and Croat political parties remained central to the Bosnian Muslim strategies during the interwar years. But, situated within different a institutional framework to the ones existing in the former Ottoman and Habsburg Empires, these could only lead to unprecedented constructions of identity. As its name indicates, the JMO supported the Yugoslav idea, and declared in its program that it regarded 'Yugoslavism [*jugoslovenstvo*] as the most appropriate path towards rapprochement and unification [of the South Slavs]'[7]. The JMO's Yugoslavism did not only correspond to its strategic choices, but also its need to escape assimilating pressures of both Serbs and Croats. Yugoslavism of the JMO therefore represented a convenient refuge rather than a genuine political choice. Already in 1920, the JMO leaders proposed to change the name of the Kingdom of

[5] See Alija Isaković, *O 'nacionaliziranju' Muslimana*, Zagreb, 1990.
[6] See Atif Purivatra, *Jugoslovenska Muslimanska Organizacija u političkom životu Kraljevine Srba, Hrvata i Slovenaca*, Sarajevo, 1974.
[7] 'Program Jugoslovenske Muslimanske Organizacije (1920)', reproduced in ibid., pp. 596–7.

Serbs, Croats and Slovenes into the Kingdom of Yugoslavia. At the same time, however, they denounced the 'Yugoslav nationalism' of the Democrats allying themselves with the Radicals, who showed more respect for their communitarian practices. Tactical Yugoslavism and a lack of national determination were thus perceived as complementary for the preservation of a Bosnian Muslim identity still constituted in a pre-national way.[8]

The escalation of the Serbo-Croat political conflict directly affected Bosnia's Muslims. Already in the mid-1920s, the divisions between the pro-Croat and pro-Serb Muslim intellectuals grew deeper, as was demonstrated by the existence of two rival Muslim cultural societies: *Gajret* (The Effort) and *Narodna uzdanica* (The People's Hope).[9] In 1929, the transformation of the Kingdom of Serbs, Croats and Slovenes into the Kingdom of Yugoslavia took place in parallel with the division of Bosnia-Herzegovina into four different *banovinas*, and the suppression of the religious autonomy obtained twenty years before[10]. The JMO leaders first joined the protests of the united opposition, but agreed in 1935 to enter the government and to dissolve itself within the Yugoslav Radical Union (JRZ), in exchange for the restoration of some autonomy for the Islamic Religious Community (*Islamska vjerska zajednica*).[11]

---

[8] Scholars have noted that some JMO leaders declared themselves Serbs or Croats, questioning their reasons for doing so. None of them seems to have paid attention to the fact that Muslim leaders, whether they declared themselves as 'Serbs' or as 'Croats', by conviction or by tactic, never called upon all Bosnian Muslims to follow them and do the same.

[9] See Ibrahim Kemura, *Uloga 'Gajreta' u društvenom životu Muslimana*, Sarajevo, 1986; Ismail Hadžiahmetović, *'Narodna uzdanica' u kulturnome i društvenome životu Muslimana Bosne i Hercegovine*, Tuzla, 1998.

[10] At the same time, the different Islamic religious institutions of Bosnia-Herzegovina, Serbia and Montenegro were unified under one single Islamic Religious Community (IVZ) which covered the whole Kingdom of Yugoslavia, and was dominated by the Bosnian *ulemas*. The Yugoslav authorities unsuccessfully tried to use them to assimilate the non-Slav Muslim populations of Kosovo and Macedonia. See Aleksandar Popović, *L'islam balkanique. Les musulmans du sud-est européen dans la période post-ottamane*, Berlin-Wiesbaden, 1986, pp. 318–9; Ismail Ahmeti, 'Institucionet e kultit islamik në Kërçovë gjatë viteve 1939–1950' in Masar Kodra (ed.), *Shqiptarët e Maqedonisë*, Skopje, 1994, pp. 457–64.

[11] The JRZ was formed by fusion of the JMO, a majority faction of the Radical Party and the Slovene People's Party (SLS). Its president was Milan Stojadinović,

Three years later, they suffered an unexpected electoral defeat against the candidates of the Muslim Organisation (*Muslimanska organizacija*), a small political party linked to the HSS.[12] From a refuge, Yugoslavia increasingly turned during the 1930s into a threat for the Bosnian Muslim community. It is therefore not surprising that its political representatives tended more and more to reject it. United in their opposition to the Cvetković-Maček Agreement of August 1939, which granted Croat-populated regions of Bosnia to the newly-formed *banovina* of Croatia, the Muslim élites founded a Movement for the Autonomy of Bosnia-Herzegovina, which constituted the first organised manifestation of a nascent Muslim nationalism.[13] Some intellectuals, denying their previous pro-Croat or pro-Serb loyalties, promoted a neo-*bošnjaštvo*, which applied the national name 'Bosniak' (*Bošnjak*) only to the Bosnian Muslims.[14] Meanwhile, the educated Muslim youth was divided between various pan-Islamist groups, which dreamed of uniting all Balkan Muslims into one large state[15], and the League of Communist Youth of Yugoslavia, which called for a new, Soviet Yugoslavia.[16] The JMO, however, remained in the government.

This political evolution of the Bosnian Muslims explains why in April 1941 they did not really mourn the collapse of the first Yugoslavia. Whilst some of their leaders joined the government of the Independent State of Croatia (NDH), many continued to seek

---

the Yugoslav Prime Minister, and vice-presidents Mehmed Spaho and Anton Korošec, leaders of the JMO and SLS, respectively.

[12] See Dana Begić, 'Akcije muslimanskih gradjanskih političara poslije skupštinskih izbora 1935. godine', *Godišnjak društva istoričara Bosne i Hercegovine*, Sarajevo, vol. XVI, 1965, pp. 173–89.

[13] See Dana Begić, 'Pokret za autonomiju Bosne i Hercegovine u uslovima sporazuma Cvetković-Maček', *Prilozi instituta za historiju radničkog pokreta*, Sarajevo, vol. IV, no. 4, 1968, pp. 177–91.

[14] See Muhamed Hadžijahić, *Od tradicije do identiteta. Geneza nacionalnog pitanja bosanskih Muslimana*, Sarajevo, 1974.

[15] See Sead Trhulj, *Mladi Muslimani*, Zagreb, 1990; Xavier Bougarel, 'From "Young Muslims" to the Party of Democratic Action: The Emergence of a Panislamist Trend in Bosnia-Herzegovina', *Islamic Studies*, Islamabad, vol. XXXVI, no. 2–3 (Summer-Autumn 1997), pp. 533–49.

[16] See Dubravka Škarica, 'Napredna srednjoškolska omladina Bosne i Hercegovine u revolucionarno-demokratskom pokretu 1937–1941. god.', *Prilozi instituta za historiju radničkog pokreta*, Sarajevo, vol. IV, no. 4, 1968, pp. 593–617.

autonomy for Bosnia. During the Second World War, however, the Autonomy Movement ran into some fatal contradictions. Hostile to the integration of Bosnia-Herzegovina into the NDH, it offered to collaborate with the Third Reich in exchange for the creation of an autonomous Bosnia under direct German tutelage. Despite the fact it had been created in opposition to the project of partition of Bosnia-Herzegovina, it was ready to offer, in exchange for autonomy, Western Herzegovina to the NDH, and Eastern Herzegovina to Montenegro.[17] But the NDH remained the closest ally of the Axis powers in the Western Balkans, and this proposal never came to fruition. On the ground, the Autonomy Movement did not even ensure the safety of the Bosnian Muslim population: the creation of the Bosnian Muslim SS division *Handžar* in 1943 only contributed to the cycle of violence.[18] From 1943 onwards, it was the Communist Party of Yugoslavia (KPJ) which offered the best protection to Bosnia's Muslims and which promised them political recognition in a future Yugoslavia. The KPJ thus succeeded in mobilizing the Muslims for its own Yugoslav project.

The Second Yugoslavia and the Muslim 'national affirmation'

Initially, the Partisan Movement in Bosnia-Herzegovina recruited its fighters mainly among the Serb population. But in order to expand its base, it was always careful to take into account the multiethnic character of the Bosnian society. The Partisans promised 'full equality of rights between all Serbs, Muslims and Croats' and foresaw Bosnia-Herzegovina as a republic of the future Yugoslav Federation.[19] The Partisans also allowed the creation of separate 'Muslim brigades',

[17] See Rasim Hurem, 'Pokušaj nekih gradjanskih muslimanskih političara da Bosnu i Hercegovinu izdvoje iz okvira Nezavisne Države Hrvatske', *Godišnjak Društva Istoričara Bosne i Hercegovine*, Sarajevo, vol. XVI, 1965, pp. 191–220; Rasim Hurem, 'Koncepcije nekih muslimanskih gradjanskih političara o položaju Bosne i Hercegovine u vremenu od sredine 1943. do kraja 1944. godine', *Prilozi instituta za historiju radničkog pokreta*, Sarajevo, vol. IV, no. 4, 1968, pp. 533–48.
[18] See Enver Redžić, *Muslimansko autonomaštvo i 13. SS divizija*, Sarajevo, 1987.
[19] 'Resolution of the first session of the Provincial Anti-Fascist Council of the National Liberation of Bosnia-Herzegovina (ZAVNOBiH)', held on 25 and 26 Nov. 1943 in Mrkonjić Grad, quoted in Dubravko Lovrenović, *Istina o Bosni i Herzegovina—činjenice iz istorije BiH*, Sarajevo, 1991, p. 76.

where the main principles of Islam were respected, and integrated some former leaders of the JMO and the Autonomy Movement into the Anti-Fascist Councils for the National Liberation of Bosnia-Herzegovina (ZAVNOBiH) and of Yugoslavia (AVNOJ), created on 25 and 29 November 1943, respectively.[20]

During the Second World War, the Communist Party of Yugoslavia had thus recognized Bosnia-Herzegovina as a separate territorial entity, and recognised the existence of the Bosnian Muslim community, although without specifying its exact nature (religious or national). But this recognition was soon called into question after the war: the Communist Party first suppressed the Muslim Committee (*Muslimanski Odbor*) existing within the National Liberation Front[21], and then carried out a campaign against the IVZ. In 1947, the abolition of Islamic courts, the nationalisation of the *vaqufs* (religious-charitable foundations and the closure of the *madrasas* (religious schools) led to the disappearance of the very institutions which had formed the backbone of the Bosnian Muslim community. Finally, in 1949, the Muslim cultural society *Preporod* (Revival) was dissolved, only three years after its foundation. After having instrumentalized the communitarian modes of the Bosnian Muslims to its own advantage, the Communist Party of Yugoslavia set about dismantling them.

In the medium term, however, these decisions of the Yugoslav authorities facilitated the transformation of the Bosnian Muslim community into a modern nation. By making Bosnia-Herzegovina one of the six constitutive republics of Yugoslavia, the Communist Party had put a brake on Serb and Croat nationalist claims, and created the necessary space for the crystallization of Muslim national identity. The 'identity void' which appeared at that time is shown by the census of 1953, in which 93.8 per cent of the Bosnian Muslims

---

[20] Atif Purivatra, 'Stav Komunističke Partije Jugoslavije prema nacionalnom pitanju Muslimana u toku narodnooslobodilačkog rata' in *Nacionalni i politički razvitak Muslimana*, Sarajevo, 1969, pp. 65–129; Attila Hoare, 'The People's Liberation Movement in Bosnia-Herzegovina, 1941–45: What Did it Mean to Fight for a Multinational State?', *Nationalism and Ethnic Politics*, vol. II, no. 3, autumn 1996, pp. 415–45.

[21] The National Liberation Front was created during the war by the Communist Party of Yugoslavia. It became the National Front in 1945, and the Socialist Alliance of the Working People in 1953.

declared themselves as 'nationally undetermined Yugoslavs', only 3.8 per cent declared themselves as Serbs, and 1.7 per cent as Croats.[22] At the same time, rapid modernisation of the Bosnian society and the formation of new political and intellectual Muslim élites strengthened the position of the Bosnian Muslims within the Communist Party (League of Communists since 1952). In the context of growing 'ethnicisation' of the political system, the League of Communists of Bosnia–Herzegovina declared on 17 May 1968 that:

> The practice has shown the harmfulness, in the past period, of the different forms of pressure and injunction aiming to make Muslims declare themselves nationally as Serbs or Croats, since it has appeared in the past, and it is confirmed by the present socialist practice, that Muslims form a distinct nation.[23]

The 'national affirmation' of the Bosnian Muslims, endorsed at the federal level by the Constitution of 1974, represented a turning point of their political evolution and was followed by the (re)discovery of their own past and culture. The strong attachment they demonstrated at that time to the Yugoslav idea has to be examined in this context, and can be related to two distinct phenomena. On the one hand, the socio-economical and cultural modernisation of Bosnian society resulted in the partial disappearance of traditional communitarianism, manifested by a rapid increase in the number of mixed marriages. Amongst the educated middle class and certain parts of the working class, it was therefore not uncommon for the Yugoslav identity to become stronger than Muslim, Serb or Croat national identities.[24] On the other hand, Yugoslav federalism represented not

---

[22] On the other hand, 61.5 per cent of the Muslim communist leaders mentioned in the the 1956 edition of Yugoslavia's *Who's Who* declared themselves as Serbs, 16.6 per cent as Croats, and only 8.6 per cent as 'nationally undetermined Yugoslavs'. See David Dyker, 'The Ethnic Muslims of Bosnia—Some Basic Socio-Economic Data', *Slavonic and East European Review,* vol. 50, no. 119, Apr. 1972, pp. 238–56.

[23] Resolution of the 12th Session of the Central Committee of the League of Communists of Bosnia–Herzegovina, quoted in Atif Purivatra, *Nacionalni i politički razvoj Muslimana,* op. cit., p. 30.

[24] In the census of 1981, 7.9 per cent of the inhabitants of Bosnia–Herzegovina declared themselves as 'Yugoslavs'. See Duško Sekulić, 'Who were the Yugoslavs? Failed Sources of a Common Identity in Former Yugoslavia', *American Sociological Review,* vol. CIX, no. 1, Feb., 1994, pp. 83–97.

only a protection against Serb and Croat nationalisms, but also a favourable framework for the affirmation of the specific identity and interests of the young Muslim nation. It is therefore no surprise that in addition to the Muslim political leaders within the League of Communists and Marxist intellectuals linked to the process of 'national affirmation' (such as Atif Purivatra or Muhamed Filipović), the Muslim population at large and even the *ulemas* of the IVZ became strongly committed to Tito's Yugoslavia.[25]

This attachment should certainly not be perceived as an unconditional one. The Bosnian Muslim communist leaders were actively involved in the 'clientelistic' conflicts opposing the different communities and nations of Yugoslavia, as shown by the '*Agrokomerc* affair' in 1987.[26] The intellectuals worked fervently for the promotion of Bosnian Muslim history and literature, and even occasionally called even for the recognition of a separate Bosnian language. They also discreetly denounced the fact that the Muslim nation had neither its own national institutions nor its own republic, since Bosnia–Herzegovina had three constitutive nations: the Muslims, the Serbs and the Croats. The *ulemas*, for their part, took advantage of the increasingly important role of the Islamic Community (IZ), which was de facto a substitute national institution.[27] However, none of them put into question the existing Yugoslav political and institutional framework. At that time, to use the words of Alija Izetbegović, 'Yugoslavia embodied not only the interest, but also the love of a large majority of Bosnian Muslims'.

[25] See Steven Burg, 'The Political Integration of Yugoslavia's Muslims: Determinants of Success and Failure', *Carl Beck Papers in Russian and East European Studies*, no. 203, Pittsburgh, 1983.

[26] The '*Agrokomerc* affair' began as a financial scandal involving Fikret Abdić, the director of a powerful agricultural and food production conglomerate in Cazinska Krajina (the area surrounding Bihać). But this scandal took quickly a political dimension after Abdić was accused of having created a wide nepotistic and clientelistic system, thanks to the protection of Hamdija Pozderac, an important communist leader originating also from Cazinska Krajina, who was then the representative of Bosnia–Herzegovina in the Yugoslav collective presidency.

[27] See Zachary Irwin, 'The Islamic Revival and the Muslims of Bosnia–Herzegovina', *East European Quaterly*, vol. XVII, no. 4, January 1984, pp. 437–58. In 1969 the IVZ dropped 'vjerska' (religious) from its name to become just the IZ (Islamic Community).

The main exception to this rule was the Bosnian pan-Islamist movement, which was reorganized in the 1970s within the Islamic Community, and whose informal leader was Izetbegović himself.[28] In 1983, with twelve other persons, he was accused of 'endangering the fraternity and unity of the Yugoslav nations', and of advocating the creation of an 'ethnically pure' Bosnia-Herzegovina. He retorted that his *Islamic Declaration* contained only general opinions on the Muslim world, and did not concern Yugoslavia itself.[29] Striclty speaking this was true, since the *Islamic Declaration* was a mere summary of the themes present in Islamic literature all over the world.[30] However, the fact that the *Islamic Declaration* proposed as a political model the Islamic Republic of Pakistan, a country which was born out of the violent partition of a larger multiethnic country, and which national identity is based on Islam, was an indirect, but clear message to all Yugoslav Muslims. Therefore, the Communists' accusation that the members of the Bosnian pan-Islamic movement argued for 'the creation of a united Islamic state that would incorporate the territories of Bosnia-Herzegovina, the Sandžak and the Autonomous Province of Kosovo'[31] was not completely absurd. What remains unclear is how much this episode had contributed to the transformation of Izetbegović and his collaborators as leaders of Bosnian Muslims several years later.

The SDA and the break-up of Yugoslavia

The Party of Democratic Action (SDA) was founded on 27 March 1990. Several of its founders were linked to the Bosnian pan-Islamic movement, but it soon expanded to incorporate a number of former Communists. Amongst the three SDA representatives elected on 18 November 1990 to the collective Presidency of Bosnia-Herzegovina, only Alija Izetbegović belonged to the pan-Islamic movement, while Fikret Abdić and Ejup Ganić used to be the members of the League of Communists. Similarly, out of eighty six

[28] Bougarel, 'From "Young Muslims" to the Party of Democratic Action', op. cit.
[29] Abid Prguda, *Sarajevski proces. Sudjenje muslimanskim intelektualcima 1983. g.*, Sarajevo, 1990.
[30] Alija Izetbegović, *Islamska deklaracija*, Sarajevo, 1990.
[31] *Oslobodjenje*, 22 July 1983.

SDA deputies elected to the Bosnian Parliament, only a dozen can be regarded as close to the pan-Islamic movement. But the pan-Islamists kept hold of the party apparatus itself, as shown by the exclusion of Adil Zulfikarpašić[32] and the promoters of neo-*bošnjaštvo* in September 1990, or the election of Izetbegović as President of the Bosnian Presidency three months later, despite the fact that he had received a much smaller number of votes than Fikret Abdić.[33] In the next few years, most political decisions made by the SDA were strongly influenced by its pan-Islamic hard core, which had of course to take into account the balance of power within the SDA, the Bosnian Muslim community, but also in the wider Bosnian and Yugoslav context.

To understand the attitude of the SDA leaders towards the breakdown of Yugoslavia, it is first necessary to distinguish between Yugoslavism as a national identification and Yugoslavism as an institutional framework, or, as Izetbegović put it, between Yugoslavia as a 'love-object' and Yugoslavia as an 'interest'. In 1990, it was already clear that the SDA leaders, or at least those linked to the pan-Islamic movement, were hostile to Yugoslavism, certainly its first form. During the electoral campaign, their most virulent attacks were directed at the Alliance of the Reformist Forces of Yugoslavia (SRSJ), founded by the Yugoslav Prime Minister Ante Marković. A few months later, during the new population census, they described Yugoslavism as an 'artificial national creation'.[34] On the other hand,

---

[32] Adil Zulfikarpašić, a former member of the Communist Party, who fled to Western Europe in the late 1940s, advocated the adoption of the national name Bosniak (*Bošnjak*) by the Bosnian Muslims since the 1960s. He was also a member of the Democratic Alternative, a pro-Yugoslav group of eminent Yugoslavs in exile, found in the early 1960s. Zulfikarpašić joined the SDA in 1990, but soon came into conflict with the pan-Islamic faction and was expelled from the party in Sept. 1990, together with his supporters. He then founded the Bosniak Muslim Organisation (MBO), which only received 1.1 per cent of the vote in the Nov. 1990 general elections.

[33] In the election to the Presidency of Bosnia-Herzegovina, Fikret Abdić received 1,040,307 votes, and Alija Izetbegović only 874,213. But, the SDA leaders decided that the latter should be nevertheless elected as President of the Bosnian Presidency. Izetbegović's election was eventually also approved by the Serb Democratic Party (SDS) and the Croat Democratic Community of Bosnia-Herzegovina (HDZ), the parties of Bosnian Serbs and Croats, respectively.

[34] Džemaludin Latić, 'Borba za bolju političku poziciju', *Muslimanski Glas,* Sarajevo, vol. 1, no. 3, 20 Feb. 1991, p. 3.

their attitude towards the Yugoslav Federation as an institutional framework remained much more complex and fluid. During the electoral campaign, the SDA leaders remained elusive on the subject. They stated their attachment to Yugoslavia but, at the same time, insisted on the sovereignty of Bosnia-Herzegovina, occasionally mentioning Bosnian independence. They also refused to take clear sides in the debate that took place at that time between the 'federalist' republics (Serbia and Montenegro) and the 'confederalist' ones (Slovenia and Croatia). There were two main reasons for this ambiguous attitude of the SDA. Firstly, it was a traditional position of Bosnian Muslims vis-à-vis Serbo-Croat arguments, and the SDA was to a degree following the path of the JMO during the interwar period. But, more importantly, the SDA leaders had to reckon with the strong attachment of Bosnian Muslims to Yugoslavia: in an opinion poll in Bosnia-Herzegovina at the end of 1989, 62.2 per cent of Muslims supported the strengthening of federal institutions, while only 9.5 per cent wanted further autonomy for the republics.[35] Therefore, the second reason for the SDA position was the fear that it might lose popular support if it clearly sided with the 'confederalist' bloc.

Shortly after the elections of November 1990, the SDA declared itself in favour of a confederal solution[36], and submitted to the Bosnian Parliament a 'Declaration on the sovereignty and indivisibility of Bosnia-Herzegovina', which did not even mention Yugoslavia.[37] It is thus too simplistic to pretend that the SDA leaders have abandoned the Yugoslav idea only under the pressure of circumstances of the early 1990s, after the collapse of Yugoslavia. What is certainly true of the Bosnian Muslims at large is not necessarily so of their political leaders. Perhaps paradoxically, but it was above all the vehement reaction of Radovan Karadžić's Serb Democratic Party (SDS), mounting tensions between Croatia and Serbia, and the first talks between Slobodan Milošević and Franjo Tudjman about the

[35] See Ibrahim Bakić, 'Gradjani BiH o medjunacionalnim odnosima', *Sveske Instituta za proučavanje medjunacionalnih odnosa,* Sarajevo, vol. VIII, no. 28–29, 1990, p. 299.
[36] See Džemaludin Latić, 'Zašto se izvršni odbor SDA odlučio za konfederaciju', *Muslimanski glas,* vol. II, no. 5, 20 March 1991, p. 3.
[37] 'Deklaracija o državnoj suverenosti i nedjeljivosti Bosne i Hercegovine', reproduced in *Muslimanski glas,* vol. II, no. 3, 20 Feb. 1991, p. 1.

partition of Bosnia-Herzegovina, which led the SDA to withdraw its proposition to declare Bosnia-Herzegovina a sovereign republic, and to fall back onto the proposition of an 'asymmetrical [Yugoslav] confederation', presented by Alija Izetbegović and Kiro Gligorov of Macedonia in May 1991.

After the declaration of independence of Slovenia and Croatia on 25 June 1991, however, the essential question was no longer how to reorganise the dying Yugoslav federation, but whether Bosnia-Herzegovina should remain in a rump Yugoslavia, reduced to Serbia and Montenegro, or should it declare independence, too. In August 1991, the SDS and the Muslim Bosniak Organisation (MBO), led by Zulfikarpašić, made public a Serb-Muslim 'historical agreement' (*historijski sporazum*), which, implicitly, exchanged the maintenance of Bosnia-Herzegovina in a rump Yugoslavia for the preservation of its territorial integrity.[38] After a few days of hesitation and confusion, the SDA leaders rejected the proposal, and set themselves irreversibly on the road towards independence. They continued for some months to advocate a 'Yugoslav community' which would include both Serbia and Croatia but, in the context of a Serbo-Croat war going on in Croatia, this position was just meant to ease Bosnia's exit from Yugoslavia, by securing the support of the European Community and of the non-nationalists at home for Bosnian independence. As soon as European diplomats started to consider recognition of the secessionist republics, the SDA passed on 15 October 1991 a 'Memorandum on sovereign Bosnia-Herzegovina' through the Bosnian Parliament, and on 20 December demanded the international recognition of Bosnia-Herzegovina, despite Fikret Abdić's strong opposition.

The controversies that still surround the Serb-Muslim 'historical agreement' testify to its importance. Was the agreement originally

---

[38] The agreement stated that 'Yugoslavia is historically fully legitimate as a common state of republics and nations, completely equal in rights, and we engage ourselves to preserve and develop this community'. Concerning Bosnia-Herzegovina, it declared that 'the basis [of the agreement] is the mutual recognition of each nation's sovereignty and the full preservation of the territorial integrity and political subjectivity of our republic, Bosnia-Herzegovina'. At the end it added that, 'whatever the situation of the Republic of Croatia, inside or outside Yugoslavia, the Croats of Bosnia-Herzegovina constitute a nation [of Bosnia-Herzegovina] with equal rights [with Muslims and Serbs]', and were therefore called to join this agreement. See 'Sporazum MBO-SDS', *Oslobodjenje*, 2 Aug. 1991.

supported by Izetbegović and/or by Abdić?[39] Was its final rejection by the SDA due to pressures of a pro-Croat faction within the SDA, or to a 'friendly advice' of the American diplomacy?[40] Could it have protected Bosnian Muslims from war or would it have handed them over to Serb hegemony? Whatever the answers, the rejection of the 'historical agreement' by the SDA marks the definitive break of the Bosnian Muslim political élites, not only with the Yugoslav idea, but also with all the strategies which had been elaborated after 1878. Until then, in order to facilitate tactical alliances, Muslim political élites had always avoided any direct confrontation with either Serb or Croat political groups, occupying an intermediate space between them. By opting for independence, the SDA leaders made a clear stand against the SDS, and had therefore to rely on the support of the Croatian Democratic Union (HDZ). It was the turn of the Croat nationalist party to occupy an intermediate position: close to the SDA because it was supportive of the independence of Bosnia-Herzegovina, but also close to the SDS because it favoured division of Bosnia into several ethnic territories. Moreover, when risking and ultimately failing to secure Bosnia's territorial integrity, the SDA broke with another tradition of their predecessors among Bosnian Muslim leaders. The SDA clearly gave priority to the Muslim nation's own sovereignty, at the risk of a territorial partition of Bosnia-Herzegovina. From this point of view, it is revealing that the MBO justified the Serb-Muslim 'historical agreement' on the grounds that it would lessen 'the risk of civil war and territorial partition [of Bosnia] between Croatia and Serbia',[41] whereas the SDA rejected it because it argued that it implied Bosnia joining a 'rump Yugoslavia in which the Serbs would be number one, and the Muslims number two.'[42]

The consequences of such political choices were felt very quickly. In September 1991, the SDS began proclaiming 'Serb autonomous regions' throughout Serb-populated regions of Bosnia, and the HDZ

[39] See Milovan Djilas and Nadežda Gaće, *Bošnjak: Adil Zulfikarpašić*, Zürich, 1994, pp. 203–14; Fahira Fejzić, 'Tronožac pada kad je na dvije noge', *Muslimanski glas*, vol. II, no. 15, 2 Aug. 1991, p. 2.

[40] See Djilas and Gaće, op. cit., pp. 203–14

[41] MBO, *Uz prijedlog srpsko-muslimanskog sporazuma*, Sarajevo, 1991, p. 2.

[42] Fahira Fejzić, 'Takozvani istorijski srpsko-muslimanski dogovor', *Muslimanski Glas*, vol. II, no. 15, 2 Aug. 1991, p. 2.

did the same two months later. Of course, this does not mean that the SDA leaders at that time favoured a partition of Bosnia-Herzegovina. In the spring of 1991, Alija Izetbegović rejected propositions to divide the republic from Slobodan Milošević and Franjo Tudjman and, from the autumn of 1991, the SDA and the non-nationalist forces gathered around the principle of Bosnia's territorial integrity. However, partition was not totally absent from the minds of the SDA leaders, as shown by their lasting fascination with the Pakistani experience or, more concretely, by their support to the demand for the 'political and territorial autonomy of the Sandžak [region of Serbia], with a right to attach itself to one of the sovereign republics [of the Yugoslav federation]'.[43] But the partition envisaged by the SDA leaders was that of Yugoslavia, not of Bosnia-Herzegovina. It just remains unclear to what extent they were aware that, due to the demographic, political and military balance of power within Yugoslavia, the former was very likely to lead to the latter.

[43] Cited from election leaflets distributed for the plebiscite on Sandžak's autonomy organised by the SDA on 25 Nov. 1991, *Borba*, Belgrade, 25 Oct. 1991.

MACEDONIANS AND ALBANIANS AS YUGOSLAVS

Hugh Poulton

Vardar Macedonia and Kosovo were the last territories of future Yugoslavia to be 'liberated' from the Ottoman Empire. After the Balkan Wars of 1912–13 they both became part of Serbia, which in turn formed the core of the first Yugoslav state, created after the First World War. Despite slipping from Yugoslav (and Serbian) control for much of the Second World War, the two regions were again incorporated into the second, Communist Yugoslavia—Macedonia as one of the six republics of the Yugoslav federation and Kosovo as Serbia's autonomous region. As I argue, despite in the main sharing initially hostile attitudes to incorporation into Serbia and the inter-war Yugoslavia, the Macedonians and Albanians had gradually developed divergent views vis-à-vis Yugoslavia and Yugoslavism.

The Macedonians

Before Yugoslavia. The identity of the Slav Macedonians (henceforth Macedonians) has been a tendentious question. While Greece historically claimed both the area and saw its Orthodox inhabitants as Greeks (or potential Greeks), and continues to insist on copyright for all things 'Macedonian', the predominantly-Slav population made Greek arguments weak.[1] The Greek claim was essentially based on shared Orthodoxy and the Ottoman *millet* system, whereby the

---

[1] In southern, Aegean Macedonia, the Greek state has successfully assimilated most, although not all, the Slav population. The assimilation was aided by the settlement of large numbers of Greek refugees from Asia Minor. Hugh Poulton, *Who are the Macedonians?*, 2nd edn, London, 2000, pp. 85–9, 108–15, 162–71.

population was divided by religious affiliation rather than ethnicity or language. Until the founding of the Bulgarian Exarchate in 1870, the Greek Patriarchate controlled the Orthodox subjects of Macedonia (and Bulgaria). Although the illiterate peasants in the countryside spoke the Slav vernacular, the urban educated spoke Greek and were gradually Hellenicized. The emergence of modern nationalism however saw a Slav revival in the area. Both Bulgarians and Serbs claimed Macedonia's Slavs on 'ethnic' and 'historic' grounds. Macedonia had been the core of the 'second' Bulgarian Empire, while the capital of the short-lived Serbian Empire was in Skopje, the capital of the present-day Macedonian state. Identity (or identities?) of local Slav population, although probably much closer to the Bulgarian one, was fluid and 'unfixed' enough to enable rival Serbian claims.[2]

The majority of Macedonia's Orthodox population who supported the establishment of the Bulgarian Exarchate saw themselves as Slavs and rejected Greek tutelage. But did this mean they were Bulgarians? Certainly there were many who did feel Bulgarian and anti-Ottoman uprisings and bloody reprisals witnessed repeated movements of Macedonians to Bulgaria. However, there were also some who regarded themselves as Macedonians, distinct from Bulgarians. These two views were reflected in competing wings of the main 'liberation' movement: the Internal Macedonian Revolutionary Organisation (VMRO). Both aimed at autonomy for Macedonia as a first step, but while the Bulgarian-based wing openly favoured eventual annexation by Bulgaria, the group based within Macedonia was more ambivalent.

During the first Balkan War of 1912 Serbia took control of Vardar Macedonia while Greece occupied Aegean Macedonia. This left Bulgaria, whose forces had taken the brunt of the fighting in an attempt to capture Istanbul from the Ottomans, the relative loser; it gained only Pirin Macedonia in the south-west of historic Macedonia. In the second Balkan War of 1913 Bulgaria tried to reverse this division of the spoils but was soundly defeated. It joined Germany and Austro-Hungary in the First World War, and as a reward it was granted most of Vardar Macedonia as well as Eastern Aegean Macedonia by

[2] See ibid.

the end of 1915. The occupation appeared to have been popular in
Vardar Macedonia as the majority of its Slav population probably
identified themselves as Bulgarians. Persecution by Bulgarian forces
there was on a much smaller scale than in parts of Serbia and
Kosovo which also came under Bulgarian control.[3]

In the Yugoslav kingdom. Defeat of the Central Powers meant that
Vardar Macedonia (henceforth Macedonia) returned to Serb control, this time in Kingdom of Serbs, Croats and Slovenes (in 1929
renamed Yugoslavia). Serbian was compulsory in schools of, as it
was officially called, Southern Serbia. The Macedonians (or Bulgarians) were not recognised and attempted Serbianization of the population took place. In September 1920 the unification of the new
state's Orthodox Churches was proclaimed. The Macedonian Orthodox community was placed under the jurisdiction of the Serbian
Orthodox Church—the Constantinople patriarchate was prepared
to sell out its control for a payment of 800,000 francs on 19 September 1919.[4]

Restoration of the Serbian rule in 1918 over Vardar Macedonia
(which now included the formerly-Bulgarian Strumica district)
meant that once more Bulgarian clergy and teachers were ousted,
all Bulgarian signs and books removed and schools and societies
closed. Personal names were compulsorily Serbianized and there
was a wave of repression, although this time there were fewer killings, the authorities preferring the arrest, detention and internment.
The VMRO leader Ivan Mihaylov claims in his memoirs that in the
1918–1924 period there were 342 killings, 47 disappearances and
2,900 political arrests—with the Kratovo area especially affected
with 62 killings, 6 disappearances and over 1,100 arrests.[5]

The alienation of the Macedonians from the new state was
shown by their rejection of the mainstream parties and the large
protest vote for the Communists. In reality, VMRO remained the
most potent force in Macedonia. It commanded 1,675 active armed
bands in 1923 and its main zone of operations were the east bank of

[3] Ivo Banac, *The National Question in Yugoslavia: Origins, History, Politics,* Ithaca, NY,
1984, p. 318.

[4] Ibid., p. 221.

[5] Ivan Mihaylov, *Spomeni. Osvoditelna borba, 1919–1924,* Brussels, 1965, p. 680.

the Vardar—the west bank which led into Albanian dominated territory remained mostly outside its control—with a central zone from Tetovo to Kyustendil in Bulgaria and Radoviš, and a southern zone from Bitola to Pirin which oversaw operations in Greece.[6] According to Yugoslav sources, from 1919 to 1934 there were 467 attacks by VMRO activists in which 185 Yugoslav officials were killed and 235 wounded; 268 civilians were similarly killed or wounded by VMRO actions, while VMRO casualties were 128 dead, 13 wounded and 151 arrested in the same period.[7] In January 1923 VMRO massacred some 30 Serb settlers in the Ovče Polje region, and assassinated Spasoje Hadži Popović, a Serb newspaper director in Bitola in 1926 and General Mihailo Kovačević in 1927 in Štip.[8] Violent Serb counter-measures like the killing of all males from Garvan (Radoviš) village in March 1923 and the excesses of the 'Association Against Bulgar Bandits', founded in 1922 in Štip, merely tended to cement local support for VMRO in the 1920s.

However, the 1930s witnessed a change. With VMRO's effectiveness severely curtailed by the clamp-down on it within Bulgaria (where until 1934 it had operated with impunity) and its degeneration into mere banditism, it began to loose support among the young in Vardar Macedonia. There was an emergence of more marked calls for Macedonian autonomy within Yugoslavia, which Tito was to build upon so skillfully after the Second World War. As an official report to Prime Minister Milan Stojadinović stated in May 1938:

[The] liquidation of the Bulgar revolutionary committee [VMRO], our good relations with Bulgaria, and finally, our relations with Italy and Austria (ending their aid to Croat separatism)—all of that contributed to a certain reorientation of Macedonians, who are manifesting [preferences for] a certain reformed autonomy without conspiracies, or rather Macedonia for Macedonians…[Their] slogan is: come to the parliament in the

---

[6] Ivan Katardžiev, *Vreme na zreenje: Makedonskoto nacionalno prasanje megu dvete svetski vojni (1919–1930)*, vol. 1, Skopje, 1977, pp. 176–7 and 203, quoted in Banac, op. cit., p. 322.

[7] Aleksandar Apostolov, 'Specifičnata položba na makedonskiot narod vo kralstvoto Jugoslavija', *Institut za nacionalna istorija: Glasnik*, vol. 16 (1972), p. 55, in Banac, op. cit., p. 323.

[8] Banac, op. cit., p. 323, using Mihaylov (p. 141) and Apostolov (p. 56) as sources.

greatest possible numbers regardless of the party, and fight there for separatism within the frontiers of Yugoslavia.[9]

This 'Macedonia for the Macedonians' strain meant in many ways an acceptance of the state of Yugoslavia and an attempt to gain autonomy within it. However it should not be overstressed. Many Slavs in Macedonia, perhaps the majority, still harboured Bulgarian consciousness and were antithetical to a Yugoslav state dominated by Serbia, as once again became clear during the Second World War, in the initial period of the Bulgarian occupation.

The Second World War.   Following the partition of Yugoslavia after the brief April 1941 war, Bulgaria was granted once again the Serbian share of Macedonia. The initial reaction among the population was to greet the Bulgarians as liberators. Even the local communist cadres, led by Metodi Šatorov, viewed the occupation as 'natural' and looked to the Bulgarian Communists for leadership in preference to Tito's Communist Party of Yugoslavia (KPJ). While Macedonian Communists considered the Bulgarian authorities as 'bourgeois-fascists', they did not tend to regard them as foreign occupiers. Even staunch KPJ supporters admitted that in May 1941 the Macedonian Communists wanted to unite with their Bulgarian comrades.[10] The Comintern, on the other hand, favoured the Yugoslav over the Bulgarian Communists' claims in Vardar Macedonia.[11]

While Hitler did not allow the Bulgarians to formally annex the parts they now controlled, and the new border between the Italian- and Bulgarian-controlled parts of the first former-Yugoslavia was not defined—leading to periodic tensions between the two—Bulgaria was given a free hand in the areas under its control. Initially Sofia pursued policies, especially in education, which were welcomed by Macedonia's population. Over 800 new schools were opened and a

---

[9] Cited in Banac, op. cit., p. 327.

[10] Mihailo Apostolski, 'The Antifascist Council for the National Liberation of Yugoslavia and the Macedonian Question', *Contemporary Macedonian Statehood*, Skopje, 1994.

[11] Stevan K. Pavlowitch, *Tito: Yugoslavia's Great Dictator. A Reassessment*, London, 1992, p. 42.

university was established in Skopje.[12] However, the honeymoon
period did not last long as the Bulgarians soon fell into the old trap
of centralisation. The new provinces were quickly staffed with officials from Bulgaria proper who displayed arrogance towards the
local inhabitants. In March 1942 the government in Sofia took
absolute control over the new territories. High level of corruption,
however, further alienated the local population. Particularly insen-
sitive, in view of the long and close association in the Balkans
between religion and nationality, was the influx of Bulgarian Orthodox bishops who displayed the same negative features as the government bureaucrats. Resentment and a growth in autonomist feelings
were the result.[13]

In Communist Yugoslavia. Resentment against the Italians and the
Bulgarians led to a number of uprisings in 1942 and to the establishment of temporary liberated areas. By 1943 the anti-Bulgarian
feeling among the Macedonians was such that Tito felt it was a
good opportunity to dispatch his dynamic trouble-shooter Svetozar
Vukmanović-Tempo to the area. Tito's aim seems already to have
been a united Slav Macedonia, not just the pre-war Yugoslav section, under his control. However, the time was not ripe yet for
Tempo's dynamism and he was withdrawn in September 1943.[14]

While a communiqué from the Macedonian communist command of October 1942 did mention the Macedonian nation,[15] the
First Congress of the Anti-Fascist Council for the National Liberation of Yugoslavia (AVNOJ) held at Bihać in November 1942 did
not specifically talk about the Macedonians. The crucial step was
taken at the Second AVNOJ congress held in Jajce on 29 November
1943. Here the Macedonian nation was affirmed and Macedonia
was given equal status with the other five federal units (Serbia,
Croatia, Slovenia, Montenegro and Bosnia-Herzegovina). However,
the equality was still somewhat qualified at this stage. Macedonia

---

[12] Richard Crampton, *A Short History of Modern Bulgaria*, Cambridge University
Press, 1987, p. 5.
[13] Ibid.
[14] For his own detailed account see Vukmanović-Tempo, *Struggle for the Balkans*,
London, 1990.
[15] Apostolski, op. cit. p. 21.

was not at Jajce given any wider autonomy than Bosnia-Herzegovina and it only had a Central National Liberation Committee while the other future republics already had full Anti-Fascist Councils of National Liberation. Moreover, perhaps showing the weakness of the KPJ in Macedonia, there were no Macedonians on the AVNOJ's 17-member supreme executive body or provisional government (the National Liberation Committee). While the Partisan movement in Macedonia lagged behind other parts of Yugoslavia, by mid-1944 Tito was confident enough to set up the Anti-Fascist Council of National Liberation of Macedonia (ASNOM). On the symbolic date of 2 August (the *Ilinden* Uprising day) 1944 the first ASNOM assembly was convened at the Prohor Pčinjski Monastery. It proclaimed 'Macedonia as a federal state in the new Democratic Federation of Yugoslavia' and issued a 'Manifesto' which described the position of Macedonia under the old Yugoslavia as that of a colony, before declaring the 'brotherhood and unity' with the other peoples of Yugoslavia.

The Stalin-Tito split of 1948 and the defeat of the Communists in the Greek Civil War ended Tito's dream of uniting whole of Macedonia under his rule. With Bulgaria once more reverting to denial of Macedonians as separate nation from Bulgarians, and the victorious anti-Communist Greek forces adamant in their own denial, the new Yugoslavia remained the only concrete medium for Macedonian aspirations to nationhood and quasi-statehood.

For the first time the Macedonians were recognised as a distinct nation, with their own language and history. Initially the spoken dialect of northern Macedonia was chosen as the basis for the Macedonian language, which was however deemed too close to Serbian, so the dialects of Bitola-Veles became the norm.[16] These were closer to Bulgarian, but as literary Bulgarian was based on eastern Bulgarian dialects, it allowed just enough differentiation to pass as a distinct language. The alphabet was accepted on 3 May 1945 and the orthography on 7 June. The first primer in the new language appeared in 1946 and a grammar in 1952. History was more problematic as many of the Macedonians' historical figures were also claimed by Bulgarians. However, this was to a large extent solved by the Communist

---

[16] Elizabeth Barker, *Macedonia: its Place in Balkan Power Politics*, London, 1951.

system with its censorship and control on information, and 'suitably edited' history. Religion was another key tool for the new authorities. The revival of the ancient archbishopric of Ohrid in 1958 was an important step along the path to Macedonian nationhood—and a rare occurrence of atheist state co-operation with organised religion. This move was resisted in vain by the Serbian Orthodox Church, as was the final declaration of the autocephalous status of the Macedonian Orthodox Church on 18 July 1967.

With such policies the new Yugoslav authorities largely overcame the residual pro-Bulgarian feeling among much of the population, and survived the split with Bulgaria in 1948. Pro-Bulgarians among Macedonians suffered severe repression as a result. Bulgarian sources assert that thousands have lost their lives since 1944, with over 100,000 being imprisoned under 'the law for the protection of Macedonian national honour' for opposing the new ethnogenesis.[17] However, while occasional trial continued throughout the life of Communist Yugoslavia, the vast bulk took place in the late 1940s. The new authorities were successful in building a distinct national consciousness based on the available differences between Macedonia and Bulgaria proper, and by the time Yugoslavia collapsed in the early 1990s, those who continued to look to Bulgaria were very few indeed.[18] The change from the pre-war situation of unrecognised minority status and attempted assimilation by Serbia to one where the Macedonians were the majority people in their own republic with considerable autonomy within Yugoslavia's federation/confederation had obvious attractions. The authorities were also aided

---

[17] *Memorandum*, Union des Associations Macédoniennes en Bulgarie VMRO-SDS to Copenhagen Conference 1990.

[18] However, in Macedonia today there remain those who identify themselves as Bulgarians. Hostility to them remains, even if less than in Communist Yugoslavia, where it was forbidden to proclaim Bulgarian identity with the partial exception of the Strumica region where the population was allowed more leeway and where most of the 3,000–4,000 Bulgarians in Macedonia in the censuses appeared. Examples of the continuing hostility are: the Supreme Court in January 1994 banned the pro-Bulgarian Human Rights Party led by Ilija Ilijevski and the non-registration of another pro-Bulgarian group in Ohrid and other harassment. Nationalist Greek émigré circles claim that similar pressures continue to be brought against Greeks in Macedonia although there appears little evidence to back this up.

by the comparative lack of attraction for its population of Bulgaria, which, unlike Yugoslavia, had remained within the Soviet block.

Understandably, most Macedonians' attitude to Communist Yugoslavia, where they were recognised as a distinct 'nation of Yugoslavia', and the federal state apparatus helped finance and support their culture, was in marked contrast to their attitude to Royalist Yugoslavia, where they were faced with a policy of forced Serbianisation. The first Yugoslavia's break-up was welcomed by many in Macedonia, while in the final death throes of the second Yugoslavia the Macedonian leadership, led by Kiro Gligorov, was in the forefront (with Alija Izetbegović of Bosnia), in trying to preserve the old state in some form of confederation, repeatedly playing down calls for outright independence. Indeed, the independence referendum of 8 September 1991 left room for Macedonia to enter an 'alliance of sovereign states of Yugoslavia' at some time in the future.[19]

However, this support for Yugoslavia did not equate to widespread identification as 'Yugoslav' rather that 'Macedonian'. In population census the number of people in Macedonia giving their national affiliation as 'Yugoslav' was very low (only Kosovo had a lower figure and percentage).[20] Moreover, the pro-Yugoslav stance of the Gligorov government and the wording of the independence referendum can be seen as expressions of the Macedonian Communist élite who were traditionally more pro-Serb and pro-Yugoslav than the bulk of the population.

[19] Tanjug, 8 Sept. 1991, in BBC SWB EE/1173, 10 Sept. 1991.

[20] For example in 1971 the numbers declaring themselves 'Yugoslavs' were: in Bosnia-Herzegovina, 43,796 (1.2 per cent); Montenegro, 10,943 (2.1 per cent); Croatia 84,118 (1.9 per cent); Macedonia, 3,652 (0.2 per cent); Slovenia 6,744 (0.4 per cent); Serbia as a whole, 123,824 (1.5 per cent)—Serbia 'proper', 75,976 (1.4 per cent), Vojvodina, 46,928 (2.4 per cent) and Kosovo 920 (0.1 per cent). In both Macedonia and Kosovo the incidence of intermarriage between the two largest groups—in both cases predominantly Muslim Albanians and Orthodox Slavs—was almost negligible. Where intermarriage between major groups occurred on a significant level, the incidence of 'Yugoslavs' was high. (For instance, in Vojvodina the percentage of self-declared Yugoslavs was the highest, and the province also had the highest incidence of intermarriage: 28 per cent). Intermarriage between a dominant group and weaker one, for example between Macedonians and Vlachs, tended towards assimilation with the progeny adopting the identity of the former, i.e. dominant group.

The break-up of Yugoslavia witnessed (or was caused by?) an increase in nationalist feeling amongst many sections of the state's ethnic mosaic. While later than for example Croatia or Slovenia, Macedonia was affected, too. Open calls, initially for a unified Macedonia but also for independence surfaced in late 1989. In October 1989 slogans such as 'Solun [Salonika] is ours!', 'Prohor Pčinjski [in Serbia] is Macedonian!', 'Ćento!' (a Macedonian nationalist leader tried by the communists after the war), and 'We fight for a united Macedonia!' began to be chanted by football supporters of 'Vardar', Macedonia's leading football team.[21] Similar slogans also appeared on the walls of Skopje.

On 4 February 1990 the founding assembly of the Movement for All-Macedonian Action (MAAK) was set up mainly by the Macedonian intelligentsia with the head of the Writers Union, the poet Ante Popovski, as its initial leader. MAAK stated that it had no territorial ambitions on Macedonia's neighbours, but still expressed criticism of Bulgaria and Greece over the treatment of their Macedonian minorities. In July 1990 local MAAK leaders from Strumica met with delegates from the UMO Ilinden movement in Bulgaria (a persecuted pro-Macedonian organisation) to discuss co-operation.[22] On 20 February large demonstration of Macedonians (estimates vary from 30,000 to 120,000 people), had taken place in Skopje to assert their identity and protest at perceived oppression of Macedonians in Bulgaria, Greece and Albania. The rally was apparently timed to coincide with Greece's Prime Minister Constantin Mitsotakis's visit to Belgrade.[23] A more radical nationalist party than MAAK emerged in June 1990; it was the Internal Macedonian Revolutionary Organisation-Democratic Party of Macedonian National Unity (VMRO-DPMNE), which was supported by the Macedonian diaspora. The name choice was significant and VMRO-DPMNE, led by Ljupčo Georgijevski, pledged to carry on the principles of the Ilinden uprising of 1903 and work for 'the ideal of all free Macedonias united' in a Macedonian state.[24] VMRO-DPMNE also expressed the desire for improvements in relations with Slovenia and Croatia

[21] *Politika*, Belgrade, 27 Oct. 1989.
[22] *RFE Weekly Record of Events*, 16 July 1990.
[23] *RFE Weekly Record of Events*, 20 Feb. 1990.
[24] *Oslobodjenje*, Sarajevo, 23 June 1990.

and for the return of some territories currently in Serbia. On 2 August 1990, to mark the Ilinden uprising, it held a demonstration of over 100 members at Prohor Pčinjski Monastery which Serbian police had to forcibly disperse.[25] In the first multi-party elections of November 1990 VMRO-DPMNE emerged as the largest party with 37 seats in a 120-seat Assembly. However, the successors to the Communists succeeded in remaining in power until elections of October 1998, when VMRO-DPMNE finally triumphed.

In conclusion of this section, Yugoslavism, as an ethnic label, was very weak in Macedonia. The attraction of the Yugoslav state was in that it allowed and supported the Macedonian identity and that without it Macedonia might be torn apart by 'the four wolves'.[26] It is possible that in time, if the Yugoslav state had survived, greater numbers of Macedonians, more secure with their own identity would have declared themselves 'Yugoslavs' but this remains conjecture. In the event, the approaching end of the Yugoslav state saw an increase in Macedonian nationalism and a sharpening of the desire for an independent state for the first time in modern history.

The Albanians of Yugoslavia

Before Yugoslavia.   Albanian nationalism was a late-starter on the Balkan stage due in part to the majority of Albanians sharing the religion of their Ottoman rulers.[27] Indeed, the leaders of the League of Prizren, established in 1878 by intellectuals to raise national consciousness among Albanians, were Christians, or Bektashis. A prime motive for the League was to combat the threat of Albanian-inhabited lands being partitioned between Serbia and Greece and possibly Bulgaria as well. An independent Albania was proclaimed in November 1912, and was recognised at the 1913 Treaty of London. However, a large number of ethnic Albanians remained outside

---

[25] *RFE Weekly Record of Events*, 2 Aug. 1990.

[26] This depiction of Macedonia threatened by four wolves (Bulgaria, Greece, Serbia and Albania) was often used in the early independence period by Macedonian politicians.

[27] Thus within the *millet* system Muslim Albanians could and did attain high posts in the Ottoman hierarchy which at that time was not specifically Turkish by ethnicity.

the newly created Albanian state—possibly equalling the number of Albanians living in Albania. A vast majority of them lived in the Kingdom of Serbia, mostly in present-day Kosovo and Macedonia, but also in the Kingdom of Montenegro. Kosovo, a place of historic and cultural importance to the Serbs, was, despite its Albanian majority, partitioned between Serbia and Montenegro, as a result of the Balkan Wars of 1912–13.

In the kingdom of Yugoslavia. From the start, as shown by both names for the new state (Yugoslavia means the land of the South Slavs and thus tacitly excludes Albanians and other non-Slavs), the Albanians were not seen as its integral members. During the interwar period an estimated 40,000 Orthodox Slav peasants (mostly Serbs and Montenegrins[28]) moved into Kosovo. During the same period, large numbers (perhaps as many as half a million) ethnic Albanians were forced to emigrate from Kosovo. The new settlers received good land and benefits from the authorities. This resulted in the formation of two separate communities: a small, relatively prosperous Serb settler community, and a mass of less well-to-do Albanians.[29] The Serbo-Croat language was compulsory in all schools and for official purposes, and irregular Serbian troops insured Serbian dominance. Albanians were forced to adopt Serbian name suffix '-ić'. Similar pressures were brought to bear in Montenegro and in Macedonia against the Albanians.

Although the religious divide between Orthodox Serbs and predominantly Muslim Albanians was a profound one, the conflict was essentially ethnic. The Serbs saw the Albanians as ethnic competitors to Kosovo, and the Serbo-Croat speaking Muslims living in the area were not seen as such a threat (they were believed to be ethnic Serbs who converted to Islam). Initially, there were state-sponsored attempts to assimilate the Albanian minority. To aid this, Bosnian

---

[28] Montenegrins are Serbian speaking inhabitants from Montenegro, which was an independent Kingdom before joining the first Yugoslav state at its inception in 1918. In Tito's Yugoslavia they were recognised as a separate 'nation of Yugoslavia' although many, perhaps even a majority, continued to identify with the Serbian nation.

[29] Elez Biberaj, 'Kosovo: the Struggle for Recognition', and Stevan K. Pavlowitch, 'Kosovo: An Analysis of Yugoslavia's Albanian Problem', both in *Conflict Studies*, No. 137/138, 1982.

Serbo-Croat speaking Muslim teachers were brought to the area, again illustrating that ethnicity not religion was of paramount importance to the state.[30] However, this changed after it became apparent that instead of aiding assimilation, the policy was educating a potential opposition élite. The Albanians turned the so-called 'Turkish' schools, where the only official language of instruction was in the Arabic of the Koran and Turkish, into centres of Albanian opposition to the state and began to run an underground parallel Albanian education.[31] This resort to the setting-up of a parallel education system in times of crisis has remained a reoccurring feature of Albanian national resistance to Serb oppression.[32] Faced with failure to achieve their aims in Kosovo with the education system, the authorities continued with the more successful policy of 'colonisation' and pressure to make Albanians emigrate.

Thus, in the first Yugoslavia, the Kosovo Albanians were seen essentially as alien interlopers living in Serbia's heartland. Similarly, the attitude of the Albanians to the state and this blatant Serbian repression was unremittingly hostile.

The Second World War. The Albanian hostility to the first Yugoslav state generated support for the brief incorporation of most of present-day Kosovo and western Macedonia into the Italian puppet Kingdom of Albania during the Second World War. The Italians capitalised on this support by establishing an Albanian language administration as well as Albanian schools and newspapers. During this period the Serbs suffered harsh treatment from the embittered Albanians who now pressured them to leave. An Albanian SS Division *Skenderbeg* was created, indiscriminately killing Serbs and Montenegrins and expelling up to 10,000 Slav families from Kosovo. New

[30] Banac op. cit., p. 299. Some Serb nationalists claimed that many of the Albanians (including the legendary Albanian hero Skenderbeg) were really Serbs, and that this policy was one of a re-Serbianization of 'denationalised brothers'. Ibid., p. 295.

[31] Ibid., p. 299.

[32] And, in the 1990s, against the Macedonian oppression. The Macedonian Albanians have resorted to setting up of private education after the Macedonian authorities forbade the opening in Feb. 1995 of an Albanian University in Tetovo. See *Nova Makedonija* (Skopje, 28 Feb. 1995) for reports of classes held clandestinely in local mosques.

Albanian colonists arrived from the poorer regions of northern Albania. As Hitler's forces withdrew from Kosovo at the end of 1944, Tito's Partisans moved in. Tito's previous attempts to attract Kosovo Albanians into his Partisan forces had not been a success.[33] He realised that only by retaining Kosovo within Serbia could help win over the Serbs to support communism and the Partisans launched a large-scale military campaign in Kosovo to consolidate their rule. The Albanians reacted with a general insurrection forcing the new authorities to declare martial law in the region in 1945. Because of their co-operation with the Axis forces, the Yugoslav Albanians were seen as politically unreliable and thus a possible threat to the stability and territorial integrity of Communist Yugoslavia.

Kosovo Albanians in Communist Yugoslavia: from repression to autonomy

The post-war period witnessed improvements in the official status of ethnic Albanians in Yugoslavia as a whole, although a large number, claiming to be Turks and thus taking advantage of emigration agreements between Ankara and Belgrade, emigrated to Turkey. For the first time (not only in Yugoslavia) the Albanian language primary schools were established and there were no attempts to assimilate the Albanian minority. These gains, however were undermined by repressive pro-Serb policies of the security forces headed by the Serb politician Aleksandar Ranković. Under the 1946 Constitution, Kosovo (or Kosovo-Metohija as it was officially called) was an Autonomous Region of Serbia.[34] The Constitutional changes of 1953 saw a further reduction of powers of Kosovo and Vojvodina, which both de facto became ordinary districts of Serbia.

[33] For a detailed account of Kosovo during the Second World War see Vukmanović-Tempo, *op. cit.* and Reginald Hibbert, *Albania's National Liberation: the Bitter Victory*, London, 1991.
[34] Under this constitution, Vojvodina was granted the higher status of 'Autonomous Province' while Kosovo-Metohija (as it was then called) had the lower status of 'Autonomous Region'. This meant that Kosovo was denied any modicum of independent decision making (albeit within the centralised communist system of that time) in its local administrative units.

However, during this period even republics enjoyed little real autonomy in the highly centralised Yugoslav state. Yet, the 1963 Constitution gave the republics the right for the first time to establish autonomous units on their own (i.e. it was a republican prerogative and not a federal one) and the status of Vojvodina was restored to that of 1946, while that of Kosovo–Metohija was upgraded to the same level.

Kosovo is rich in mineral resources, but economic decisions made in Belgrade were essentially politically motivated. Following the Tito–Stalin split of 1948, Kosovo was considered too vulnerable a site for the construction of major industrial projects. Instead it was to be a supplier of raw materials for other (wealthier) parts of Yugoslavia. Economic development witnessed regional interests becoming increasingly identified with the national interests of each republic's nominative nation. On the other hand, the official 'brother-hood and unity' ideology, promoted by central authorities, encouraged a patriotic Yugoslavism. This was followed by a review of the 'minorities' question' by the Executive Committee of the League of Communists of Serbia in 1959 after which the 'minorities' were officially referred to as 'nationalities'. In spite of these cosmetic changes, the Albanians remained discontented. In Kosovo, the display of any Albanian national symbol or flag, and the commemoration of Albanian national holidays were prohibited, and the teaching of Albanian history, traditions and literature was considered a 'nationalist deviation'.[35]

The purging of Ranković by Tito in 1966 allowed Albanian dissatisfaction to be more openly voiced and there were large-scale demonstrations in Priština in November 1968 calling for Kosovo to be granted republican status within Yugoslavia. As a result, constitutional amendments in 1968 granted Kosovo and Vojvodina some republican prerogatives while Kosovo was also allowed to fly the national Albanian flag (which was identical to the flag of the Republic of Albania). This compromise was confirmed in constitutional amendments of 1971 and in the 1974 Constitution. Kosovo became an autonomous *province* within Serbia, with a predominately

---

[35] Ali Hadri, *The National and Political Development of Albanians in Yugoslavia*, Zagreb, 1970, vol. 1, p. 551.

Albanian communist leadership and gained, *de facto* if not *de iure*, many of the powers of a republic within the federation. Development of cultural contacts with Albania was encouraged so that Kosovo might serve as a 'bridge' between Belgrade and Tirana. The adoption of the basically Tosk literary Albanian by the Gheg speaking Kosovo Albanians[36] in 1968 paved the way for Albanian cultural penetration into Kosovo, and Albanian textbooks and publications were imported from Albania.

At the same time Kosovo experienced significant demographic changes due to the extremely high birth rate of the Albanians, combined with the emigration of over 30,000 Serbs and Montenegrins between 1971 and 1981.[37] The high Albanian birth rate saw their number virtually double between 1961 and 1981 while that of the Serbs and Montenegrins declined. According to the 1981 census the Albanians made up 77.5 per cent of the population of Kosovo and their share of the province's population continued to grow.

The rise of Albanian nationalism in Kosovo

Although naturally rich in resources, Kosovo remained economically one of the most backward regions of former Yugoslavia, and the economic problems exacerbated nationalist unrest. The setting up of an Albanian university in Priština in 1968 compounded this as huge numbers of Albanians enrolled as a way of avoiding unemployment. However, the university helped create for the first time a large, and largely unemployed, Albanian intelligentsia. In 1984 unemployment in Kosovo was 29.1 per cent compared with a national average of 12.7 per cent and only 1.8 per cent in Slovenia—economically the most advanced of former Yugoslav republics. In Kosovo, 70 per cent of those unemployed were 25-year-old or younger.[38]

Albanian nationalist discontent simmered throughout the 1970s with Priština University becoming a breeding ground for nationalists,

[36] There are two main Albanian dialects, Tosk which predominates in the central and southern regions and which is the basis of literary Albanian, and Gheg which predominates in northern Albania and Kosovo.
[37] *Opština*, Belgrade, no. 8–9, Aug.–Sept. 1983.
[38] *Rilindja*, Priština, 25 June 1984.

despite the province gaining self-rule in 1974.[39] The situation exploded in 1981 with a massive wave of unrest in Kosovo sparked off by university students. The main demand quickly became for Kosovo to be granted republican status within the Yugoslav federation, though some Kosovo Albanians called for outright unification with neighbouring Albania. The demonstrations were put down by the army, and there were dead.[40] Nationalist discontent continued throughout the 1980s with thousands of Kosovo Albanians— predominately male students and young school teachers, but also many schoolchildren—imprisoned for activity in support of republican status for Kosovo.[41] There was also a severe purge among university lecturers and school teachers.

However, in the early 1980s the Kosovo Albanians were not repressed culturally. Kosovo was in effect an Albanian polity with the Albanian language in official use, Albanian television, radio and press, and with an ethnic Albanian government. Even the courts which were used to persecute those calling for a republic for Kosovo were staffed by ethnic Albanian judges. The system was still ostensibly a communist one and one where open religious attachment was seen as suspect for party officials. Thus while mosques were open and Islamic religious practice was not banned, there were pressures against overt religious attachment.

During the 1970s until the rise of Slobodan Milošević in the second half of 1980s the Albanians of Kosovo had the best situation in terms of representation and cultural autonomy that they had in any time since the collapse of the Ottoman Empire. However, the refusal by authorities to grant them republican status, despite their

[39] See Hugh Poulton, *The Balkans: Minorities and States in Conflict*, London 1993, p. 61.

[40] Official sources stated that nine or eleven had died, but the Central Committee of the League of Communists of Serbia was reportedly told that over 300 had been killed. See *Yugoslavia: Prisoners of Conscience*, Amnesty International, AI Index EUR 48/20/85.

[41] Amnesty International reported in 1989 that over 7,000 Albanians had been arrested in Kosovo in the 1980s with many given prison sentences of six years or more for nationalist activity. See *Yugoslavia: Recent Events in the Autonomous province of Kosovo*. Amnesty International, EUR/48/20/85. For full details of both the nationalist forces and the state repression in this period see Poulton, *The Balkans*, op. cit., pp. 61–6.

numerical superiority over other less numerous Slav 'nations of Yugoslavia' who did have their own republic within the federation, illustrated that Yugoslavia's Albanians remained *de facto* second class citizens. In the 1980s Kosovo's Serbs and Montenegrins began to complain of physical attacks and intimidation by Albanians. The Kosovo Albanians were accused of creating 'ethnically pure zones' by a combination of pressure on Serbs to emigrate and their high birth rate. Economic backwardness significantly contributed to the emigration, but position of the Serbs in Kosovo began to come to the fore in mainstream Serbian public opinion by the end of 1985. This helped to fuel Serbian nationalism.[42] Slobodan Milošević rode the upsurge of aggrieved Serbian feeling and took power in Belgrade signalling a fundamental shift in policy. This was that the position of Kosovo and Vojvodina as effective republics within the Serbian republic as laid out in the 1974 constitution was anomalous and should be changed. In October 1988 the Vojvodina party leadership was overthrown and replaced by Milošević's appointees. This was followed in 1989 with the stripping of Kosovo's autonomy by constitutional changes. Troops were again sent into Kosovo to deal with the resulting protests. The Kosovo Albanian leadership was purged and special measures were imposed in the province by the federal Presidency. Despite Milošević and the Serbs' leading role in this, the other, non-Serb members of Yugoslavia's collective Presidency acquiesced in this blatant demolition of the 1974 constitutional set-up and the ensuing *de facto* military rule in Kosovo.[43]

---

[42] The best example of this was the Jan. 1986 petition on behalf of the Kosovo Serbs which was sent by 200 prominent Belgrade intellectuals—representing a wide range of opinion from former leading Marxists to Orthodox Priests— alleging 'genocide' against the Serbs by the Albanians. In 1987 another such petition was signed by 60,000 Kosovo Serbs—see Poulton, op. cit., pp. 66–8.

[43] Even the leading Yugoslav dissident Milovan Djilas supported Milošević in this stating: 'I agree with the policy of sorting out the relations of Serbia with her Province [Kosovo]. I think he is right in this respect and the mass meetings [Milošević organised a number of mass street demonstrations by his supporters to force the pace of his changes] were a positive thing...'. Djilas went on to underline the importance of Kosovo to the Serbs, saying: 'Wipe away Kosovo from the Serb mind and soul and we are no more...if there had been no battle at Kosovo, the Serbs would have invented it for its suffering and heroism.'

In early 1990 a further wave of demonstrations and violent clashes took place with 32 Albanians killed by the end of February. In April the federal authorities lifted the 'special measures' and removed most of the federal troops leaving the Serbian republican authorities to take over direct police control. Over 200 members of the erstwhile, mainly Albanian, provincial police force were suspended and some 2,500 Serbian policemen drafted in. By May 1990 all ethnic Albanian members of Kosovo's government had resigned in protest at the Serbian take-over and the Kosovo Assembly which still had an Albanian majority was in deadlock. The Albanian deputies attempted to hinder Serb moves at ending what was left of Kosovo's autonomy and in July 1990 declared Kosovo an independent republic. In retaliation the Serbian Parliament on 5 July suspended Kosovo's Assembly, taking control of local government as well as some 60 leading economic enterprises, sacking over 15,000 Albanian functionaries by September that year.[44] The same month, a two-third majority of ex-Kosovo Assembly delegates met in secret in Kačanik and adopted a new constitution for a republic of Kosovo. An underground government and legislature was formed.[45] This was the basis of the continuing underground government body which attempted to fulfil the requirements of a 'normal' government even claiming to take in the roles of defence and police matters.[46] It also discussed economic co-operation and even signed a protocol on agreement on legal matters with Albania.[47] In October 1991 the Albanians held a referendum, despite official censure and harassment, on the issue of Kosovo being an independent republic and they claimed that 940,802 people out of a possible, 1,051,357 took

---

Unpublished interview with Milovan Djilas by G. Ćirjanić, Belgrade, Feb. 1989.

[44] Helsinki Watch, *Yugoslavia: Human Rights Abuses in Kosovo 1990–1992*, Washington, DC, Oct. 1992, p. 58.

[45] The 'Kačanik Constitution' described the 'republic of Kosovo' as 'a democratic state of the Albanian people and of members of other nations and national minorities who are its citizens: Serbs, Muslims, Montenegrins, Croats, Turks, Romanies and others living in Kosovo.' Tanjug, Belgrade, 13 Sept. 1990.

[46] Croatian Radio, Zagreb, 8 Feb. 1992.

[47] Albanian Radio, Tirana, 14 July 1992 and Albanian Telegraph Agency, Tirana, 25 Sept. 1992.

part with over 99 per cent voting in favour. A provisional government was elected with Bujar Bukoshi as prime minister and Ibrahim Rugova as would-be president.[48] In May 1992 they held further underground elections using a system of proportional representation with a 3 per cent threshold vote.

The Serbian constitutional amendments of September 1990 vested all effective control of political, economic, judicial and security institutions in Belgrade, leaving only cultural and educational institutions under control of local Serbs and Montenegrins. The combination of Serbian purges and Albanian non-violent resistance resulted in almost complete removal of Albanians from all decision-making and executive bodies. The Kosovo Supreme Court, the Public Prosecutor's Office of Kosovo and other courts were abolished and some 200 Albanian judges, district and public attorneys discharged and replaced by 75 Serbs and Montenegrins.[49] Replying to the UN Special Rapporteur Tadeusz Mazowiecki's 1992 report on human rights in rump Yugoslavia, the authorities stated that only 90 out of 284 employees in the provincial state administration were Albanians[50]—and these mostly in menial positions.

Ibrahim Rugova, the leader of the main Kosovo Albanian party, the Democratic League of Kosovo (LDK), opted for essentially non-violent resistance, setting up parallel Albanian institutions. With the dissolution of Yugoslavia, the Albanians argued that Kosovo, too, as one of the territorial units recognised under the 1974 Constitution, should have the right to secede, just like the republics.

The non-violent approach achieved little, and the stage was set for the emergence of radicals among the Kosovo Albanians. The Kosovo Liberation Army fought the Serb security forces, civilian population being the main victim of their fighting. However, the Kosovo war and the NATO intervention fall outside of the scope of this chapter. What is clear is that the Kosovo Albanians remained deeply distrustful of the Yugoslav state throughout its existence. Despite achieving self-rule after 1974, expressions of 'Yugoslavism'

[48] Croatian Radio, Zagreb, 19 Oct. 1991.
[49] A.A. Gashi (ed.), *The Denial of Human and National Rights of Albanians in Kosovo*, New York, 1992, p. 106.
[50] Tanjug, Belgrade, 20 Nov. 1992.

among Kosovo Albanians was virtually non-existent, largely limited to the Albanian Communist leadership. Even Kosovo Serbs, unlike Serbs living in other parts of Yugoslavia, in the heated atmosphere of Kosovo rarely declared themselves as Yugoslav.[51]

---

[51] Indeed most Serbs in Kosovo saw the 1974 Constitution as a betrayal of their interests and so looked more to Serbia rather than the state as a whole.

Part III. LEADERS AND INSTITUTIONS

(DIS)INTEGRATING YUGOSLAVIA: KING ALEXANDER AND INTERWAR YUGOSLAVISM[1]

Dejan Djokić

King Alexander of Yugoslavia, dressed in an admiral's uniform decorated with numerous orders and medals, prominent among them the *Légion d'Honneur*, was waving his hand acknowledging the cheers of a large Marseilles crowd which had come to greet him on his state visit to France. The car, an old police vehicle, had its windows open so that the King and his host, the French Foreign Minister Louis Barthou, could enjoy a warm and sunny October afternoon. Only moments later, after allegedly telling his host that he was 'very happy to be in France', both the King and Barthou were shot dead by a Macedonian revolutionary hired by the Croat émigré Ustaša organisation. According to a contemporary account: 'There was blood now everywhere except on the face of the King, which was as white as marble…Some last thought was on his face, but it was not fear of death, no, nor spasm of mortal agony.'[2]

The 'last thought' that Stephen Graham, author of the above account, refers to was alleged to have been Alexander's concern for the unity of his country. Bogoljub Jevtić, the Yugoslav Foreign

[1] I am indebted to Wendy Bracewell and Stevan K. Pavlowitch for many useful comments on this chapter. My gratitude is also due to the Central Research Fund of the University of London, which funded a research trip to Croatia in the summer of 2001, where I have gathered some of the source material used in this work.
[2] Stephen Graham, *Alexander of Yugoslavia: Strong Man of the Balkans*, London, 1938, p. 60. For the full account of the King's arrival and the assassination see pp. 51–62.

Minister who accompanied the King on the visit to France in
October 1934, reported that Alexander's final words were 'Preserve Yugoslavia!' *(Čuvajte mi Jugoslaviju!).* Although there is no
evidence that the dying King said something to this effect, or
indeed anything, given that his death was immediate, the alleged
last words were propagated by the régime as Alexander's 'political
testament'. It incited patriotic, pro-Yugoslav feeling across the
country, but it also sent a clear message to the Yugoslav public that
despite the monarch's death there would be a continuation of his
dictatorship introduced less than six years previously and, with it, of
the official ideology of 'integral Yugoslavism'. In an Orwellian
fashion, the late ruler was to be kept 'alive' in public memory, his
virtual presence guaranteeing the preservation of the régime and
even the nation.[3] When Jevtić became Prime Minister of Yugoslavia in December 1934, his career no doubt propelled by his role as a
'messenger' of Alexander's 'testament', one of the new government's
first declarations, presented to the *Skupština* on 3 January 1935, stated:

Preserving Yugoslavia, preserving the unity of the Yugoslav nation and the
state, is the highest order for everything and everyone, it is a duty for our
present and future generations. The Kingdom of Yugoslavia is a territorial,
political and moral creation of many generations; it is a holy bequest of the
King-Martyr, which must be preserved and, once strengthened, handed
over to future generations.[4]

[3] A similar discourse emerged in the second Yugoslavia after President Tito died in
1980, with his Communist successors promoting slogans such as 'After Tito-
Tito!' and 'Comrade Tito, we swear not to deviate from your path!'. Indeed, several parallels between Alexander's and Tito's reigns can be drawn. The King
intervened against party divisions and the President against divisions within the
Party; they both tried to 'preserve Yugoslavia', imposing ideology from above:
Alexander promoted 'integral Yugoslavism' and Tito 'self-managing socialism'.
See Stevan K. Pavlović, 'Jugoslavija 1918–1991: Poraz jednog identiteta i jedne
nestabilne političke kulture', *Istorija XX veka* (Belgrade), vol. 14, no. 1, 1996,
pp. 7–20, pp. 15–6.
[4] *Stenografske beleške Narodne skupštine Kraljevine Jugoslavije, (vanredan saziv za 1935,
zapisnik sa sjednice od 3. januara 1935.),* cited in Ferdo Čulinović, *Jugoslavija
izmedju dva rata,* Zagreb, 1961, 2 vols, vol. 2, p. 75 (all translations from Serbo-
Croat are mine). Jevtić only held his new position until June 1935 when he was
dismissed by Prince Regent Paul following poor results for the government list in
the May 1935 elections. See Todor Stojkov, *Vlada Milana Stojadinovića, 1935–
1937,* Belgrade, 1985, pp. 13–18.

On 1 December 1918, a delegation of the political representatives
of Croats, Serbs and Slovenes from the former Habsburg territories
had come to Belgrade to invite Alexander, the then Prince Regent
of Serbia, to proclaim their union with the Kingdom of Serbia
(itself just united with the Kingdom of Montenegro), and thus formally to declare the formation of the Kingdom of Serbs, Croats and
Slovenes. Although there was a general support among South Slav
political élites for a united Yugoslav state and a general agreement
among them that the Serbs, Croats and Slovenes made up a single
nation[5], disagreements over how the new state should be internally
organised and even how it should be called, emerged even before its
formation. There was an added confusion between the two key concepts of unitarism, or integral Yugoslavism (i.e. the belief in the 'national oneness' of Serbs, Croats and Slovenes) and centralism. In this
chapter I argue that unitarists were not always centralists and vice
versa—not all centralists were (genuine) unitarists.

While the Serbs generally favoured a centralist Constitution, to
which they were accustomed in the pre-war Kingdom of Serbia,
the Croats preferred a de-centralized constitutional arrangement,
or at least a dualist one, modelled on the now former Austria-
Hungary. The Serbian argument eventually won, but only just,
thanks to the Croat boycott of the Constituent Assembly and to a
political deal between the largest Serbian and Bosnian Muslim parties. (The Radical Party secured support for their constitutional
proposal from the leaders of the Yugoslav Muslims in exchange for
economic and political concessions.)[6] As Beard and Radin argued,
'there was no majority in the country for any plan of the government;
the Constitution represented in the main the work of the Serb

[5] In the former-Yugoslavia, like in the rest of Eastern and Central Europe, the
'nation' has an ethnic, not a civic meaning and this is how it is understood in the
context of this work.
[6] The standard work on the formative years of the Kingdom of Serbs, Croats and
Slovenes is Ivo Banac's *The National Question in Yugoslavia: Origins, History, Politics*,
4th edn, Ithaca and London, 1994 (first published 1984). I found three contemporary works on the subject particularly useful: Charles A. Beard and George
Radin, *The Balkan Pivot: Yugoslavia. A Study in Government and Administration*,
New York, 1929; Josip Horvat, *Politička povijest Hrvatske*, vol. 2, Zagreb, 1990 (first
published as *Politička povijest Hrvatske 1918–1929*, Zagreb, 1938); and Slobodan
Jovanović, *Ustavno pravo Kraljevine Srba, Hrvata i Slovenaca*, Belgrade, 1995 (first
published in 1924).

minority.'[7] Yet, the promulgation of the Constitution of 'the Serb minority' on 28 June 1921, or St Vitus' Day (*Vidovdan*), the Kosovo Battle anniversary and a sacred day in the Serbian national calendar, symbolised not just the subsequent Serb-domination of the first Yugoslav state, but also marked the beginning of a long political crisis. The Serb primacy in the new state was also reflected in the country's official name: the Kingdom of Serbs, Croats and Slovenes. The paradox was that the centralists, who strongly opposed any territorial divisions of the country, wanted the state name to preserve the 'tribal' identities, while the anti-centralists, who argued for the protection of individual identities, preferred the name 'Yugoslavia'.[8] These early misunderstandings and conflicts led some historians, such as Ivo Banac, the foremost authority on the subject, to 'blame' the way Yugoslavia was united for later national conflicts and the country's seemingly perennial instability.[9]

In the following chapter I suggest that although the 1920s and 1930s were undoubdtedly marked by a political contest between Serbian and Croatian visions of the common state, it would be too simplistic to reduce the Yugoslav politics of the period to the Serbo-Croat conflict. Political conflicts as well as cooperation and alliances more often than not ignored ethnic boundaries. It would be equally simplistic to argue that throughout the interwar years Croats and other non-Serbs represented the opposition to Serb governments. There were significant Serb political groupings opposing the régime, just like there were non-Serbs, including the Croatian Peasant Party, participating in or supporting the government.

Another contention of this chapter is that there existed several variants of Yugoslavism during the interwar period. I look at the contest between 'official' and 'opposition' Yugoslavism, and show how both the Yugoslavism promoted by the state and by the oppo-

[7] Beard and Radin, op. cit., p. 54.

[8] Jovanović, op. cit., pp. 89–90. Banac, in my opinion, goes too far when he accuses the Radicals of hoping that the Serbs' primacy, reflected in the centralist Constitution and the state name, would eventually result in the assimilation of non-Serbs. Banac, op. cit., pp. 162–3. Apart from Macedonians, who were considered 'Southern Serbs', the largest Yugoslav group did not envisage assimilation of other Yugoslavs, certainly not Croats and Slovenes, except, in some cases, Bosnia's Muslims.

[9] Banac, op. cit., esp. pp. 403–5.

sition evolved during the two interwar decades. The interrelationship between these different variants of Yugoslavism shaped decisively the politics of the Yugoslav Kingdom. In this chapter I concentrate on King Alexander's Yugoslavism, but I also look at the period which preceded the King's dictatorship and at its aftermath, when in the late 1930s the state abandoned Alexander's concept of integral Yugoslavism. The 1939 *Sporazum*, which led to the creation of an autonomous Croatia, marked not just the beginning of the devolution of the central power, but also of the official Yugoslav ideology.

The idea of Yugoslav unity originated in the 1830s, when a group of Croat intellectuals began promoting cultural unity between Croats and Serbs. It was a reaction to a growing threat of Magyarization and its most immediate result was cultural integration of the Croats, who had been divided not only territorially but also linguistically. The early development of the Yugoslav idea is therefore inseparable from the development of modern Croatian national integration. Parallel to the Yugoslav idea, the Croats developed a separate Croatian national ideology, based on the 'historic right' to statehood. The emerging Serbian state had little understanding for Yugoslavism, a somewhat narrower idea of pan-Serbian liberation and unification dominating the official discourse of nineteenth-century Serbia. The Croatian and Serbian national ideas did not differ much from other Romantic nationalist ideologies of the time, including the Yugoslav idea. They posed a threat to Yugoslav unity, but were not in as sharp a contradiction with it as it might seem from today's perspective. Conflicting claims of Croatian and Serbian nationalists and sometimes even denial of each other's existence were based on the two nations' linguistic and cultural similarities, not fundamental differences.

The Yugoslav idea survived the nineteenth century and its updated version formed the basis of the programme of the Croat-Serb Coalition, which dominated the politics of Habsburg South Slavs in the years preceding the First World War. At the same time, Yugoslavism, hitherto largely rejected, became accepted by Serbia's intellectuals and, increasingly, politicians. Proponents of Yugoslavism at the beginning of the twentieth century argued that Serbs, Croats and Slovenes were 'tribes' of one *ethnic* nation with three names (*troimeni narod*).

The history, idea and programme of this 'national oneness' version of Yugoslavism are best summarised in a series of pamphlets published in London during the war by the Yugoslav Committee, a group of exiled Habsburg South Slav politicians of the Croat-Serb Coalition and pro-Yugoslav intellectuals.[10] Members of the Yugoslav Committee argued that Yugoslavs—i.e. Serbs, Croats and Slovenes—were and had always been one nation, kept apart only by divisions imposed by their foreign rulers. However, they also argued that, like other national ideas, 'the idea of Southern Slav unity was modern in its essence', and that its development may be divided into several phases. Employing a remarkably modern language, the author(s) of an essay published by the Committee stressed that national ideas demand 'clear self-consciousness, a wide mental outlook and an enlightened intelligentsia'. According to them, the birth of the Yugoslav idea began in the sixteenth century, but its 'final phase' started in 1903 (the dynastic change in Serbia, the death of Benjámin Kállay, the administrator of Bosnia, and the end of *ban* Khuen-Héderváry's rule in Croatia), and that it would be only completed with the unification of the three 'tribes' into one political entity.[11] Although there were disagreements between the Yugoslav Committee and the Serbian wartime government over the question of whether the future common state should be a centralized or a decentralized one, the notion of *narodno jedinstvo* (national oneness) was accepted by both sides. Thus, for instance, the Corfu Declaration, issued in July 1917 by the Serbian Government and the Yugoslav Committee, stated that 'our trinominal nation' shared 'the same blood' and 'spoken and written language', and despite external pressures, 'the idea of its [Yugoslav nation's] unity could never be extinguished'.[12]

[10] [The Yugoslav Committee], *The Southern Slav Library*, nos 1–6, London, 1915–16.

[11] 'Idea of Southern Slav Unity', ibid., no. 5, 1916; 'modern in its essence', p. 7; 'final phase', p. 20.

[12] 'Krfska deklaracija od 20. (7.) jula 1917' in Ferdo Šišić, *Dokumenti o postanku Kraljevine Srba, Hrvata i Slovenaca, 1914–1919*, Zagreb, 1920, pp. 96–9, pp. 96–7. Terms such as 'national unity', 'our race', 'the Serbo-Croat-Slovene nation' can

When it was created in 1918, Yugoslavia was viewed both from inside and outside as a Serbo-Croat-Slovene nation state, in which the South Slavs formed some 82 per cent of the country's population.[13] For instance, the foremost British expert on the South Slav history and a close supporter of the Yugoslav Committee, R.W. Seton-Watson, wrote in 1911, three years before the war broke out, that Serbs and Croats belonged to one, Yugoslav, 'race' which would eventually unite, just like the Italian and German 'races' had done in the nineteenth century.[14] In fact, the formation of the Kingdom of Serbs, Croats and Slovenes would be facilitated by the principle of self-determination of the peoples, the key to President Wilson's 14 points. Inside the new country, even the Communists, despite the Comintern's anti-Versailles, and therefore anti-Yugoslav stance, did not oppose the concept of Yugoslav ethnic unity. Aleksa Djilas has argued that 'Yugoslav Communists saw no contradiction between their devotion to the Yugoslav idea, which was "national", and their general ideological opposition to nationalism and belief in interna-

---

be found in the official proclamation of the Kingdom of Serbs, Croats and Slovenes of 1 Dec. 1918. See 'Delegati Narod.[nog] Vijeća pred Regentom Aleksandrom' in ibid., pp. 280–3.

[13] According to the 1921 census the Kingdom of Serbs, Croats and Slovenes had a population of around 12 million. The census did not distinguish between the South Slavs in terms of ethnicity, but only in terms of religion and language. In the case of the latter, the South Slavs could state as their maternal language either 'Serbian or Croatian' or 'Slovene'. Therefore it is difficult to distinguish between Serbs, Croats and Slovenes, or Bosnian Muslims, Macedonians or Montenegrins, the nations recognised after 1945. A recent study, by the statistician Bogoljub Kočović, estimates the population of the South Slav kingdom in 1921 at 11,985,000, out of which 4,813,000 (40,1 per cent) were 'Serbs and Monte-negrins', 2,797,000 (23.3 per cent) Croats, 1,020,000 (8.5 per cent) Slovenes, 740,000 (6.2 per cent) [Slav] Muslims, and 465,000 (3.9 per cent) Macedonians, or in total 9,835,000 (82 per cent) Yugoslavs (Kočović provides round figures). See Kočović, *Etnički i demografski razvoj u Jugoslaviji od 1921. do 1991. godine (po svim zvaničnim a u nekim slučajevima i korigovanim popisima)*, Paris, 1998, 2 vols, vol. 2, pp. 332–3.

[14] R.W. Seton-Watson, *The Southern Slav Question and the Habsburg Monarchy*, New York, 1969 (first published in 1911), p. 336. Seton-Watson continued to regard Serbs and Croats as one nation in his later writings—see for instance his article 'The background of the Jugoslav Dictatorship', *Slavonic (and East European) Review*, vol. 10, no. 29, Dec. 1931, pp. 363–76.

tionalism.'[15] Nor did the Croatian (Republican) Peasant Party reject Yugoslavism, although it opposed the way the unification was carried out and boycotted the new state's interim institutions. Its leader, Stjepan Radić, while calling for a Croatian state *within* Yugoslavia, proclaimed not long after the unification that 'we, Croats, Slovenes and Serbs really are one nation, both according to our language and our customs.'[16]

In the aftermath of the unification the debate between centralists and decentralists gradually turned into a Serbo–Croat disagreement.[17] Yet, even then the lines were not so clear. On the one hand, it was a disagreement between Belgrade, or the pre-war Serbian tradition on the one side, and the former Habsburg territories of the new state on the other side. On the other hand, it was a conflict between different beliefs what was best for the new country, regardless of ethnic background. Stojan Protić, the first prime minister of the Kingdom of Serbs, Croats and Slovenes[18] and a leader of the [Serbian] People's Radical Party (NRS) argued in favour of local autonomies, while Svetozar Pribićević, a Croation Serb was among the staunchest centralists.

It was Stjepan Radić's vision of Yugoslavism which would pose the strongest challenge to the official *Vidovdan* Yugoslavism embodied in the centralist Constitution promulgated on St Vitus' Day (*Vidovdan*) 1921. Although Radić's views are not always easy to pin down, and although during the 1920s (before he was shot in the

---

[15] August Cesarec, a leading Croatian Communist, described the unification as a 'national revolution'—as Djilas noted, this was 'the highest compliment a Marxist can pay to a historic event'. Aleksa Djilas, *The Contested Country: Yugoslav Unity and the Communist Revolution, 1919–1953*, 3rd edn, Cambridge, MA., 1996, p. 59.

[16] Stjepan Radić, 'Hoćemo u jugoslavenskom jedinstvu svoju hrvatsku državu' ('We want our Croatian state within the Yugoslav unity'), in Stjepan Radić, *Politički spisi: Autobiografija, članci, govori, rasprave*, compiled by Zvonimir Kulundžić, Zagreb, 1971, pp. 319–22, p. 319.

[17] How a political and constitutional debate came to be perceived as a national, Serbo–Croat conflict is described in Horvat, op. cit., pp. 158–98.

[18] Protić only became the Prime Minister because Alexander had blocked Pašić's election to the post. This was not only an early omen of the future King's undemocratic tendencies, but also another example of an *intra*-ethnic (i.e. Serb-Serb) conflict.

Skupština by a [Serbian] Radical Party deputy in 1928) he manoeuvred between 'hard opposition'[19] and participation in the government, it is nevertheless possible to define some lasting aspects of Radić's Yugoslavism. Essentially, he envisaged a Yugoslavia within which the Croats would get maximum autonomy, but he did not reject the idea of a Yugoslav state, or even of a common South Slav identity. Because Radić was the undisputed leader of the Croatian Peasant Party (HSS), by far the largest Croat party, his repeated conflicts with Serb-dominated governments have led most historians to equate Radić with the Croats as a whole and to argue that the first Yugoslavia was plagued by the Serbo-Croat conflict. While this view is in many respects correct, I suggest that we look at the period as a contest between two Yugoslavisms: a highly centralist one, favoured by Serb-dominated Belgrade governments, and an anti-centralist one, whose staunchest advocates were Stjepan Radić, and, after 1927, Svetozar Pribićević, formerly the most vocal proponent of centralism, who left the government in 1925, ironically because Radić's Peasant Party had joined it.

Pribićević, a leading Croatian Serb and one of the founders of the Democratic Party (DS), was initially opposed to any alternative vision of Yugoslavia to his favoured centralist-unitarist one. His inability to tolerate calls for decentralisation is often rightly blamed for the almost instant alienation of Croats from the new state. When the Democrats, under Ljubomir-Ljuba Davidović began to move against centralism and closer to the HSS position, Pribićević left them in 1924 to found the breakaway Independent Democratic Party (SDS) and enter the government of Nikola Pašić, leader of the Radical Party. As mentioned above, Pribićević resigned from the government because of the Pašić-Radić alliance. The Independent Democrats' leader, a firm believer in both unitarism and centralism, refused to cooperate with Radić, who had previously rebuffed the *Vidovdan* Constitution and boycotted the *Skupština*.

However, Radić also left the government, less than two years after his 'historic' agreement (*sporazum*) with Pašić, unable to form a genuine partnership with the Radical leader and his successors.[20]

---

[19] To use the phrase coined by Banac in op. cit.

[20] Pašić died in 1926, aged eighty-one, not long after a heavy row with King Alexander.

In 1927, in a volte face suppressing even the 1925 pact with the Radicals, Radić joined forces with Pribićević. The two leading *prečani*[21] politicians became co-presidents of the newly formed Peasant Democratic Coalition (SDK)—the main, Serbo-Croat opposition bloc to the government in Belgrade. Although Pribićević continued to believe in the national oneness, his rejection of centralism made possible the coalition with Radić, who, as already argued, did not reject the notion of a common Yugoslav identity. Thus, it may be argued that the Yugoslavism of the opposition (especially if we include Davidović, who remained outside the government until his death in 1940, except for a few months in 1928) was 'greater' than the official Yugoslavism of the Radical-dominated position, which placed more emphasis on centralism than unitarism. The common Radical 'enemy' made the cooperation between Pribićević and Radić even more likely, although Radić's decision to fight for the Croat rights in the parliament (as opposed to outside it, as he did prior to 1924 when the HSS boycotted the state institutions) also played a role in forging the once most unlikely of alliances.

Throughout the 1920s, the Yugoslav political scene continued to be cross-cut by *inter-*'tribal' as well as by *intra-*'tribal' contests between political parties. No party or party coalition was able to form a stable government on national or supra-national lines and tensions in the *Skupština* gradually rose. In June 1928 the crisis reached its culmination, when a Radical deputy fired revolver shots at a group of HSS deputies, killing two and mortally wounding Stjepan Radić.[22] Boycott of the *Skupština* by the SDK and failure of two more governments, one headed by an army general and another by Anton Korošec (the Slovene Clericals' leader and the only non-Serb Prime

---

[21] *Prečani* means those from across (*preko*)—this is how Serbs of pre-1912 Serbia called Serbs and other Yugoslavs who lived across the border in Austria-Hungary. The term survived the unification and during the interwar years the co-operation between the HSS and the SDS was often called the *prečanski front*.

[22] One of the shot HSS deputies was Radić's nephew. For a detailed account of Yugoslavia's party politics throughout the 1920s see Branislav Gligorijević's *Parlament i političke stranke u Jugoslaviji, 1919–1929*, Belgrade, 1979. For Pribićević's political career see Hrvoje Matković, *Svetozar Pribićević i Samostalna demokratska stranka do šestojanuarske diktature*, Zagreb, 1972 and Ljubo Boban, *Svetozar Pribićević u opoziciji (1928–1936)*, Zagreb, 1973. For a recent study in English on Radić see Mark Biondich, *Stjepan Radić, the Croat Peasant Party and the Politics of Mass Mobilization, 1904–1928*, Toronto, 2000.

Minister in the interwar period), before the end of the year, apparently persuaded the King that there was no other option but for him to take matters into his own hands. In early January 1929 Alexander received leading political and public figures, including Pribićević and Vladko Maček, Radić's successor as the HSS president, asking them for their opinion on the future of the state. The two *prečani* leaders argued for wide autonomy of 'historical provinces', united in a federal Kingdom with 'the common King, common state borders, common army, common foreign affairs, common financial policy and common customs and trade policies.'[23] However, to Alexander anti-centralisation amounted to anti-Yugoslavism and was therefore unacceptable. He apparently also threatened the 'amputation' of Croatia (minus its Serb-populated territories), but given the obvious impracticalities of such an action, it is not clear how seriously the King considered it.[24] Anyhow, instead of disintegrating the country, Alexander opted to integrate it through his personal rule. If the politicians could not unite the nation, the King hoped a strong state apparatus under his control would. On 6 January 1929, the Orthodox Christmas Eve, he dissolved parliament, banned all political parties and declared that 'the moment has arrived when there can, and should, be no intermediary between nation and King'.[25]

The *šestojanuarska diktatura* ('the Sixth of January dictatorship'), as Alexander's régime is usually known after the date on which it was proclaimed, was meant to put an end to the country's disunity by enforcing an integral Yugoslav identity from above. The initial

---

[23] *Arhiv Jugoslavije* (Archives of Yugoslavia, Belgrade, hereafter AJ), 335–15 (Papers of Vojislav Jovanović Marambo), Minutes from a meeting of the Executive Committee of the SDK, 21 Dec. [1928].

[24] Pribićević wrote later that the King indeed told him during their meeting following the *Skupština* murders of July 1928 that he would rather opt for the 'amputation' of Croatia than a federation, proposed by the SDS leader. Both Pribićević and Radić were against the 'amputation'. See Svetozar Pribićević, *Diktatura Kralja Aleksandra*, Belgrade, 1953 (first published as *La dictature du roi Alexandre*, Paris, 1933), pp. 73–5.

[25] For an English translation of the 6 Jan. 1929 proclamation see Snežana Trifunovska (ed.), *Yugoslavia Through Documents: From its Creation to its Dissolution*, Dordrecht, 1994, pp. 190–1.

discourse blamed political, not national conflict, for the crisis in the country. In his proclamation of 6 January, Alexander accused politicians, not 'nationalist leaders', that their

> blind *political* passions have begun to misuse the parliamentary system...to such an extent that it has become a hindrance to any fruitful work in the State...It is my sacred duty to preserve the unity of nation and State by all means; and I am determined to fulfil this duty to the end without hesitation.[26]

According to contemporary accounts, the King's view that political parties and their leaders were to be blamed for political instability was shared by many Yugoslavs, including Croats. The royal proclamation was initially also supported by some political parties, notably the Croatian Peasant Party (HSS) and their allies, the Independent Democrats (SDS), who had long campaigned against the *Vidovdan* Constitution.[27] Foreign diplomats also believed that the failure of political institutions had put Alexander in a position when something had to be done. Howard W. Kennard, of the British legation in Belgrade, wrote to Austen Chamberlain, the British Foreign Secretary, a few days after the King's proclamation:

> Quite apart from the questionable manner in which this absolute autocracy has been introduced, it was essential, as I have frequently reported in

[26] 'Royal proclamation abrogating the Constitution and dissolving the Parliament of the Serb-Croat-Slovene Kingdom', Belgrade, 6 Jan. 1929, in ibid. Emphasis added.

[27] Mood among Croats: 'Izvještaji o promeni raspoloženja naroda', *Hrvatski državni arhiv* (Croatian State Archives, Zagreb—hereafter HDA), *Grupa XXI, Politička situacija, 1910–41, Kutija 26, inv. br. 1559* (Group 21: Political situation, 1910–41, box 26, inventory number 1559). For instance, a report from Jastrebarsko, a town near Zagreb, stated that people thought that 'politicians managed to compromise themselves over the last 10 years', and that with the royal proclamation 'a knot was cut off, so there will be no more demands made in the party name, and what is most important there will be no more party arbitrariness and terror'. The same report offers an interesting analysis of the reaction of local politicians: the HSS and SDS welcomed the abolition of the *Vidovdan* Constitution, and believed that Radić's wish, that there should be only the King and the people, had now been achieved. Sreski poglavar Grubić, Jastrebarsko, Velikom županu zagrebačke oblasti, Zagreb, 'Proklamacija novog stanja, raspoloženje naroda', Jastrebarsko, 9 Jan. 1929, ibid.

recent despatches, that some drastic action of a radical nature should be taken to free the Administration from the *political* incubus which has crippled it and finally brought it so low a level that it was hardly functioning at all.[28]

However, the prime goal of the dictatorship was to solve the 'national question', understood as essentially a dispute over the Constitution between the HSS and SDS on the one hand and the government and the Crown in Belgrade on the other. Vladko Maček even issued a statement welcoming the abolition of the *Vidovdan* Constitution and expressing his belief that thanks to 'the great wisdom of His Majesty the King', the Croats would now achieve autonomy.[29] But Alexander's vision of Yugoslavia was somewhat different from Maček's—instead of gradually decentralizing power, the King believed that centralism as well as unitarism were essential for the country's survival. At the New Year's dinner party in 1929, Alexander told his Ministers that the new Yugoslavia was to:

represent that higher synthesis of our national expressions and characteristics, which would in our internal harmony enable the development of all beautiful distinguishing features of our race, while showing to the outside world the strength of unity and unyielding will of the same-blooded [Yugoslav] nation. In such a Kingdom of Yugoslavia, [only] those institutions, state government and state structure which are best suited to general needs of the nation and of state interests, will be established.[30]

[28] Emphasis added. Kennard also expressed his doubts over Gen. Živković, writing in the same despatch that 'one must doubt whether the King has chosen the best instrument with which to purge the Augean stable.' Public Record Office, London (hereafter PRO), FO 371/13706, Kennard to Chamberlain, Belgrade 14 Jan. 1929.

[29] Horvat, op. cit., p. 362. In this statement Maček used the then well known metaphor: 'the vest [*lajbek*] is unbuttoned', arguing that in 1921 the 'vest' (i.e. the Constitution) was wrongly 'buttoned', and that the King's Manifesto presented a chance to now 'button' Serbo-Croat relations all over again, but 'properly' this time. The metaphor was originally used by Ferenc Deák, the Hungarian politician, to describe the Austro-Hungarian Compromise of 1867, so Maček's use of it is another indication that he wanted Yugoslavia to be a dual Serbo-Croat state, thus resembling the former Austria-Hungary. Maček often openly stated this idea; see for instance Stenographic notes from Maček's trial, Belgrade, 11 March 1933, in *Vodja govori: Ličnost, izjave, govori i politički rad vodje Hrvata Dra. Vladka Mačeka*, compiled by Mirko Glojnarić, Zagreb, 1936, pp. 178–83.

[30] AJ, 74–38–56 (The Royal Court Papers), 'Govor [Kralja Aleksandra ministrima] na večeri [na Dvoru] 31. dec[embar] 1929 g.'.

On 3 October 1929 the country's official name was changed into the Kingdom of Yugoslavia, and it was divided into nine *banovinas* (provinces), which cut across old historic borders and were, at least in theory, based on geographic, rather than ethnic criteria. The new name was more than just an act of convenience, given that the state had already generally been called 'Yugoslavia'. It was meant to reflect 'the complete state and national oneness [...] and to express symbolically the idea of total unity, equality and brotherhood of us South Slavs—Serbs, Croats and Slovenes', in the words of the then Yugoslav Prime Minister and the King's closest ally, General Petar Živković.[31] Looking back at the significance of the October 1929 changes, a government manifesto issued the following year stressed:

The ethnic and ethical substance of our historical and national development has definitely been formulated by the [new] name of our Kingdom, which has been accepted throughout the country with great enthusiasm. The administrative division [into 9 *banovinas*] has forever erased historic borders and [removed] all obstacles to our national formation and development [...] This Law [of 3 October 1929] has laid foundations for the following absolute principle: *a single nation and single sense of national belonging.*[32]

Despite the new internal division into the *banovinas,* meant to satisfy growing (mostly Croat) demands for federalization, the country remained as centralized as it had been throughout the 1920s.[33] At the same New Year's speech the King told his ministers that the main aim of his personal rule was to 'improve national unity, [which was] sacred, and to put the state above anything else'.[34] In practice

---

[31] *Politika* (Belgrade), 4 Oct. 1929.

[32] 'Historički zaključci Ministarskog Savjeta', *Novo doba* (Zagreb), 5 June 1930. Emphasis in original.

[33] Not that centralism was peculiar to Yugoslavia. Mark Mazower points out in his recent history of Europe in the twentieth century that in the interwar period 'only in Germany and Austria [before Hitler and Dollfuss] was the new state constructed on a federal rather than unitary basis, and in those cases not until a long struggle, not for very many years.' *Dark Continent: Europe's Twentieth Century,* London, 1998, p. 7.

[34] AJ, 74–38–56, 'Govor [Kralja Aleksandra ministrima] na večeri [na Dvoru] 31. dec[embar] 1929 g.'.

that meant that there were no longer Serbs, Croats or Slovenes, but only *Yugoslavs*. Alexander's 'integral' Yugoslavism placed more emphasis on unitarism and represented a slight shift from the pre-dictatorship Yugoslavism, when *internal sub-identities* within the nation were tolerated (as reflected in the country's pre-1929 official name). So, instead of the autonomy they were hoping for, the Croats soon discovered that the new order promised as much centralisa-tion as the old, with an additional danger: integral Yugoslavism could turn out to be an effective way to de-nationalize (and Serbianize?) them. As for Serbs, while they were generally more sympathetic to the King and the new régime, once they realised that the dictator-ship was not going to be a short-term measure, they began to call for a return of democracy. As Stevan Pavlowitch argued, while the Croats accused them of hegemony, the Serbs felt that they had to sacrifice perhaps the most important legacy they brought to Yugo-slavia—the liberal-democratic institutions 'they had come to appre-ciate in the old kingdom during the decade preceding the First World War.'[35]

Alexander's Yugoslavism ultimately failed. It was particularly rejected by Croats, among whom the HSS had become a *de facto* national movement, with strong grass roots support in Croat-populated areas. Perhaps the main problem was that Alexander's Yugoslavism was too easily associated, both institutionally and ideo-logically, with the largest of the three Yugoslav 'tribes'—the Serbs. There is evidence that Alexander adopted a Yugoslav identity even before the creation of Yugoslavia.[36] Yet, the Karadjordjević dynasty was seen by non-Serbs (and many Serbs) as primarily a Serbian dynasty. As already argued, centralism was associated with Serbia's tradition, but more importantly it also meant that in the interwar

[35] Stevan K. Pavlowitch, *Yugoslavia*, London, 1971, p. 81.
[36] See Ivan Meštrović, *Uspomene na političke ljude i dogadjaje*, Zagreb, 1993, pp. 82–5. While not always the most reliable source, Meštrović's memoirs are amusing and because of its author's acquaintance with many leading Yugoslav personalities they offer a good insight into Yugoslav politics in the first half of the twentieth century. At the time of the writing of his memoirs, in the 1960s, Meštrović had long been disillusioned with Yugoslavism, so his treatment of Alexander is not very sympathetic. For other examples of Alexander's Yugoslavism see Šišić, *Dokumenti*, op. cit, pp. 60–4. Following the unification, as an act of symbolism, Alexander gave his second son a Croat name (after the greatest Croatian medi-eval King) and his third son a Slovene name.

period all the powers were concentrated in the state capital Belgrade, which in Croatia symbolised Serbia and Serbs, rather than a new Yugoslav synthesis.

Ideologically, many of the Serbian national myths were linked too closely with the post-1929 Yugoslavism, despite the régime's rejection of 'tribal' names and national symbols. Serbian sacrifices in the First World War were turned into one of the main founding myths of the Yugoslav state. Heroic as it were, the Serbian struggle during the war was not so easily identifiable with the non-Serbs, not only because the Habsburg South Slavs were officially on the enemy side during the war. The key danger of the 'Kajmakčalan ideology'[37] was that it implied—often explicitly—that because the Serbs suffered most during the war in order to liberate *all* Yugoslavs, they were entitled to lead, if not dominate the new state. The 1389 Kosovo battle—around which developed the key Serbian national myth—was celebrated as a pan-Yugoslav myth, as well as anniversaries of the two Serbian uprisings against the Ottomans of the early nineteenth century.[38] It is in this lack of common Yugoslav national mythology that one should also look for reasons why integral Yugoslavism ultimately failed.

Yugoslav integral ideology also failed because it became synonymous with the régime. The public realized that many politicians who supported the post-Sixth-of-January order became Yugoslavs overnight, out of pragmatic considerations. Because it became compulsory, because it could not exist outside its official form and

---

[37] Kajmakčalan was the site of a major battle of the First World War in the Balkans, where the Serbian army, in 1916, defeated Bulgarian forces, suffering heavy losses.

[38] Thus every 28 June was celebrated throughout the country, and a newspaper which championed the integral Yugoslavism was called *Vidovdan*. Also Karadjordje, the leader of the First Serbian uprising (1804–13) and the founder of the Karadjordjević dynasty was turned by integral Yugoslavs into the progenitor of the Yugoslav idea. It would be wrong, however, to presume that only Serbs identified with the key events of the Serbian history. Many pro-Yugoslav Croats, such as the sculptor Ivan Meštrović, saw in the Kosovo myth a symbol of suffering and moral victory of all Yugoslavs, while the Croatian historian Ferdo Šišić, in his book *Jugoslovenska misao: Istorija ideje narodnog ujedinjenja i oslobodjenja od 1790–1918*, Belgrade, 1937, lists Karadjordje among proto-Yugoslavs. But, most Croats and other non-Serbs were unable to identify with the Serbian national mythology.

because it was associated with many of the same corrupt politicians who compromised the democratic institutions of the 1920s, Alexander's Yugoslavism lost much of its potential to appeal to the masses. Even some unquestionably Yugoslav figures close to the King reacted against the way the official Yugoslavism was promoted by the state, at the expense of other, narrower identities. In the Upper House (Senate) of the National Parliament, Želimir Mažuranić, a pro-Yugoslav Croat, spoke for many:

The feeling of being a Croat grows stronger and becomes more resolute when someone tries to prove to me that that I am not [a Croat], or when they try to force me to admit that Croatdom does not imply a nation, but just a tribe… When someone tells me today that the Croats are a Yugoslav tribe, I have nothing against it because it is true […] But if they tell me that Croats are not and have never been a nation, that they are just a tribe, then I feel resistance to it and I then insist that it is a name for a nation, not a tribe.[39]

Alexander's death provoked a reaction opposite to the one his assassins had hoped for. Instead of breaking up after its leader's death, Yugoslavia appeared more united than ever since 1918, if only for a brief period. The Croat-populated areas were swept with a mixture of sorrow, anxiety and fear.[40] Although by 1934 the King had realised that the integral Yugoslavism had failed to achieve its main aim and was apparently planning to solve the Croat question upon his return from France,[41] it is not clear how he intended to do so. Was he prepared just to decentralize the power, or to abandon integral Yugoslavism as well? Maček had made it clear that the Croats

[39] *Stenografske beleške Senata Kraljevine Jugoslavije (saziv za 1932. i 1933. godinu)*, vol. 3, Belgrade, 1933, p. 50. Cited in Nikola Dugandžija, *Jugoslavenstvo*, Belgrade, 1985, p. 127n.
[40] HDA, *Grupa XXI, Politička situacija, 1910–41, Kutija 58*.
[41] This is confirmed by Vladko Maček in his memoirs. The Croat leader, who was in prison at the time for publicly opposing the régime, received a message from the King through Ivan Šubašić, a senior member of the HSS, who was also close to the Court. The King apparently told Šubašić: 'Tell Dr. Maček…that I shall free him as soon as I return from France. But then I shall deal with him in person.' Vladko Maček, *In the Struggle for Freedom*, London, 1957, p. 154.

demanded not only decentralisation of the country, but also recognition of their 'individuality'. Although not against Yugoslavia as a state, Maček, unlike Radić, rejected the notion of a common Yugoslav nation. In a newspaper interview he stated that: 'The ideology of national oneness was based on the notion of linguistic unity. But life has taught us that linguistic unity is not enough for national unity'.[42] In another interview the Croat leader was even more explicit in his rejection of the national oneness Yugoslavism:

> There existed a Croatian nation, a Serbian nation, a Slovene nation and a Bulgarian nation, each with a developed national consciousness...nations are created and abolished by God, and not by ministers or dictators. Only what springs up from the people can be long-lasting.[43]

During the years of the Royal Regency (1934–41), which under Alexander's first cousin, Prince Paul, ruled in the name of the minor King Peter II (until it was deposed on 27 March 1941), the Crown and the government eventually began the federalisation of the country and also abandoned Alexander's brand of Yugoslavism. Under the terms of the 1939 *Sporazum* (Agreement) between the Crown and the government on the one hand and the HSS on the other, an autonomous *banovina* of Croatia was established. Maček became the deputy prime-minister in the Yugoslav government of Dragiša Cvetković, while five other members of the SDK (four were from the HSS and one from the SDS) also entered the government. The establishment of an autonomous Croatia reflected the realisation on behalf of authorities in Belgrade that the Croat question could only be settled if the country was decentralised, but also if the Croats' separate identity was recognised. In other words, by the end of the 1930s the solution of the Croat question was only possible outside the concept of integral Yugoslavism. The latter *de facto* came to an end with the *Sporazum* of August 1939.

On 10 March 1939, a month after replacing Milan Stojadinović as Yugoslavia's Prime Minister, Dragiša Cvetković declared to the

[42] Maček's interview with a journalist from *Slovak* (Bratislava), no date, in *Vodja govori*, op. cit., pp. 268–9.
[43] Maček's interview with a journalist from *Zora* (Sofia), 4 Aug. 1935, ibid., p. 229.

Skupština that the prime aim of his government was to re-establish the lost confidence of the Croats in the Belgrade government, and that past mistakes must not be repeated. This was a clear sign that the régime was not going to continue to insist on the notion of national oneness, and that Croat, Serb and Slovene separate, if closely related, identities would be recognised. Cvetković said as much when he told the *Skupština*:

Certain parts of our homeland had in the past been culturally and geographically separated, they have developed their national individuality, which is still, twenty years after living in the common state, strongly manifested. We have to recognise this fact and seek a solution, within the borders of Yugoslavia, which would enable a normal coexistence.[44]

But the *Sporazum* was not realized before the SDK and Serbian opposition parties united in a common opposition bloc which strongly challenged the government lists in the 1935 and 1938 elections. Historians rightly emphasize the international crisis as a key motivation behind the 1939 agreement—both Prince Paul and Maček were aware that a stable Yugoslavia was a necessity at the time when the Second World War was looming.[45] However, the Cvetković-Maček *Sporazum* could not have been achieved without the Serbo-Croat *Sporazum* of November 1937, when the Bloc of National Agreement was formed by the SDK and Serbian opposition parties: the DS, the NRS (its Main Committee) and the Agrarian Union (SZ).[46] The united Serbo-Croat opposition bloc gave the

---

[44] Dragiša Cvetković, 'Srpsko-hrvatsko pitanje i putevi Sporazuma', *Dokumenti o Jugoslaviji*, vol. 3, Paris, 1952, p. 20.

[45] For the 1939 agreement see Ljubo Boban, *Sporazum Cvetković-Maček*, Belgrade, 1965.

[46] Most historians erroneously call the Aug. 1939 *Sporazum* the *Serbo-Croat* agreement, whereas it was an agreement between the largest Croatian party, in coalition with the party of Croatian Serbs on the one hand and the Crown and the Yugoslav Radical Union (JRZ), the government party, which was a *de facto* coalition of the Radical faction led by the Prime Minister Milan Stojadinović, the Slovene People's Party (SLS) and the Yugoslav Muslim Organization (JMO), the main Slovene and Bosnian Muslim parties, respectively, on the other hand. The Pašić-Radić *Sporazum* of the mid-1920s and the 1937 Bloc of National Agreement (both of which were also branded as *Sporazums* by contemporaries), were political agreements much more deserving of the label *Serbo-Croat*.

government list a close run in the elections of December 1938. Although the three Serbian parties (and a fourth one, as the SDS was predominantly a Croatian Serb party) believed that the solution to the Croat question was in the democratisation of the country, they also, to varying degrees, accepted the need for federalisation. More importantly, the Serbian opposition parties had strong support among the masses. Not only did they do well in the elections, but when Maček visited Belgrade in August 1938, a year before the *Sporazum*, tens of thousands people came to greet him. Thus, in the second half of the 1930s, until he became the deputy Prime Minister in August 1939, Maček was more than just a Croat leader—he was also the leader of the pan-Yugoslav opposition, even if his political ambitions did not go far beyond achieving a maximum autonomy for the Croats within Yugoslavia. It may be therefore argued that the strength of the Serbo-Croat democratic opposition prompted Prince Paul just as much as the international crisis to solve the Croat question.

The 1939 *Sporazum* satisfied a majority of Croats, if not the extreme right and left, and it also marked the first step towards the federalization of the country and the solution of Yugoslavia's national question. Many Serbs—both those living in the newly formed Croatian *banovina* and those in the rest of Yugoslavia—sought to 'rally together'[47] all their compatriots in a Serbian unit, and both Slovenes and Bosnia's Muslims called for the creation of their own *banovinas*. Integral Yugoslavism, which in 1929 was introduced to stabilise and save Yugoslavia, was, only ten years later abandoned by most Yugoslavs, even by its most enthusiastic supporters, the Serbs.[48] If the solution of the Croat question led to the opening-up

[47] The slogan of a movement which emerged at the time and which was suported by a group of Serbian intellectuals around the Serbian Cultural Club (SKK) was 'Serbs, rally together!' (*Srbi na okup!*).

[48] Slobodan Jovanović, a leading Serbian intellectual and one of the founders of the SKK, argued in a lecture delivered in Dec. 1939 in the SKK, that instead of integral Yugoslavism, Serbs and Croats should revert to the original Yugoslavism of the Illyrians, which was a reaction against a threat from a larger nation (Hungarians). According to Jovanović, Yugoslavia should be based on the self-interest of Serbs and Croats to live in a common state, which would best protect them from their neighbours and biger powers. See Aleksandar Pavković, *Slobodan Jovanović: An Unsentimental Approach to Politics*, Boulder, CO, 1993, pp. 199–204.

of the Serbian one, and put an end to the democratisation of the
country, the beginning of federalisation promised to bring long-
term stability. The Second World War destroyed the Yugoslav
state, but when it re-emerged after the war, it was as a federation,
albeit a Communist one.

YUGOSLAVISM AND YUGOSLAV COMMUNISM: FROM TITO TO KARDELJ

Dejan Jović

'The name Yugoslavia is somehow heard less lately while people write and talk mostly of the 'federation'. We must lay more stress on Yugoslavia. We are Slovenes, Croats, Serbs, Macedonians, but all of us together are also Yugoslavs, all of us are citizens of socialist Yugoslavia. In this sense, we must strengthen the sense of belonging to the Yugoslav socialist community of equal nations and nationalities. This is not Yugoslavhood in the unitarist sense that denies the nation or endeavours to diminish its role. We have fought energetically against Yugoslavhood in the unitarist sense and must strive in the future against every, even the slightest tendency towards unitarism that has inherent in it the hegemony of any nation whatsoever. What I refer to is the need to deepen awareness of belonging to Yugoslavia, of the fact that the strengthening of our Yugoslav community is the concern of all our nations and nationalities and that only if strong can it guarantee them true prosperity.'[1] (Josip Broz Tito)

'In brief, the essence of today's Yugoslavism can be only the socialist interest and socialist consciousness... Socialist forces would be making a big mistake if they allowed themselves to be carried away by futile ideas of creating some new kind of nation.'[2] (Edvard Kardelj)

This chapter focuses on differences between Josip Broz Tito and Edvard Kardelj's understanding of Yugoslavia and Yugoslavism. Although both were Marxists, by the late 1960s they understood

---

[1] Josip Broz Tito, 'No compromise with nationalism' (1969) in his *The National Question*, Belgrade, 1983, p. 156.

[2] Edvard Kardelj, 'The Development of the Slovene National Question: Preface to the second edition', 1957; in *The Nations and Socialism*, Belgrade, 1981, p. 127.

and interpreted Marxist doctrine of state—and, crucially, of the Yugoslav state—somewhat differently. While Kardelj abandoned the 'brotherhood and unity' concept, which envisaged Yugoslavia as primarily a state of South Slavs, Tito hesitated to view Yugoslav unity through ideology only. Following the acceptance of Kardelj's concept during the constitutional debate of 1967–74, Yugoslavia was defined primarily as an ideological, not ethnic project. Tito's position was reduced to a 'tolerated exception', not to be continued by anyone else after his death. This change enormously contributed to gradual weakening of the Yugoslav state in the last fifteen years of its existence. In fact, it led Yugoslavia to a no-win situation. The success of Kardelj's anti-statist project led to weakening of the state, thus making it vulnerable and unable to defend its unity. Yugoslavia was first weakened from within, by its own ideological concept of 'withering away of the state'. Democratisation posed a challenge not only to the régime, but also to the weakened state, which reduced the basis of its unity merely to the ideology.

Unlike liberal states, which never allow civil wars but rather use instruments of coercion to prevent them, the socialist anti-statist 'state' found itself incapable of reacting to challenges from within.[3] Although external pressure (from the international community), nationalism, economic crisis, cultural and social differences between its constituent nations and nationalities were all important elements in the process of disintegration, it was the ideology of anti-statism that had crucially contributed to the fall of Yugoslavia. Thus, a wider aim of this chapter is to contribute to the debate on what caused the break-up of Yugoslavia. In order to do that, however, it is necessary to also briefly explore the relationship between the Yugoslav Communists' understanding of Yugoslavism and their taking of power at the end of the Second World War.

Tito's Brotherhood and Unity Federalist Yugoslavism

The post-1945 ('New') Yugoslavia was to be totally, i.e. revolutionary, different from everything that the pre-war Yugoslavia had been.

---

[3] The Yugoslav army indeed became an 'army without a state'. In a state based on an anti-statist concept, the Army was increasingly turning into an 'extra-systemic' institution, the most conservative representative of statism, which was to be defeated. See Veljko Kadijević, *Moje vidjenje raspada*, Belgrade, 1993.

While the pre-war Yugoslavia was based on the liberal concept of nation-state, with a Yugoslav nation in the process of being promoted and consolidated by the state, the post-war Yugoslavia was based on the Marxist concept of nations and states. Communist movement was 'national in form', and it promised liberation of smaller Yugoslav nations from various forms of oppression by greater nations and their élites. The state was to change its character and ultimately to be destroyed from within society (by its 'subjective forces', i.e. the Communist party and its satellite-organisations) as an 'instrument of class exploitation'. The ultimate goal of socialist revolution was to create a stateless form of social order. As formulated in the programme of the League of Communists of Yugoslavia, the 'historic task' of the Yugoslav Communists was to 'transform the contemporary social scene, which bears all the marks of the transition period, into one in which classes and all traces of exploitation and the oppression of man by man will disappear', to create 'a society without a state, classes, or parties'[4].

If the state is to wither away in general, then in Yugoslavia this ought to happen too. In addition to their commitment to the Marxist theory of state, the Yugoslav communists were to decentralize the state also because they wanted to be radically (i.e. revolutionary) different from the inter-war Yugoslav kingdom, which was—in their interpretation—a highly centralised state, dominated by the 'Great-Serbian' bourgeoisie. The promise they gave to the Yugoslavs was that 'New Yugoslavia' would be different on both accounts, as a de-centralised republic, with no dominant ethnic group. For the Yugoslav communists, integral Yugoslavism and Pan-Slavism were not much more than a cover that had hidden what they viewed as the great-Serbian hegemony in interwar Yugoslavia. The social injustice and inequality among the nations could be defeated only by socialist revolution, not by agreement between Serbian and other segments of the political élites.[5] Both Kardelj (in his 1939 book *The Development of the Slovene National Question*) and Tito (in a 1942 article)[6] conditioned the existence of any Yugoslavia

---

[4] *The Programme of the League of Yugoslav Communists*, Belgrade, 1958, pp. 266–7.
[5] It was on these grounds that the Yugoslav Communists criticised the *Sporazum* of 1939.
[6] Josip Broz Tito, 'The National Question and the Liberation Struggle', *Proleter* 17:3 (1942), *The National Question*, Belgrade, 1983, pp. 43–53.

upon being socialist, i.e. just in terms of social and national questions. The concept of justice they followed defined justice as 'justice for disadvantaged', for the underprivileged. In terms of Yugoslavia's national question, a just society is only that one in which smaller nations are no longer underprivileged. It is not surprising, thus, that the Marxist understanding of justice among nations was appealing to smaller Yugoslav nations (Slovenes and Croats), and to those who had not been recognised as nations in the interwar period (Montenegrins, Bosnian Muslims and Macedonians).

During the Second World War, however, it looked as if the idea of national emancipation was emphasised much more strongly than the idea of social justice and revolution. In doing so, the Yugoslav communists demonstrated not only political pragmatism, but also loyalty to its major allies in Moscow and London, who urged them to eliminate or suppress their revolutionary ideology for the sake of Yugoslavia's liberation. For a long period of time, the Yugoslav communists, including Tito himself, hesitated to reveal publicly their ideological background, speaking only of Yugoslav patriotism. But their definition of 'patriotism' was new and it included both social and national justice as compulsory elements of any Yugoslavia worth fighting for. The slogan of 'brotherhood and unity' expressed the complexity of the new notion of patriotism in the most graphic way. 'Brotherhood' was not only an ethnic category, but also a socialist demand for solidarity, equality and fraternity among the Yugoslav peoples. The programme of social and national justice, combined with a promise to re-unite (and re-organize) Yugoslavia contributed to a wide popular support for Tito's Partisans. The notion of *new* Yugoslavia, and the open rejection of the 'old' one appealed to the non-Serbs. At the same time the *Yugoslav* orientation of the Partisan movement attracted many Serbs (especially those from the Independent State of Croatia—present-day Croatia and Bosnia-Herzegovina) to Tito's Partisans.

For most of the war and in its immediate aftermath, the idea of the 'new Yugoslavia' was a 'catch-all' formula, which to many sides offered something and to none everything. Those who wanted more changes, particularly non-Serbs, emphasised its 'new' character. Just like in two other communist federations, Czechoslovakia and the USSR, the smaller nations linked themselves closer to socialist ('new') character of state, which offered them also a 'new solution' of the national question. Those more ideological among the members of Yugoslav élite and public, had hoped the state would be decentralised in order to wither away quickly. On the other hand, the Serbs joined Partisans more for patriotic rather than ideological reasons. Although 'new Yugoslavia' was a socialist state, many among the participants of the 1941 Partisan uprising believed that it should remain above all a 'Yugoslav *state*'. The new generation of leaders (who emerged under influence of Marxism as thought in schools and other public institutions) as well as those from the smaller nations, believed that the state should indeed be permanently weakened in order to eventually 'wither away'. The conflict between the 'statist' and the 'socialist' interpretation of the meaning of the 'catch-all' formula of a new 'socialist state' was from the very beginning of the post-war period linked with ideological, ethnic and generational differences. It culminated in the 1962–71 period, with the dismissal first of the main representative of the 'statist' interpretation (Aleksandar Ranković), by the younger generation of socialist leaders, who were eventually replaced, as well. The Croatian Spring was entirely led by the young generation of ideologically-motivated leaders from a potentially disadvantaged nation. The main rhetoric of this movement was indeed another interpretation of the socialist + nationalist formula.

Most Yugoslav political conflicts in the post-war period were of ideological, not ethnic nature. They were conflicts between different interpretation of various ideas, including the idea of Yugoslavism. It is about interpretation of Marxist understanding of nation and state that most of these conflicts focussed. The first in the line of ideological conflicts was initiated by an external factor—Stalin in 1948—but it had enormous consequences for internal structure of Yugoslavia. The 'war of words' with Stalin soon turned into an ideological war between what the Yugoslav communists called 'statist' and 'self-managing' ('non-statist') understanding of the objectives of socialism. New reading of Marx (in order to refute accusation of being 'revisionists') reminded the Yugoslav communists of the crucial notion of Marxist theory of state—that the state should 'wither away' as communism approached. Those who had taken Marxism more seriously than others (for example Edvard

Kardelj and Vladimir Bakarić, later to be followed by Milan Kučan and Stipe Šuvar), argued that Yugoslavia simply could not avoid the process of 'socialisation' (*podruštvljavanje*). The 'statists' (Aleksandar Ranković, to be followed by Slobodan Milošević) were less enthusiastic.

The history of post-1948 Yugoslavia could be best interpreted as a process of defeating the 'statist' and introducing 'anti-statist' trends. Being Stalinists, the Yugoslav Communists were in 1948 still to a large extent 'statists' themselves. In fact, paradoxically, they seemed to be more Stalinist than Stalin himself.[7] In addition, Tito hesitated to abandon the notion of the South Slav political unity. Although he opposed Yugoslav centralism of the interwar period, he believed, as Milovan Djilas witnessed, that all South Slavs should live one country because...they were South Slavs.[8] This idea of South Slav unity motivated him to propose closer links with the only South Slav country outside Yugoslavia—Bulgaria. In his speech at the Founding Congress of the Communist Party of Serbia on 11 May 1945 Tito said:

With the Bulgarians we are trying, and they are trying as well, to make our relationship of brotherhood and unity firm. We have deeper ambitions with the Bulgarians and we have wanted to realise them, but the English and the Americans have not allowed it. Fine, we shall not [do it] now. But, no one can stop us in this. We are Slavs, and they are Slavs as well, and they have always been in the hands of the reaction. It is up to us, the Yugoslav Communists to develop the consciousness that we need to live with the Bulgarians in the closest relationship, so that between us and the Bulgarians there should not be any greater differences than between Serbs, Croats and Slovenes. We shall act so that the Bulgarian people will be happy, as we shall be too, when we unite in a country of the South Slavs.[9]

---

[7] In hindsight, it seems paradoxical that the notion of Yugoslavia as (strong) state and of Yugoslavism (South-Slavism) as the main component of its identity was among the main causes of Stalin's criticism of Yugoslav political élite in 1948. Stalin criticised Yugoslavs for being unreasonably 'nationalistic' in their foreign affairs (the Trieste crisis) and not sufficiently 'ideological' in domestic politics (the idea of 'Popular Front' becoming the main political organisation—which was potentially indeed a step towards weakening the role of the Party and of the state).

[8] Vladimir Dedijer, *Novi prilozi za biografiju Josipa Broza Tita*, Rijeka and Zagreb, 1981, p. 76.

[9] Josip Broz Tito, 'Govor na osnivačkom kongresu Komunističke Partije Srbije', in *Osnivački kongres Komunističke partije Srbije (8–12 maja 1945.)*, Belgrade, 1972, p. 214.

Not only did the two countries share South Slav ethnic origins, but they were united by the common goal of building socialism. If the South Slav concept and the revolutionary idea were the two cohesive elements for the Yugoslavs, why should Bulgaria remain outside such a state? Yugoslavs and Bulgarians therefore entered serious negotiations, signing an agreement on a new federation in 1948[10], which was immediately vetoed by Stalin. Tito's ambitions to unify and lead all the South Slavs (and one day, if Georgi Dimitrov's 'incautious' remark about an 'East European Federation' were to be realised—possibly of all East European Slavs or even all East Europeans) made Stalin think that Tito was primarily a nationalist and a rival socialist leader[11]. In Tito's hesitation to abandon the ethnic dimension of new Yugoslavia's identity, Stalin recognised a deviation from internationalist principles and the remnants of the 'old' Yugoslav (South-Slavonic, and possibly even Pan-Slavonic) nationalism. At the same time, the revolutionary dimension of the new Yugoslav identity distanced Tito from the other world power 'entitled' (by the Moscow Conference in 1944) to control the region: Britain.

The hesitation of the Yugoslav Communists to entirely abandon the South Slav concept of Yugoslavia caused, however, serious problems with the Albanians in Kosovo. The Albanians felt alienated from any concept of South Slav Yugoslavia.[12] Although during the war and in its aftermath (until 1948) the Yugoslav Communists had a very close relationship with the Communists in Albania, and in spite of Stalin's sugestion that Yugoslavia should 'swallow' Albania, it never happened. A federation between Albania and Yugoslavia

[10] Edvard Kardelj, *Reminiscences*, London, 1982, pp. 94–7.

[11] Dedijer, op. cit., pp. 167–8, and Kardelj, ibid. pp. 104–12.

[12] One may of course offer here a counterfactual 'evidence': the only time when Albanians were not totally dismissive about Yugoslavia was exactly at the time when Yugoslavia ceased to be South-Slavonic (i.e. ethnic), and became an ideological project. Only in the post-1974 (Kardelj's) Yugoslavia, they did not openly protest. With its collapse, and especially as the demands for return to the pre-Kardelj's (or even interwar) Yugoslavia grew in the 1980s (not only by Milošević, but increasingly so with him), their disatisfaction with Yugoslavia re-emerged. Despite Koča Popović's conclusion that the Albanians could have become Yugoslavs, but not Serbs, one may argue that they could have been good Yugoslavs only when Yugoslavia was not South-Slavia any longer.

would definitely have disturbed the South Slav concept of Yugoslav unity. The preference that Yugoslav Communists gave to their
links with Bulgaria over links with Albania was a strong indicator of
their *brotherhood* and unity concept, which did not abandon the
South Slav dimension.

Paradoxically, the communist (and as some would argue, even
Stalinist) character of Yugoslavia became more obvious as the Yugoslavs embarked into an open conflict with the Soviet Union. The
firm centralisation and coercion that took place followed in the
1948–53 period was in contrast with what Yugoslav communists
had preached. As a Communist federation, the new Yugoslavia was
firmly led by the Communist party leadership. Despite its federalist
claims, and although its leadership was composed of people from
different nations, in practice Yugoslavia developed a political system
which allowed no more than regional cultural autonomy combined
with the most rigid political centralisation. The detention camp in
Goli Otok and overall repression against political opponents simply
could not be reconciled with idea of 'withering away of the state',
and even less with the notion of 'people's democracy'. Nor could
centralisation be brought in line with the wartime promises of 'home
rule' for all, especially smaller Yugoslav republics.

This created a new paradox: in words and ideology, the Yugoslavism of the Yugoslav Communists was fundamentally different from
that of the official Yugoslavism of the interwar period. Yet, it was
equally centralised and even less democratic (in the sense of representative democracy) than the Yugoslavism of King Alexander and
Prince Paul. And it was still based on 'South-Slavism', a local form
of 'Pan-Slavism'. Did Communists not promise to Yugoslavia 'no
return to the past'? Was it not supposed to mean, no return to centralism in any form, either as 'Great-Serbian' or any other, including
the 'Great-Statist'? The concept of 'South Slav' (Yugoslav) unity
could secure some level of cohesion domestically. But, how different then were they becoming from their interwar predecessors? If
they, on the other hand, abandoned the concept of Yugoslav unity
for the sake of (international) revolution, would they not in fact
have recognised that Stalin had been right when he argued that
there should be only one centre of the 'world revolution'—Moscow? And how would this reflect on popular support enjoyed by

Tito, and foreign (Western) support for his new government? If they really argued that Yugoslav socialism was so different from the one developed under Stalin, then the Yugoslav communists had to decentralise and socialise functions of the state. The decentralisation was, therefore, the *conditio sine qua non* of the new Yugoslav identity, the one that is not only different, but completely opposite to both the inter-war Yugoslavism and Soviet-style state socialism.

Although the first signs indicated that some Party leaders might have been willing to move towards a partial if not a full democratization (for example, Milovan Djilas, but not he alone), and in spite of being encouraged by the West to do so, they never reached the breaking point with the one-party monopoly and revolutionary logic. The ideology was for Yugoslav Communists always more than just a formal justification of their political actions—it was the very core of their policies. Instead of abandoning it, the Yugoslav Communists attempted to show that it was the Soviets and not they who had deviated from Marxism. To the accusation of being 'revisionists', they replied with the same counter-accusation against the Soviets. The Yugoslav identity was now created against not only the past concepts of Yugoslavism, but also against the Soviet concept of socialism. These two *Others* (the inter-war bourgeois Yugoslavia and the Soviet type of socialism) became the two landmarks against which the Yugoslav mirror-image was to be created. The new Yugoslavia became constructed as an antipode to its own past and to the other model that claimed to be the blueprint of socialism.[13]

A new reading of Marx proved to be extremely fruitful for the identity-building of the new phase of socialism in Yugoslavia. In 1952, the Party name was changed to the League of Communists of Yugoslavia (inspired by Marx's Communist League of 1848). The idea of self-management came out of this reading in 1950. It was not a finished project, but more a slogan for the new, Yugoslav road to Communism. However, it had a relevant symbolic value in the early 1950s. Finally, as regards foreign policy, Yugoslavia moved from

[13] This had enormous consequences for the final years of Yugoslavia in the 1980s. Once the Soviet model ceased to represent a real threat, only the fear of a renewal of inter-war Yugoslavia remained. In Milošević's attempts to re-unite Yugoslavia, Slovenian and Croatian leaders saw such an intention.

the idea of uniting all South Slavs into one state, towards leading the 'oppressed' and underprivileged nations in global arena. The idea of non-alignment (formulated between 1956 and 1960), not only gave Tito a distinctive and prominent role worldwide, but also had a role of the 'Fourth International', the 'consciousness of mankind'. Because of its central role in the non-aligned movement, Yugoslavia, not the USSR, was the world leader in fighting global injustice.

Although the concept of brotherhood and unity had not been completely abandoned (especially not by Tito), it was gradually being replaced by the idea of 'Yugoslav socialist patriotism',[14] which emphasised the socialist over the South Slav dimension of Yugoslav identity. The notion of socialism was further emphasised when the country changed its name (in 1963) from the *Federal* People's Republic of Yugoslavia to *Socialist* Federal Republic of Yugoslavia, in a move which demonstrated that the ideological character of the state became more important than its territorial (and thus also ethnic) structure. Now that its borders had become safe due to the world power balance and that 'internal enemies' had been finally defeated, the existence of Yugoslavia was no longer in question. It was a time for social change which would definitely eliminate the last vestiges of the national question.

The national question was re-opened in the 1960s by the political élite itself, and was not the result of pressure to the élite from the population. Its re-emergence was in no way whatever linked with any 'ancient ethnic hatred' and only marginally it was a result of the economic crisis in the 1960s. Its reappearance was due to initiative by the most prominent members of the 'ideological' (anti-statist) wing of the Party élite, which felt that the relatively favourable circumstances both domestically (in economic and political sense) and internationally should be used in order to further advance the anti-statist socialism. In the early 1960s, to most 'ordinary' Yugoslavs it looked as if the national question was (finally) off the agenda and as if Yugoslavia was entering a period of stability after years of post-war austerity and post-1948 military and political danger. Even the middle-ranked politicians of the time, such as Milka Planinc (later Yugoslav Prime Minister, 1982–6) were surprised when the national

[14] See Steven L. Burg, *Conflict and Cohesion in Socialist Yugoslavia*, Princeton, NJ, 1983.

question emerged from the top of the 'socialist pyramid'. She recalled in April 1998:

We were all, including myself, Yugoslavs, and we did not have, even in our most private thoughts, any idea that Yugoslavia could disintegrate. I remember how shocked I was when it was reported that Vladimir Bakarić, a very experienced politician, said somewhere in Belgium in the mid-1960s that what we were doing was re-structuring Yugoslavia, but that only the future would show how long it would last as a common state. To me, this statement came as a big surprise. I asked myself: 'How could he say this? Does he really think that there could be something else but Yugoslavia?' We all believed that, in principle, the national question had been resolved, and that the misunderstandings we occasionally had would decrease as economic development progressed.[15]

But was really the 'Yugoslav nation' what Yugoslav project of socialism ought to create? To those who were less ideological, and to many among the population, it indeed looked as if there was a real possibility for a new 'Yugoslav (socialist) nation' to be promoted as result of economic, political and international success of the Yugoslav socialism. And this is what socialist ideologists found difficult to accept. The 'national question' in the mid-1960s was resurrected by the 'ideologists' in their attempt to defeat the 'statists' (often identified as potential allies of the USSR, Stalinists and even of the 'Great-Serbian' tendencies domestically). The conflict between the 'ideologists' and 'statists' more often than not crossed over the ethnic lines, although the focus on the national question often blurred that fact.[16] And, as one would expect in a highly ideological (socialist) society, the 'ideologists' had won over the 'statists'.

---

[15] In an interview with the author of this chapter.

[16] The Croatian Spring is interpreted as an 'ethnic conflict'. However, it was primarily a conflict within Croatian political élite, in which both sides were Croats (Vladimir Bakarić and Josip Vrhovec vs. Savka Dabčević-Kučar and Miko Tripalo). The same applies to the 1972 conflict within Serbia's leadership (Draža Marković and Petar Stambolić vs. Latinka Perović and Marko Nikezić). Almost all political conflicts in the post-1945 Yugoslavia were intra-ethnic, i.e. ideological: for example Ivan Stambolić vs. Slobodan Milošević (in 1987), or Stipe Šuvar vs. Mika Špiljak (in 1984–8).

Kardelj's concept of Yugoslavism

The conflict within the élite was fuelled by the fact that President Tito was approaching an advanced age (he was seventy in 1962), and that he had already been in office for seventeen years (in addition to the four war years). Although nobody openly challenged his undoubtedly exceptional position, everyone was thinking of the post-Tito period. Both within the country and abroad, the question of what would happen to Yugoslavia after Tito was being asked.

Edvard Kardelj believed that the main danger to post-Tito's Yugoslavia would come from the renewal of a centralised state, either in its interwar (bourgeois) form or in a form of Soviet statist ('Stalinist' or—as Kardelj called it—'Great-Statist') socialism. If this happened, Kardelj argued, the results of the Yugoslav revolution would be annulled. Within this context, he attacked those within the élite (then yet unnamed) who were promoting 'Pan-Slavist and Yugoslav illusion' that a new, Yugoslav nation was emerging out of the Yugoslav state. Socialism, just like any other ideology, can neither make nor deny the existence of nations, Kardelj stated in the preface to the second (1957) edition of his (1939) book *The Development of the Slovene National Question*. Furthermore, he concluded, it was unrealistic to expect nations to wither away soon.[17] In 1962 he warned that 'our federation is not a framework for any new Yugoslav nation, nor for any national integration about which in their time some advocates of hegemony and denationalizing terror used to dream'[18]. In *The Development of the Slovene National Question* Kardelj had argued that the Communists were the only force that

[17] In this conclusion the second edition (1957) differs from the first (1939). While in 1939 Kardelj fully shared Stalin's definition of the nation as the result of the bourgeois epoch, which is present in socialism only as a remnant of this old epoch, in 1957 he defines nation as a 'product of the socio-economic relations of the epoch of capitalism' which is a product of 'the social division of labour'. Since under socialism the division of labour still exists, so does the nation. Kardelj himself admits that the second edition dropped elements of Stalin's influence. For the importance of this change, see Muhamed Filipović, *Nacionalno pitanje u jugoslavenskoj teoriji i praksi—doprinos Edvarda Kardelja*, Banja Luka, 1979, pp. 157–63.

[18] Edvard Kardelj, 'The Federation and the Republics. Speech to the National Assembly, 20 September 1962', in *The Nations and Nationalism*, Belgrade, 1981, pp. 137–40.

could offer a viable solution of the national question in Yugoslavia. But, also, under the new circumstances, it was from the ranks of the Communist bureaucracy that the main danger could potentially come. It is, therefore, the struggle with bureaucracy that should be given high priority in party and state policy.[19]

Under new circumstances, even the idea of socialist Yugoslavism was no longer feasible, since the Yugoslav nations had became fully constituted nations.[20] Yugoslavia had helped them to reach the level at which they wanted to have their own nation-states, staying in Yugoslavia as long and only as long as it suited their common interests. These interests, Kardelj concluded in 1970, could arise mostly in three areas: first—in the common defence policy; second—in the common goals of the revolutionary transformation of the country; and third—in developing a common market area. In all other areas, Kardelj said, the countries of Yugoslavia had became mature enough to take care of their own interests. A multi-ethnic state which would not protect the independence and state structures of small nations would not be in their interest.

Although Kardelj was an advocate of the existence of a Yugoslav state, Yugoslav unity in his concept now became conditional on the agreement of its constitutive parts. Already in 1957, Kardelj used words such as 'today' and 'at this moment'[21] when concluding that Yugoslavia was in the interest of all Yugoslav nations. And it existed because nations were 'complete national organisms wishing to live in a community with all other peoples, and especially with the Yugoslav peoples'.[22] Yugoslav unity was neither a matter of ethnic

---

[19] The anti-bureaucratic rhetoric of Slobodan Milošević in his 'anti-bureaucratic revolution' was in fact a copy of Tito's (successful) attempt to place 'bureaucrats' in a sandwich between himself and the people.

[20] Kardelj used term *completed* or *fully constituted* nations ('*dovršene nacije*'), emphasising that the republics in Yugoslavia became states after the socialist revolution in 1945. Observing from his Slovenian experience of living in two multi-ethnic states which treated their ethnic groups as cultural, but not political entities (Austria-Hungary and the Kingdom of Yugoslavia), Kardelj was a fierce opponent of any similar attempts in post-war Yugoslavia.

[21] Kardelj, 'The Development of the Slovene National Question', in *The Nations and Socialism*, Preface to 2nd edn (1957), Belgrade, 1981, pp. 47, 62.

[22] Kardelj, 'Yugoslavia—the Socialist Self-Managing Community of Equal Peoples [1969]' in ibid., p. 226.

similarities, nor of ideals, but of interests and historical necessities.
'The unity of the peoples of Yugoslavia is not based so much on
their ethnic relatedness as on joint interests deriving from a common destiny and above all on their joint struggle for socialist relations among men and nations'.[23] And—it was also more result of
necessity in contemporary world, than of ethnic similarities among
the South Slavs. Kardelj, the Slovene, believed that small nations
could not remain independent in the world of imperialism:

Above all, unity was to their advantage in safeguarding their very existence
and independence. In the modern world, the power of the reactionary
force of imperialism and political hegemony is still extremely great. The
Yugoslav nations would need each other's support to be able to guarantee
their economic and political independence.[24]

In 1967 Kardelj argued that the American policy towards Vietnam
was a good example of what would happen to small independent
states after the potential disintegration of Yugoslavia. They would
become 'a provincial appendage of the imperialist world, which is
today again showing its true face in Vietnam'.[25] The unnamed
Slovenian separatists, whom he often criticised, were 'cutting the
branch on which they themselves were sitting'[26] and were 'killing
the ox for a pound of meat'.[27] In the world of the two blocs, it would
have been virtually impossible for Slovenia (or for any other Yugoslav nation) to be independent to the degree that it was in Yugoslavia. At the same time, however, he warned the Yugoslav 'unitarists'
not to provoke ethnic separatism but to allow all nations to create
their own states within Yugoslavia. Only when this happened,
when all Yugoslav nations really governed themselves, would ethnic
separatism be finally defeated.[28]

[23] Kardelj, 'Cultural and Economic Aspects of Relations Among Nationalities
[1975]' in ibid., p. 141.
[24] Kardelj, 'Thirty Years After the Founding Congress of the Communist Party of
Slovenia [1967]' in ibid., p. 54.
[25] Ibid., p. 203. The argument was strengthened when, in 1968, the USSR intervened in Czechoslovakia.
[26] Kardelj, 'Yugoslavia—The Socialist Self-Managing Community of Equal Peoples [1969]' in ibid., p. 237.
[27] Ibid. p. 238.
[28] Kardelj, 'The Development of the Slovene National Question'. Preface to the
Second Edition (1957) in ibid., p. 47.

Kardelj's writings and speeches in the 1957–66 period met, if not with open criticism, then certainly with serious resistance among the statists, the defenders of Yugoslavism and South Slavism within the party and the state leadership. The most prominent among these was Yugoslavia's vice-president Aleksandar Ranković, who controlled domestic affairs.[29] Even Tito himself seemed puzzled by Kardelj's writings. Deep in his heart, wrote Milovan Djilas, Tito believed that one day all the differences between the Yugoslavs would disappear, both in the social and in the national sense. He recalls a discussion on Yugoslavism with Tito in 1953: 'Tito believed that the nationalities of Yugoslavia would ultimately merge into one true nation. When I remarked that King Alexander Karadjordjević thought so too, he retorted: "Ah, but there was no socialism then."'[30]

Tito could have hardly ever abandoned his Yugoslav beliefs. The ideology of socialism was for him a tool of securing unity of Yugoslavia. To Kardelj, on the contrary, the unity of Yugoslavia was an instrument of advancing socialism, both in Yugoslav nations and globally. Yugoslavia was a space in which the new project of socialism was to be developed, in order to demonstrate that only socialism can finally resolve the 'national question'. Tito understood importance of being different from both the interwar centralism and Soviet state-socialism, but, once the socialist self-management is developed,

[29] While Ranković was certainly the most prominent member of the 'statist' wing of the party, it was Dobrica Ćosić, then member of the Central Committee of the League of Communists of Serbia who most directly resisted Kardelj's ideas. Ćosić sent a letter to Tito, urging him to review his decision to remove Ranković from the office, and in 1968 he openly opposed the 'new course', arguing that 'since the [Socialist] Republic of Serbia was established, up until the present, the leading political forums of the Republic of Serbia have, in general and in historical perspective, conducted a democratic and internationalist policy.' Ćosić believed that what was worrying was 'the bureaucratic nationalism which keeps replacing Marxist internationalism and universalism', as well as 'the ideology which equates socialist self-management and national, i.e., state sovereignty'. See *Četrnaesta sednica CK SK Srbije—autorizovani zapisnik, 29 i 30 maja 1968*, Belgrade, pp. 102, 105.
[30] Milovan Djilas, *Tito: The Story from Inside*, London, 1981, p. 134. In his memoirs, the former Yugoslav Foreign Secretary Mirko Tepavac concludes that 'Tito was a Yugoslav in the good meaning of this word, and even a unitarist. To him, even Yugoslavia as it was, was somehow too small'. See Tepavac, *Sećanja i komentari*, 1998, Belgrade, p. 154.

'the forces of the past', including nationalists, would be defeated. Although at the 8th LCY Congress elections (in 1964) Tito for the first time declared himself a Croat (rather than a Yugoslav), he opposed 'witch-hunts' against Yugoslav patriotism, as seen in his passionate speech against Croatian nationalism in December 1971. 'What does it mean to be against Yugoslavism?', he asked his colleagues in the party leadership:

> If it means to be against the old Yugoslavism of King Aleksandar, then of course I am against this sort of Yugoslavism. But, if it means to love my country, to feel a Yugoslav in the first place and to be proud of it, then I must tell you that I am Yugoslav. Of course, as you know, I am from Croatia, but I am also a Yugoslav and I have spent all my life working for Yugoslavia.[31]

On another occasion, Tito opposed Bakarić's idea of recognising the 'national working classes', arguing:

> In Yugoslavia there is only one working class, the working class of the whole of Yugoslavia…The working class is one for a number of reasons, especially ideological ones…In a word, what I mean is that we cannot divide the working class up by republics. The working class is Yugoslav.[32]

It was not only because Tito was a pragmatist who understood well the importance of real instruments of power that he emphasised importance of unity of the working class. It was also because he did believe that Yugoslavia should remain united, and that the unity of the working class was the key to the Yugoslav unity. He certainly had no intention of destroying the state, in which he had played the crucial role. But, on the other hand, Kardelj asked, what were the prospects for socialism if the nations of Yugoslavia were not satisfied regarding their national demands? And what was the future of Yugoslav independence if Yugoslavia were not able to create an effective and radical alternative to Soviet 'state socialism' and interwar Yugoslavism?

[31] J.B. Tito, 'No republic can be sufficient unto itself [1971]' in *The National Question*, Belgrade, 1983, p. 161.
[32] J.B. Tito, 'Yugoslav sovereignty—the sovereignty of all the republics [1971]' in ibid., p. 179.

The conflict between Ranković and Kardelj (who enjoyed support of the younger generation of political leaders) in many ways was Kardelj's ideological (and enormously cautious) conflict with Tito too. It looked indeed in the late 1960s, immediately after the removal of Ranković, that this was the only period in his 35 years of power when Tito looked weak and vulnerable. He restored his position only when he placed other members of the élite in a 'sandwich' between himself and masses (chiefly after the 1968 Belgrade student protests) and when re-allying with the military élite in the Yugoslav People's Army (after being strongly advised by them to halt the Croatian reformist and nationalist movement in 1971). Tito's decision to support (though not wholeheartedly) Kardelj, rather than Ranković, is to be attributed to younger generation of political leaders, who had all identified Ranković as a threat to both their own careers and to the project of Yugoslav socialism. As the leading Serbian politician of the 1960s and 1970s, Petar Stambolić, said:

Ranković's whole line was conservative. In Serbia, we felt him to be a heavy burden…Tito exercised full control over foreign policy and the Army, while Ranković controlled the Party and the police. We wanted to put the lid on this… Everything that Kardelj initiated and promoted in our political system, distinguished us from the East and it was a guarantee that we would not return to the past. In general, he was a reformist and a Yugoslav.[33]

The young cadres shared Kardelj's disappointment with bureaucracy, and sought more autonomy for their republics and more security for their positions in the post-Tito era. Since none of the republics (not even Serbia) had a majority of votes to control the federal leadership on their own, all of them preferred the 'second best' option: to have as much autonomy as possible in their own territories and to prevent any drastically unfavourable outcome. If they could not influence the federal politics for as long as Tito was alive, then they certainly could limit the powers of the federation and secure that there would be no 'new Tito' after Tito.[34] In order to

[33] Quoted in Slavoljub Djukić, *Kako se dogodio vodja*, Belgrade, 1992, p. 212.
[34] On a symbolical level, a good illustration of this shift is Kardelj's decision to move from Belgrade to Ljubljana in the early 1970s. The Croatian leader Vladimir

remain in power for as the rest of his life, Tito had to accept the process of 'detitoisation', which started with the 1974 Constitution, only to continue after his death in 1980. He also had to accept much of Kardelj's initiative for further decentralisation, which was probably the only programme which managed to unite otherwise divided groups in all eight leaderships of republics and provinces.[35]

The victory of Kardelj's concept in the constitutional debate of 1967–74 marked the beginning of the last phase of the history of socialist Yugoslavia. Kardelj's main argument linked ideology of anti-statism with identity and sovereignty of Yugoslavia. He argued that Yugoslavia would not be different from the two antipodes (inter-war Yugoslavism and Soviet socialism) unless it was further decentralised. The main goal of socialism was that everyone decided upon the results of their labour. This principle applied to nations as well.[36] The de-centralisation of Yugoslavia was a pre-condition for self-management to work. Since self-management was the only real democracy, de-centralisation was a precondition for democratisation

---

Bakarić had never moved his house to Belgrade, but had always, even when a member of the Yugoslav Presidency (1974–83), lived in Zagreb. In the 1970s Belgrade was left to Tito, federal ministers and federal administration, while real politics shifted to republican (and provincial) capitals.

[35] When it comes to issues of further decentralisation, there were no differences between the Croatian leadership before 1971 and after 1971, just as the Serbian leaders before 1972 and after 1972 remained both committed to Kardeljism. Their relations with Kardelj were very warm, and they respected him more than they respected Tito. See Marković, op. cit.

[36] This explains why Yugoslavia refused to accept the Soviet supreme authority and to join the Warsaw Pact. Since the Yugoslav nations were considered 'completed', Yugoslavia itself came close to becoming a 'pact' between the newly created national states on its territory. It is not only that various republics therefore spoke of Belgrade (the federal centre) as a supra-national force with no right to 'intervene' in their 'domestic affairs', but Kardelj himself contemplated Yugoslavia more as an international conglomerate than a state in any 'classic sense'. Once it arrived in 1991–92, full state independence was perceived by the non-Serbian republics of Yugoslavia (primarily Slovenia and Croatia), in rather similar terms to the non-Soviet countries of the bloc, as 'liberation' from a supra-national centre. For the majority of the Serbs, of course, this was not a valid interpretation, since they certainly did not see themselves as 'the Soviets' of the Yugoslav 'bloc'. On the contrary, their leaders, such as Ivan Stambolić, often pointed out that Serbia felt disadvantaged in Yugoslavia. See his book *Rasprave o SR Srbiji*, Belgrade, 1988.

too. On the other hand, the continuation of a centralised Yugoslav state would endanger both the national and socialist dimensions of the Yugoslav revolution. Finally, Kardelj underlined that the state was withering away in the transitional period and that the model of governance should be transformed towards direct democracy.

Tito, who believed that the key to socialist transformation lay in the Party, not in the state, unwillingly accepted that the state should be decentralised, but requested that the Party should remain united. He also allied himself more closely with the Army, strengthening its presence in the Central Committee at the Tenth LCY Congress in 1974. Tito now relied on Kardelj's 25-year-old attack on the 'theories of spontaneity' in his argument against Milovan Djilas (1953–4). The process of 'withering away' of the state, Tito argued, has to be guided by the vanguard (Party) and other 'subjective forces of socialism'.

Another reason why Tito might have accepted a compromise was in his firm belief that the dissolution of Yugoslavia was not a realistic option because it would change the whole international balance of power. If this was so, then separatist nationalism(s) had no chance for as long as the communists remained in power. Kardelj agreed with this, adding that this would be so, for as long as the communists demonstrated they could offer more independence to nations than either 'imperialist forces' or 'the forces of (Soviet) statist socialism'. Since, in principle, there could be no 'return to the past', the real danger originated in a different, statist type of socialism.

Kardelj warned against 'hegemonic forces', i.e. the Soviet-type communists who would 'naturally' rely on the strongest nation, the Serbs. He insisted that these forces must be denied any possibility of succeeding to the Presidency and that Tito's role in achieving this was crucial. No other 'social critics' (as Kardelj called them in 1965) represented such a real danger for the Yugoslav project of socialism as those who advocated different 'directions of the development of socialism'.[37] Neither the liberals nor the separatists could succeed, both because of 'objective laws' of social development and because of international and domestic reality. The future of Yugoslavia, thus, ultimately depended on who would define socialism. The future of

[37] Edvard Kardelj, 'Notes on Social Criticism in Yugoslavia [1965]' in *Science and Social Criticism*, Belgrade, 1980, pp. 23–144.

Yugoslavia, in other words, Tito and Kardelj agreed, depended on the strength of the Party.[38]

The victory of Kardelj's concept over the one symbolised by Ranković in 1966 marked the end of Tito's concept of Yugoslavia. The new concept, based on Kardelj's interpretations of Marxism and of Yugoslav political reality, was defined in the 1967–1974 Constitutional debate and codified in the 1974 Constitution. After a long and controversial debate, it was accepted by regional political élites in all parts of Yugoslavia, including Serbia. Tito, however, had never accepted it enthusiastically. In 1971, he practically admitted that this was done under pressure coming from republics. At the same time, he warned republican leaders not to 'divide up statism among the republics.'[39]

In many ways, Kardelj's concept marginalised Tito, making his position an exception to the rule, which would be fully implemented only after his death. Tito was still allowed to defend 'Yugoslavism', but no other politicians would escape the 'unitarist' label if they attempted the same. The 1974 Constitution prevented anyone from becoming a 'new Tito' after Tito's death. Although still the main arbiter in conflicts between republican and provincial élites, Tito was increasingly becoming a symbol, an icon with great influence but little power. Indeed, the de-Titoisation of Yugoslavia began in 1974 not in 1980. Consequently, this is why the 'transfer of power' was so smooth when Tito actually died in 1980. There was no much real or constitutional power left in him by then.

In 1969 Kardelj declared that the Yugoslav state was not a 'classic' state, but rather a 'self-managing community of working people, nations and nationalities', and that therefore terms like 'federation' and 'confederation' were no longer applicable to describe the new Yugoslavia. Although the state was still named the Socialist *Federative*

---

[38] Ironically, their belief that the future of Yugoslavia depended on the future of Party and—ultimately—on the Yugoslavs themselves today sounds almost like prophecy. Despite the optimistic predictions of the last Yugoslav Prime Minister Ante Marković and of most Western analysts, the disintegration of Yugoslavia indeed followed the collapse of the Party in January 1990.

[39] See J.B. Tito, 'No republic can be sufficient unto itself [1971]' in *The National Question*, Belgrade, 1983, p. 162.

Republic of Yugoslavia, 'federation' was—Kardelj said—an 'outdated category, which can solve nothing in our system'.[40] The same applied to the term 'confederation'.

Finally it was not only that words to describe the institutions of *new Yugoslavia* had to be invented, but the entire structure of the state was unique. The functions of the Yugoslav Federal state were drastically reduced mainly to common defence and foreign policy, but even in these areas the federation itself became 'more the initiator, executor and agent of adjustment ... than an autonomous decision—maker'.[41] Federal bodies were not independent of the republics, but formed directly by them. The republics handed over to the exercise of the federation only those powers which they 'explicitly determined in the federal constitution', which could be amended only with the consent of all members of the federation. 'The power of the federation... derives from the republics, not the other way round', was the principle realised in the Yugoslav legislature.[42]

So, what were the consequences of such an understanding of Yugoslavia? Since the system of representation through federal units (and hence, to a large extent, through ethnic identities) had been taken to be decisive for any political participation, there could be little place for those who ceased to belong to such a system. The sense of belonging to Yugoslavia, so important for any country to survive, was now weakened by a systemic action from political system itself. Any expression of belonging to Yugoslavia first, above and before belonging to any separate ethnic group, republic or province, was treated with great suspicion, as an attempt to promote unitarism and great-statist centralism. Expressions of Yugoslavism now became almost an anti-socialist activity. Consequently, as Jovan Mirić argued:

As long as a citizen remains an outsider, an unrecognised element of the community, the awareness of belonging to this community will not develop. A community (in contrast to a society) can be built and destroyed

[40] Kardelj, 'Yugoslavia—the Socialist Self-Managing Community of Equal Peoples [1969]' in *The Nations and Socialism*, Belgrade, 1981, p. 248.

[41] Kardelj, 'Performance of the Functions of the Federation [1974]' in ibid., p. 292.

[42] Kardelj, 'The National Question in Yugoslavia and Its Foreign Policy [1973]' in ibid., p. 279.

in our own minds. It cannot be constructed externally, from somewhere
outside ourselves.[43]

But the concept of citizenship that Mirić had in mind was a liberal
concept, and, therefore, was not acceptable to Kardelj.[44] As he
explained in his 'Notes on Social Criticism' in 1965, the Yugoslav
political system should not be based on the liberal notion of
'abstract citizens', because an 'abstract man' is 'non-existent'.[45] He
existed only in liberal models, which 'try to transform man into a
God' instead of accepting that man's life was dependent on both
society and on nature. Instead of basing their criticism on man as he
was, they criticised him from the position of man 'such as he ought
to be'.[46] On the contrary, Kardelj believed that his concept should
enable representation of *existing* (i.e. real) interests, making sure that
the long-term interests of the working people were satisfied. It was
because of these beliefs that he saw no problems in basing the entire
structure of the Yugoslav political system on separate interest groups,
rather than on the equality of abstract citizens. It was also in his
opposition to inter-war official Yugoslavism, and centralised state
socialism (such as in the USSR) that one needs to look for roots of
the anti-Yugoslavism in Kardelj's texts.

The fact that the citizens of Yugoslavia were politically non-
existent was, therefore, the logical result of Kardelj's (but not only
his) Marxist beliefs as well as of his views on the national question.
Since the idea of a 'Yugoslav nation' was condemned as 'great-state,
nationalistic, unrealistic and profoundly harmful and reactionary',
people who wanted to declare themselves as ethnic 'Yugoslavs' could

---

[43] Jovan Mirić, *Sistem i kriza*, Zagreb, 1985, p. 45.
[44] There should be, therefore, little surprise that Mirić's book initiated a wave of
attacks on him by Kardeljists. His warnings about dangerous consequences of
the 1974 Constitution were declared the worst attack on socialism after Milovan
Djilas' writings in 1954. It is by defending Mirić's views that Slobodan Milošević
made his first important political speech, at the 18th Session of the CC LCS, in
November 1984. See Slobodan Milošević, 'Srpski narod nema razloga za osećanje
krivice zbog ponašanja srpske buržoazije u prošlosti [1984]' in *Godine raspleta*,
Belgrade, 1989, pp 30–6.
[45] Kardelj, 'Notes on Social Criticism in Yugoslavia [1965]' in *The Nations and
Socialism*, op. cit., pp. 74.
[46] Ibid., p. 73.

register only as 'undeclared Yugoslavs', not as a separate ethnic group.[47] Unlike the recognised 'constitutive nations', and even the 'nationalities' and 'national minorities', they were not represented in politics.[48] This was a legal expression of Kardelj's belief that 'socialist forces would be making a big mistake if they allowed themselves to be carried away by futile ideas of creating some new kind of nation', since 'this would only intensify nationalism and chauvinism in the existing nations'.[49]

When it emerged with its full strength, in the 1980s, the increase in number of ethnic 'Yugoslavs' was evidence of discontent with the system, not the evidence of its success. In fact, the growing number of Yugoslavs (as ethnic group) caused an outrage among the main 'defenders of the [1974] Constitution', especially since it was reported that if the trend continued, more than 20 per cent of the Yugoslav population would declare themselves 'Yugoslav' by 1991.[50] Those who promoted Yugoslavism were semi-dissidents, an alternative to the establishment, such as the film director Emir Kusturica, the musician Goran Bregović, and others. The latter's attempts to symbolically

---

[47] Kardelj, 'Cultural and Economic Aspects of Relations among nationalities (1975)' in ibid., p. 147.

[48] For example, while Sinan Hasani, an ethnic Albanian, became the President of Yugoslav Federal Presidency in 1985 as a representative of Kosovo and Ali Shukria (also an Albanian from Kosovo) became the head of the LCY Presidency in 1984, no person who declared himself/herself a 'Yugoslav' ever succeeded in occupying these posts. In none of four 'elections' for the Presidency of Yugoslavia (1974, 1979, 1984, 1989) was a single 'Yugoslav' appointed by any republic or province.

[49] Kardelj, 'The Development of the Slovene National Question: preface to the second edition, 1957' in ibid., p. 127. A similar type of circular argument was later used by Milošević and Kučan. They were both 'saving Yugoslavia' by 'satisfying' national demands, in order to 'prevent' ethnic nationalists taking power and destroying Yugoslavia. Milošević was also 'saving' Yugoslavia from 'anarchy', arguing that anarchy would lead to a totalitarian response.

[50] The number of citizens who declared themselves as 'Yugoslavs (ethnically undeclared)' rose from 320,853 in 1971 to 1,209,045 in 1981. Some demographic estimates in early 1981 projected a further growth of this population to 5 million people (about 20 per cent) in 1991. This estimate played some role in fostering fears among the nationalists. Mirić demonstrated that only one quarter of the Yugoslavs were children from 'ethnically mixed' marriages, while on average they represented the most educated 'ethnic group' in the country. See Mirić, op. cit.

'reconcile' accords of Croatian and Serbian national music with Yugoslav national anthem was a matter of concern, rather than of support by the most conservative segment of political élite.

Such an opposition to Yugoslavism, however, provided a context in which Slobodan Milošević's pro-Yugoslav rhetoric emerged in Serbia in the 1984–89 period. Milošević's main demand was to re-establish Yugoslavia by returning to the pre-1966, pre-Kardeljist concept. Ranković was rehabilitated, Tito defended from public attacks, while Kardelj became the most unpopular figure in new, Milošević's Serbia. The Yugoslav problems were interpreted as if they began in 1966, when Kardelj's concept won over the one of the 'statists'.

However, the anti-statist rhetoric of Kardelj's Yugoslavism did not strengthen statism only in Serbia, but also in Croatia and Slovenia. The weakening of the state made nationalist demands for a strong state (whether Yugoslavia, or separate nation-states of constitutive nations) plausible. This is why nationalism (and not, for example, the liberalism of the minimal state) grew as the main alternative to the 'self-managing' system. Contrary to popular interpretations, which link the existence of 'strong states' run by Communists with people's demands for strong (nationalist) states after Communism, I argue that it was the weakness of the state that provoked an alternative. Post-Communism (as anti-Communism) was about establishing the state that was missing, not about preserving the one that already existed. This is why it is so important not to underestimate significance of ideas and ideologies. The fall of Yugoslavia and what happened in its aftermath was not result of either changes in the international politics, nor of the economic crisis or cultural differences. Although all these elements played a significant role by providing a context in which it happened, the disintegration of Yugoslavia was in the first place a consequence of 'revolutionary political changes' introduced by Kardelj and his proteges among the younger generation of the Yugoslav political élite.

Being convinced that the future must come in the way they predicted, the 'anti-statists' underestimated the real danger from the real world. Their vision of the future blurred their ability to view the present. Their almost religious belief in the power of words and beliefs made them react by moral condemnation, resolutions and propaganda, rather than with measures that belonged to the world of real politics. Defending their vision of the future, the Yugoslav Communists in the end lost touch with the present. Once they realised the vision itself was not adequate to explain and change reality, they lost both the present and the future.

THE TWO YUGOSLAVIAS AS
ECONOMIC UNIONS
PROMISE AND PROBLEMS

John R. Lampe

Post-mortems and criminal investigations predominate in recent publication on the former Yugoslavia. How and why did Tito's postwar federation die, and who in the post-Tito period killed it? While the Milošević régime in Serbia and the Tudjman régime in Croatia richly deserve investigation, any post-mortem tempts us to assume that death was inevitable. But to maintain that Yugoslavia was doomed to die from its earliest days, as I have argued elsewhere, makes no more scholarly sense than to posit that its creation was inevitable, in the fashion of postwar Titoist historiography.[1]

Let us therefore reconsider both Yugoslavias, interwar and postwar, as potentially viable states. Of the three state-building rationales that might have made Yugoslavia an enduring entity, two of them worked against each other. For both states, the rationale for a centralized, authoritarian régime to provide military security in a hostile international environment helped to make the other rationale—a single but geographically representative government—seem too risky. The idea that a single Yugoslav identity would emerge to remove the risk failed both times, as ethnic convergence among Serbs, Croats and Slovenes for the first Yugoslavia and as a broader supra-national, socialist identity for the second. Ironically, no conceivable domestic defense, however broadened from its Serbian-dominated core, could have saved the first Yugoslavia and its royal

---

[1] John R. Lampe, *Yugoslavia as History: Twice there was a country*, Cambridge, 2nd edn, 2000, pp. 4–6.

army from the overwhelming Nazi attack that destroyed them both in 1941. Nor could Tito's large Yugoslav People's Army (JNA) maintain its odd balancing act between anti-Western ideology and anti-Soviet preparations after his death and then the end of the Cold War and the USSR itself.

The third state-building rationale, the promise of an economic union, could not have stopped Hitler in 1941. But it might well have stopped Milošević and Tudjman in 1991. This chapter addresses the promise and problems of Yugoslavia as a single economic unit. First between the two world wars and then in the much longer Communist period, our inquiry finds less theoretical concern with pursuing integration than the often inadvertent practice of economic interconnection. Still, we ask how or to what extent political leadership, in power and in opposition, regarded economic growth and integration as promising to creating a viable Yugoslavia? More portentously, what role did economic integration actually play in the growth that was achieved and how did the absence of integration limit or distort growth?

Let us be clear that by integration into an economic union, we mean not just the creation of a customs union with a common external tariff and the elimination of internal barriers to trade. We also mean an economy which facilitates, and not just permits, the free movement of capital and labor to any area offering a commercial advantage. From the American experience, we would expect labor to be almost as geographically mobile as capital. From the European experience, however, we would assume a mobile labor force only if the majority's initial shift from rural to urban were still under way. That shift had barely begun for the first Yugoslavia but then proceeded, rapidly if unevenly, during the postwar régime. We therefore address the mobility of labor as well as capital, realized or forgone, in the integration of a single, 'national' economy and the comparative advantage, thereby taken or missed, in international trade.

Ivo Bićanić has concluded that over its two lifetimes, Yugoslavia was 'a loosely integrated, administratively run economy…[with] an extraordinary capacity to adjust without changing'.[2] Our inquiry

---

[2] Ivo Bićanić, 'Fractured Economy' in Dennison Rusinow (ed.), *Yugoslavia: A Fractured Federalism*, Washington, DC, 1988, pp. 138–9.

will not much dispute that verdict. But we emphasize the almost
insuperable set of obstacles that post-1918 settlement and the brief
interwar period placed in front of the first Yugoslavia. And for the
second Yugoslavia, we find an initially Stalinist theory of economic
integration giving way to a struggle between market enterprise and
political management conducted largely at the republic level. There
and in the central government, Yugoslavia's Communist leaders
did consider but never actually decided to turn away from political
management. The political priorities of one-party rule and military
security were simply too strongly felt. In the process, those leaders
forfeited the integrative processes of economic union that might
have preserved Yugoslavia once the political rationale and strategic
justification for one-party rule had so completely vanished between
1989 and 1991.

Obstacles to integrating the first Yugoslavia

Born as the Kingdom of Serbs, Croats and Slovenes in 1918, royal
Yugoslavia began its brief lifespan facing a formidable series of barriers to economic integration. The pre-1914 entities of Croatia-
Slavonia, Bosnia-Herzegovina, Dalmatia, Vojvodina, and Slovene
Carniola within the Habsburg monarchy had all experienced rapidly rising external trade and some industrial stirrings as well since
1900. So had the independent states of Serbia and Montenegro as
well as the Ottoman territories (until added to Serbia in 1912) of
Macedonia and Kosovo. But very little of that trade moved between
these entities; barely one per cent of Serbia's and Croatia-Slavonia's
foreign trade was one with the other. What imperial, Western or
native capital arrived in one entity, moreover, failed to provide con-
nections to the others, most conspicuously for east-west rail links.
The considerable migration of upland peasant labor from Croatia,
Herzegovina, Dalmatia, Carniola and also Macedonia went abroad,
or at least as far as Trieste, Prague or Salonika.[3]

The first years of political unification after 1918 made economic
integration still more difficult. Without a constitution until 1921, the
first Yugoslavia started with four railway networks, five currencies

[3] John R. Lampe and Marvin R. Jackson, *Balkan Economic History, 1550–1950:
From Imperial Borderlands to Developing Nations*, Bloomington, IN, 1982, pp. 278–322.

and six legal systems and customs unions to connect. In addition, the wartime damage to Serbian industry and infrastructure dwarfed the disruption of Croatian agriculture by Habsburg requisitions. But the immediate postwar years witnessed widespread peasant unrest in Croatia and the burden of accepting the conversion of its now defunct Austro-Hungarian currency into Yugoslav dinars at a rate of five to one (rather than the one to one rate that its representatives initially demanded and the ten to one rate initially offered by the new central bank in Belgrade, the old Serbian central bank that became the *Narodna Banka Jugoslavije* [National Bank of Yugoslavia]). This disagreement only encouraged the commercial banks of Zagreb to ignore the credit soon available from Belgrade's *Narodna Banka*. They would rely instead on the funds flowing out of the retreating financial houses of Budapest and Vienna. The Zagreb banks were thereby able to facilitate rising agricultural exports to the desperate economies of truncated Austria and Hungary. Meanwhile, Serbia struggled to rebuild with war reparations from the Central Powers that never arrived in the expected amounts. Hence the 'misery and early misunderstandings', as I have characterized the first years of the first Yugoslavia elsewhere.[4]

Nor did the Belgrade government's two major economic initiatives of the 1920s—land reform and the stabilization of the dinar—serve the advance of integration. The redistribution of some 10 per cent of the entire territory's agricultural land, including 20 per cent of its arable, from large estates to full one quarter of all peasant households did not in itself reduce efficiency, as was initially assumed. Once clear title to these new or enlarged smallholdings had been established and credit cooperatives were in place, grain yields in Croatia and Slavonia, the areas most affected and with the best land, rose from well under prewar levels to well beyond. But because prewar Serbia had few large estates and was therefore least affected by the redistributions, their imposition from Belgrade roused even the Croatian Peasant Party (HSS) of Stjepan Radić to oppose a process they might otherwise be expected to favor.[5] Political opposition

---

[4] John R. Lampe, 'Unifying the Yugoslav Economy, 1918–1921: Misery and Early Misunderstandings' in Dimitrije Djordjević (ed.), *The Creation of Yugoslavia, 1914–1918*, Santa Barbara, CA, 1980, pp. 139–56.

[5] Charles A. Beard and George Radin, *The Balkan Pivot: Yugoslavia*. A study in Government and Administration, New York, 1929, pp. 23–32. On the disillusion

also came from the Bosnian Muslims and Albanians, especially where their less efficient sharecropping tracts were transferred to Bosnian Serbs or to the Serbian or Montenegrin veterans who came as colonists to Kosovo or Macedonia. Only in the latter location did they record good economic results. Overall, colonist families were less than 10 per cent of the 518,000 receiving land, but their resettlement in just these contested regions further discredited the land reform as a project for political integration on Serbian terms.[6]

As an economic policy, however, the land reform encouraged the vast majority of peasants to stay just where they were. The agriculturally occupied share of the first Yugoslavia's population hardly moved during the course of the 1920s, from 78.9 in 1921 to 76.5 per cent in 1931. The separate cooperative networks, most successful in Slovenia and Croatia, did not cooperate with each other. Thus there was no state-wide integration of best-practice, let alone migration to the more successful regions. As for industry, the modest urban growth of Belgrade, Ljubljana and especially Zagreb owed something to new employment in manufacturing but never to the extent of introducing a national labor market. At least for Zagreb, a growing demand for factory labor helped to make up for the loss of official employment. Like Sarajevo and Skopje, it had been a provincial capital before the war. Timber, textile, metallurgical and other manufactures already put 6 per cent of the Kingdom's industrial labor force in Zagreb by 1923. The city's enterprises drew their credit and financial capital from Zagreb's aforementioned commercial banks rather than the *Narodna Banka* or any other Belgrade bank. Italy, Austria and Hungary were initially more attractive markets for their products than the wider Yugoslav market.

The stabilization of the dinar in 1925–6 admittedly made those foreign markets less attractive. It was 'overvalued' at a high rate of exchange for the French franc that made the country's exports more expensive and its imports less expensive than they had been. An overvalued, convertible currency should however carry the advantage of attracting private foreign investment. As is well known, that

---

of Dalmatia's Croat peasantry with the new Yugoslav state in general specifically because of the shortcomings of land reform, see Alexander Jakir, *Dalmatien zwischen den Weltkriegen. Agrarische und urbane Lebenswelt und das Scheitern der jugoslawischen Integration*, Munich, 1999, pp. 130–215.

[6] Lampe and Jackson, op. cit., pp. 150–2.

was a commodity conspicuous by its absence for all the new East European states during the 1920s. In addition, that was not a goal of the stabilization's principal architect, Milan Stojadinović. Rising through the Finance Ministry to be Director of Budget Control and then its Minister, Stojadinović was an economist trained in the classic British liberalism that preached balanced state budgets and non-intervention in the economy as ends in themselves.[7] In order to cut the *Narodna Banka*'s debt to the state run up by his predecessor, he trimmed its note issue by one third. His deflationary strategy did succeed in establishing a stable and convertible dinar by 1926. In the process, however, industrial firms dependent on exports and peasants dependent on an already limited supply of agricultural credit were adversely affected.

These hardships added to the burden of a state budget that was twice the real per capita value of prewar Serbia's. Its largely administrative expenditures had added barely 300 miles of new railway track by 1930, with no attention to connecting the previously separate entities. Indeed, ruling coalitions led by the National Radical Party paid little attention in general to issues of economic policy. A proposed Economic Council did not even convene until 1927, while Serbia's leading public intellectual, Slobodan Jovanović, ignored economic issues in his otherwise detailed commentary on the new Yugoslav state.[8]

Stjepan Radić, who had opposed the state's formation in 1918, and his Croatian Peasant Party (HSS) were however greatly interested. Radić had long railed against direct and turnover taxes whose per capita collection for Croatia (and Slovenia too) was twice Serbia's average. Just before his assassination in 1928, Radić proposed a geographic reorganization to equalize both taxation and political representation. From 33 administrative districts bound to the center by a Belgrade-appointed set of prefects, he advocated consolidation into four largely autonomous units. They were Serbia, Slovenia, a separate one for Macedonia/Kosovo, and, to Serbia's further disadvantage, an Adriatic-Danubian, in fact former Habsburg entity that

---

[7] L. Pejić, 'Ekonomska ideja Dr Milana Stojadinovića i balkanski privredni problemi', *Balkanica*, VII, 1976, pp. 240–65.

[8] Beard and Radin, op. cit., pp. 111, 235–7; Aleksandar Pavković, *Slobodan Jovanović: An Unsentimental Approach to Politics*, Boulder, CO, 1993, p. 23, pp. 193–207.

would combine Bosnia-Herzegovina and Vojvodina with Croatia
and Dalmatia.[9]

King Alexander presented his actual administrative consolidation
of what became the Kingdom of Yugoslavia in 1929 as rational economic integration rather than rational decentralization. But the
nine *banovinas* he centered on river valleys, supposedly as focal points
for interconnection, were chosen (and perceived) as no less politically biased than the abortive Radić proposal. The new provincial
borders they imposed conveniently divided Bosnia-Herzegovina
among four *banovinas* so that none had a Bosnian Muslim majority.
They also configured Kosovo, Macedonia and Vojvodina so that all
had Serb majorities. No discussion of integrating the *banovinas* with
each other followed in the face of the Great Depression of the
1930s that hit Yugoslavia's agricultural economy especially hard.

Nor did the Depression and the partial recovery afforded by rear-
mament generate policies that promoted integration even inadvertently. Quite the reverse. First, the central *Narodna Banka* in Belgrade
allowed the crisis for commercial bank credit in Central Europe
that culminated in the collapse of Vienna's Kreditanstalt in 1931 to
drag down the leading Zagreb banks with it. A new state agency for
agricultural credit, Prizad, favored the Serbian areas, leaving an
expanded HSS network of cooperatives to provide some rural
recourse in Croatia. Then the Belgrade government's commitment
to support the League of Nations' trade sanctions against Italy in
1935, following Mussolini's invasion of Ethiopia, curtailed export
earnings for neighboring Dalmatia and Slovenia in particular. After
King Alexander's assassination in October 1934, Milan Stojadinović
had emerged as a now powerful Prime Minister. He set aside his liberal economic orthodoxy of the 1920s in favor of state intervention.
A bilateral clearing agreement privileged Germany, and therefore
Vojvodina's agricultural exports, in Yugoslavia's foreign trade. New
state investment in metallurgy and arms production privileged Serbia and Bosnia. These decisions were strategically defensible but
also served, inadvertently as best I can judge, to make the economic
impact of the decade all the more disadvantageous for Croatia and
Slovenia. Such state enterprise accounted for fully half the rise in

---

[9] Mark Biondich, *Stjepan Radić, the Croat Peasant Party and the Politics of Mass Mobilization, 1904–1928*, Toronto, 2000, pp. 228–35.

industrial production for 1929–38, attracting Western as well as German capital and becoming Yugoslavia's largest industrial employer.[10]

The promise and problems of the second Yugoslavia

Tito's Yugoslavia began its economic life in 1945 with a clean slate. The Nazi-led attack and occupation in 1941 had destroyed all prewar institutions. The course of the Second World War also discredited the political leaders and the very divisions of prewar territory put in place by the now defeated occupiers. And this second Yugoslavia needed to be rebuilt as well as reunited. Nearly one half of prewar industry had been destroyed, half of prewar livestock killed, and infrastructure hit harder still. Only a single, centrally controlled strategy for recovery made immediate economic sense. Yet the spectacular success of that recovery by 1947 owed more to local Communist initiative and to largely American UNRRA aid than to Tito's Politburo.

That did not prevent the party leadership from pushing ahead with a Soviet-style Five Year Plan for 1947–51. Its procedures for central coordination quickly generated several tons of paper reports. It promised a fivefold increase in industrial production and 700 miles of new rail lines by 1951. Minimal investment in a largely private agricultural sector would presumably push peasants into a burgeoning industrial sector supported by low-cost delivery of machinery and raw materials from the emerging Soviet bloc. Its success would have launched the formation of an economic union, at least on the autarkic Soviet model. Its spectacular failure was already clear before the Tito-Stalin split of 1948 reduced deliveries from Eastern Europe to a trickle the following year.

As is well known, the split prompted no quick turn to the West. The Titoist leadership tried instead to repair both its own ideological image and the Plan's prospects by pushing through the full-scale collectivization of agricultural holdings. In addition, what Ljubiša Adamović has aptly called 'a siege mentality' took hold of economic decision-makers.[11] The strategic threat to the régime's survival led

[10] Lampe, *Yugoslavia as History*, pp. 176–84.
[11] John R. Lampe, Russel O. Prickett and Ljubiša S. Adamović, *Yugoslav-American Economic Relations since World War II*, Durham, NC, 1990, p. 74.

not only to the autarkic neglect of export capacity but also to industrial concentration on military production located far from the borders so rapidly overrun in 1941. Thus Bosnia and the Serbian interior were again the most favored locations, Croatia and Slovenia the least favored.

As is less well known, the subsequent economic decentralization and turn to Western trade did not reverse any of these trends until the late 1950s. The elimination of the Planning Ministry and a massive central plan in 1950 did see much economic decision-making transferred downward but not to the new workers' councils mandated for each 'socially-owned' enterprise. Those powers were transferred instead to the local leadership of what now became the League of Communists of Yugoslavia (SKJ). The local party leaders in some 3,834 *opština* (municipalities) were responsible not only for appointing enterprise managers but also for collecting the extra tax contributions (or *doprinosi*) from each enterprise. These contributions would remain a burden on reinvestible funds throughout the history of the second Yugoslavia. The allocation of new capital, moreover, remained concentrated in Belgrade, in a new General Investment Fund. By 1953 the US agricultural and military assistance that began flowing to the Tito régime in 1950 had turned much less into an investment fund than a mechanism for covering debt service and an import surplus. (Fully $1.75 of the $2.5 billion in US grants and soft loans to Yugoslavia were provided during the period 1953–64). American representatives did press the Yugoslav leadership in 1953–4 for a new investment strategy that would favor exports and reduce the duplication of investment in every branch of industry in each republic. But the Yugoslav response was to cut the number of investments for consumer goods or exports in each republic, leaving them all with sizeable sectors of heavy industry. The régime could thereby continue to starve light industry and also agriculture, where collectivization had now been abandoned.[12]

The period that followed, from 1954 to 1969, can rightly be called the decisive years for Tito's Yugoslavia if it were to become an economic union and reap the attending advantages. Let us recall that those advantages, since the Act of Union in 1707 which

---

[12] Lampe, *Yugoslavia as History*, pp. 257–76.

created a single British economy, have been external as well as internal. For the free movement of capital and labor as well as goods takes not only absolute advantage of the larger domestic market but also comparative advantage in international trade. Soviet-style central planning, which involved virtually no foreign trade during its heyday of the 1930s, was obviously ill-suited to take any international advantage. But Yugoslavia's commerce opened significantly to trade the West. First came the initial jump in trade with the United States after 1950 and then the much larger and longer-lasting shift to trade with Italy once the dispute over Trieste was settled in 1954. Soon joined by substantial trade with West Germany, the Western share of Yugoslav exports and imports would stay well over 50 per cent through the 1960s, and also well ahead of the share with the Soviet bloc even after political relations were repaired in 1955–6. By 1961, Yugoslavia had cut tariffs and devalued its overvalued, multiple-rate dinar to a single exchange rate in order to qualify as associate member of the GATT (General Agreement on Trade and Tariffs). The régime promised to make enterprise management and workers' councils more responsive to market signals. The distribution of short-term credit had already been transferred from the central *Narodna Banka* in Belgrade to some 380 new communal banks.[13]

The Yugoslav practice of 'market socialism', as it was sometimes called, could not however fulfil the promise of economic union. That promise, as is plain from the success of the individual West European economies that has made possible their participation in ascending European integration, demands that enterprises, banks and other economic institutions be largely free from political monopoly and management. Simply decentralizing a single-party monopoly, as occurred in Yugoslavia, failed to provide the freedom of movement that is the major advantage of a larger economic space.

The crucial fifteen-year period that we have identified for the 'Yugoslav experiment', to recall another once popular phrase, began with significant overall growth in a system that had barely begun to experiment. Gross Domestic Product (GDP) grew by 35 per cent from 1957 through 1959. Recapturing that sort of advance would

[13] Ibid. pp. 277–83.

remain an argument for hard-line opposition to market reform throughout these years. True enough, some earlier forced investments in heavy industry were paying off by the late 1950s. But we should also note the good fortune of favorable weather and several fine harvests during those same years. They eased the transition to a smaller agricultural population. Massive movement to town and factory had cut the rural share of the labor force from 67 per cent in 1948 to 50 per cent by 1961.

Despite the growth of the late 1950s and a temporary advantage in the country-wide availability of industrial labor by the early 1960s, two new problems pushed the Tito régime closer to market-based reform by the last half of the decade than any Soviet bloc régime would ever be. One came from the un-socialist appearance of inflation, approaching 20 a year per cent by 1964. Prices rose in part because the workers' councils took advantage of their new power to divide net enterprise profit between wage bonuses and new investment by voting themselves large bonuses. Also fuelling inflation was the easy recourse to new investment capital afforded the local party leadership and the enterprise managers they appointed. The communal banks the local SKJ also controlled were simply lending large amounts of low-interest short-term credit whose repayment the enterprises were rolling over year after year, thereby transforming them into long-term loans.[14]

A second problem prompting first intensive economic debate and then the 1965 *Reforma* was however the demise of an integrated Yugoslavia as the party's ideological and cultural goal. Tito himself had tried to make the case for a unitary socialist Yugoslavia in a famous speech at Split in 1963. His remarks made no reference to Yugoslavism as an economic idea. He also failed to address the accumulating economic problems, other than a revived warning against 'the class enemy'. This phrase only raised anxiety about a return to the repressive régime of 1948–53. Tito would thereupon drop the subject and concentrate on insuring each republic's loyalty to single, unchallenged party. Despite stipulations in the new 1963 Constitution meant to restrain the individual republics, their leaders and interests set the framework for the apparently bold measures of 1965.

---

[14] Ibid., pp. 284–9.

The watchword of the reform was 'de-étatization' rather than decentralization, which might have prompted a still reluctant Tito to exercise his unchallengeable veto. The key measures were financial. Enterprises were allowed to keep a larger share of their gross income (up to 70 per cent), but the many communal banks were abolished in order to restrict access to inflationary credit. In their place, a limited number of regional banks were created, all republic-based but intended to lend to the most economically qualified customers across all of Yugoslavia. But the new banks quickly made it clear that they would rarely if ever lend outside their republic borders. At the same, the three large Belgrade banks for investment, export and agriculture that replaced the state's General Investment Fund failed to convince borrowers outside of Serbia that they were not favoring that republic. By 1972 the largest of the three, the Investment Bank, had been broken up into republic-based number of essentially separate institutions. The promise of a new law on foreign investment also failed to materialize. When finally passed in 1967, it kept too much control of management or access to profits out of foreign hands to attract the significant amount of Western investment that might have expanded or integrated what was a set of republic capital markets.

The central bank in Belgrade stood by while the money supply mushroomed up. Inflation averaged 18 per cent a year for the 1970s, while the rate of interest on domestic lending stayed fixed at six per cent. Borrowing at such a negative rate of interest prompted a rise in bank credit to account for 45 per cent of social sector investment across the decade. Joining this stimulus to disconnected, politically driven investment was a flood of short- and medium-term Western credit. By the time that its misuse threatened to cut off more loans in the early 1980s, the Federal Executive Council (SIV) in Belgrade had to rely on an American accounting firm to determine the country's total debt. Although the Western rescheduling of repayment eased its burden, the reduced access to external credit put enough pressure on domestic sources to drive the rate of inflation steadily upward, to 63 per cent by 1984–5 and then beyond. Only the last Prime Minister of the SIV and a Croat, Ante Marković, had the political courage to empower the Belgrade-based central bank to reign in the money supply and establish a stable, convertible dinar across all of Yugoslavia.[15] But that was in the fateful year of 1989, too late to save any single-party régime in Eastern Europe.

Nor had the movement of labor out of agriculture favored the creation of an economic union more than the mobilization of capital. That movement had proceeded from the 50 per cent left in agriculture in 1961 down to 38 per cent in 1971 and to 20 per cent by 1981. But total internal migration in the 1960s had been barely half of the external flow of temporary labor to Western Europe. When the larger part of that 800,000 outflow returned during the 1970s, too many went to large enterprises or small towns in their native republic, or in the case of Bosnian Serbs and Croats, to Serbia and Croatia. The overly capital-intensive growth of large enterprises, especially in heavy or military industry, and labor's limited mobility from small towns made a major contribution to a rate of unemployment in social enterprises that reached 14 per cent by 1978. Susan Woodward has called this 'socialist unemployment' the fatal economic failing of the second Yugoslavia and blames it primarily on the connection to Western credit, proffered and then withdrawn.[16]

I would argue instead that such unemployment points to a wider failure to prevent the politically encouraged growth of regional disparity and disconnection. That was the real Faustian bargain that the Titoist régime made, not with Western lenders for economic advantage, but with republic and local party leaders to preserve their common political monopoly. John Allcock has rightly concluded that it was 'the *post*-war process of state-directed industrialization that gave the greatest stimulus to the creation of regional disparities'.[17] By 1988, Yugoslavia's disparity based on regional variation in GDP per capita was twice that of Italy and three times that of Spain. Inter-republic trade declined during the 1980s and was also failing to provide the efficient flow of components needed for the few manufacturers that had attracted foreign investment. Witness the delayed or defective deliveries to the Yugo auto enterprise

[15] Lampe, Pricket and Adamović, op. cit., pp. 148–95.
[16] Susan L. Woodward, *Socialist Unemployment: the Political Economy of Yugoslavia, 1945–1990*, Princeton, NJ, 1995.
[17] John B. Allcock, *Explaining Yugoslavia*, London, 2000, p. 95. Also see Dijana Pleština, *Regional Development in Communist Yugoslavia: Success, Failure and Consequences*, Boulder, CO, 1992.

in Kragujevac.[18] International trade was in any case a smaller share of GDP than for comparable European countries, prompting the post-mortem from two European Investment Bank economists to call Yugoslavia a 'trade-diverting community', rather than an economic union.[19] If the economic consequences of this diversion and disparity were inflation and unemployment, the political consequences for the party that had willingly paid those prices for so long would indeed prove fatal after 1989.

[18] Michael Palairet, 'The Rise and Fall of Yugoslav Socialism: A Case Study in the Yugo Auto Enterprise, 1954–1992' in David Good (ed.), *Economic Transformations in East and Central Europe: Legacies from the Past and Policies for the Future*, London, 1994, pp. 93–109.

[19] Daniel Ottolengi and Alfred Steinherr, 'Yugoslavia: Was it a winner's curse?', *Economics of Transition*, vol. 1, no. 2 (1993), pp. 236–7.

RELIGION IN A MULTINATIONAL STATE: THE CASE OF YUGOSLAVIA

Radmila Radić

The main aim of this chapter is to assess the relationship between the former Yugoslav state and its three main religious institutions— the Serbian Orthodox Church, the Roman Catholic Church and the Islamic Religious Community, and to look at the attitude to and the role of the three religious institutions in the creation of Yugoslavia in 1918, the development of Yugoslavia and Yugoslavism in the inter-war and post-war periods, and the country's collapse in the early 1990s. The inter-relationship between the three religious institutions is also analysed. It will be argued that they never, during the seventy years of Yugoslavia's existence, established genuine co-operation, and that this was one of the factors behind the break-up of the Yugoslav state. While it is beyond an scope here to analyse the role of religion in Yugoslavia's disintegration, this important topic has not yet received sufficient treatment by scholars, with the notable exception of Paul Mojzes.[1]

Interwar Yugoslavia

The Kingdom of Serbs, Croats and Slovenes was formed in 1918 as the South Slavs' nation state. Only religious differences between Serbs, Croats and Slovenes, the three 'tribes' of *one*, Yugoslav nation, were officially recognized.[2] However, there was not in the 'first'

---

[1] See Paul Mojzes, *Yugoslavian Inferno: Ethnoreligious Warfare in the Balkans*, New York, 1994, and his edited book, *Religion and War in Bosnia*, Atlanta, GA, 1998.

[2] There were, according to the 1921 population census, 46.6 per cent Orthodox, 39.4 per cent Roman Catholics and 11.2 per cent Muslims.

Yugoslavia (let alone its post-1945 socialist successor) a prominent advocate of Yugoslavism among religious leaders (in the mould of Josip Juraj Strossmayer, a leading nineteenth century Yugoslav ideologue).

The Serbian Orthodox Church (SPC) greeted the creation of Yugoslavia not only because most of its believers now lived in one state, but also because with the unification of South Slav territories the Church united, as well.[3] The SPC, however, lost the status of a 'state religion' it enjoyed in pre-war Serbia and Montenegro—in the new kingdom all religions were nominally equal—and often found it difficult to accept its new, 'reduced', status.[4] Paradoxically perhaps, the Serbian Church, while supporting the centralized 1921 Constitution, faced internal dissent, particularly in Bosnia and Vojvodina, over the highly centralized structure of the new Patriarchate. Moreover, voices were heard from within the Church demanding its emancipation from the state. The 1921 Constitution abandoned the principle of 'state church', but it did not separate the church from the state.[5]

The SPC leadership supported the dictatorship introduced by King Alexander in January 1929. Patriarch Varnava stressed the importance of 'state-building' and encouraged 'the implementation of complete unity of brethren of the same blood'. He argued that the Yugoslav idea was 'the national faith of all Serbs, Croats and

---

[3] The restoration of the Serbian Patriarchate, abolished by the Ottomans for the second time in 1766, was ceremoniously proclaimed in 1920, following long preparations.

[4] The *Vidovdan* Constitution of 1921 adopted the principle of full freedom and equality of all religions. All confessions recognised by the law had the right to independently manage their internal affairs and manage their societies and funds. It was prohibited for all confessions and their representatives to use their spiritual authority for political purposes. See *The Constitution of the Kingdom of Serbs, Croats and Slovenes*, Belgrade, 1921, Article 12.

[5] Radmila Radić, *Verom protiv vere. Država i verske zajednice u Srbiji, 1945–1953*, Belgrade, 1995, p. 20. According to the 1931 Constitution the state exercised even more control over religious communities. Neither the 1921 nor the 1931 Constitutions guaranteed religious communities financial aid from the state, but it was provisioned that an amount of money from the state budget would be used for religious purposes. It was to be divided among the respective religious communities in proportion to the number of believers and their needs.

Slovenes', and promoted the slogan 'every brother is dear, whatever faith he might be'.[6] Only after the assassination of the King
in 1934 and the formation of the government of Milan Stojadinović in 1935 would relations between the Serbian Orthodox Church
and the Yugoslav state deteriorate. The SPC increasingly accused
the government that it favoured the Catholic Church. Relations
between the Orthodox and Catholic Churhes consequently also
deteriorated in the 1930s, especially during the Concordat crisis of
1937.[7]

　　Like the SPC, the Roman Catholic Church (RKC) in Croatia
and Slovenia supported the unification of Yugoslavia, even though,
just like its Serbian counterpart, it lost the dominant status it had
enjoyed prior to 1918, in the Habsburg Empire. The RKC in fact
appeared to be initially very enthusiastic about the new state. Its
clergy had hoped that the predominantly Catholic areas of the new
country would enjoy a high degree of autonomy. Furthermore,
Yugoslavia offered the best protection against Italy's territorial
demands in Dalmatia and against the Bolshevism. According to
recent research, the RKC support for Yugoslavia was also based on
a 'dangerous self-deception' that 'the Croats would run the new
state, i.e. that the Catholic element would prevail'.[8] However, misunderstandings between the RKC and the state in the sphere of
culture and education began as early as 1919, and this conflict, as

[6] Nikola Žutić, 'Narodnosna (nacionalna) politika crkava u Kraljevini Jugoslaviji',
in Bogdan Djurović (ed.), *Religija—Crkva—Nacija—Vreme posle rata*, Niš, 1996,
pp. 364–9.
[7] But even before the Concordat crisis, tensions were high. In Dec. 1932 a pamphlet attacking 'the insatiable [Serbian Patriarch] Varnava' was secretly distributed
in Zagreb. It had provoked a fierce debate between Catholic and Orthodox newspapers. The authorities attempted to curb further 'tribal' arguments by deciding
to ban publications which could insult religious feelings of any of Yugoslavia's 'tribes'. Arhiv Jugoslavije (Archives of Yugoslavia, Belgrade) (hereafter AJ),
Ministarstvo pravde, poverljiva gradja, 'Izveštaj Komande Beograda (od 2. 12.
1932.) Ministarstvu vojske i mornarice' and 'Izveštaj Ministarstva unutrašnjih
poslova Kraljevine Jugoslavije (od 3. 12. 1932. i 9. 1. 1933.) Ministru pravde, AJ–
63–13–2–933 and AJ–63–13–185–933, respectively.
[8] Zlatko Matijević, 'Politika katoličkog jugoslavenstva (1912–1929)' in Hans-
Georg Fleck and Igor Graovac (eds), *Dijalog povjesničara-istoričara*, Zagreb, vol. 1,
1998, pp. 155–71.

well as the one over the agrarian reform and the Concordat, would continue throughout the interwar period.

Perhaps the main initial obstacle to the establishment of cordial relations between the Catholic Church and the Yugoslav state was in that the former was too closely associated with the Habsburg Empire in view of the latter. It did not help that the régime suspected that some Croatian bishops could not reconcile themselves with the disappearance of the Dual Monarchy.[9] Furthermore, although the Croatian Peasant Party (HSS) was anti-clerical, relations between the Catholic Church and the HSS improved in the 1930s, when the HSS was led by Vladko Maček. During the decade, public and religious manifestations in Croatia gradually acquired Croatian, rather than Yugoslav character. During the interwar period the Catholic Church became almost as 'national' among the Croats, as the Serbian Orthodox Church was among the Serbs.

It is difficult to trace the development of the Yugoslav idea among the Muslim South Slavs, not least because the pre-1918 Yugoslavism was essentially a Christian, Serbo-Croat-Slovene idea. The Muslims, mainly living in Bosnia-Herzegovina, were considered either Serbs or Croats, and it was assumed that they would eventually return to their 'original' religion and their 'original' identity. Nevertheless, the Muslim leadership generally welcomed the unification of Yugoslavia.[10]

Yugoslav Muslims form the largest Sunni Muslim community in Europe. Until the Royal Dictatorship of January 1929, all Muslims of Bosnia-Herzegovina (and of Croatia and Slovenia) were placed under the supreme authority of the *reis-ul-ulema* in Sarajevo, while the Muslims of Serbia and Montenegro were headed by the supreme *mufti* in Belgrade. Soon after the Yugoslav unification, there gradually emerged a rivalry between the Sarajevo *reis-ul-ulema* and the Belgrade *mufti* over the leadership of all Yugoslav Muslims. The Yugoslav government recognised the *reis-ul-ulema* Džemaludin Čaušević as the religious head of all Yugoslavia's Muslims, although

[9] See for instance a letter of the Yugoslav *chargé d'affaires* to the Vatican, M.M. Jovanović to the Yugoslav Foreign Minister M. Ninčić, 19 Jan. 1926, AJ–69–7–12.
[10] Milorad Ekmečić, *Stvaranje Jugoslavije, 1790–1918*, Belgrade, 1989, vol. 2., p. 802.

it did not allow him to interfere much into Muslim religious affairs outside Bosnia.[11]

The Muslims of Bosnia-Herzegovina, as the South Slavs, were the dominant group among Yugoslavia's Muslims (the other large Muslim community being the Albanian one). The Islamic Religious Community (IVZ) was closely connected to the main Bosnian party, the Yugoslav Muslim Organisation (JMO). The JMO, founded in 1919 and led by Mehmed Spaho, a minister in several interwar governments, listed the protection of the Islamic faith, customs and consciousness in its party programme, arguing for 'equality between Islam and Christianity and other religions'.[12] The JMO supported the 1921 *Vidovdan* Constitution (in fact, without its support it would not have been voted in the parliament) and remained loyal to the state throughout the period. Another Bosnian Muslim group, the Muslim National Organisation, formed in February 1924, also stressed in its draft programme that it supported the national unity of Serbs, Croats and Slovenes, as well as the Constitutional monarchy under the Karadjordjević dynasty.[13]

The IVZ itself mostly restricted its activities to religious affairs, leaving politics aside. Muslim religious leaders accepted Yugoslavism because its concept offered protection from Serbian and Croatian nationalisms. Yugoslav identity was much more appealing to Muslims than Serb or Croat identity, because it allowed for religious freedoms. On the contrary, only an Orthodox South Slav could be a Serb, and only a Catholic one was considered a Croat. By the strength of its organisation and its financial power, the IVZ was in an inferior position when compared to the RKC or the SPC. Still, on the eve of the Second World War, it had around 1,500,000 believers, 2,200 *hodžas* and over 2,000 mosques, its own schools and a university.

The Law on the Islamic Religious Community was passed in 1930. It abolished the Muslims' religious and educational autonomy, and the Justice Minister became the supreme administrative authority supervising the entire work of the IVZ. The *reis-ul-ulema* was

---

[11] Radić, op. cit., p. 28.
[12] 'Program Jugoslovenske muslimanske organizacije', Sarajevo, 1919, in Branko Petranović and Momčilo Zečević (eds), *Jugoslovenski federalizam: Ideje i stvarnost, 1914–1943. Tematska zbirka dokumenata*, Belgrade, 1987, p. 204.
[13] 'Nacrt programa Muslimanske narodne organizacije', in ibid., p. 239.

forced to retire because he opposed the Law, and his successor's seat was moved from Sarajevo to Belgrade, where it was closer to the watchful eye of central authorities.

Milan Stojadinović, appointed Yugoslavia's Prime Minister in the summer of 1935, invited Mehmed Spaho to join his government. In exchange for entering the government, the JMO leader demanded a full autonomy for the IVZ from the state—a request eventually granted in February 1936. The new *reis-ul-ulema* became Fehim Spaho, the brother of Mehmed, and his seat was moved back to Sarajevo. He remained in this post until his death in 1942.

Negotiations over the Concordat between the Vatican and the Yugoslav state began in 1922, but were completed only in 1935, with the signing of a draft agreement in Rome. Although the full text of the Concordat had not been published, the SPC immediately criticised the Rome agreement, accusing the state of favouring the Catholic Church. Serbian opposition parties took the opportunity to attack the government and Prince Regent Paul. Stojadinović had long delayed submitting the Concordat to the Parliament, but when he finally did it, in the summer of 1937, it sparked perhaps the most serious crisis of his years in government (1935–9).

Passing of the Concordat in the Parliament provoked street demonstrations in Belgrade, led by the Serbian Orthodox Church, and there were clashes with the police. To make matters even worse, on the very night the Parliament passed the document, Patriarch Varnava died. Rumours immediately spread that he was poisoned by the government.[14] After several months of protest the government was forced to withdraw the Concordat from the parliamentary procedure and the situation finally calmed down. In his memoirs,

---

[14] The sudden illness and death of the Patriarch was never properly investigated by the police. The official verdict was that he died of poisoning. Within a few days both his brothers died under similarly unclear circumstances. There were even rumours that the late Patriarch had originally been named as one of the Royal Regents in King Alexander's 'real' testament, which had allegedly been destroyed by Prince Paul. For more on these conspiracy theories and on the Concordat crisis see Miloš Mišović, *Srpska crkva i konkordatska kriza*, Belgrade, 1983, p. 162 and *Zatamnjena istorija. Tajna testamenta kralja Aleksandra i smrt patrijarha Varnave*, Belgrade, 1994, p. 127; and Ivan Mužić, *Katolička crkva u Kraljevini Jugoslaviji*, Split, 1978, p. 133.

Stojadinović blamed the Serbian Church for the crisis, arguing that its main problem was in its inability to accept that other religions had equal rights.[15]

Whatever the reasons for the SPC over-reaction, the crisis only widened the gap between Serbs and Croats, whose political leaderships were working on organising a common opposition front to the government. Interestingly, the Catholic episcopate remained relatively neutral during the crisis, although it used it to highlight its apparently difficult position within Yugoslavia.[16] The Croatian Peasant Party and its leader Vladko Maček also showed little interest in the Concordat question. Maček argued that the Serbo-Croat conflict was not a religious one.[17]

Stojadinović had expected that the Concordat would help his government solve the Croatian question. He hoped to erode Maček's support among Croats and also to establish closer ties with Italy and the Vatican, thus islotating the extremist émigré Ustaša organisation. Yet, his plans had misfired and the failure to solve the Croat question would be the key reason for his dismissal by Prince Paul in early 1939.

The new Serbian Patriarch Gavrilo Dožić established friendlier relations with the government, but this rapprochement lasted only until August 1939, when the new Yugoslav government of Dragiša Cvetković formed an autonomous *banovina* of Croatia. In its Christmas message in January 1940, the Holy Sinod of the SPC warned against drawing internal boudaries in the country, especially as a large Serb minority remained inside the Croatian *banovina*. The Serbian Orthodox Church argued that despite creating Yugoslavia, Serbs

[15] Milan Stojadinović, *Ni rat ni pakt*, Rijeka, 1970, pp. 481, 518.
[16] AJ, 'Predstavka katoličkog episkopata upućena Milanu Stojadinoviću sa plenarne sednice Biskupske konferencije od 10. 1. 1937, Ministarstvo pravde Kraljevine Jugoslavije, Pov., 63–3–75–37; 'Informacija o delovanju katoličkog episkopata', *Jugoslovenski list*, Sarajevo, 12 Oct. and 29 Oct. 1937; 'Nadbiskup Stepinac o položaju Katoličke crkve u Jugoslaviji', *Hrvatski tjednik*, Vinkovci, 19 Feb. 1938.
[17] In an interview to the Czechoslovak newspaper *Slovak*, published on 8 Aug. 1937, Maček said: 'The demonstrations and their initiators together with Patriarh Varnava, us Croats interest very little. You must differentiate between Orthodox and Serbs. There is no conflict between the Orthodox and Catholics—our problem is not a religious one. Our disagreements with the Serbian Orthodox Church are only because it supports the idea of a Greater Serbia.' AJ, Central Press Bureau, 38–199–346.

now found themselves divided within their own country. The atmosphere was especially heated during the December 1940 talks between representatives of the church and the state in the Patriarchate, when the former claimed that Yugoslavia was turning into an anti-Serbian state.[18] The March 1941 events, which brought down the Cvetković–Maček government after it had joined the Tripartite Pact, marked another rapprochement between the SPC and the Yugoslav state. But it was a short-lived one, because first Yugoslavia ceased to exist following a brief April war of 1941 against the Axis Powers. Partiarch Gavrilo and his clergy supported the exiled monarchy and the government throughout the war, although there were some Orthodox priests who joined the Communist-led Partisan resistance.

The Second World War

On the eve of the Second World War in Yugoslavia, the RKC was preparing to celebrate thirteen centuries since the Croats' conversion to Christianity. The war which broke out in April 1941, was seen as 'a great deed of Providence', while the Archbishop of Zagreb, Alojzije Stepinac described the proclamation of the Independent State of Croatia (NDH) on 10 April as 'the most important event in the history of the Croatian people'. Stepinac visited representatives of the Ustaša régime before the Yugoslav army, acting on orders of the government, capitulated on 17 April, although he had taken an oath to the monarchy at his consecration.[19] Maček's indirect and Stepinac's direct cooperation with the new régime lent the Ustašas legitimacy they had clearly lacked, being brought to power by their German and Italian allies. The Vatican did not condemn the aggression against Yugoslavia and reduced, although did not sever, relations with the Yugoslav government-in-exile. However, Ante Pavelić, the Ustaša leader, never managed to obtain anything more than a *de facto* recognition from the Holy See.

The Ustaša plan for solving the 'Serb question' (there were nearly 2 million Serbs living in the NDH, which in total had a population

---

[18] Mihailo Konstantinović, *Politika Sporazuma. Dnevničke beleške, 1939–1941; Londonske beleške, 1944–1945*, Novi Sad, 1998, pp. 240, 617–18.

[19] Stella Alexander, *Church and State in Yugoslavia since 1945*, Cambridge, 1979, p. 19.

of some 6 million) was to expel one third, to kill the other and to
convert to Catholicism the final third. In principle, the Catholic
clergy welcomed conversion of thousands of Orthodox Serbs into
Catholicism. It believed that the Orthodox schismatics should
return to their mother Church, although there were prominent
Catholic priests who opposed the Ustaša terror against the Serbs.

On 25 April 1941 Ante Pavelić sent a message to the *reis-ul-ulema*
expressing his desire that Muslims should feel 'their own men in
their own country', free and independent state of Croatia. Fehim
Spaho welcomed the creation of the NDH and received Pavelić in
the Gazi Husrev-beg Mosque in Sarajevo on 11 May 1941.[20] Soon
after the establishment of the NDH, a group of prominent Muslim
leaders went to Zagreb to pay homage to Pavelić. Subsequently,
they issued a proclamation, calling on all Muslims in the NDH to
be loyal to the new régime.

Conflict over the Ustaša claims that all Muslims were in fact
Croats, rather than a separate ethnic group, soon arose. In addition,
when they realised the extent of the Ustaša terror, many Muslim
leaders distanced themselves from crimes committed against Serbs.
In the summer of 1941 they issued protest notes and resolutions
against the mass murder of Serbs (but also against Serb reprisals
against Muslims).[21] Fehim Spaho died in 1942, and was not replaced,
so the Muslims of the NDH remained without their spiritual leader
until the end of the war.

Socialist Yugoslavia

The post-1945 Communist régime treated all religious communities equally. Although the Communists were against religion, they
did not ban it. Initially, they attempted to find a *modus vivendi* with
church leaders, partly because their power was still not consolidated
and partly because they needed international support. But the Communists made sure that even in this initial period they had control
over the leaderships of the three religious communities, reducing

[20] Enver Redžić, *Muslimansko autonomaštvo i 13. SS divizija. Autonomija Bosne i
Hercegovine i Hitlerov Treći Rajh*, Sarajevo, 1987, p. 11.
[21] Radić, op. cit., p. 83.

their activities strictly to spiritual affairs. Under the 1946 Constitution the church was separated from the state, while religious education in schools was banned. Funds from the state were radically reduced and gradually all three churches were marginalized. The secret police kept a close watch over the clergy, who were often intimidated. The Catholic Church faced most pressure, undoubtedly because of its links with the former Ustaša state. The trial of Archbishop Stepinac came, however, more as a result of his refusal to cooperate with the new régime, than because of his alleged collaboration with Pavelić. Sentenced to house arrest, Stepinac became a Croat martyr and his grave in the Zagreb Cathedral would become the major shrine of Croatian nationalism.

The Serbian Orthodox Church suffered the greatest human and material loss during the war of all the three main churches. Its position in the new Yugoslav state was not easy either, as the Communists saw in it a symbol of Serbian interwar hegemony. The SPC regarded the creation of federal Yugoslavia as an attempt to divide the Serb nation and also its Church (a separate Macedonian Orthodox Church would eventually be created in the 1960s).

Muslim dignitaries did not show much affection for the Communist régime, either. Some even called for an independent Bosnia, but they were in a minority and abroad.[22] The position of the Islamic community somewhat improved in the 1960s, when it had played a role in Yugoslavia's emergence as a Third World leader, within the Non-aligned movement. Also, by the early 1970s the Bosnian Muslims were recognised the sixth Yugoslav nation.

The hostility of the Vatican towards socialist Yugoslavia put the Yugoslav Catholics in a difficult situation. Diplomatic relations

---

[22] A Bosnian Muslim committee in Cairo sent in April 1948 an appeal to the British Prime Minister in the name of all Bosnian Muslims, explaining that throughout the centuries Bosnia preserved its special character and individuality. Bosnian Muslims were described as the main victims of the Yugoslav Communist régime, mostly supported by Orthodox Serbs, 'the natural allies of the Russian Bolsheviks'. The committee asked for British help in their struggle against Communism, reminding the British people that if they send help to the 'small Muslim nation in Europe', they would have friendship and favour of the whole world. Similar demand was sent also at the end of Jan. 1949 from Damascus, and was signed by Derviš Ćehović and Mahmut Kapetanović. Public Record Office (London), FO 371/78680.

between Yugoslavia and the Holy See were severed in 1952. The policy of the Holy See started to change more visibly during the Second Vatican Council, between 1962 and 1965. Council defined new place and role of the Church in modern world, especially in relation to socialist countries. The Second Vatican Council also contributed to the establishment of a closer relationship between the RKC and the SPC in the 1960s. Hitherto, the two churches hardly had any contact—for instance the Catholic Archbishop of Belgrade had for twenty years never met with the Serbian Partiarch, who also resided in the Yugoslav capital. The SPC expected a public apology from the RKC for its role in the NDH, when hundreds of thousands Serbs were killed.

The apology came from the Bishop of Banja Luka Pichler, in his Christmas message in 1963. Pichler confesed that 'brothers of the Orthodox fate' were killed in the past only because of their religion, and condemned the Ustašas, who in his view were not the real Catholics. His apology was badly received among the Catholic clergy. However, contact between the two would intensify in the next few years. In 1967 the Serbian Patriarch German met with the Croatian Archbishop Šeper in 1967—this was the first post-war meeting between Yugoslavia's Orthodox and Catholic leaders. The previous year Belgrade and Vatican re-established diplomatic relations.

The strict party control over religious institutions loosened after the Brioni plenum of July 1966. The plenum represented an important turning-point in Yugoslav political life. It led to the fall of Aleksandar Ranković, the country's vice-president and in charge of the secret police; it weakened centralism and brought short-term liberalization of Yugoslav politics. An autocephalous Macedonian Orthodox Church was established in 1967, while Muslim Slavs were recognised as the sixth Yugoslav nation in 1971. The Serbian Church's dissatisfaction with these developments was obvious, through its increasingly open resistance to cooperation with the state authorities. The change was also visible in Catholic regions, especially Croatia, despite the raprochement between Yugoslavia and the Vatican. The late 1960s and early 1970s witnessed an upsurge in Croatian nationalism, the so-called 'Croatian Spring'. In Slovenia, however, the Church remained quite. Generally, in this republic the link between religion and national identity has not been as strong as in Croatia.

The return of conservative party figures in the mid-1970s was followed by renewed attacks on religion, because of nationalism, clericalism, regressive influence on inter-ethnic relations, the overstepping of constitutional rights. At the same time, the religious communities criticized the state for disturbing their activities, for the state's discrimination against believers, and for violating human rights.

Yugoslav sociologists of religion noticed a resurgence of religious feelings among all Yugoslavs in the 1980s. The growing nationalist opposition saw the church as a symbol of the pre-Communist times. Some religious figures also openly adopted a nationalist rhetoric. With the deepening of general crisis and the breaking-up of the old system of values, Orthodoxy, Catholicism and Islam became increasingly important for cultural and national distinctiveness of Serbs, Croats and Muslims and their ethnic homogenization. This process did not take place symultaneously or under identical circumstances, but among all Yugoslav nations religion became vital part of their resurgent nationalisms. The crisis in the mostly Albanian-populated Serbian 'holy land' of Kosovo, which erupted in the early 1980s, provoked strong feelings within the SPC, which became a main pillar of modern Serbian nationalism. The Orthodox clergy increasingly spoke the nationalist language, clearly trying to play a more prominent role in Serbia, now under the control of the new Communist leadership led by Slobodan Milošević. Notions such as democracy, liberalism, the freedom of conscience, western culture—all part of a new discourse in Slovenia—were seen as alien and anti-Orthodox. The Church supported Milošević's attempts to re-centralize Yugoslavia, although its rhetoric was often anti Yugoslav. The Vatican's open support to the secession of Slovenia and Croatia was, in the eyes of the SPC clergy, a final confirmation of an Vatican-sponsored 'anti-Serbian' and anti-Yugoslav conspiracy.

Religion in the former-Yugoslavia never represented a cohesive force, but struggle between religious organisations on behalf of 'their' nations contributed to intolerance, and even open hostility between Orthodox, Catholic and Muslim Yugoslavs, and eventually to the break-up of their common country.

THE MILITARY AND
YUGOSLAV UNITY

Mile Bjelajac

The Yugoslav army, just like the Yugoslav state, was multi-ethnic, and as such it had experienced various crises, including that of its identity. It evolved from victorious armies of the two world wars. In 1918 the basis for its formation was the Serbian army, and in 1945 the Partisan National Liberation Army. Preserving ethnic balance within the army had been of special concern to both King Alexander and President Tito, both also Commanders-in-Chief. The two leaders faced similar questions and dilemmas: how to safeguard results of the war and secure legitimacy for the new state and régime? How to create a reliable military force able to withstand external and internal threats, while at the same time preserving its multi-ethnic character? How to exercise post-war reconciliation as one of key preconditions for the legitimacy of the new order?

Both Alexander and Tito had enjoyed unquestionable loyalty of their army officers and of army as a whole. Both the King and the President gained further legitimacy with the army through internal political conflicts that challenged the Yugoslav unity. The Yugoslav army had always been seen as the ultimate guarantor of Yugoslavia's integrity. As a result, there had been a number of myths or one-sided interpretations of the military's role in Yugoslav history, including the one that the army was not truly Yugoslav. It is the main aim of this article to critically examine such myths, by assessing the degree of Yugoslavism in the army of both Yugoslavias. In the first part I look at the official Yugoslavism in the army of the Royal Yugoslavia. The second part deals with the Yugoslav Army in Homeland led by General Mihailović, which claimed to be a successor of the pre-war army, heavily defeteated in the brief war against the Axis Powers in

April 1941. The third part will analyse the Yugoslavism of the army of the second, Socialist Yugoslavia.

Yugoslavism of the Yugoslav [Royal] Army

While it would be erroneous to claim that inter-ethnic relations within the army of the first Yugoslavia did not pose any problems, there is no reliable documentary evidence to suggest that Serbian leadership of the interwar Yugoslav army had chauvinistic or intentionally chauvinistic intentions towards the army's non-Serbs. A number of confidential recommendations clearly show that their authors—war ministers, top army generals and other officers—were fully aware that harmony within the army was a necessary precondition for a high combat morale and the army's loyalty to the state. Predominantly Serb leadership of the Yugoslav Army understood that any such signs would nourish anti-Serb and anti-Yugoslav sentiments both in the army and whole society.[1]

Before the Yugoslav volunteers from Russia reached the Salonika front, the Chief-of-Staff of the Serbian Army's Supreme Command, General Petar Bojović, had issued a special order to Serbian officers emphasizing the importance of 'harmony', 'respect', 'tolerance' and 'brotherhood', between Serbs, Montenegrins and other Yugoslavs. He particularly stressed that it was vital that Serbs of the Kingdom of Serbia do not attempt to dominate other Yugoslavs, not just in order to counter the enemy propaganda. The officers and non-commission officers were ordered to avoid any actions that could offend pride and dignity of newcomers or cause suspicion among them. Those who disobeyed were to be put on trial.[2] Bojović's successors, Generals Mihailo Rašić and Stevan Hadžić, as well as various Ministers of War who held the office in the formative period of the Kingdom of Serbs, Croats and Slovenes, frequently issued orders

---

[1] See Mile Bjelajac, *Vojska Kraljevine Srba, Hrvata Slovenaca, 1918–1921* (hereafter *Vojska KSHS, 1918–1921*) Belgrade, 1988, passim, and *Vojska Kraljevine SHS/ Jugoslavije, 1922–1935* (hereafter *Vojska KSHS/Jugoslavije, 1922–1935*), Belgrade, 1994, passim.

[2] The full text of the order is reproduced in Mile Bjelajac, *Jugoslovensko iskustvo sa multietničkom armijom, 1918–1991* (hereafter *Jugoslovensko iskustvo*), Belgrade, 1999, pp. 7–10.

to officer corps in regard to relationship between Serbian and former Habsburg officers and soldiers, demanding tolerance and mutual
respect.[3]

The new officer corps was created by officers from the former
Serbian, Montenegrin, Austro-Hungarian and Russian armies.[4] They
were not only educated in different countries, but also in many
cases fought each other in the First World War. However, by the late
1930s, the Yugoslav army had some 10,000 officers, 85 per cent of
whom had received military education in Yugoslavia. The relatively
slow and painful incorporation of the former enemy officers into
the new army, at whose core was the former Serbian army, led to
many criticisms of the new Yugoslav military establishment.[5] While
undoubtedly there were numerous difficulties in the initial period
after the unification, the military and political leadership of the
Kingdom of Yugoslavia placed high hopes on new generations of
officers trained in the spirit of Yugoslav unity. In fact, the new
Yugoslav army proved more tolerant and inclusive of the former
enemy officers than the Italian army had been after the unification
in 1870, or Polish after 1918, or West German in the case of the reunited Germany, to take a more recent example.[6]

Official Yugoslavism in the Yugoslav army emphasized the tradition of liberation wars, mostly associated with Serbian and Montenegrin nineteenth century history. However, prominent pro-Yugoslav
Croat and Slovene historical figures (such as *ban* Josip Jelačić, Bishop
Josip Juraj Strossmayer, General and poet Petar Preradović, counts
Zrinski and Frankopan) formed integral part of the new army's
patriotic discourse. This was particularly the case with the navy, as
most vessels were named after Croatian and Slovene historical figures and place names. While the régiments stationed in predominantly

---

[3] For examples of such orders see Bjelajac, *Vojska KSHS, 1918–1921*, pp. 271–6,
286–7, 312–14, and 323–6.

[4] There were 3,500 officers from the former Serbian army, 2,590 from the former
Habsburg army, 469 from the Montenegrin army and 12 from the Russian Tsarist
army.

[5] See Mile Bjelajac, 'Military Élites—Continuity and Discontinuities: The Case of
Yugoslavia, 1918–1980' (hereafter 'Military Élites') in Wolfgang Hoepken and
Holm Sundhaussen (eds), *Éliten in Suedosteuropa. Rolle, Kontinuitaeten, Brueche in
Geschichte und Gegenwart (Suedosteuropa-Jahrbuch)*, no. 29, Munich 1998, pp. 229–41.

[6] Bjelajac, *Jugoslovensko iskustvo*, pp. 15–6.

Serbian areas celebrated the traditional Serbian *slavas* (this tradition was established by the old Serbian army), most régiments based in Croatia and Slovenia observed Croatian or Slovene traditional festivities.[7]

The commanding language of the army was Serbo-Croat, but with the Serbian variant being predominantly used, in order to avoid Croatian military terms which bore too close an association with the Habsburg military tradition. In everyday life officers and soldiers were free to use their native speech, with the exception of those of ethnic German background, as the usage of German in the army was forbidden immediately after the war. The military authorities were obliged to use the Latin alphabet in correspondence with civil and religious authorities in Slovenia, Croatia or Bosnia, except in predominantly Serb areas or if the correspondence in question was with the Orthodox church. The books and manuals, as well as official acts, were published both in Latin and Cyrillic. Sometimes articles in military publications appeared in Slovene, too. The language used in military schools and textbooks, when it was referred to events of the First World War, was intentionally neutral as far as the former-Habsburg Yugoslavs were concerned. Terms such as 'the enemy, 'Austro-Hungarians', and *Švabe* (Swabians, which in Serbo-Croat slang refers to all Germans) were used, so any reference to those Croats, but also Serbs, who committed atrocities in the occupied Serbia was avoided.[8] The army's Yugoslavism was also based on the myth of 'enslaved brothers'—Croats and Slovenes still living in Italy and Austria.

From November 1919, every year some 4,500 recruits were sent to the 7,500 men strong Royal Guard from the whole country. The authorities made sure that there was an equal representation. For instance, four Bosnian districts of Banja Luka, Travnik, Sarajevo and Tuzla were obliged to send 55 recruits to the Royal Guard each year, 30 of whom were supposed to be Muslims. Each year the Ministry of War required from military districts of Prizren, Kosovska Mitrovica and Priština 80 ethnic Albanians for the Royal Guard.[9]

[7] Ibid., pp. 40–1.
[8] Bjelajac, *Vojska KSHS/Jugoslavije, 1922–1935*, p. 162.
[9] 'Razrez regruta', Ministarstvo vojske i mornarice, Pov. Br. 40598, Belgrade, 5 Nov. 1919 (The Distribution of Recruits, Ministry of War, Classified). *Arhiv Vojnoistorijskog Instituta* (Archives of the Institute for Military History, Belgrade), P 6, kutija 656.

During King Alexander's dictatorship (1929–34) twelve military districts from pre-1912 Serbia sent 54 per cent out 4.617 recruits. In regard to Montenegrin recruits for the Guard, military authorities in Montenegro were obliged to respect equality in representation of each Montenegrin clan. The religious structure within the Guard almost corresponded to the one in the state. The ethnic composition of the Guard's career officers was also mixed, as well as of Royal aides-de-camp and orderly officers. The Royal congratulations for Catholic, Muslim and Orthodox religious occasions and holidays were usually published on the front page of the *Official Military Gazette*, and commanders were obliged to read it in front of their troops.[10]

Some two thirds of Serbian officers came from a tiny bourgeois class.[11] Others' social background was more obscure, although we know that most reserve officers had at least secondary education, whereas non-commissioned officers usually had six years of schooling. The Balkan wars and the First World War badly affected Serbia's officer corps in terms of numbers. For example, of those who graduated from military schools between 1899 and 1914, 38.1 per cent died (490 out of 1,286) during the 1912–18 period.

Let us now turn to the former Habsburg officer corps admitted into the newly created Yugoslav Army. According to Istvàn Deàk, in 1910 there were only 2.4 per cent Serbs, Croats and Slovenes, or in total 427 out of 17.808 Habsburg officers in active service. That shows a decline of 1.5 per cent in comparison to 1897. In the same period there were only 35 South Slav officers in all classes of the Military Academy, seventeen of whom were Serbs. In November 1918 there were 25 South Slavs out of 375 active Generals (6.6 per cent).[12]

Imperial and Royal Navy (the Habsburg *Kriegsmarine*) had by June 1914 almost 2,000 officers and 17,000 enlisted men. While the

---

[10] Bjelajac, *Vojska KSHS, 1918–1921*, pp. 75–6 and *Vojska KSHS/Jugoslavije, 1922–1935*, pp. 93–4, 292.
[11] *Spomenica sedamdesetpetogodišnjice Vojne akademije 1850–1925*, Belgrade, 1925 (hereafter *Spomenica*); Milić Milićević, 'Reforma srpske vojske 1897–1900', unpublished MA dissertation, University of Belgrade, 1996; Mile Bjelajac, 'Slučaj tajnog raporta pukovnika Mašina 1906', *Vojno-istorijski glasnik*, Belgrade, no. 1, 1997, pp. 55–79, p. 64.
[12] Istvàn Deàk, *Beyond Nationalism: a Social and Political History of the Habsburg Officer Corps, 1848–1918*, Oxford, 1990, p. 188.

officer corps was dominated by the Germans and Magyars, the Croats were the largest national group among the enlisted men, making up about 30 per cent of total number (the Magyars made up about 20 per cent and Germans about 16 per cent).[13] Despite the complaints by non-Austrians, German was the official language of instruction and command.[14] In contrast to that, in the Yugoslav Kingdom, Croats and other Habsburg Yugoslavs dominated the Navy. During the first few years after unification, some 269 former Habsburg naval officers were accepted into the new Navy. Two of them were admirals and another ten would rise to the same rank before 1941. In March 1941 the share of non-Serbs in the Navy Officer Corps was 82.41 per cent (or 567 out of 688).[15]

Despite some claims that former Habsburg officers were neglected and humiliated in the Yugoslav army,[16] statistics suggest more profound conclusions. For example, in the early 1920s, former Habsburg officers formed 36.76 per cent out of the Yugoslav officer corps. In 1924 they formed only 4 per cent among all generals and admirals and 9.7 per cent among colonels, but 15.8 per cent among lieutenant-colonels and 42.2 per cent among majors. Twelve years later, in 1936, the figures grew to 6.5 per cent for generals and admirals, 33.35 per cent for colonels, 34.66 per cent for lieutenant-colonels and 47.76 per cent for majors. On the eve of the Second World War 23 per cent of active general corps were formerly officers of the Habsburg army.[17] According to the French military

[13] At the same time the Croats made up 7 per cent of the Habsburg officer corps.
[14] Luis Gebhard, 'The Croats, the Habsburg Monarchy and Austro-Hungarian Navy', *Journal of Croatian Studies*, vol. XI–XII (1970–1), pp. 152–4. In 1901 there was only one Croat admiral, 7 per cent of all officers were Croats, and 34 per cent of all enlisted men in the navy. The number of Croatian officers increased to 10 per cent in 1918. The Croatian delegates in both Austrian and Hungarian parliaments frequently complained about the low number of Croatian cadets attending the Naval Academy in Rijeka.
[15] Bjelajac, *Vojska Kraljevine SHS 1918–1921*, p. 79; Stevan K. Pavlowitch, 'How many non-Serbian Generals in 1941?', *East European Quarterly*, vol. XVI, no. 4, Jan. 1983, pp. 447–52, p. 449.
[16] In Deák's words, 'Croats were systematically hounded out of the army', op. cit., p. 209, after Ivo Banac, *The National Question in Yugoslavia: Origins, History, Politics*, Ithaca, NY, 1984. Richard Crampton also accepts this argument in his *Eastern Europe in the Twentieth Century*, London and New York, 1994, p. 132.
[17] Bjelajac, 'Military Élites', p. 236

attaché to Belgrade, General Bethouart, in 1940 the Croats constituted one quarter of the personnel in the General Headquarters.[18]
The same year Croats and Slovenes occupied 63.6 per cent of all
military attaché posts. The Croat Colonel Vladimir Kalečak was
the head of the military intelligence service in 1940–1.[19]

The Serbs did dominate the Yugoslav Army, particularly the
General corps. However, there were 12 former Montenegrin and
64 former Habsburg officers, as well as two non-Serbs, Karlo Silvi
and Ignjat Kirhner, from the former Serbian army among generals
and admirals (the total figure was 506). The percentage of Generals
who were former Habsburg officers gradually increased throughout
the interwar period.[20]

Mihailović's Home Army

During the brief April 1941 war, Yugoslavia's army was defetead, its
government and the royal family fled to the Allied territory, while
the country itself was partitioned. A majority of Yugoslav career
and reserve officers were sent to Germany or Italy as prisoners of
war. Because Croatia was officially an ally of the Axis, most, though
not all, Croat officers were soon released, while others, mostly Serbs,
remained in captivity throughout the war. Several hundred Yugoslav troops, mainly officers of the Air Force and the Navy, fled to the
Middle East. The Ministry of War, active in exile, attempted, with
the British help to organise a Yugoslav army-in-exile and planned
to recruit Yugoslavs living in the United States, Canada and Australia.
However, very little came out of these plans.

In Yugoslavia itself, a group of officers who refused to surrender,
led by the general staff colonel Dragoljub–Draža Mihailović, became
a nucleus of the soon-to-be-established Yugoslav Army in the

[18] Antoine Bethouart, *Des Hecatombes glorieuses au desastre 1914–1940*, Paris 1972,
pp. 154–66.
[19] For more details on distribution of the highest posts in regard to officers' ethnicity see Bjelajac, *Jugoslovensko iskustvo*, pp. 41–4.
[20] 'Stručna rang lista oficira, službenika i ukaznog osoblja Kraljevine SHS, Beograd
1922 (1926), Službeni kartoni oficira i vojnih činovnika Vojske Kraljevine
Jugoslavije, *Arhiv Vojnoistorijskog Instituta*, Belgrade; Pavlowitch, op. cit., pp. 447–
52.

Homeland, or the Home Army. These formations were also known as the Četniks or the 'Ravna Gora Movement', after the Ravna Gora mountain in western Serbia, where Mihailović established his headquarters in May 1941. By the end of the year, the Četnik leader was promoted to the rank of a general, and in January 1942 he became the war minister and the Chief-of-Staff of the Supreme Command in the Homeland, in the new cabinet headed by Professor Slobodan Jovanović. Thus, although the Yugoslav army collapsed together with the state in April 1941, Mihailović's Home Army was a legal successor to the old army, providing a symbolic continuity with the pre-war state.

What was Mihailović's attitude towards the Yugoslavism of the inter-war period? He was among some seven thousand Serbian officers who had fought in the First World War. When Yugoslavia was created as a result of the war, Mihailović was loyal to the new country. There is no evidence to suggest that he was a Serb nationalist during the interwar period. Among his close friends there were both Serbs and non-Serbs. While serving in Slovenia between 1937 and 1939 Mihalović's anti-German statements led to his being moved to Belgrade by the then Defence Minister General Milan Nedić. Disappointed by the army's conservatism and by anti-Yugoslav sentiments among some non-Serbs, he proposed that the army be reorganized into separate Serb, Croat and Slovene units and be trained for a guerrilla warfare. Because of these views he was arrested by military authorities, spending 30 days in an army prison in the late 1930s.[21]

The embarrassing military defeat of April 1941, left Mihailović bitter and resentful towards his superiors who quickly gave up fighting, and towards those who deserted the country and the army. But, unlike some other Serbian officers, he did not openly criticise the Yugoslavism of the interwar years.[22] In a 1942 memorandum

[21] Bojan Dimitrijević and Kosta Nikolić, *Djeneral Mihailović. Biografija*, Belgrade, 2000, pp. 82–3. In 1938 Mihailović's personal involvement in efforts to suppress pro-Nazi demonstrations earned him a recall from the position as Chief-of-Staff of the Drava Division.

[22] For instance General Bogoljub Ilić, Mihailović's predecessor as the Minister of War, disappointed and horrified by the crimes committed against Serbs in the Independent State of Croatia, came to believe that the 1939 Agreement (*Sporazum*), which established an autonomous Croatia, must be reconsidered under new circumstances. See his letter to the Prime Minister, General Dušan Simović,

entitled *Polazno stanovište*, (The Starting Point) Mihailović stated
that the Kingdom of Yugoslavia never seized to exist, and that
although the first battle had been lost, the war had not been lost yet.
As the war minister he called upon all Yugoslavs to obey eventual
calls for mobilization by his Supreme Command. He envisaged
establishment of secret organizations that would gather all Yugoslav
patriots. In a paragraph dedicated to the strategy against the Partisan
movement, Mihailović foresaw gathering of all Yugoslav-oriented
and anti-Communist Serbs, Croats and Slovenes. In the document
there is no mention of Yugoslavia's post-war internal borders,
although Mihailović did talk about the enlargement of Yugoslavia
by 'liberation' of South Slavs under the Italian and Austrian rule.[23]

While in the initial period of the war Mihailović was officially
unquestionably a Yugoslav, his Yugoslavism became more evident
in the last stages of the war, in 1944–5. He renounced German and
Ustaša propaganda that Četniks would undertake mass revenge
against all Croats. And he issued more regular calls on Bosnian
Muslims and Croats to join his troops.[24] In this period Mihailović
came to support the idea of a Yugoslav federation consisting of
three units—Slovene, Croat and Serb—thus abandoning a straight
return to the old order. At a Congress held in Ba, in January 1944,
sponsored by Mihailović, presided over by Živko Topalović, leader
of the small Socialist Party, and attended by representatives of most
pre-war parties, including the Croatian Peasant Party, a resolution
was passed calling for an internal reorganization of Yugoslavia into
the three units after the war. The resolution also called for the

---

Cairo, 8 Nov. 1941, in Bogoljub Ilić, *Memoari armijskog generala 1896–1942*,
Belgrade, 1995, Appendix No. 2, pp. 236–41.

[23] Milan Vesović, Kosta Nikolić and Bojan Dimitrijević (compilers), *Dragoljub
M. Mihailović: Rat i mir Djenerala. Izabrani ratni spisi*, Belgrade, 1998, 2 vols, vol. 2,
pp. 7–9 (source: *Arhiv Vojnoistorijskog Instituta*, CA 16–1–22, 1942). The document also contains Mihailović's recommendations regarding the punishment of
deserters and criminals within the Home Army, and his call for a struggle against
the Ustašas by all means. As far as Serbia's collaborationist régime of General
Nedić was concerned, Mihailović ordered that all those who collaborated with
it be closely monitored and that records of their collaboration be kept, so that
their personal responsibility for collaboration with the enemy can be proven
after the war.

[24] Ibid., pp. 17–36.

abolition of the 1939 *Sporazum*. Future borders between Serb and Croat units were not drawn, but it was emphasized that

> In tomorrow's Yugoslavia, which we are adopting as our state and existential framework, the union of all Serb lands must be realized. Serb lands are all those where Serb blood was spilled and where Serb heads fell, because by their very sacrifice they irrefutably marked the boundaries of Serbdom.[25]

Mihailović, however, never managed to attract mass following among non-Serbs and his movement was eventually defeated. In early stages of the war he was linked with Greater Serbian programmes of the lawyer Stevan Moljević and of young, pro-Četnik intellectuals who met in December 1942 in Šahovići, Montenegro. The Šahovići meeting called for the establishment of a Greater Serbia.[26] His association with those who openly advocated Greater Serbia was certainly a key factor behind his movement remaining predominantly, if not exclusively Serbian.[27] Mihailović was also perceived as someone who fought for the restoration of the old order, which had been, even before the war, largely discredited, especially among the non-Serbs. Mihailović furthermore discredited his movement by tolerating collaboration of his commanders with Italian troops in Dalmatia. The government-in-exile was of little help in promoting Mihailović's as an all-Yugoslav resistance and an alternative to the Partisan movement. All these factors, combined with the Partisans' successful resistance campaign, contributed to both inability of Mihailović to attract a significant non-Serb support and to his ultimate failure. His arrest in 1946 and a show-trial at which he was

---

[25] Kosta Nikolić, 'Dragoljub Draža Mihailović', in Peter Radan and Aleksandar Pavković (eds), *The Serbs and their Leaders in the Twentieth Century*, Ashgate, 1997, pp. 219–20.

[26] For Moljević's programme see Jozo Tomasevich, *War and Revolution in Yugoslavia: The Chetniks*, Stanford, CA, 1975, pp. 155–65. For the Šahovići meeting and the argument that it was not directly linked with Mihailović see Branko Petranović, *Srbija u Drugom svetskom ratu*, Belgrade, 1992, pp. 214–16.

[27] Mihailović established good relations with the Croatian Peasant Party. In mid-1944, the former Yugoslav Generals Matija Parac and Dragutin Kuzmić and Colonel Luka Šarić were appointed commanders of the Home Army for Croatia, Slavonia and Bosnia. See Vesović *et al.* (compilers), op. cit., p. 34. In 1944 there were some 4,000 Bosnian Muslim troops under Mihailović's command. Slovene troops under General Karlo Novak also fought under Mihailović's command.

sentenced to death, marked a symbolic end of the interwar Yugoslav Army and the beginning of a new era in history of Yugoslavia's
military.

Brotherhood and Unity within the Yugoslav People's Army (JNA)

With the collapse of the royal Yugoslav Army's resistance and dismemberment of Yugoslavia in April 1941, the Communist Party of
Yugoslavia organized the Partisan resistance movement which after
the war grew into the Armed Forces of the Socialist Yugoslavia of
some 800,000 troops. The army also provided the core of the post-
war party that grew from some 12,000 members in 1941, to a membership of 140,000 by the end of the war.[28]

To a much greater degree than in 1918, Yugoslavia was again a
land of reconciliation after a civil and liberation war. The new army
took in a large number of officers who fought against it during the
war or who spent it as German and Italian POWs.[29] The admission
began on a larger scale in late 1944, and accelerated in the spring of
1945. Among the Croat officers formerly serving in the Croatian
army, there was a number of the former Habsburg officers, who
were admitted to the Yugoslav Army after the creation of Yugoslavia. Such was for example the Chief of the new Air Force, General
Franjo Pirc, and the Head of the Military Intelligence and member
of the Supreme Command in late spring of 1945, General Vjekoslav
Klišanić.[30]

---

[28] Robin Alison Remington, 'The Yugoslav Army: Trauma in Transition', in
Constantine Danopoulos and Daniel Zirker (eds), *Civil-Military Relations in
Soviet and Yugoslav Sucessor States*, Boulder, CO, 1996, p. 156.

[29] There were 2,016 former prisoners of war, mostly Serbs, 1,963 former officers
of the army of Independent State of Croatia, mostly Croats, 727 former
Mihailović's officers, again, mostly Serbs, 322 Bulgarians, 215 Germans, 124 Italians, 18 Hungarians, 17 former Yugoslav Army officers who spent the war in the
Middle East and 4 officers of the Albanian pro-Italian militia.

[30] Klišanić was later transferred to the post of Chief of Education Department of
the Ministry of Defence. See *Razvoj oružanih snaga SFRJ, 1945–1985*, vol. 15,
'Kadrovi i kadrovska politika', classified edition published by the JNA, Belgrade,
1986.

The Yugoslav Communists brought into socialist Yugoslavia much of their political heritage from the interwar period. They believed that the main problem with the old kingdom was the Serb hegemony. They hoped that the problem of legitimacy in a multiethnic society would be overcome by appropriate representation of non-Serbs among generals and the officer corps in general. However, they faced same or similar problems as the interwar authorities. The commanding structure of the Partisan army was predominantly Serb. Also, there was a lack of interest in pursuing a military career among the under-reprsented nations, particularly Croats and Slovenes. Thus, in 1985 for instance, the Serbs, who made 36.3 per cent of Yugoslavia's population, formed approximately 57.17 per cent of the officer corps. Among the army generals their share was 46 per cent. When, 15 years previously, the percentage of Serb generals was almost equal (46.6 per cent), they held only 33 per cent of the highest military posts.[31] At the same time, the Croats with some 22 per cent of the country's population, formed 14 per cent of the officer corps. There were, however, 19 per cent of Croats among generals, and as many as 38 per cent of highest posts went to Croats. In addition, while generals from Croatia constituted 39.07 per cent of the general corps, those from Montenegro 17.56 per cent and from Slovenia 6.09 per cent, the share of those from Serbia 'proper' (without the provinces) was only 13.98 per cent.[32]

There were legal provisions within the Yugoslav People's Army (JNA) for a balanced regional recruitment into professional military ranks. The equal representation was even guaranteed by the 1974 Constitution, which made Yugoslavia unique in the world.[33] According to the 1974 Constitution, 'the composition of the officer corps and promotion to senior commanding and directing posts in the Yugoslav People's Army, the principle of the most proportional representation of the Republics and Autonomous Provinces will be applied.'[34]

[31] By 'highest post' I mean Chief of the General Staff, deputies of the Minister of Defence, commanders of Air Force, Navy, Army Districts, Chief of the Security of Armed Forces, Secretary of the League of Communists in the JNA, Chiefs of departments within the Ministry of Defence and General Staff.

[32] Bjelajac, *Jugoslovensko iskustvo*, p. 56. Figures in 1980 show increase in the cases of Serbia (28.47 per cent) and Slovenia (9.72 per cent).

[33] Anton Bebler, 'The Military and the Yugoslav Crisis', *Südosteuropa*, vol. 40, no. 3–4, 1991, pp. 132–3.

[34] *Federal Constitution of SFR of Yugoslavia* (1974), Article 242.

The JNA was thus mandated to come as close to proportional composition (if not representation) as possible, in its upper echelons.
But the Yugoslav military had been only partly successful in implementing the above mentioned constitutional provision, in spite of
considerable efforts on behalf of the authorities.[35]

Yugoslavism of the JNA was based on the 'brotherhood and
unity' myth. Essentially, it meant that all Yugoslav nations equally
contributed to the victory against the foreign occupiers and domestic collaborators (the blame was also evenly distributed). In fact, the
myth about the heroic Partisan struggle grew into the myth about
the JNA, often regarded by Yugoslavs and non-Yugoslavs as one of
the most powerful forces in post-war Europe. The JNA was perceived by both the régime and by the Yugoslav population as the
defender of the country from outside danger. Indeed, it remained
the last pan-Yugoslav institution. But ultimately, just like the country, it was destroyed from inside. Not immune to the influence of
nationalists, the Army experienced several serious crises in the 1980s
and early 1990s and gradually ceased to be a common military force
of all Yugoslav citizens. Both Admiral Branko Mamula and General
Veljko Kadijević, as well as many others from the top who remained
committed to a united Yugoslavia, eventually regreted the support
they lent to Slobodan Milošević. Milošević's aggressive brand of
Serb nationalism in their opinion nourished Slovenian and other
potential nationalisms and separatisms.[36]

Just like the 'third' Yugoslavia (Serbia-Montenegro), its Army of
Yugoslavia (VJ) is more multiethnic than armies of other Yugoslav
successor states. According to the then Chief-of-Staff general Momčilo
Perišić, in early 1994 Serbs and Montenegrins made up 75.6 per cent
of the VJ officer corps, declared 'Yugoslavs' 9.7 per cent and 'others'
14.7 per cent. Approximately, only 66.8 per cent were born in the
Federal Republic of Yugoslavia.[37] But the brotherhood and unity
and the Communist ideology, the pillars of common identity in

[35] Bebler, op. cit, p. 133.
[36] Remington, op. cit., p. 166; Louis Sell, 'The (Un) Making of Milošević', *Wilson Quarterly*, summer 1999, pp. 24–5; Branko Mamula, *Slučaj Jugoslavija*, Podgorica, 2000, pp. 109–21; Veljko Kadijević, *Moje vidjenje raspada*, Belgrade, 1993, passim.
[37] Remington, op. cit., p. 167 (after *NIN*, 13 May, 1994, p. 20). Perišić was purged in 1998 and later joined the opposition to the former President Milošević. At the time of writing he was vice-premier in the Serbian government.

socialist Yugoslavia, have been replaced in the army by once forgotten myths about Serbian and Montenegrin heroic military traditions, although the Partisan values still remain important.[38] The
transformation of Yugoslavism of the new Yugoslav army will,
however, very much depend on whether the third Yugoslavia will
survive. At the time of writing, this question remains wide open.

---

[38] *Negovanje i vrednovanje tradicija u vojsci Jugoslavije*, Belgrade, 1993.

Part IV. INTELLECTUALS

SOUTH SLAV INTELLECTUALS AND THE CREATION OF YUGOSLAVIA

Ljubinka Trgovčević

In the early twentieth century, a dominant idea among South Slav intellectuals and educated youth was the idea of Yugoslavism, or Yugoslav unity. In an overwhelmingly rural area, such was the future (now former) Yugoslavia, intellectuals were bound to form a tiny minority, but their influence on South Slav societies far exceeded their number. The Yugoslav idea originated in the nineteenth century, it had its ups and downs, and it had many variations. Its 'founders' had been the Croatian 'Illiryanists', who turned to the Serbo-Croat linguistic and cultural unity as a defensive mechanism against Budapest's increasingly Magyarizing policies. In some cases, however, the Yugoslav idea also included the Slovenes to the north of the Croats and sometimes the Bulgarians, to the east of the Serbs. By the beginning of the twentieth century Yugoslavism (*jugoslovenstvo*) emerged as a political movement among the Habsburg South Slavs and became increasingly accepted in Serbia. At its core was the notion of 'national oneness' (*narodno jedinstvo*) of Serbs and Croats (and Slovenes). Yugoslavism was modelled on the ideas of Italian and German unificationist movements. At the same time, its advocates looked towards the United States for a model of a hybrid nation.

In this chapter I concentrate mainly on Serbian intellectuals and Yugoslavism, because the role of Croat intellectuals in the development of the Yugoslav idea has been the subject of several studies in English.[1] While by no means ignoring Croatian and Slovene

---

[1] For instance Elinor Murray Despalatović, *Ljudevit Gaj and the Illyrian Movement*, New York, 1975; Mirjana Gross, 'Croatian national-integrational ideologies from the end of Illyrism to the creation of Yugoslavia', *Austrian History Yearbook*, vol. 15–16, 1979–80, pp. 3–33.

intellectuals, the following pages will critically examine the attitude of Serbian intellectuals towards the Yugoslavism in the years before and during the First World War. While the role played by the Serbian government and the army and the Yugoslav Committee during the First World War in the process of the creation of Yugoslavia has also been studied elsewhere[2], Yugoslavism of Serbia's intellectuals has received relatively little attention from scholars, both in the former-Yugoslavia and the West.[3]

The first part of this chapter provides an overview of the development of the Yugoslav idea among Serbian and other South Slav intellectuals and their understanding of Yugoslavism as a (mostly) cultural union of kindred, but separate nations. It will be argued that while the Yugoslav idea gained ground in the early twentieth century, Serb and other South Slav intellectuals did not foresee the Yugoslav unification in a near future. Only the Balkan Wars of 1912–13 and especially the First World War made the unification of Yugoslavia imminent. In the second part I briefly examine different views of the future state among Serbian intellectuals, who were mostly divided on centralists and federalists, although dualist (i.e. Serbo-Croat) and 'Greater Serbian' options were also discussed.

Cultural bonds

Encouraged by the results of their scholarly research into linguistics, ethnography, history and literature, intellectuals were the ablest promoters of the Yugoslav idea. Although their arguments often fell on deaf ears, particularly among the rural population, and were opposed by some intellectuals, it was difficult to dispute that Serbs, Croats and Slovenes had much in common, particularly culture- and language-wise.[4]

---

[2] See for instance Dimitrije Djordjević (ed.), *The Creation of Yugoslavia 1914–1918*, Santa Barbara, CA, and Oxford, 1980.

[3] An exception is Ljubinka Trgovčević, *Naučnici Srbije i stvaranje jugoslovenske države, 1914–1920*, Belgrade, 1986.

[4] Distinct features of the Slovene language, as opposed to the Serbo-Croat, were recognised. At the time Slav populations of Montenegro, present-day Macedonia and Muslims in Bosnia-Herzegovina were not regarded as separate from Serbs and Croats.

Virtually all leading Serbian intellectuals accepted Yugoslavism by the beginning of the twentieth century. A common Yugoslav identity was still to be created however, and they all, while emphasising similarities, recognised certain differences. The differences were not seen as incompatible or unbridgeable. Jovan Cvijić, a famous Serbian geographer and ethnologist, recognised a number of distinct cultures and traditions and different levels of national consciousness among the South Slavs, but argued that due to migrations these differences were becoming less pronounced, and that these peoples were in fact one nation.[5] Stojan Novaković, Serbia's leading historian and eminent politician, wrote in 1911 a futuristic essay entitled 'After One Hundred Years: Belgrade, 15 May 2011', predicting a united Yugoslav state in 2011. While accepting the national oneness, Novaković, like Cvijić, recognised that there existed differences between Serbs and Croats. He wrote that 'broadly observing, Serbs and Croats seemed to be the same people, but when looked at from a close proximity they were two peoples.'[6]

A well known historian of literature, Jovan Skerlić, believed that the Serbs and Croats were one people which spoke one language, but had parallel literatures, which arose from their different spiritual and cultural development[7] The leading Serbian linguist, Aleksandar Belić, argued that while there were clear differences between the Serbo-Croatian and Slovene, together they formed a linguistic whole.[8]

The pro-Yugoslav Croat politicians accepted these arguments. Frano Supilo, one of the leaders of the Croat-Serb Coalition and of the wartime Yugoslav Committee, stated in 1911:

Serbs and Croats are one people with two names. They may have two names, two religions, two traditions, two cultures... they may kill, they

[5] Jovan Cvijić, 'Antropogeografski problemi Balkanskoga poluostrva', *Govori i članci*, vol. 4, Belgrade, 1987; and *Jedinstvo Jugoslovena*, Niš, 1915 (the latter was published under the pseudonym Dinaricus).

[6] Stojan Novaković, 'Nakon sto godina. Beograd, 15. maja 2011', in Ivo Tartalja, *Beograd XXI veka. Iz starih utopija i antiutopija*, Belgrade, 1989, p. 255 (first published in: *Hrvatsko-srpski almanah za 1911*, Zagreb and Belgrade, 1911, pp. 9–19).

[7] Midhad Begić, *Jovan Skerlić-čovek i delo*, Belgrade, 1966, p. 328.

[8] Aleksandar Belić, *Srbija i jugoslovensko pitanje*, Niš, 1915.

may kiss each other, but in spite of that, from the ethnic point of view, Serbs and Croats are the same people, because they are the children of the same Slavic race and because they have the same national language.[9]

The argument about one nation with one language presented a problem in relation to the Slovenes who clearly spoke a different, if closely related language, and who insisted on preserving their linguistic individuality. A notable exception was the Slovenian ethnologist Niko Župánič, who lived and taught in Belgrade since 1907. During the war he joined the Yugoslav Committee, and wrote in 1915 that 'the true homeland is language, and for the one Yugoslav language, there can only be one, Yugoslav fatherland'.[10]

As for the Yugoslav literature, it was often understood to include both Serbian and Croatian literatures. Yugoslav intellectuals anticipated that over time these literatures would fully merge, although different dialects would be kept for local and popular needs. A notable supporter of this idea was the Bosnian Serb writer and philosopher Dimitrije Mitrinović.[11]

The issue of a unified language and a common script was often discussed in the years prior to the First World War. Skerlić proposed in an article written in 1913 for the *Srpski književni glasnik* (Serbian Literary Review) that the common language should be based on the *ekavski* dialect (spoken in Serbia), and written in Latin (used in Bosnia, Croatia and Slovenia; Serbs and Montenegrins wrote in Cyrillic).[12] Fearing a controversy, he suggested that his proposal is left to the judgement of time. In a survey conducted by the same paper, an agreement was reached concerning the script, but not concerning the dialect. Another survey, conducted by the Slovene journal *Veda* (Knowledge) in 1913, showed that Skerlić was right to be cautious: *Veda* asked its readers whether they would be willing to

---

[9] Frano Supilo, *Politički spisi*, Zagreb, 1970, pp. 401–2.

[10] Niko Župánič, *O Slovencima*, New York, 1916. The introduction to the pamphlet was written by one of the most prominent Yugoslav intellectuals and a member of the Yugoslav Committee, the famous sculptor Ivan Meštrović.

[11] Dragomir Gajević, *Jugoslovenstvo izmedju stvarnosti i iluzija. Ideja jugoslovenstva u književnosti početkom XX veka*, Belgrade, 1985, p. 54.

[12] Jovan Skerlić, 'Istočno ili južno narečje', *Srpski književni glasnik*, vol. XXXI/10, 16 Nov. 1913, pp. 756–70.

give up their language in the name of the Yugoslav cultural unity and all answers received were negative.[13]

Writers, poets and critics from Ljubljana, Zagreb and Belgrade increased their cooperation in the years prior to the war. *Srpska književna zadruga* (Serbian Literary Cooperative), a publishing house from Belgrade, published works by Croatian and Slovenian authors such as Stanko Vraz, Nikola Tommaseo, Petar Preradović, August Šenoa and Andrija Kašić Miočić. This institution assumed the role of *Matica*—a Slav cultural organization—establishing close ties with *Matica Slovenska* and *Matica Hrvatska* (Slovene and Croatian *Maticas*, respectively). It considered publishing books in both Cyrillic and Latin alphabets. A number of Croats and Slovenes, such as Ante Trumbić, Josip Smodlaka, Ivo Tartalja, Julije Gazari and Fran Ilešič (president of the *Matica Slovenska*), became members of this Serbian institution.[14]

Just before the war preparations began for publishing a Yugoslav Encyclopaedia jointly by the Yugoslav Academy of Arts and Sciences of Zagreb and the Serbian Royal Academy of Belgrade, but the outbreak of the war interfered with the initiative.[15] The idea was renewed by South Slav émigré intellectuals in 1917, who argued that the Encyclopaedia should describe 'the past, the present, [and] moral and material power of Serbs, Croats and Slovenes'.[16] As already argued, promoters of cultural unity respected diverse cultural traditions. An example was *Književni jug* (The Literary South), a journal established by younger, pro-Yugoslav Croats in Zagreb, in January 1918. Its editorial policy was to promote the Yugoslav unity while respecting linguistic and cultural differences.[17]

Four meetings of writers and journalists from Serbia, Croatia, Slovenia and Bulgaria were held between 1904 and 1906, with participation of some of the most renown names of these literatures:

---

[13] Gajević, op. cit., p. 60.

[14] Ljubinka Trgovčević, *Istorija Srpske književne zadruge*, Belgrade, 1992, p. 282.

[15] Dragoslav Janković, 'Jedna srpsko-hrvatska akcija 1910–1914. Pokušaj izdavanja Enciklopedije Jugoslavije', *Jugoslovenski istorijski časopis*, vol. 22, no. 3, Belgrade 1987, pp. 77–83.

[16] Ljubinka Trgovčević, 'Pokušaj pisanja Jugoslovenske enciklopedije tokom Prvog svetskog rata', *Istorijski časopis*, vol. 29–30, Belgrade 1983, pp. 513–25.

[17] Gajević, op. cit., p. 60.

Ivan Vazov, Ksaver Šandor Djalski, Vladimir Vidrić, Ante Tresić-Pavičić, Jovan Skerlić, Petar Kočić, Bora Stanković, Bogdan Popović, Ivan Hribar and others. At their Second Congress in Sofia in August 1906 they decided to work towards 'unification of South Slavs in the cultural field'.[18]

At the annual assembly of Croatian writers in February 1906, Ksaver Šandor Djalski stated that he had become 'aware of the necessity of cultural unity among Yugoslavs', because without that unity, the Croatian literature cannot develop successfully either. He stressed that in literary terms it is impossible to survive within narrow limits of either of the four South Slav literatures (Serbian, Croatian, Slovenian and Bulgarian). According to Djalski, it was time for Yugoslavs to unite spiritually and to create a unique culture and literature, which would enable them to assume their place among other developed European nations.[19]

Leading Croatian poet, Antun Gustav Matoš, stated that 'no matter how different, Serbian and Croatian political ways and interests, unity of literary language [independently of us] point to the unity of culture'.[20] Yet, his argument about inferior (Serbian) and superior (Croatian) cultures, meant that his views were somewhat self-contradictory.[21] The young Croatian poet Augustin-Tin Ujević, who lived in Belgrade prior to the First World War, was another adherent of the idea that Serbs and Croats were the same people (the so-called integral Yugoslavism), underlining their common ethnic origins and language. Religious differences could not endanger their instinctive feeling of unity. According to Ujević, 'Yugoslavia is not the consequence of an empty desire to change borders on geographic maps, but...an inner need of our souls, which craves for

---

[18] Ibid., p. 85.

[19] Ibid., p. 45.

[20] Anton Gustav Matoš, *Djela*, vol. 8, Zagreb, 1938, p. 93.

[21] For instance he once said that 'as long as our culture is anational, non-Croatian, Yugoslav—Serbian culture, though inferior, will continue to act and create confusion among us until our culture becomes national and free, like the Serbian culture'. Cited in Ivo Banac, *Nacionalno pitanje u Jugoslaviji. Porijeklo, povijest, politika*, Zagreb, 1988, p. 103. The part of the sentence referring to inferiority of the Serbian culture was omitted in the original English version of the book. See *The National Question in Yugoslavia: Origins, History, Politics*, Ithaca, NY, 1984, p. 100.

unification of our hitherto diverse cultural elements in harmony…
our tendencies are spiritual'.[22]

Bulgarian, Croatian, Serbian and Slovene painters who formed
Lada—the Association of South Slav Artists—also argued for a
'spiritual confederation'. In 1904 some 100 artists took part in the
Lada's first collective exhibition, held in Belgrade. According to its
Draft Statute adopted in Sofia the same year, *Lada*'s main aim was to
work on cultural preparation for a '[South Slav] spiritual confederation'. Before the First World War, *Lada* organized four large exhibitions in Belgrade, Sofia, Zagreb and again in Belgrade.[23]

The Yugoslav idea found particularly fertile ground among
South Slav students who started to increasingly frequently visit each
other and to organize various South Slav student and other societies. The 'Progressive Croatian Youth' saw as its only task paving the
way towards the unification of Serbs and Croats. A group known as
'Young Croatia', whose member was Ujević, also turned pro-Yugoslav.
The more radical groups went a step further: 'Our national thought
is Croato-Serbian, our nationality is Serbo-Croat'[24], were the words
from the program of the Zagreb student magazine *Val* (Wave). The
Belgrade journal *Slovenski jug* (Slavonic South) in its early stages
advocated cultural unification with recognition of all differences
and with a federal state as a common ideal.

Advocates of spiritual unity also emerged in Bosnia, including
young writers such as Ivo Andrić and Pero Slijepčević and a slightly
older poet Aleksa Šantić. When in 1908 Dimitrije Mitrinović became the editor of the Sarajevo journal *Bosanska vila*, many pro-
Yugoslav authors gathered around it and supported the idea that
joint publishing and education will contribute to knowing each
other better.[25]

Among the Slovenes, the idea of political unity prevailed over the
idea of cultural unification, because the Slovenes feared that their
language and culture would be suppressed by the dominant Serbo-
Croat one. The leading Slovene writer, Ivan Cankar, thought that

[22] Gajević, op. cit., p. 47.

[23] See *Suoyuzut na yuzhnoslavyanskite hoodozhnitsi 'Lada' (1904–1912)*, Sofia, 1994.

[24] Cited in Mirjana Gross, 'Nacionalne ideje studentske omladine u Hrvatskoj uoči
I svjetskog rata', *Historijski zbornik*, vol. 21–22, 1968–9, Zagreb, pp. 75–143, p. 106.

[25] See Predrag Palavestra, *Dogma i utopija Dimitrija Mitrinovića. Počeci srpske književne
avangarde*, Belgrade, 1977.

four distinct cultures already existed and that they need not be unified.[26] Advocating another extreme, some Bosnian intellectuals argued
that 'one national culture is impossible without a national society,
and a national society is impossible without a nation-state'.[27]

Towards political unification

To a majority of South Slav intellectuals at the beginning of the
twentieth century a political union seemed a distant future. They
believed that young nations naturally tended first to create their
own nation-states and thus unite their ethnic territory. Political
unification of all South Slavs was seen as a second step, a logical
conclusion of calls for cultural unity and the only way for smaller
peoples, such as the Yugoslavs, to jointly defend themselves from
domination of large neighbouring states, in their case the Habsburg
and Ottoman Empires. Thus for example, the Serbian leading literary critic, Bogdan Popović wrote to R.W. Seton-Watson that: 'Croats
and Slovenes are defending Serbian borders in the west, while we
are defending Croatian and Slovenian borders in the east'.[28] Stojan
Novaković expressed the same view when he wrote that 'the one
on the Timok river [in eastern Serbia] is defending his fellow coun-
trymen on the Adriatic'.[29]

Yugoslavism was not always clearly defined ideology, and was
often understood by its advocates as a long and evolutionary process. Its proponents among intellectuals believed that Yugoslavs
would first achieve kind of a loose alliance or a customs union. A
proper state would be the next step, but it was envisaged only in a
distant future. The above mentioned essay by Stojan Novaković,
who predicted a unified South Slav state in a 100 years, is an excellent example of such views.

The Balkan wars, which strongly resounded among Habsburg
South Slavs, had a particularly significant impact on the idea of

---

[26] See Ljudmila Bezlaj, 'Ivan Cankar und das nationale Programm der slowenischen
Sozialdemokratie', *Oesterreichische Osthefte*, vol. 25/1, Vienna 1983, pp. 56–94.
[27] Cited in Vladimir Dedijer, *Sarajevo 1914*, vol. 1, Belgrade, 1978, p. 277.
[28] Letter from London, 5 Oct. 1915, in French, *R.W. Seton-Watson i Jugoslaveni.
Korespodencija 1906–1941*, vol. 1, Zagreb and London, 1976, p. 247.
[29] Novaković, op. cit., p. 263.

Yugoslavism. Serbia became a model for many, raising hopes of other South Slavs that their liberation was becoming possible. The unification with Serbia seemed not only closer but also desirable, because it was hard to reasonably expect that the Habsburg South Slavs alone could succeed from Austria-Hungary. With the Croat-Serb Coalition dominating the *Sabor*, Serbian military victories were celebrated publicly in many cities.[30] After the Balkan wars, the Croatian poet Matoš noted the achievement of the 'synthesis of all our great political concepts: democracy and traditionalism, nationalism and Yugoslavism'.[31] Not even the final exclusion of Bulgaria from a future South Slav union, because of its war with Serbia over Macedonia, could spoil the enthusiasm felt among the Yugoslavism's advocates.

The Yugoslav idea, as its name suggests, was the idea of a South *Slav* unity. Even when reference was made to a 'Balkan federation', it included only the mentioned four South Slav peoples: Slovenes, Croats, Serbs and Bulgarians. Its aim was to gather in one state *Christian* South Slavs. This *Christian Slav* solidarity was seen as the only way of escaping from the Orient (i.e. the Ottoman past) and to integrate into Europe. Matoš wrote in 1912, during the Balkan Wars, that Balkan Slavs were exercising their old mission, 'namely, to defend the Cross from non-Christians, to defend Europe from Asia, [...], culture from barbarianism'.[32] A few years later, when the First World War already broke out, the Serb Orthodox theologian and bishop Nikolaj Velimirović wrote to Seton-Watson:

Serbia fought and died once for Christianity and Civilisation. It was 500 years ago [at the 1389 Battle of Kosovo]. Serbia is today again fighting and dying for Christianity and Civilisation ...Serbian soldiers are now also doing their sacred duty...She is not fighting in this moment for a Greater Serbia, but for a greater World, for a greater Humanity and Christianity.[33]

---

[30] Ivo Vukić Lupis wrote to R.W. Seton-Watson in September 1912 that 'last Sunday 10,000 people in Split and 6,000 in Šibenik with mayors and deputies paraded streets, sang and hailed Balkan armies and rulers'. In *R. W. Seton-Watson i Jugoslaveni*, op. cit., vol. 1, p. 118.

[31] Matoš, op. cit., vol. 11, Zagreb, 1940, p. 296.

[32] Cited in Viktor Novak, *Antologija jugoslovenske misli i narodnog jedinstva*, Belgrade, 1930, p. 647.

[33] Letter to R.W. Seton-Watson, 29 Oct. 1915, *R. W. Seton-Watson i Jugoslaveni*, op. cit., p. 251.

Yugoslavism clearly excluded non-Christian Balkan peoples— Slav or non-Slav—who lived together with the Christian South Slavs. How were than Muslim Slavs, mostly living in Bosnia and Herzegovina, to be integrated into a future Yugoslav state, which would inevitably incorporate the two provinces? The pro-Yugoslav Serb and Croat intellectuals believed that the solution was in the Muslim Slavs going back to their former ethnic origin (i.e. Serbo-Croat, or Serb or Croat). The non-Slav Muslims, such as Albanians, were largely left out of any serious discussion.

The war which broke out in the summer of 1914 caught the advocates of Yugoslavism by surprise. Nobody could envisage that Austria–Hungary would disintegrate, thus opening up the way for the Yugoslav unification. In Serbia in particular, but also in Croatia and Slovenia, the crucial question was how to preserve the 'national territory' against Austro-Hungarian, Italian and Bulgarian territorial claims. Croats and Slovenes had three options: autonomy within the Habsburg Empire, the independent states or unification with Serbs and creation of Yugoslavia. All three options had their supporters in political and intellectual circles, but by far the most important political force in Croatia before the war was the Croat-Serb Coalition, which advocated the unification with Serbia.

The unification with Serbia also had its supporters among intellectuals outside the Coalition, particularly among the Slovenes. At the beginning of October 1914, editor of the Trieste daily *Jugoslavija*, Andrej Munih, wrote with his colleague Leopold Lenard a memorandum to the Serbian Government, stating their wish for Slovenia's unification with Croats and Serbs.[34] Some of the advocates of unification among the Habsburg South Slavs were interned, such as Ivan Cankar, while others, such as Ivan Meštrović or Bogumil Vošnjak emigrated, continuing to work from abroad for the Yugoslav cause. Some intellectuals moved to Serbia before or at the beginning of the war. Niko Županič, for instance, wrote in December 1914 a pamphlet arguing that the Slovenes were an integral part of the trinominal Serbo-Croato-Slovene nation, advocating its political unification.

The situation in Serbia was different. Mounting pro-Yugoslav sentiment naturally required that unification be stressed as the

---

[34] Janko Pleterski, *Prvo opredeljenje Slovenaca za Jugoslaviju*, Belgrade, 1976, p. 48.

official war aim. When the war began, the Serbian government
assembled the country's leading intellectuals, asking them to prepare scholarly pamphlets which would support the government's
Yugoslav policies. Majority of these intellectuals had already been
'converted' to Yugoslavism before the war. Some of them were
dispatched to special propaganda missions to the Entente capitals.
Others wrote scholarly or propaganda pamphlets, some of which
will have a more lasting value. During the war Professor Pavle
Popović wrote a study on Yugoslav literature under that very same
title. Tihomir Djordjević with his ethnological and Jovan Radonić,
Jovan Tomić and Stanoje Stanojević with their historical essays,
helped spread the pro-Yugoslav propaganda. On the basis of his
research, the linguist Aleksandar Belić claimed that Serbian and
Croatian are the same language with dialectal differences. Perhaps
the greatest contribution was that of Jovan Cvijić through his studies
of geography and ethnographic characteristics of the South Slavs.[35]

Among Yugoslav intellectuals active outside Serbia the most
renown was the sculptor Ivan Meštrović, who already in 1911, at
the World Exposition in Rome exhibited in the Serbian pavilion.
In 1907 Meštrović began working on the *Vidovdan* (St. Vitus in
Latin, St. Guy in English) Temple, dedicated to the Kosovo battle of
1389. He considered Kosovo a symbol of all defeats in which the
Yugoslav peoples lost their medieval states. Kosovo was, according
to him, the Yugoslav 'sacred place', which best symbolised their
unity. At the opening of his exhibition in Victoria and Albert
Museum in London on 24 June 1915, Meštrović stated that all
Yugoslavs had their Kosovos: 'In the entire Yugoslav nation, every-
one shivers at the mention of Kosovo and feels deep sorrow at their
hearts'.[36] In 1917, a 'Yugoslav exhibition' was organized in the
Grafton Gallery in London, where works on Kosovo themes by
Croatian painters Mirko Rački ('The Jugović Mother', 'The Nine

[35] Pavle Popović, *Jugoslovenska književnost*, Cambridge, 1918; Jovan Cvijić, *La Péninsule balkanique. Géographie humaine*, Paris 1918; J. Cvijić, 'Unité etnique et nationale des Yougoslaves', *Scientia*, vol. 23, no. 74, June 1918, Bologna-Milan, pp. 455–67; Stanoje Stanojević, 'Šta hoće Srbija?', *Savremena pitanja*, no 1, Niš, 1915.
[36] Ivan Meštrović, 'The Opening Address at the London Exhibition of 1915', cited in Novak, op. cit., p. 718.

Jugović Brothers', 'The Kosovo Maiden' and 'Miloš Obilić) and Jozo Kljaković ('Boško Jugović') were exhibited.[37]

Serbian intellectuals kept close ties with mostly Croatian and Slovenian politicians and intellectuals gathered around the Yugoslav Committee, which operated in exile. They held several meetings across western Europe. But links were also held with those who had different ideas about the unification. Thus, Božidar Marković, the Serbian law professor, associate of the Yugoslav Committee and organiser of its Press Bureau met twice with Fran Barac, a Croatian religious scholar, in Switzerland, in the autumn of 1915 and 1917. Although Barac did not oppose unification, he believed that Croatia should first establish its own nation-state before it eventually enters a Yugoslavia.[38] Barac gathered a group of Croatian intellectuals who adopted the principle 'being our own, but making alliances with others'. In other words, they demanded resolution of the Croatian national question before wider alliances are made.[39]

Just like the politicians, the Yugoslav intellectuals did not always agree on the method of unification and form of future government. While most pro-unification intellectuals from Croatia and Slovenia opted for a kind of local autonomy for their lands, separate states or federation,[40] and were sceptical towards the ruling Serbian dynasty, most Serbs refused to renounce the Karadjordjević dynasty, and held different views in regard to the future form of government.

Most Serb intellectuals believed that the future Yugoslav government was to be modelled on the existing Serbian one.[41] The centralists argued that Yugoslavia should be a parliamentary monarchy. In their view, the monarchy would preserve the unity of the state, and most

---

[37] See Ljubinka Trgovčević, 'The Kosovo Myth in the First World War', *Sveti mesta na Balkanite*, Blagoevgrad, 1996, pp. 331–8; Branka Prpa-Jovanović, 'Rasprave o nacionalnom umjetničkom stilu', *Srbija 1917. godine*, Belgrade, 1988, pp. 255–63.

[38] Milada Paulova, *Jugoslavenski odbor (Povijest jugoslavenske emigracije za svjetskog rata od 1914–1918)*, Zagreb, 1925, pp. 351–8.

[39] Janko Pleterski, *Prvo opredeljenje Slovenaca za Jugoslaviju*, Belgrade, 1976, p. 98.

[40] For example, Slavist Matija Murko wrote in 1915 that it was necessary to first strengthen Croatia within its present borders, and only than unite all Croat lands. Cited in Pleterski, op. cit., p. 87. During the war a group of Yugoslav federalists published the journal *La Yougoslavie* which opposed both the Yugoslav Committee and the Serbian government.

[41] See Ljubinka Trgovčević, *Naučnici Srbije*, pp. 249–82.

that certain regions could be allowed was the British-style self-governance, because at the time it was considered to be the highest degree of self-governance within a unified (i.e. centralized) state. Slobodan Jovanović, a leading Serbian jurist and historian, was an advocate of this view. He claimed that Serbs had no affinity for decentralization and that federalism was 'alien to their political mentality'.[42] Another two Belgrade University Professors, the jurist Lazar Marković and historian Ljubomir Jovanović, both members of the ruling Radical Party, held similar views. Some monarchists and those who perceived Serbia as a South Slav Piedmont looked to Germany for a model. They argued that Serbia, just like Prussia, should have a degree of hegemony.

However, not all Serb intellectuals supported centralism. Stojan Novaković wondered in 1914 whether the future Yugoslav state should be 'a confederation of South Slav states, or perhaps a dual state, such as the Habsburg monarchy'.[43] He considered all options, and argued against a centralized state that would make Serbia's hegemony possible. Božidar Marković demanded in 1916 an equal community of three peoples and warned that 'the relationship now existing between Zagreb and [Buda]Pest must not be permitted to develop between Belgrade and Zagreb'.[44]

Although the Serbian federalists were prominent individuals, they were small in number and enjoyed little influence in real politics. The most prominent among them, in addition to Novaković and Božidar Marković were Jovan Cvijić, the philologist Ljubomir Stojanović and geologist Jovan Žujović; all three had occupied the post of the president of the Serbian Royal Academy and all three were prominent republicans. Stojanović argued that future Yugoslavia can only be a republic with an American-style presidential and parliamentary system. Cvijić, agreeing with him, wrote on 6 October 1918 that 'Yugoslavia must be a federation, with full equality of

---

[42] Archives of Slovenia, Ljubljana, Priv. A-LVIII: War diary of Bogumil Vošnjak, 26 June, 1917.

[43] Stoyan Novakovitch, 'Problèmes Yougo-Slaves', offprint from *La Revue de Paris*, 1 Sept. 1915, p. 27.

[44] Archiv Jugoslavije (Archives of Yugoslavia, Belgrade, hereafter AJ) Collection of papers of Jovan Jovanović, 80–37–336, B. Marković to J. Jovanović, 15/28 Oct. 1916.

certain regions—the United States of Yugoslavia'.[45] According to this group, the federation should consist of voluntarily united independent states, which would transfer some of their powers to a central federal authority. Although Slobodan Jovanović opposed the argument from a legal point of view, pointing out that Yugoslavia could not be formed in such a way because the only formerly independent states were Serbia and Montenegro, supporters of federation nevertheless thought that former historical provinces (Croatia, Slovenia, Dalmatia, Bosnia), could form units of a future federal state. The Serbian federalists argued that four most important state functions—foreign policy, army, monetary system and transportation—should be transferred to the federal state, while provincial governments would assume all other powers. Similar ideas were held by intellectuals gathered around the short-lived Yugoslav Democratic League, which under Cvijić's presidency in 1919, gathered many intellectuals from the territory of then already united Kingdom.

The American model of the federal state was closest to Serbian republicans, while the German model of a federal state and a unitary state appealed to monarchists. All, however, often used the example of the Swiss confederation as a proof that living together was possible. A dual state made up of Serbia and Croatia was mentioned only in autumn 1914 when a proposal was put forward that Serbian king be crowned with the Croatian crown, too, but it was soon abandoned due to negative experiences of the Habsburg monarchy.[46]

Finally, the so-called 'Greater Serbia' project had not been seriously considered in intellectual circles, although there were those who feared that in a large Yugoslav state, the Serbs would become a minority, that their name and statehood would be lost, and that they would be outvoted. Jovan Žujović stated these fears in the spring 1915, but evetually he came to support the creation of a Yugoslav federal republic.[47]

---

[45] Cited in Ljubinka Trgovčević, 'Jovan Cvijić i Ljubomir Stojanović o budućoj jugoslovenskoj državi. Prepiska iz 1917. i 1918. godine', *Godišnjak grada Beograda*, vol. 37, Belgrade, 1990, pp. 193–205, p. 202.

[46] AJ, Collection of papers of Jovan Jovanović, 80–4–574: minute of B. Marković, 27 Oct. 1914. See also Andrej Mitrović, *Srbija u Prvom svetskom ratu*, Belgrade 1984, pp. 148–50.

[47] Trgovčević, *Naučnici Srbije*, pp. 260–1.

The Yugoslav idea was among the integrating national ideas that marked Europe's nineteenth century. Emerging at the time when other nation states were in the process of creation, it was understood in intellectual circles as an attempt to create a united South Slav state that would rest on 'two corner-stones: freedom and equality'.[48] Yugoslavism opposed the outdated concept of a multiethnic state based on historical rights. Instead, its model was the liberal nation-state. Stojan Novaković perhaps best elaborated this view in late 1914:

Yugoslavism is the product of modern democratic processes, because the new state is not going to be based on the conqueror's rights of medieval miniature states, nor on force, nor on any inherited or historical right, but [...] the sole basis for linking [will be] national rights.[49]

Novaković, Cvijić and others who shared their Yugoslavism, believed that modern technologies would help connect diverse geographic territories populated by the South Slavs. They emphasized geostrategic advantages of a large state and benefits of cultural interaction. Except for the revolutionary pro-Yugoslav youth, very few thought that the South Slavs would melt completely, especially in a near future. Therefore, local differences were to be respected. However, the fact that the three 'founding nations', Slovenes, Croats and Serbs were already formed, while the process of national development was in infant stages among other peoples living on the same territory, had not been given due consideration.

The Yugoslav state, established on 1 December 1918, failed to fulfill all the expectations of those who advocated its creation. Perhaps in 1918 Yugoslavia was premature because even the most educated of the Serbs, Croats and Slovenes did not know each other very well. It was believed that over time the three 'tribes' would get to know each other better, that their linguistic and cultural closeness would unify them, while historical and religious divisions would be overcome. Those who argued this are today often criticized for being too idealistic. Yet the Yugoslav state was nevertheless formed, and in spite of brutal temptations brought about by the

[48] Novaković, *Nakon sto godina*, p. 258.
[49] Novaković, 'Problèmes Yougo-Slaves', op. cit., p. 25.

Second World War, it survived for more than seven decades. Those who above all desired cultural cooperation were perhaps idealistic, but they also ultimately turned out to be right—despite the tragic wars of the last decade the South Slav 'cultural closeness' remains a reality, as well as a need for those who lived and continue to live in what used to be Yugoslavia.

IVAN MEŠTROVIĆ, IVO ANDRIĆ AND THE SYNTHETIC YUGOSLAV CULTURE OF THE INTERWAR PERIOD

Andrew B. Wachtel

When the unified Kingdom of the Serbs, Croats, and Slovenes was created in the immediate aftermath of the First World War, even the most optimistic adherents of the Yugoslav idea would have admitted that no Yugoslav nation yet existed to live in the new Yugoslav state. But they recognized that, as had been the case in Italy, the new state would thrive only if élite-led efforts to create a unified Yugoslav nation succeeded.[1] Questions almost immediately arose, however, regarding what sort of nation the Yugoslavs could or should be and what approaches should be tried to convince them that they did indeed belong to a single nation however defined.

Difficulties faced by those who wished for a unified national culture, which ultimately proved insurmountable, have been treated extensively elsewhere, and it is not the aim of this chapter to analyze them again. These difficulties included the historical, cultural, and religious differences among the majority Slavs of the Kingdom, the presence of large groups of non-Slavic Yugoslav citizens, the difficult internal and external political situation of the country in the inter-war years, and the paucity of resources for implementing any unifying cultural schemes.[2] If, however, we focus not on the

---

[1] As one prescient observer put it a few months after the new state was created: 'The basic problem of our revolution is not state-building, social or economic development. It is—for on this rests the possibility of a satisfactory answer to the aforementioned questions—to a much greater extent national and cultural.' Branko Tkalčić, 'Srednja škola kao rasadište jugoslavenske misli', *Jugoslavenska njiva*, year III, no. 17, 26 Apr., 1919, pp. 263–4.

[2] The classic treatment of the political problems in the formative period of inter-war

obstacles to creating a unified Yugoslav culture but rather to the extant models for cultural unification in inter-war Yugoslavia, we discover that they can be broken down into three groups which coexisted in the inter-war period: 1) an existing culture (most likely Serbian as Serbs were the largest and most politically powerful group in the country) could be chosen as the standard; 2) a new culture could be created that would combine elements of the existing 'tribal' cultures (i.e., Serbian, Croatian, Slovene, and possibly Bosnian Muslim as well); 3) a new culture not based on existing tribal cultures could be created.

In this essay devoted to the sculptor Ivan Meštrović (1883–1962) and the writer Ivo Andrić (1892–1975) I will concentrate on the second model, for these two figures were, in my view, its central partisans. Before focusing our attention on them, however, it is necessary to say a few words about the other potential models. The idea that South Slavs would become culturally unified by assimilating to the culture of one of the groups (Serbian culture) was explicitly or implicitly the central model for nineteenth century Yugoslav thinkers. It underlies, for example, the decision by the Croatian 'Illyrians' to adopt as their standard the štokavian dialect of Croatian (the dialect closest to the Serbian standard) despite the fact that most of them spoke kajkavian.[3] It also helped incline the greatest of the Illyrian writers, Ivan Mažuranić, to choose an episode from Montenegrin rather than Croatian history for his verse epic *The Death of Smail-Aga Čengić*. This romantic vision of a Yugoslav national culture based primarily on Serbian culture had, however, more or less played itself out by around 1900. In the inter-war years, it was difficult to find any strong backers of this approach, even in the ranks of the Radical Party which has generally been accused of attempting

---

Yugoslavia is Ivo Banac, *The National Question in Yugoslavia: Origins, History, Politics*, Ithaca, NY, 1984. For a full treatment of cultural problems of the period, see Ljubodrag Dimić, *Kulturna politika Kraljevine Jugoslavije, 1918–1941*, 3 vols, Belgrade, 1996–7.

[3] For a survey of efforts to bring Serbian and Croatian closer together in the second half of the nineteenth century, see Peter Herrity, 'The Problematic Nature of the Standardisation of the Serbo-Croatian Literary Language in the Second Half of the Nineteenth Century' in Ranko Bugarski and Celia Hawkesworth (eds), *Language Planning in Yugoslavia*, Columbus, OH, 1992, pp. 162–75.

to impose a Serbian political model on the Kingdom.[4] Still, it existed in the background, and could surface particularly when political backers of a strong Yugoslavia turned to nineteenth-century models for inspiration. Such was the case, for example, in some of the rhetoric surrounding the 1925 celebrations in honour of the great Montenegrin writer Prince-Bishop Petar Petrović Njegoš.[5]

The other potential cultural model to be mentioned briefly is a Yugoslav national culture that would ignore existing 'tribal' affiliations and create a supranational Yugoslav culture to supersede them. In the thought of cultural figures, two different versions of this model can be discerned. One was to align Yugoslav culture with West European culture by creating a true modernist literature in the Serbo-Croatian or Slovenian language. Any number of inter-war writers could be examined in this context, including the Croatians Tin Ujević and Antun Šimić, the Serbians Miloš Crnjanski and Marko Ristić, or the Slovenian Oton Župančič. A different path to the creation of a supranational Yugoslav culture lay through a turn to the East, whereby the 1930s Soviet cultural propaganda promised a path to universal proletarian culture through an art that would be 'national in form, socialist in content.' And although universalist Socialist Realism as a model for Yugoslav culture did not achieve hegemony until after the Second World War (and then only for a very limited time), writers such as the Croatian August Cesarec provided inter-war models.

For Ivan Meštrović and Ivo Andrić, however, as for the majority of Yugoslav artists and intellectuals in the first decade after the First World War, neither Serbianization nor supranational culture was attractive. Rather, they worked within the dominant cultural paradigm of this period: a synthetic Yugoslav culture that would join the existing tribal cultures into a new and dynamic national culture

[4] As Dimić puts it: 'The political parties that participated in the government [in inter-war Yugoslavia] did not as a rule have well-developed party programmes in the realm of cultural politics. This question was of absolutely no interest to the Radicals.' Dimić, op. cit., vol. 3, p. 419.
[5] For a discussion of these celebrations, see Andrew Wachtel, *Making a Nation, Breaking a Nation: Literature and Cultural Politics in Yugoslavia*, Stanford, CA, 1998, pp. 105–6.

suitable for the new state. Ljubodrag Dimić describes the thinking behind this goal as follows:

At the foundation of modernizing ideas relating to the political, national, and cultural unity and integration of the Yugoslav peoples that obsessed writers, artists, scholars, and the intellectual élite was most often a fear of foreign assimilating tendencies (Germanization, Hungarianization, Italianization), religious and national schisms, particularization and the tradition-bound mindset of...the Balkan cultures...Tending toward romanticism, utopianism, and insufficiently rational thinking in which artistic fiction and reality were mixed, they dreamed of a Yugoslav culture and a Yugoslav state that would be a kind of 'absolute ideal,' more universal than national, confessional, or political...capable of enveloping, pacifying, and synthesizing all that was best in Serbian, Croatian, and Slovenian culture.[6]

And although support for this model waned gradually in the inter-war period, both Meštrović and Andrić remained faithful to it.[7]

Ivan Meštrović and Ivo Andrić shared a number of key biographical details that help to explain their devotion to a synthetic vision of Yugoslav culture. Both were born in Roman Catholic families and thus by present-day standards could have identified themselves exclusively as Croats. But neither came from Zagreb, the centre of Croatian intellectual life. Instead, both were strongly connected to Bosnia—Meštrović because his father's family hailed from Bosnia originally, and Andrić because he was born and raised in the Bosnian towns of Travnik and Višegrad, respectively. That is, both artists were aware from childhood of the variety of peoples who lived on the territory of what was later to become Yugoslavia. Both matured in the waning years of Austro-Hungarian rule, the period when the synthetic model of Yugoslav culture was developed, and the period in which it captured the imagination of a good portion of young South Slav intellectuals.

[6] Dimić, op. cit., vol. 3, p. 411.

[7] I will not discuss the post-war period in this essay. However, it should be recalled that Andrić, who chose to stay in Yugoslavia during and after the war, became the most visible artistic spokesperson for Yugoslavism in Tito's Yugoslavia. Meštrović, who emigrated to Western Europe during the war and to the US in 1947, more or less dropped out of Yugoslav post-war discourse. For a discussion of Andrić's post-war work in the context of Yugoslav cultural debates, see my *Making a Nation, Breaking a Nation*, pp. 156–72.

In the case of Meštrović, this cultural ideology was expressed in artistic work early on (the famous 'Kosovo Temple' to be discussed below), while for the somewhat younger Andrić it first found an outlet in the political arena. Their cosmopolitan outlook was furthered by educational experiences in Vienna, the cultural capital of the polyglot Austro-Hungarian Empire. In the inter-war period, both Meštrović and Andrić were closely connected with the royal government. Meštrović accepted subsidies and a raft of commissions from the government and made no secret of his admiration for King Alexander, while Andrić served in the diplomatic corps, eventually rising to very high positions in the immediate pre-war period. Most importantly, both men embodied a synthetic Yugoslav vision in their artistic work, thereby providing powerful examples of cultural Yugoslavism for their contemporaries.

Meštrović burst onto the Yugoslav and the international scene with his controversial exhibition at the Rome Exposition of 1911. He had been expected to show his work at the pavilion of the Habsburg Empire, but refused to do so unless a separate pavilion was provided for South Slav artists. When this was denied, he and his compatriots arranged to exhibit their work at the Serbian pavilion.[8] The mere fact of a Viennese-trained, well-respected artist turning his back on central European culture to throw in his lot with the Serbian 'barbarians' was sensational enough. But the work he exhibited in Rome, fragments from his so-called Kosovo or St Vitus Day temple (it was on St Vitus Day 1389 that the Battle of Kosovo was fought), was even more sensational. From the outside the temple had a monumental, classical feel, although it was embellished by such typical secessionist touches as caryatids and sphinxes. In form it combined Catholic and Orthodox elements (it was built on the pattern of a Roman Catholic cross, but the dome looked like that of a Byzantine rather than a Catholic church). Inside were displayed Meštrović's figures inspired by the heroes of South Slav oral poetry. Even today these sculptures retain their monumental presence and, in the case of the male figures, the pent-up strength that seems about to spring from sculpture directly into life.

---

[8] For details on the controversy surrounding the choice of a site for Meštrović's work at the 1911 exposition, see Milan Marjanović, 'Genij jugoslovenstva Ivan Meštrović i njegov hram,' *Jugoslovenska biblioteka*, no. 1, New York, 1915, pp. 115–16.

As it happened, sculpture was an ideal choice for the expression of the new Yugoslav synthesis. First, sculpture was practically unknown in Serbian culture, which, like other Orthodox traditions, permits painted icons but discourages three-dimensional figures. It had, however, been quite well developed in the Dalmatian cities, especially on the exteriors of the region's Venetian inspired churches. As a result, when he chose to carve the figures of epic poetry, Meštrović automatically achieved a bold melding of cultural traditions. Furthermore, figurative sculpture is much more easily accessible than high literature, and it does not depend on translation to reach an international audience.

For many of Meštrović's contemporaries, these figures also symbolized the entire miraculous spirit of the Yugoslav awakening. As one contemporary put it:

Meštrović's temple has deep national significance. In this sense it towers above all previously existing artistic monuments from ancient times until today. What the pyramids were for the Egyptians, pagodas for the Indians, the Parthenon for the Greeks, the Coliseum for the Romans, what the Gothic cathedrals were for the Middle Ages, the luxurious palaces for the Renaissance, what the National Gallery is for today's Englishmen and the Louvre is for the French, that is what Meštrović's temple is for the Southern Slavs. But it must be pointed out: not a single one of the monuments mentioned above is in as close touch with the national soul as the Temple is with our soul, the Yugoslav soul.[9]

Meštrović himself made no secret of his Yugoslav views. In an article in the Zagreb journal *Nova Evropa* (New Europe), he explained that he wanted to provide 'a single synthesis of the popular [South Slav] folk ideals and their development', and to express 'in stone and architecture how deeply rooted in all of us are the memories of the greatest moments and most significant events of our history'. He argued that the temple 'cannot be dedicated to any one confession or separate sect, rather to all of them together, to all who believe in the ideals expressed in our folk songs.'[10]

[9] Kosta Strajnić, 'Umetnost Meštrovića.' *Savremenik*, vol. 10, 3–4 Apr. 1915, pp. 115–16.
[10] Ivan Meštrović, 'Zamisao Kosovskog hrama,' *Nova Evropa*, book 1, no. 13, 1920, pp. 447–8.

While Meštrović was embodying a synthetic Yugoslav ideology in his early sculpture, Andrić was still a schoolboy in Sarajevo. At that time, however, Andrić founded and presided over the 'Sarajevo Secret Youth Organization'. The organization had links with other similar youth societies in Belgrade which worked at 'spreading and strengthening the idea of freedom and unity with Serbia among Serbian and Croatian youth.'[11]

Andrić's earliest literary work, in the form of lyric poetry, reflects a personal and intimate point of view rather than an overt expression of a Yugoslav point of view. Nevertheless, his connection to groups agitating for Yugoslav union led to his arrest almost immediately after Austria-Hungary's 1914 declaration of war on Serbia.[12] The experience of being a prisoner and internee between 1914 and 1917 had a profound affect on the tubercular, hyper-sensitive young writer. His first substantial work, a series of prose poems entitled *Ex Ponto* (published in the summer of 1918) can in fact be seen as a kind of extended meditation on the theme of loneliness, exile, and suffering. Perhaps not surprisingly, early critics of Andrić's work, while impressed by his immense talent, hoped that he would produce a work more in keeping with the spirit of the times. In his 1921 review of *Ex Ponto*, for example, the critic Milan Bogdanović noted Andrić's works produced thus far did not live up to his talent:

Fragments of this type, no matter how much they show a fine psychological and lyric sense and no matter how perfect they are from a stylistic point of view, cannot have the value of a work of broad conception and boldness…Ivo Andrić is a much bigger talent [than this] and the novel and perhaps the drama awaits him.[13]

And indeed, the synthetic 'Yugoslav' direction in Andrić's work would only be fully realized in the novels he wrote during the Second World War (particularly *The Bridge on the Drina* and *A Bosnian*

---

[11] Vanita Singh Mukerjee, *Ivo Andrić: A Critical Biography*, Jefferson, NC, 1990, p. 7.

[12] The arrest was, however, motivated at least in part because his poem 'Prva proljetna pjesma' ('First Spring Poem', published in the Zagreb journal *Vihor* in 1914), was interpreted by the authorities as a call for a Serbian invasion of Habsburg territory. See the notes to Ivo Andrić, *Sabrana djela*, Sarajevo, 1984, vol. 11, p. 282.

[13] Branko Milanović (ed.), *Kritičari o Ivi Andriću*, Sarajevo, 1981, p. 42.

Chronicle, both published after the war, in the second Yugoslavia). But the direction his talent would take was already evident in his first published short story 'Djerzelez u hanu' (Djerzelez at the Inn). The story appeared in a remarkable journal, *Književni jug* (Literary South), which began publication in January 1918 and continued until the end of 1919. Andrić was a member of the four-man editorial board of the journal, whose contributors included practically every major writer from Serbia, Croatia and Slovenia. Each issue published literary work in Serbo-Croatian and Slovenian, and employed both the Cyrillic and Latin alphabets. The first issue, published on 1 January 1918, left no doubt that the central goal of the editorial board was to create a synthetic Yugoslav culture. It opens with a photograph of a sculpture by Meštrović. The lead article is entitled 'Zadaci vremena' ('Tasks of the Time') and sets out the basic objectives of the publication:

We now see hundreds of practical tasks: the question of a unified literature, of a unified language with a single literary language and orthography... If we get to know one another through the popularization of Slovenian writing among the Croats and Serbs and vice versa; if we accustom our people truly to look at our literature as a single whole; all of that would be a great deed. In this way, greater assimilation would occur all by itself, as would the purification of our language and our pride in a great literature.[14]

Andrić's story (which was published in August 1918) involves the eponymous hero, a legendary figure drawn from Yugoslav Muslim culture, who is known more for his strength than for his intelligence and whose impulsive personality is reminiscent of that of the South Slavic folk hero Marko Kraljević. In this story, Djerzelez is made a fool of by a number of travelers at the inn, who convince him first of all that a beautiful Venetian woman guest is available for the taking, and who devise a sham footrace to demonstrate who among them is most worthy of her. To the delight of all, Djerzelez runs like a madman, his lust and desire to perform a heroic feat having blinded him completely to the reality of the situation. At the end of the story, a dejected Djerzelez is compelled to saddle his own horse and flee the site of his humiliation. For our purposes, the story

[14] *Književni jug*, vol. I, no. 1, 1 Jan. 1918, pp. 3–4.

is significant because in it Andrić extends the range of subject matter considered as part of an implied Yugoslav world, depicting an imagined Yugoslavia far broader than the Serbian Orthodox/Croatian Catholic axis of Meštrović's work. The story takes place at an inn near the Bosnian town of Višegrad, where a broad cross section of individuals has gathered:

> Suljaga Dizdar with three tax collectors traveling on business; two Franciscan friars from Kreševo who were going to Istanbul regarding some kind of suit; an Orthodox monk; three Venetians from Sarajevo with a young and beautiful woman. It was said that they were ambassadors from Venice traveling overland to the Porte—they were carrying a letter from the Pasha in Sarajevo and were accompanied by a bodyguard, but they held themselves aloof and looked dignified and suspicious. There was a trader from Serbia with his son, a tall quiet youth with a sickly red face...[15]

To be sure, Andrić ultimately depicts his Muslim hero ironically, but in placing him at the center of his story he opens for consideration the question of how the Muslim heritage can be incorporated into the Yugoslav synthesis.[16]

Through the 1920s and 1930s, as many intellectuals and writers gradually abandoned the synthetic Yugoslav model in favour either of supranational Yugoslav models or of separatist Croatian or Slovenian cultural nationalism, both Meštrović and Andrić continued to produce work in the synthetic Yugoslav spirit. Meštrović was the more visible of the two on the cultural scene, receiving a series of important commissions, private, clerical, and public. The journal *Nova Evropa* functioned as a kind of unofficial propaganda machine for Meštrović, devoting numerous articles and one entire issue (15 August, 1933, vol. 26, no. 8) to the sculptor and his work.

The central theme of the majority of inter-war writing on Meštrović was his role precisely as a synthetic Yugoslav. Thus, in a

---

[15] *Književni jug*, vol. II, no. 3, 1 Aug., 1918, p. 83.

[16] The question of Andrić's attitude to Muslims (some Bosnian critics accused him of harboring an anti-Muslim bias) and therefore the worthiness of his work to be a symbol for Yugoslav cultural synthesis began to be raised in the 1960s. For a consideration of this topic that convincingly refutes this claim and illustrates the cultural thinking underlying it, see Bogdan Rakić, 'The Proof is in the Pudding: Ivo Andrić and His Bosniak Critics', *Serbian Studies*, vol. 14, no. 1, 2000, pp. 81–91.

brochure produced in Split in 1929 and devoted to Meštrović's monument to Gregory, the Bishop of Nin, we read:

> From time immemorial Meštrović has been a penetrating prophet of the needs and yearnings of his people and his time...That is why, after the collapse [of the Austro-Hungarian Empire], Meštrović erected a statue in Zagreb to Strossmayer, the champion of Yugoslav solidarity and union alongside the Monument to Victory designated for Belgrade. That is why he gave Split monuments to Marulić, a testimonial to the cultural work of the Croatian nation during the period of Venetian domination, and to Gregory of Nin, a defender of the nation's interests in the even earlier period of the middle ages. The crowning glory of Meštrović's work will be the 'King's Stone,' on the sea coast in Split. This work will, in a significant synthesis, depict on one side the face of King Tomislav and on the other King Petar [Karadjordjević] the Liberator.[17]

This last statue, which as far as I am aware never made it past the idea stage, would indeed have stood as a visual symbol of the culture that Yugoslav synthesizers dreamed of. A single stone, inscribed with a medieval Croatian king and the last Serbian and first Yugoslav king would have linked the two nations into an indivisible whole while simultaneously emphasizing their distinct histories.

Insofar as one wishes to consider a 'Yugoslav' monument that Meštrović actually executed, one should examine 'Tomb of the Unknown Soldier' at Avala, some ten miles outside of Belgrade. Benedict Anderson has of course noted the central importance of cenotaphs and tombs to Unknown Soldiers in nationalist imaginings.[18] By commissioning a tomb to the unknown Yugoslav soldier in the 1930s, King Alexander was clearly trying to cash in on the unificatory symbolism that such a monument was supposed to provide.[19] And

---

[17] Ljubo Karaman, *O Grguru Ninskomu i Meštrovićevu spomeniku u Splitu*, Split, 1929, pp. 24–5.

[18] Benedict Anderson, *Imagined Communities: Reflections on the Origins and Spread of Nationalism*, London, 1983, p. 17.

[19] Meštrović recollected events surrounding this commission in his usual off-hand style: 'In the Fall the King asked me to come and see him...He told me that in imitation of the French everyone had begun paying homage to the graves of "unknown soldiers" and that here all foreign delegations were going to the base of Avala, where some peasants had erected an ugly headstone and given it the name "tomb of the unknown soldier" because they had found there the skeleton

what better way for a king from the pre-war Serbia's dynasty to show his Yugoslav feeling than by asking the Croatian sculptor Meštrović to plan and build it?

In its very layout, the tomb was meant to symbolize Yugoslavia's role as mediator between east and west, for the monumental portals, supported by gigantic caryatids clad in folk clothing from various regions of Yugoslavia, face in those directions. The diversity of the caryatids' origins not only recalls the variety of the peoples of Yugoslavia but implies that all have contributed their part to the unity that is symbolized by the presence of a single unknown soldier (rather than one from each part of the country). In its inclusion of avowedly non-Serbian figures, the tomb indicates that Meštrović's multicultural conception of Yugoslav culture had evolved since the days of the Kosovo temple. Whereas then traditionally Serbian themes were rendered in western form, now non-Serbian material was incorporated on the thematic level as well. At the same time, the monumental figures also clearly invoke the caryatids Meštrović had carved for the Kosovo temple. In both cases, a monument to male heroism is supported and introduced by stiff, gigantic female figures which are given the task of expressing what Ivo Vojnović called 'the dumb petrified terror of century upon century.'[20]

There were, of course, multiple reasons for Meštrović to retain his belief in multi-cultural Yugoslav synthesis through the entire inter-war period. No doubt financial self interest played some role. As Dimić points out, Meštrović was best off of all Yugoslav visual artists. His yearly salary, 'arranged through the gradual purchase of his so-called Kosovo cycle, amounted to some 36,000 francs per year (82,500 dinars—equivalent to a ministerial salary)', and the state also regularly paid 'for the organization of his exhibitions (for example, expenses relating to his exhibition in America in 1929 cost the state around 250,000 dinars and $40,000).'[21] At the same

---

of some buried soldier wearing Serbian boots. He was embarrassed by this poor grave and, what is more, he owed a debt to fallen warriors. So he asked me to make a plan for a suitable tomb for an unknown soldier.' *Spomini*, Ljubljana, 1971, pp. 293–4.

[20] Ivo Vojnović, 'Chords' in Milan Ćurčin (ed.), *Ivan Meštrović: A Monograph*, London, 1919, pp. 25–6.

[21] Dimić, op. cit., vol. 3, p. 296.

time, Meštrović's personal friendship with King Alexander must also have played a role. Finally, his own artistic temperament, his family background, and the history of the development of his own oeuvre must have been significant as well.

Some of these same reasons can be adduced when considering Ivo Andrić's decision to throw in his lot with the Yugoslav diplomatic corps and to continue his literary work in a synthetic Yugoslav mode. Again, there is no doubt that self interest was involved to a certain extent. The diplomatic corps was a popular workplace for any number of writers in inter-war Yugoslavia, presumably because the nature of the work allowed time for one's own writing, particularly if one occupied a relatively low-level position in one of the sleepier capitals of Europe. According to Dimić, some 5 per cent of the diplomats, ambassadors, senators and ministers in inter-war Yugoslavia were writers, including such important figures as Jovan Dučić, Milan Rakić, Rastko Petrović and Isidor Cankar.[22] In effect, diplomatic positions functioned as sinecures for writers in a country that had few other resources to support financially its cultural figures. Andrić, however, was in career terms one of the most successful of the writer/diplomats, rising to the rank of Yugoslav minister plenipotentiary and extraordinary in Berlin, where he presented his credentials to Hitler in April 1939.[23]

In part because he was not as consistently in Yugoslavia, in part because he did not have the time to devote to literary activity, and in part because he did not have the propaganda machine that *Nova Evropa* was for Meštrović, Andrić's Yugoslav-oriented literary work was not as visible as it might otherwise have been in the inter-war period (and as it would become in the aftermath of the Second World War when he took Meštrović's place as Yugoslavia's principal artist). Nevertheless, literary criticism of the inter-war period never failed to identify Andrić as a Yugoslav writer of synthetic bent. Thus, Velimir Živojinović concludes his lengthy 1931 review of Andrić's work as a short story writer as follows:

[In Andrić's work] Orthodox priests, Catholic friars, Turks and Gypsies of the *kasaba*...are all subject to the same law. And because that law is a

[22] Ibid., p. 291.
[23] Mukerjee, op. cit., p. 35.

general one with deep roots, it is not tied to the narrow territory on which the events in the stories play themselves out. Rather it holds for our entire race (at least for the Dinaric strain). Thus Andrić's stories escape from a narrow regional orbit and take on a national character.[24]

Not surprisingly, as Yugoslavism in general and synthetic Yugoslavism in particular lost support in the course of the inter-war period, both Meštrović and Andrić came under attack for their positions. Again, because Meštrović was the more public figure in this period, controversy surrounding him was more overt. A feel for the difficulty of Meštrović's position by the late 1930s can be derived from the words of the sculptor's friend and supporter, Milan Ćurčin, the editor of *Nova Evropa*. In an article devoted to complaints about Meštrović's 'Crucifixion', Ćurčin expresses amazement that while in the advanced countries of western Europe, Meštrović is acclaimed both as a great artist and a prophet of Yugoslavism, Yugoslavs themselves are unhappy:

People from Zagreb or central Croatia, even the best educated, cannot forgive Meštrović for his early works in which he celebrates in stone 'Serbian Kosovo' and Serbian heroes…But, on the other hand, Serbians from Serbia won't accept Meštrović's folk heroes and victors in bronze as their own—they aren't wearing [Serbian] soldiers' hats and peasant shoes![25]

Although Andrić was more or less shielded from such public controversy, he certainly recognized the difficulty of his in-between position by this period as well. He made this point in a 1934 speech devoted to Prince Bishop Njegoš. Here Andrić concentrated on his great predecessor's personal situation, seeing him as a synecdoche for Yugoslavia as a whole:

The tragedy of this struggle was sharpened and deepened by the unavoidable fratricidal battles that our difficult history has frequently provided. The tragedy was all the greater for Njegoš in that from his high point of view, like all the great and light-bearing souls of our history, he could capture at a glance the totality of our nation, without differentiating between belief or tribe.[26]

[24] Milanović (ed.), op. cit., p. 87.
[25] Milan Ćurčin, 'Pred Meštrovićevim "Hristom"', *Nova Evropa*, vol. 31, no. 2, 1938, p. 37.
[26] Andrić, *Sabrana djela*, vol. 13, p. 16.

Andrić's biographer notes that this speech is closely related to a contemporaneous essay devoted to Simon Bolivar: 'Both Bolivar and Njegoš waged their wars against the political and human powers of darkness, to lead their people "to civilization and a more dignified, better life." Disillusioned with their own people and thwarted in the exertion of all their energies in these unequal battles, there were no boats to take them over the seas to realms of repose'[27] The autobiographical overtones in these essays would be hard to miss. Andrić, shuttled from one European capital to another by the foreign ministry of a failing state, must certainly have compared his own political and literary efforts with those of his predecessors.

Fortunately, the works of great artists outlive the political and cultural ideology that helped to birth them. Thus, although the idea of a synthetic Yugoslav culture has fallen into disrepute and oblivion, Meštrović's sculptures and Andrić's literary work still retain the power to move viewers and readers. And, considering what has transpired since different cultural models have come to dominate the territory that was Yugoslavia, it might well be argued that their cultural model, problematic as it may have been, had the potential to create more stability and peace in the region than did the separatist nationalist models that eventually won out.

[27] Mukerjee, op. cit., p. 33.

YUGOSLAVISM'S LAST STAND: A UTOPIA OF SERB INTELLECTUALS

Aleksandar Pavković

The Yugoslav Communist Party—officially the League of Communists of Yugoslavia—remained, until its effective dissolution in January 1990, committed to the Yugoslav federation as a common South Slav state.[1] However, by 1980, the year when its leader Josip Broz Tito died, the Party had abandoned its commitment to its earlier ideology of Yugoslavism encapsulated in the Second World War slogan: 'brotherhood and unity of the peoples of Yugoslavia'. According to this ideology, the peoples of Yugoslavia—both its constituent nations and its nationalities (national minorities)—forged their political unity during the heroic National Liberation Struggle (1941–5) led by the Communists. This political unity, based on the undefined kinship ties of 'brotherhood', was to be expressed in a federal state of equal nations and national minorities, established in early 1946 on the model of the only existing communist federation, the Union of Soviet Socialist Republics. The political power in the federation, again on the Soviet model, was concentrated in the inner leadership of the Communist Party selected by its general secretary, Tito.

By 1980 'brotherhood and unity' had been replaced by an even vaguer concept of 'togetherness' (*zajedništvo*). Yugoslavia was, according to this concept, a state in which different nations and nationalities only lived *together* but, apart from this, they had no other ties, except their alleged participation in and commitment to the system of socialist self-management which then distinguished Yugoslavia

---

[1] For an account of Yugoslav political movements and ideologies see Aleksandar Pavković, *The Fragmentation of Yugoslavia: Nationalism and War in the Balkans*, 2nd edn, London, 2000.

from the Soviet model of 'real socialism'. In contrast to the countries of 'real socialism', political power in Yugoslavia had by then been devolved to the leadership of the Communist Party of each of the six federal units (republics) and two sub-federal units (provinces). Unlike the ideology of 'brotherhood and unity,' the ideology of *zajedništvo* denied the existence of any common national or supranational identity to the citizens of Yugoslavia—all citizens were assumed to belong to a recognised nation or nationality of their birth (or were of mixed nationality) but no one could legally be a Yugoslav, as this was not a recognised national group.[2] It was an accident of history, as it were, that this state came to be called Yugoslavia—the name of the state was of no relevance to the bonds that allegedly tied its citizens together.

The Yugoslav idea or Yugoslavism was, I shall assume here, an attempt to explain or to justify a common state of the South Slavs (Yugoslavs). If so, one could argue that the later communist ideology of *zajedništvo* reduced the Yugoslav idea to a bare minimum—a mere coexistence of separate nations and nationalities within a common federal state—without seriously attempting to explain why they should so coexist. In the early 1970s, various Serb dissidents, engaged in delegitimising the Communist Party's policies and ideology, also questioned the ideology of *zajedništvo* and some, as we shall see, offered a more substantive version of Yugoslavism.[3] While they did not insist any longer on the 'brotherhood and unity' of Yugoslav peoples, their insistence on the political unity of the Yugoslav state linked their version of Yugoslavism to the earlier communist ideology of 'brotherhood and unity'.

This chapter examines three versions of post-1980 Yugoslavism: federalist and integralist versions, both articulated in the late 1980s, and a regionalist version which appeared only after the collapse of the Yugoslav federation in 1992.

---

[2] For a brief history of the Yugoslav national identity, including the communist era, see Aleksandar Pavković, 'Yugoslavism: a National Identity that Failed?' in Leslie Holmes and Philomena Murray (eds.), *Citizenship and Identity in Europe*, Aldershot, 1999, pp. 147–58.

[3] For an account of the Serb dissidence see Aleksandar Pavković, 'Intellectuals into Politicians: Serbia 1990–1992', *Meanjin*, vol. 52, no. 1, 1993, pp. 107–17.

Federalist Yugoslavism and the Memorandum of the Serbian Academy

The Constitution of the Socialist Federal Republic of Yugoslavia (which the Yugoslav Federal Assembly, controlled by the Communist Party leadership, enacted in 1974) transferred all federal powers to the republics and provinces and their representatives in the federal Presidium (or collective presidency). The only exception were foreign affairs and security and defence, which were assigned to the office of President. The office was to have only one office-bearer, namely, Tito and after his demise, these powers were to be transferred to his heir, the federal Presidium. Since each republic and province had one representative and equal vote in the Presidium, the leadership of each republic had the right of veto over any matter within federal jurisdiction. While this was never exercised during the lifetime of the all-powerful President, no federal body in Yugoslavia had any longer power of decision-making independent of the republics/provinces. Moreover, in this constitution the republics (but not the provinces) were described as 'states' suggesting that these federal units had a constitutional status similar if not identical to the federation itself. Already in 1971 the Serbian philosopher and jurist Mihailo Djurić publicly attacked these constitutional principles (which had then already been introduced in a series of constitutional amendments) as effectively replacing the Yugoslav federation with a confederation of states in which the Serb nation was split into several states instead of living in one.[4] Following his sentencing to a year in prison—the harshest punishment for a political offence meted out to a Serb intellectual since the early 1960s—any criticism of the Constitution of 1974 as a confederal document, unfavourable to Serbs, was restricted to various, closely watched, dissident discussion groups in Belgrade.

However, in 1985, faced with a prolonged economic crisis as well as continued and at times violent political protests by the Albanian population demanding the recognition of the province of Kosovo

---

[4] 'Smišljenje smutnje,' a paper read at an academic conference and then published in the student weekly *Student* and in the principal legal journal in Belgrade, *Anali Pravnog fakulteta u Beogradu*, no. 3, 1971, pp. 230–3. Reprinted in Mihailo Djurić, *Iskustvo razlike*, Belgrade, 1994, pp. 11–7.

as a republic of Yugoslavia, the Serbian Academy of Arts and Sciences selected a committee of sixteen distinguished academicians—most of whom hailed from the humanities and social sciences disciplines and were known as dissidents—to draft a memorandum addressing the causes of the economic and political crisis and proposing remedies. Their memorandum was to be considered and endorsed by the Academy before being presented to the highest Communist Party and state organs of Yugoslavia and Serbia. In its last draft the memorandum was leaked to a régime tabloid, which attacked it as a reactionary and nationalist document but did not publish it. Thus started the official campaign against the as yet unpublished draft memorandum (referred to in this paper as 'the Memorandum'), in which the highest state and party officials of Serbia, including the then president of the League of Communists of Serbia, Slobodan Milošević, took part.[5]

In its first part entitled 'The Crisis in the Yugoslav Economy and Society', the Memorandum explains the disintegration of the Yugoslav economy into the separate economies of the republics and provinces by a general transformation of

the federal state as constituted by the decisions taken at the Second Session of the Anti-Fascist Council of National Liberation of Yugoslavia and during the first decade of postwar development into a kind of confederation which became institutionalized in the most recent Constitution of 1974.[6]

That the general transformation of the Yugoslav federation into a confederation is the principal source of almost all the ills that have befallen Yugoslavia since the early 1970s was made clear throughout the Memorandum.

The Yugoslav Communist Party officially traced the origins of the Yugoslav federation to the second session, in 1943, of the Anti-Fascist Council of National Liberation of Yugoslavia—best known by its Serbo-Croat acronym 'AVNOJ'—which it fully controlled.

---

[5] On his role see Lenard J. Cohen, 'Slobodan Milošević' in Petar Radan and Aleksandar Pavković (eds), *The Serbs and Their Leaders in the Twentieth Century*, Ashgate, 1997, pp. 237–8. For an account of this campaign by two members of the Academy see Kosta Mihailović and Vasilije Krestić, *Memorandum of the Serbian Academy of Sciences and Arts: Answers to Criticisms*, Belgrade, 1995, pp. 13–38.

[6] Ibid., p. 104.

In consequence, all Communist Party and constitutional pronounce-
ments—including the Constitution of 1974—ritually referred to
this event as constitutive of the Yugoslav state. The Memorandum,
however, claimed that the most recent constitution of 1974 abandoned the foundational principles allegedly endorsed at the constitutive session of the Yugoslav state. The Memorandum's reference
to the second session of AVNOJ in 1943 is thus central to its argument that in the early 1970s the Yugoslav Communist leaders
betrayed the original revolutionary principles on which the Yugoslav state was founded during and immediately after the Second
World War. Yet the Memorandum did not specify which decisions
or principles of the second AVNOJ session, constitutive of the
Yugoslav federation, had been abandoned and betrayed in the early
1970s. It simply assumed that AVNOJ constituted Yugoslavia as a
federation in which federal institutions are the centres of political
decision-making and in which the federal units (republics) have little if any sovereign powers. Starting from this assumption, the
Memorandum proceeded to outline the sovereign powers of the
republics and provinces accorded to them by the 1974 Constitution and to illustrate their alleged widespread abuse by Communist
Party leaders.

In its second, shorter part entitled 'The Status of Serbia and the
Serbian Nation', the Memorandum argued that the abuse of these
powers had been particularly detrimental to the Serbs both in the
Republic of Serbia and in other republics because non-Serb Communist leaders used them to implement revanchist and highly dis-
criminatory policies against them. One way to remedy this, the
Memorandum proposed, was for Serbia to return to the AVNOJ
principles, provided other republics do it as well:

> While supporting the arrangement first outlined in the Anti-Fascist Coun-
> cil of National Liberation during the war, Serbia will have to bear in mind
> that the final decision does not rest with it, and that the others might prefer
> some other alternatives...By insisting on the federal system, Serbia would
> not only be furthering the equality of all national groups in Yugoslavia but
> also facilitating resolution of the political and economic crisis.[7]

While the Memorandum conspicuously failed to specify what were
the alternatives to the AVNOJ federal system, it extolled the Serbian

---

[7] Ibid., p. 140.

independent statehood and 'civil democracy' achieved in the Kingdom of Serbia, prior to 1918. This suggests that an independent
Serbian nation-state, such as the Kingdom of Serbia, may be the
best alternative to the Yugoslav federation.

The Memorandum's reference and expressed loyalty to the AVNOJ
constitutional principles are the clearest expression of its unspecified Yugoslavism—the conception of a South Slav state in which
the Serbs are only one among its constituent nations. The Memorandum's praise of the independent Serbian state and its democratic
institutions was an expression of equally unspecified and rather
rudimentary Serbism—the conception of an independent state of
Serbs. These two incompatible conceptions of the state reflect the
differences of opinion among the members of the Memorandum
drafting committee as well as of the Academy at large.[8] More
importantly, these two conceptions of state—the Yugoslav and the
Serb—determine the boundaries of the post-1986 debate among
nationally-minded Serb intellectuals over the type of state in which
Serbs should live.

A Yugoslav federation: Ćosić's utopia

In the public debate on Serb national goals, which the Slobodan
Milošević régime encouraged after the purge of his opponents from
the Serbian Communist Party in 1987, Dobrica Ćosić, a leading
Serb novelist and former dissident,[9] had, until 1992, advocated a

---

[8] For example, the Praxis neomarxist Mihailo Marković (later a vice-chairman of
Milošević's Socialist Party of Serbia) was an advocate of Yugoslav federalism
while the well-known linguist, the late Pavle Ivić, advocated an independent and
unified Serb state. For a brief account of the revival of Serbism see Aleksandar
Pavković, 'The Serb National Idea: A Revival 1986–1992', *Slavonic and East European Review*, vol. 72, no. 3, 1994, pp. 440–55.

[9] Dobrica Ćosić (b. 1921), the creator of Partisan heroic realism in literature, was
until 1968 one of the best known communist writers and confidante of Tito's
circle. In 1968 he was expelled from the Central Committee of the Serbian
Communist party for his warnings about the rise of Albanian nationalism and the
possibility of a Serbian nationalist backlash. In spite of this, the series of his novels
about a Serbian family caught up in the twentieth century turmoil was published
by mainstream publishing houses and gained a wide readership. In May 1992 he
abandoned his position of dissident to be elected the first president of the new
Yugoslavia (Serbia and Montenegro) by a parliament dominated by Milošević's

reformed Yugoslav federation as the most rational choice of state for all nations of former Yugoslavia, including the Serbs.

According to the then official communist interpretation, the second session of AVNOJ, at which each Yugoslav nation freely opted—once and for all—to live in a common state, was the culmination of a progressive process of unification of the South Slav peoples, previously divided by foreign and domestic oppressors. In contrast, in 1988 Ćosić claimed that Yugoslavia was created by 'above all… the pain and necessity of national survival, and not the progressive ideas and love among the Yugoslav nations.'[10] The necessity of national survival here refers to the need to preserve their nations' independence and identity from the dominance of foreign powers; it was this need, according to Ćosić, and not their free choice that led the Yugoslav nations to unite into a common state.

The well-known Serb jurist Slobodan Jovanović had also argued that in the nineteenth century the Croats and the Serbs realised that a common Yugoslav state was the best guarantee of their independence from foreign powers. In 1940, on the eve of the Axis attack on the Kingdom of Yugoslavia, Jovanović called for a return to this core Yugoslav idea.[11] Ćosić appears to be well acquainted with Jovanović views: in his novel *Otpadnik* (Renegade, 1989), Slobodan Jovanović, as a fictional character, propounds in conversation this very version of Yugoslavism which the real life Jovanović advanced in his speeches and essays.

From the point of view of national survival, Communist Yugoslavism, as expressed in the slogan 'brotherhood and unity' was, Ćosić claims 'rational, revolutionary and offered salvation in the genocidal

---

followers (who, on the latter's orders, dismissed him a year later). Although not a member of the drafting committee of the Memorandum, he participated in its work and the Memorandum reflects some of his Yugoslav federalism.

[10] 'Uslovi demokratske budućnosti', *Književne Novine* (Belgrade), 15 Dec. 1988, reprinted in Dobrica Ćosić, *Srpsko pitanje- demokratsko pitanje*, Belgrade, 1992, p. 168.

[11] 'Jugoslovenska misao u prošlosti i budućnosti' (1940) in Slobodan Jovanović, *Sabrana dela*, Belgrade, 1991, vol. 11, pp. 569–76. For a discussion of this argument see Aleksandar Pavković, *Slobodan Jovanović: An Unsentimental Approach to Politics*, Boulder, CO, 1993, Appendix. From March 1941 to Jan. 1942 Jovanović was a deputy prime minister and from Jan. 1942 to June 1943 the prime minister in the anti-Axis royal Yugoslav government (in exile in London from Apr. 1941).

region of Yugoslavia.'[12] However, the internal federal boundaries of the new Yugoslav federation were, in his view, set according to the principles dictated by the Communist International in Moscow. These boundaries intentionally ignored the ethnic or national divisions of Yugoslavia. As they were not determined on the basis of democratic principles and ethnic 'realities', they were, Ćosić insisted, 'historically illegitimate, therefore, conditional and temporary.'[13] In short, Ćosić accepted the general idea of a federation which the Yugoslav Communist party (of which he was a high ranking member until 1968) offered as a rational way out of the 'genocidal conflict' but rejected the boundaries of the federal units it introduced.

In 1988 Ćosić proposed a radical democratic transformation of the Yugoslav state which, like the Memorandum, he also held to have become a confederation. He called for: first, the democratic referenda of the Yugoslav nations in order to establish whether they wanted to live in a Yugoslav state community; second, the abolition of the Communist Party monopoly on political power and the introduction of pluralism and 'integral democracy'; third, the introduction of various types of ownership, including private ownership of economic assets; and, fourth, the respect for 'and further development of autochtonous values, national peculiarities and positive traditions of all nations' as well as 'the socialist features of the National Liberation Struggle' of 1941–45. In this way Yugoslavia could become a democratic, civilised and harmonious community of nations, and a free and open society; unless this was achieved, there would be no human or historical reasons for the further existence of Yugoslavia.[14]

However, as he makes clear in his later essays, Ćosić's reformed Yugoslav community should not be a confederation of the six republics—such a confederation would only increase national antagonisms and lead to war. Moreover, a confederation would negate the historical goal of the Serb people—'the unification of all Serbs into a single state'[15] which he believed to be a precondition of their

---

[12] 'Reč na skupu posvećenom pedesetogodišnjici ustanka' (1991) in Ćosić, *Srpsko pitanje—demokratsko* pitanje, op. cit., p. 223.

[13] 'Jugoslavija i srpsko pitanje' (1991), ibid., p. 207. Similarly in 'Jugoslavija—država izneverenih očekivanja' (1988), ibid., p. 184.

[14] Ibid, pp. 185–6.

[15] 'Jugoslavija i srpsko pitanje' (1991), ibid., pp. 215–17.

liberty. The same rights and liberties granted to the Serb people in the reformed Yugoslav state should also be granted to each Yugoslav nation or national group.

Ćosić's version of Yugoslavism thus appears to be that of a democratic and pluralist federation in which Serbs and all other nations would have equal rights of entry and exit as well as of political organisation, including that of organising their 'own' federal units. Consequently, the Serbs have no 'national and democratic reason' to prevent the Croats and Slovenes (and by implication other nations as well) to leave Yugoslavia and to form their own states, provided that this does not involve the 'annexation of the Serb ethnic territories.'[16] However, in his writings he did not explain how one is to determine what these Serb ethnic territories were or how the right to free political organisation of each nation is to be exercised in the territories with mixed population.

As he admitted in January 1991, this vision of a reformed Yugoslavia was only his utopia. In March 1992, as the war broke out in Bosnia-Herzegovina, Ćosić appeared to have abandoned it, arguing that Serbs, Croats and (Bosnian) Muslims there needed to form borders and divide the territory among themselves in 'as just way as possible...so as to remove reasons for the hatred and the killing and so as to be able to unite, with the least possible obstacles, in all that is mutually rational and useful.'[17] While pleading for a just partition of the Yugoslav space, Ćosić still allowed for the possibility of some future reunion. In 1995, after the NATO bombing of Bosnian Serb territories, he rejected any possibility of a Yugoslav state in the future, proclaiming it historically dead and labelling those who still believed in it 'nihilists' and 'ideologically sick people'.[18] Ćosić's utopia of a federal Yugoslavia was thus a victim of a prolonged warfare among the peoples who should, in his vision, be free to opt to live in it. His Yugoslavism was replaced by a version of Serbism, according to which the Serbs should strive for a predominantly Serb state, at the same time preserving Serb national identity of all the Serbs forced, by foreign powers, to live outside that state.[19]

[16] Ibid. p. 219.
[17] 'Kongresu srpskih intelektualaca' (1992), ibid., p. 234.
[18] 'Pogled na budućnost' in *Šta je stvarno rekao Dobrica Ćosić*, edited by Milan Nikolić, Belgrade, 1995, p. 257.
[19] For an account of his Serbism see Aleksandar Pavković, 'From Yugoslavism to

Yugoslavia as a community of language: Milorad Ekmečič and Yugoslav unity

In Ćosić's utopia of a federal Yugoslavia only some but not all of its inhabitants identify as Yugoslavs; his utopia does not presuppose any widespread supranational or national Yugoslav identity or feeling among its inhabitants, and for him Yugoslavs were only those who were inclined to endorse Yugoslavism of some sort or other.[20]

In contrast, the distinguished Bosnian Serb historian Milorad Ekmečić[21] believed that all inhabitants of Yugoslavia not only could but should identify themselves as Yugoslavs. The commonality or similarity of their language, in his opinion, determined their national identity as Yugoslavs. Emečić found the idea that a nation is a community of language in the French rationalist philosophy; according to him, Yugoslavism, as a conception of the Yugoslav nation and of its state originates in this philosophy. This linguistic concept of the Yugoslav was rational 'in the sense that nature has determined the borders of the national territory and the democratic character of the political organisation'.[22] Opposed to this rational conception is the conception of nation defined by its religion or church. This conception, based on confessional solidarity, partitions the allegedly 'natural' grouping of the South Slavs into smaller nations such as the Serbs, Croats, Slovenes and so on. Although it is a very strong political and spiritual force, the religion-based conception

---

Serbism: the Serb national idea, 1986–1996', *Nations and Nationalism*, vol. 4, no. 4, 1998, pp. 511–28, pp. 521–3.

[20] 'Jugoslavija i srpsko pitanje' (1991), in *Srpsko pitanje—demokratsko pitanje*, op. cit., p. 219.

[21] Milorad Ekmečić's (b. 1928) first book on the Christian uprising in Bosnia-Herzegovina 1875–8, published in 1960, attracted attention of historians both in Yugoslavia and abroad for its relatively unconventional approach. His later historical works, including a history of Yugoslavia, of which he was a co-author, attracted considerable controversy. A resident of Sarajevo, in the late 1980s Ekmečić was a member of both the Serbian Academy and the Academy of Bosnia and Herzegovina. After the outbreak of the war in Bosnia in 1992, he was arrested by Bosnian Muslim authorities for his alleged Serb nationalism but never charged with any offence; after his release he settled in Belgrade.

[22] Milorad Ekmečić, 'Srpska nacionalna sudbina izmedju srednje Evrope i Evrope (Srbi i jugoslovenstvo)', *Srbija izmedju srednje Evrope i Evrope*, Belgrade, 1992, p. 23.

is incompatible with the linguistic conception which Ekmečić regards as the only truly scientific conception of a nation.[23]

According to Ekmečić, the history of the South Slav unification, is a cycle of defeats and victories of one or the other of the two conceptions. The linguistic conception was, he argues, widely accepted by the South Slav revolutionaries in 1848; their defeat was also a defeat of that conception by its arch-enemy, the Roman Catholic conception of separate nations. However, in the early twentieth century the linguistic conception formed the core of unitary Yugoslavism according to which the South Slavs are a single nation with three names (Croat, Serb and Slovene), constituted of three tribes, speaking three equal variants of the same language.[24] While at the end of the First World War unitary Yugoslavism emerged as victorious, in addition to its former religious enemies (primarily, Roman Catholicism) the new Yugoslav state acquired new atheist ones: Lenin and the Bolshevik party believed that the Yugoslav state was a creation of global—and of Serbian—imperialism. In spite of this, the victory of the Yugoslav communists in 1945, was a victory, however flawed, of the linguistic/democratic conception of the Yugoslav nation.[25]

Writing in 1991, Ekmečić still believed that the contest between the two conceptions had not ended.[26] The ascendancy of the religious conception of separate nations, as exemplified in the secessionist movements in Slovenia and Croatia, did not preclude a later resurgence of the linguistic/rationalist conception of a Yugoslav state, which he confidently anticipated to happen in a few decades' time.[27] In late 1993, however, he admitted that the 'existing civil war [primarily in Bosnia-Herzegovina]…as its principal consequence has the destruction of the foundation of the unity of the Yugoslav peoples.'[28] In admitting the final defeat of the linguistic/rationalist conception

---

[23] Ibid.

[24] Milorad Ekmečić, *Stvaranje Jugoslavije*, Belgrade, 1989, vol. 2, p. 669–70.

[25] Ibid., pp. 833, 839.

[26] 'Istorijski koren i dinamika jugoslovenskog jedinstva u XIX veku', *Srbija izmedju srednje Evrope i Evrope*, op. cit., p. 87.

[27] 'Srpska nacionalna sudbina izmedju srednje Evrope i Evrope (Srbi i jugoslovenstvo)', ibid. p. 37.

[28] Milorad Ekmečić, 'O jedinstvu srpskog naroda danas' *Srpsko pitanje danas: kongresni materijali (Drugi kongres srpskih intelektualaca)*, Belgrade, 1994, p. 17.

of Yugoslav unity, he himself endorsed a rather romantic version of Serbism, arguing that the Serbs' historic perseverance in their will to unite in a single state will prevail in the end.[29]

Unlike Ćosić, in his advocacy of Yugoslavism the historian Ekmečić did not offer a blueprint for a reformed Yugoslav state. Yet his preferred—and allegedly scholarly, democratic and progressive—conception of Yugoslav unity implies that a Yugoslav state, inhabited by single Yugoslav nation should correspondingly be united in a single democratic nation-state on the model of the present-day Italy or Germany. Any conception of Yugoslavia as a multinational state or a confederation, in which each nation inhabits a federal unit, would, according to this conception, be a concession to the religious and thus allegedly unscientific conception of nationhood.

Yugoslavia as a federation of regions: Vukobrat's blueprint for reintegration

Despite its abandonment by distinguished Serb intellectuals, such as Ćosić and Ekmečić, Yugoslavism was, in the early 1990s, still a subject of debate among intellectuals in Belgrade. From 1992 to 1994, Boris Vukobrat, a successful French businessman and philanthropist of Serb origin, offered a series of blueprints for Yugoslav reintegration which were extensively discussed at a series of round tables held in Beograd, by a large group of political scientists, political theorists and economists from former Yugoslavia.[30]

In his first, 1992, proposal Vukobrat envisaged a community of an undetermined number of regions (as an example only, he listed fourteen historical regions of former Yugoslavia). Each region, on the model of Swiss cantons, would be a center of decision-making

[29] Ibid. See Aleksandar Pavković, 'From Yugoslavism to Serbism', op. cit., pp. 519–20, for a discussion of this version of Serbism.

[30] Vukobrat's proposals and these dicussions were published in English in Predrag Simić, Srdan Kerim and Mirko Stojčević (eds), *Towards a New Community: Possibilities and Perspectives for the New Settlement of South Slav Area*, Zug (Switzerland) and Belgrade, 1992; Boris I. Vukobrat, *Proposals for the New Commonwealth of the Republics of ex-Yugoslavia*, Zug and Belgrade, 1994; Predrag Simić, Nebojša Spaić and Mirko Stojčević (eds), *Crisis and Reform: State and Civil Society in Transition*, Zug and Belgrade, 1994.

powers, while the new community would exercise international sovereignty. The foundational principle of the new Yugoslav community, to be enshrined in its constitution, is its association with the (then) European Community, to be followed by its full integration. Vukobrat confidently asserted that, because of its geo-strategic position, the new Yugoslav community would become indispensable to the latter.[31] By fragmenting the 'national' territories of former Yugoslavia into separate regions and offering no role to nation-based institutions of any kind, Vukobrat's model of regional integration was obviously intended to deny any political influence or role to the existing national sentiments and ideologies. While he did not envisage the introduction of a new Yugoslav national identity (for example, on the model of Swiss national identity), he claimed that '[I]t is necessary, vital in fact, that we come together again. [T]here are very clear historical, economic, political and cultural reasons for this.'[32] No explanation was offered, however, of what these reasons were.

In his 1994 blueprint the Yugoslav community was renamed the 'Commonwealth of the Republics of ex-Yugoslavia'. Correspondingly, the republics, as states, hold the ultimate decision-making powers. A region is still the basic unit of organisation but the states/republics are to 'supervise' regions. The republics, it was conceded, will represent national interests (which his earlier blueprint intentionally ignored) but these separate national interests, in the new commonwealth, can only be optimised and not maximised. In this way, the republics would cooperate first in the economic sphere and, then, hopefully agree on a common constitution, forming a commonwealth in this way.[33]

In spite of his later concession to the new states as representative of national interests, Vukobrat's blueprints primarily aim to transfer the focus of political organisation and of the citizens' loyalty from the new nation-states to regions and then from the regions to a community of regions. The principal model for the new community is neither a federal nor unitary nation-state but an idealised European Union as a community of regions. Unlike Ćosić and

---

[31] Simić, Kerim and Stojčević (eds), op. cit., pp. 13–30.
[32] Ibid., p. 30.
[33] Simić, Spaić and Stojčević (eds), op. cit., p. 17.

Ekmečić, Vukobrat shows no interest in the re-evaluation of the past: his interest is only avoiding the past conflict, not in evaluating the 'national' achievements or failures of past political régimes.

While most participants in the debate on Vukobrat's blueprints tended to regard them as utopias or visions, those who refused to acquiesce to the necessity of creating separate nation-states out of former Yugoslavia still regarded them as worthy of consideration. Other participants, who were possibly sympathetic to one of the existing nation-state projects, showed a marked interest in the prospects for regionalisation or of cooperation in the area of former Yugoslavia offered in these blueprints. In contrast, Ćosić's and Ekmečić's essays on Yugoslavism appear to have been directed primarily at those who felt an affinity to some, however undefined, project of Serb unification as well as those who retained an affinity to a Yugoslav state.

Why has Yugoslavism persisted for so long?

The Yugoslav idea, in its various forms, appears to have retained the loyalty and interest of distinguished Belgrade intellectuals through the wars in Slovenia and Croatia in 1991, and, in its regional version, through the war in Bosnia-Herzegovina in 1992–4. The commitment of Serb intellectuals—as well as non-intellectuals—to a Yugoslav state has often been explained by the large dispersal of Serbs throughout the territory of former Yugoslavia (substantial numbers of Serbs inhabited Croatia, Serbia, Bosnia-Herzegovina and Montenegro) and by their numerical superiority over any other single national group in that state. It was argued that Yugoslavia provided for all the dispersed Serbs a single state in which they were a constituent nation (and not a minority) and that their numerical superiority enabled them to dominate its state apparatus and thus to dominate the other national groups as well. Arguments of this kind had been used, since the creation of Yugoslavia in 1918, to show that Yugoslavia serves Serb interests better than the interests of other South Slavs.

Of the three authors discussed here, it was only Ćosić who referred to arguments of this kind. He accepted that in the creation of Yugoslavia, the Serbs saw 'the realization of their centuries-long national goal—the life of the whole of the Serb diaspora in a single state'.[34] However, Ćosić denied that, for this or any other reason, the Serbs needed Yugoslavia more than any other nation.[35] He argued that only a democratic Yugoslavia in which every nation and nationality enjoys equal rights is in the Serb national interest and that, therefore, the Serbs do not and should not seek a hegemonistic, unitary and centralist Yugoslavia.[36] Within Ekmečić's integralist conception of Yugoslavia, any attempt at separating the interests of the Serbs from those of other Yugoslavs, is a concession to a retrograde religious conception of the Yugoslav nations. As we have seen, Vukobrat's blueprint of regionalisation was specifically designed to prevent the dominance of one national group over another. Each author thus argued that his blueprint furthers the interests of all inhabitants of former Yugoslavia and not of any particular national group or groups.

The persistence of the Yugoslav idea among Serb intellectuals could probably be explained also in terms of the political ideals which they endorse and with which they associate it. Ćosić and Ekmečić believe that small nations, such as the South Slavs, need a strong and independent state capable of resisting not only outright foreign occupation but any other form of foreign domination which may threaten their national identity. Theirs is the ideal of a fully independent nation or nations, free from dominating foreign ideologies, such as, for Ćosić, capitalist consumerism or, for Ekmečić, Roman Catholicism. Yugoslavia, in their opinion, was a state that came closest to this ideal; this is what made it, until the Bosnian civil war proved otherwise, a worthy cause. A Serb nation-state—whatever its boundaries—could never match Yugoslavia in its economic strength and geostrategic position and thus did not present so good a guarantee of independence. In contrast, Vukobrat's ideal is that of European federation, not of nation-states, but of regions. His concern is thus not with independence but with integration into a wider federal framework. He believes that the re-integration of Yugoslavia on regional basis was the best way of achieving his ultimate ideal, the integration into the European Union.

---

[34] 'Jugoslavija i srpsko pitanje', *Srpsko pitanje-demokratsko pitanje*, op. cit., p. 204.
[35] 'Uspostavljanje istorijskog uma', ibid., pp. 199–200.
[36] 'Jugoslavija i srpsko pitanje', ibid., p. 215.

Whether the Yugoslav idea, as a utopian ideal, will continue to attract intellectuals among the Serbs or other South Slavs probably depends, in part, on whether it will maintain its association with political or social ideals such as those two.[37]

[37] I thank Peter Radan and Kathleen Engelen of Macquarie University for their help in the writing of this chapter.

INTELLECTUALS AND THE COLLAPSE OF YUGOSLAVIA: THE END OF THE YUGOSLAV WRITERS' UNION[1]

Jasna Dragović-Soso

The first Yugoslav institution to disintegrate at the end of the post-Tito decade was not a political but a cultural one—the Yugoslav Writers' Union. It ceased to function in spring 1989, after several years of agony and more than six months before the disintegration of the League of Communists of Yugoslavia. Ironically, four years earlier, the Yugoslav Writers' Union was hailed as the carrier of a new democratic alternative, bringing together critical intellectuals from different republics around a common struggle for freedom of expression. Rather than crystallizing this initial momentum into a new integrative ideology, however, Yugoslav intellectuals for the most part showed themselves to be just as incapable as their republican leaderships in fostering a spirit of compromise and bridging national differences. Instead, they relied on a selective use of 'democratic' criteria in promoting and justifying incompatible national agendas, consequently foregoing the possibility of constructive dialogue necessary for the survival of the common state.

The Yugoslav Writers' Union as a mirror of Yugoslav politics

Culture and politics in communist Yugoslavia were always closely linked and the Yugoslav Writers' Union was never a purely professional or literary organization. Based on the Soviet model, it was

---

[1] My thanks go to Aleksandar Pavković for his comments on this chapter. All interpretations and any mistakes are, of course, my own responsibility.

created in 1945 in order to promote the values and the legitimacy of the new communist authorities.[2] Following the 1948 break with the Cominform, Yugoslavia's emancipation from the Soviet model of communism was concurrently introduced in both the political and cultural spheres. In October 1952, as the Sixth Party Congress resolved that the party would no longer play the role of 'the direct operative manager and commander in the economy, state or political life',[3] the concurrent congress of the Yugoslav Writers' Union marked the beginning of a progressive (though never complete) disengagement of the party from the cultural sphere.[4]

Despite increasing freedom of literary creation in the course of the 1950s and 1960s, the Yugoslav cultural sphere continued to reflect contemporary political debates and problems. As Yugoslavia's 'national question' reappeared in the course of the 1960s, spurred by party divisions on economic decentralization and constitutional change, it was not uncommon for writers to act as 'sounding balloons' for their respective republican leaderships, to test the acceptability and effects of specific standpoints. The best known such case was the public debate between Serbian novelist Dobrica Ćosić and his Slovenian friend Dušan Pirjevec in 1961, which focused on the relationship between the republics and the federation. Both intellectuals were encouraged by their leaderships to present their arguments in the press and the debate reflected the internal party divisions over the future of the federation: whereas Ćosić represented the Serbian leadership's commitment to 'socialist Yugoslavism' as a form of 'internationalism' that was 'constitutionally and historically overcoming the limits of nation and national belonging', Pirjevec saw the republics as 'clearly formed national organisms' whose 'national self-determination' was a logical consequence of

---

[2] In practice, however, the Yugoslav Writers' Union never had as much power as its Soviet counterpart. It had neither the large administrative apparatus, nor the funds to accomodate housing, 'rest homes', or honoraria for its writers. See Ratko Peković, *Ni rat ni mir: Panorama književnih polemika 1945–1965*, Belgrade, 1986, pp. 20–1.

[3] 'Resolution and Statute of the Sixth Congress', quoted in Dennison Rusinow, *The Yugoslav Experiment, 1948–1974*, London, 1977, p. 75.

[4] See notably the speech by Miroslav Krleža, 'Govor na kongresu književnika u Ljubljani', *Eseji*, VI, Zagreb, 1967, p. 51.

socialist development.[5] As subsequent constitutional changes showed, Pirjevec's vision eventually emerged victorious over 'socialist Yugoslavism'.[6] These changes in the functioning of the Yugoslav state were, in turn, mirrored in the cultural sphere. In 1965, following a heated debate, the Congress of the Yugoslav Writers' Union decided to change its statutes to introduce decentralization on a regional and national basis, as Slovenian writers demanded, rather than on the basis of literary affinities, as Ćosić and other Serbian writers proposed.[7]

The second important instance of culture acting as a proxy for politics took place in the 1967 Croat-Serbian 'language debate'.[8] At this time of rising Croatian national assertiveness, which was to culminate in the 'Croatian spring' of 1971,[9] one hundred and forty intellectuals representing nineteen Croatian cultural institutions, issued a 'Declaration Concerning the Name and Position of the Croatian Literary Language'. This document, widely seen as embodying the opinion not only of the Croatian intellectual élite but also of the republic's leadership, affirmed 'the right of each of our nations to protect the attributes of its national identity' and called for a constitutional change which would replace 'Serbo-Croatian' by two separate languages, making 'Croatian' the official language

[5] See Audrey Helfant Budding, 'Yugoslavs into Serbs: Serbian National Identity, 1961–1971', *Nationalities Papers*, vol. XXV, no. 3, 1997, pp. 48–62; Peković, op. cit., pp. 302–3; and Jelena Milojković-Djurić, 'Approaches to National Identities: Ćosić's and Pirjevec's Debate on Ideological and Literary Issues', *East European Quarterly*, vol. XXX, no. 1, 1996, pp. 63–73. For Ćosić's account, see Slavoljub Djukić, *Čovek u svom vremenu: Razgovori sa Dobricom Ćosićem*, Belgrade, 1989, pp. 121–37.

[6] For a good overview of the stages of Yugoslavia's development until 1980, see Lenard J. Cohen, *Broken Bonds: The Disintegration of Yugoslavia*, Boulder, CO, 1993, p. 27.

[7] For a critical discussion of the 1965 changes in the statutes of the Yugoslav Writers' Union, see Sveta Lukić, *Contemporary Yugoslav Literature: A Sociopolitical Approach*, Urbana, IL, 1972, pp. 130–7.

[8] For a more thorough analysis of this debate, see my *'Saviours of the Nation': Serbia's Intellectual Opposition and the Revival of Nationalism*, London, 2002.

[9] On the Croatian 'spring', see Steven Burg, *Conflict and Cohesion in Socialist Yugoslavia*, Princeton, NJ, 1983, pp. 121–60; George Schöpflin, 'The Ideology of Croatian Nationalism', *Survey*, vol. XIX, no. 1, 1973, pp. 123–46; and Jill A. Irvine, *The Croat Question*, Boulder, CO, 1993, pp. 258–72.

in the Republic of Croatia. The 'Declaration' received a prompt reply from forty-two members of the Writers' Association of Serbia in a 'Proposal for Reflection', which endorsed the Croatian demands but argued that the Serbs of Croatia had to be guaranteed the right to keep their 'Serbian' language.[10] In other words, if the Croats demanded cultural or—implicitly—any other kind of autonomy, then they would have to grant exactly the same level of autonomy to the republic's Serbs, thus enabling them to remain linked to Serbia. Whereas for Croatian intellectuals the 'Declaration' represented an affirmation of their nation's sovereignty, for their Serbian counterparts, it threatened to reverse their own nation's traditional goal of 'liberation and unification'. While Serbian writers saw their 'Proposal' as simply a call for the extension of equal rights to the Serbs of Croatia, Croatian intellectuals saw it as an attempt to keep Croatian independence hostage to its Serbian minority and under the 'Greater Serbian' thumb. The so-called 'language debate' was, in fact, less about linguistics than about questions of nation and state.

In 1971, as events in Croatia spiralled out of control of the republic's communist leadership, Tito decided it was time to put an end to both the national and the liberal streamings throughout the country. The crackdown in the early 1970s on the republican communist leaderships, particularly in Croatia and Serbia, was accompanied by the return of closer surveillance over the cultural sphere. A number of intellectuals were imprisoned, especially in Croatia, and others were prevented from publishing and teaching. The Party was purged of its 'unreliable elements'. Symbolizing this new course were the introduction in all public institutions of the 'moral and political suitability' criterion for employment and of communist *aktivs*—small groups of party representatives to oversee that no anti-state or anti-communist activities took place. The writers' associations, as well as the Yugoslav Writers' Union, generally toed the new line. Critical intellectuals dissociated themselves from official institutions and began to search for new outlets for their activities, outside the state's control.

[10] For both texts, see Christopher Spalatin, 'Serbo-Croatian or Serbian and Croatian? Considerations on the Croatian Declaration and the Serbian Proposal of March 1967', *Journal of Croatian Studies*, vols VII–VIII, 1966–7, pp. 6–9 and 10–11 respectively. Unlike in Croatia, the 'Proposal' was not endorsed by the Serbian political élite. See Petar Džadžić, 'Strele, jezuiti, simetrije', *Svet*, 10 Jan. 1990.

Once again reflecting what was happening to Yugoslavia as country, this revival of dogmatism in the intellectual sphere was accompanied by further regional decentralization. The six republican writers' associations increasingly functioned independently of each other, while the Writers' Union played a diminishing role. After the mid-1970s, no writers' congresses were held for ten years and activities, if any, were organized by individual associations. Furthermore, the constitutional changes that raised Serbia's autonomous provinces of Vojvodina and Kosovo to republican status in all but name were accompanied by the creation of two separate and independent regional writers' associations, along with other cultural institutions. In both provinces, the affirmation of 'particularist' regional—and in Kosovo's case, national—identities predominated over any attempts to foster cooperation within the Republic of Serbia. As a result, the Belgrade-based Writers' Association of Serbia effectively came to function as an institution of 'inner' Serbia only.

Writers' Associations and alternative politics in Serbia and Slovenia, 1981–5

During the Tito era, cultural institutions including the Yugoslav Writers' Union essentially reflected political differences and disputes in the Party leadership, but they never went so far as to openly challenge official policy. Although intellectuals at times overstepped the limits of publicly acceptable discourse, genuine dissident activities, which contested single party rule and aimed at a transformation of the system, were few and had no institutional base. It is only with the revival of repression in the 1970s that critical intellectuals began to adopt dissident methods akin to those of their counterparts in Eastern Europe: petitions demanding the respect of civil and human rights, a 'flying university' in private homes and *samizdat* journals. Belgrade, which had an ideologically heterogeneous but dynamic group of critical intellectuals and a more liberal régime, was at the forefront of such activities. In the 1980s, Ljubljana also emerged as a centre of a buoying 'alternative scene'.

Tito's death in 1980, followed by new disclosures concerning the depth of Yugoslavia's economic crisis and the divergences between the leaderships of the federal units, provided fertile soil for the blossoming, spread and radicalization of alternative politics. With the communist leaderships still unsure how to deal with these new challenges, intellectual activism was able to find a stronghold in existing cultural institutions in Serbia and Slovenia, the two most liberal republics. The two writers' associations, which had until the 1980s mainly concerned themselves with the organization of literary debates and material problems of their members, thus began to articulate an ever-more encompassing criticism of the régime.

Slovenia's critical intellectuals had two main centres, pursuing both a 'liberal' agenda of systemic transformation and a 'national' one of maintaining and extending Slovenian sovereignty. One was a group of writers, philosophers and sociologists gathered around the journal *Nova revija* and the other was the Slovenian Writers' Society.[11] As Rudi Šeligo, one of the Society's presidents during the post-Tito decade, put it: 'After 1980, the Society achieved a high degree of autonomy *vis-à-vis* the political organizations... and, in this way, gained prestige and became an important moral force in Slovenia.'[12] It gained prominence as the champion of Slovenian cultural rights and initiatives to raise consciousness of Slovenia's 'Central European' identity. Comparing their own republic to neighbouring Austria and northern Italy, feeling economically exploited by the poorer republics, resenting the influx of workers from the Yugoslav 'south' and disagreeing with Yugoslavia's Third World orientation, many Slovenian writers began calling for their republic's adherence to the 'Central European space' and for a loosening of ties with the rest of Yugoslavia.[13]

[11] See my *Saviours of the Nation*, op. cit. Slovenia also had the most active youth alternative in Yugoslavia. See particularly Tomaž Mastnak, 'From Social Movements to National Sovereignty' in Jill Benderly and Evan Kraft (eds), *Independent Slovenia: Origins, Movements, Prospects*, London, 1994, pp. 95–108, and Jozef Figa, 'Socializing the State: Civil Society and Democratization from Below in Slovenia' in Melissa K. Bokovoy, Jill A. Irvine and Carol S. Lilly (eds), *State-Society Relations in Yugoslavia*, Basingstoke, 1997, pp. 163–82.

[12] *Danas*, 21 Apr. 1987, p. 38.

[13] See, for example, Ciril Zlobec, *Slovenska samobitnost i pisac*, Zagreb, 1987; Drago Jančar, 'Srednja Evropa kao meteorološko pitanje', *Književnost*, vol. XLII, no. 6, June 1987, pp. 879–83; and Taras Kermauner, 'Pisma srpskom prijatelju', in instalments, *Borba* and *NIN*, 24 June-6 Sept. 1987.

The Slovenian writers' first battle against the political authorities came in 1982, in response to the launching of a federal proposal for Yugoslav-wide 'common core curricula' for secondary schools. The aim of this project was to revive a degree of cultural Yugoslavism, by narrowing separate 'national' curricula and republican control over secondary school teaching.[14] Slovenian writers immediately reacted against the proposal, arguing that such measures would prevent Slovenian pupils from achieving national consciousness and a sense of their specific 'spiritual, cultural, historical and social identity'.[15] They became politically active, raising public awareness and organizing conferences and debates, openly voicing disagreement with the stance of their republican authorities and lobbying support within all the echelons of power, until the League of Communists of Slovenia eventually came round to their point of view. This case inaugurated the revival of the Slovenian national question in the post-Tito era, rendered the role of the Slovenian Writers' Society 'a classical example of the impact of an interest group upon political processes'[16] and culminated in a resounding political success for critical intellectuals. As a harbinger of future 'national homogenization' in the republic, it also united the Slovenian intelligentsia and political leadership against Yugoslavia's centre for the first time since Tito's death.

In Serbia, alternative politics did not initially arise to further a 'national' cause, but in the defence of civil rights. The arrest of poet Gojko Djogo in 1982 for publishing a collection of poems containing veiled criticism of the deceased President Tito, sparked widespread protest within the Belgrade intelligentsia, spearheaded by writers. Relentless petitioning of the authorities, the creation of a Committee for the Defence of Freedom of Creation in the Writers' Association of Serbia, and a series of massively attended public 'protest evenings' signalled that unity in the intelligentsia was achievable despite internal ideological differences.[17] It also turned the writers' association into an institutional base for the intellectual opposition,

---

[14] See Zlobec, op. cit., p. 59.

[15] Ibid., p. 62.

[16] Adolf Bibič, 'The Emergence of Pluralism in Slovenia', *Communist and Post-Communist Studies*, vol. XXVI, no. 4, Dec. 1993, p. 372.

[17] See my '*Saviours of the Nation*', op. cit.

although divisions remained between those who were more prone to seeking 'cooperation' with the régime and those who adopted a stance of 'no compromise'. Djogo's release 'on medical grounds' as the opposition movement gained amplitude represented an unprecedented victory for the critical intelligentsia. By May 1983 the increasingly free press in Serbia compared the intelligentsia's activism to that of the French '*intellectuels*' in the turn-of-the-century Dreyfus case and the Writers' Association became publicly perceived as the sanctuary of democratic values.[18]

The activities of the critical intelligentsias in Slovenia and Serbia and the spread of liberal ideas and critiques of Yugoslavia's system provided the impetus to coordinate such activities on an inter-republican level. In April 1985, the Ninth Congress of the Yugoslav Writers' Union was called after ten years of nonactivity. This congress was hailed as both the intellectuals' 'exit from the ivory tower' and as the 'congress of unity' by some of its participants and the more liberal press.[19] In their official declaration, Yugoslav writers openly demanded the abolition of the 'verbal offence' from the federal penal code—the focal point of the intelligentsia's civil rights activism of the 1970s and early 1980s—in what was widely seen as an announcement of a united struggle for democratic change.[20] To more observant analysts, however, this veneer of common purpose was already overshadowed by gaping national divisions, particularly between the two most active writers' organizations: the Serbian and the Slovenian.

Already in the preparatory meetings, the president of the Writers' Association of Serbia, Miodrag Bulatović, announced that he

---

[18] *NIN*, 15 May 1983 and Drinka Gojković, 'The Birth of Nationalism from the Spirit of Democracy' in Nebojša Popov (ed.), *The Road to War in Serbia: Trauma and Catharsis*, Budapest, 2000, p. 328. On the Dreyfus case, see notably Christophe Charle, *Naissance des 'intellectuels' 1880–1900*, Paris, 1990.

[19] *Danas*, 23 June 1987, p. 37.

[20] Article 133 of the federal penal code, commonly referred to as the 'verbal offence', prohibited any attempt 'by means of an article, leaflet, drawing, speech or in some other way' to advocate or incite 'the overthrow of the rule of the working class' and the disruption of 'brotherhood, unity and equality of the nations and nationalities', as well as any 'malicious and untruthful portrayal' of the socio-political conditions in the country. See *Amnesty International Report on Yugoslavia*, 1985, pp. 21–2.

wanted the congress to be a manifestation of the 'spirit of Yugoslavism' and criticized the Slovenian stance on the 'common core curricula'. Slovenian representatives, on the other hand, opposed the
slogan 'the congress of unity', arguing that it infringed upon the
principle of national sovereignty embodied in the Yugoslav constitution.[21] The quarrel continued throughout the congress; Bulatović
lamented the creation of eight 'artificial states' in Yugoslavia and
criticized 'autocephalous writers'.[22] Ciril Zlobec, a member of the
Slovenian association's presidency, replied that he was indeed 'an
autocephalous writer and a Slovene' and warned that Slovenes
would only accept a policy based on respect of Slovenian sovereignty.[23] Although the congress ended on a more conciliatory note,
with the adoption of the common declaration endorsing the critical
intellectuals' liberal agenda, the promise of conflict over national
issues loomed large.

The Yugoslav Writers' Union and the politics of 'National Equality', 1985–8

In the second half of the 1980s, the Yugoslav Writers' Union provided the main arena in which intellectuals battled for their national
rights and entitlements.[24] The same two national issues that plagued
Yugoslavia's political élites in the post-Tito era surfaced in debates
between writers: the relationship between the Republic of Serbia
and its two autonomous provinces and that between the republics
and the federation, which manifested itself, like in the early 1960s,
primarily as a Serbian-Slovenian debate. Although the defence of
civil rights and calls for transformation of the system continued to
figure on the agenda of critical intellectuals, these common aspects
of the alternative political scene were overshadowed by the deepening divergences over the 'national question'. The struggle for freedom

<hr>

[21] Zlobec, op. cit., pp. 205–14 passim.
[22] *IX Kongres Saveza književnika Jugoslavije—Dokumenta*, Novi Sad, 1985, pp. 93–9, passim.
[23] Ibid., pp. 112–14, passim.
[24] See also the excellent unpublished paper by Audrey Helfant Budding, 'End of Dialogue: Serbs, Slovenes and the Collapse of the League of Writers of Yugoslavia' (Harvard University).

of speech did, however, leave one enduring legacy: each side couched its own demands for collective national entitlements and statehood in the 'liberal' terminology of human rights and democracy.

The question of Serbia's relationship with its autonomous provinces was initially raised in the Writers' Association of Serbia as a concern about the human rights situation of the minority Serbs in Kosovo. This subject was first broached in 1985, in a context of deepening nationalist polarization in Kosovo, explosive new disclosures concerning the scale of emigration of Serbs and Montenegrins from the province and the first manifestations of a nascent political movement of Kosovo Serbs, acting in its early stages as an independent social force.[25] In this sense, it represented a natural extension of the earlier struggle for freedom of expression to a wider notion of human and civil rights.[26] The catalyst for this new activism was the particularly sordid case of Kosovo Serb peasant Djordje Martinović, who had allegedly been 'impaled' with a bottle by two masked Albanian-speaking men.[27] Official attempts to cover up the case in fear of a nationalist backlash only had the opposite effect; for many Serbian intellectuals, as well as the population more generally, Martinović became a martyr. The first statement pertaining to Kosovo, issued by the Writers' Association of Serbia in June 1985, thus criticized the authorities' handling of the Martinović case and

[25] The causes of Serbian emigration from Kosovo are, of course, disputed between Serbian and Albanian scholars. Although the politicized nature of this issue makes it impossible to ascertain the exact proportion of Serbs that emigrated as a result of pressures and discrimination, independent surveys carried out among Serbian emigrants in the 1980s do, however, indicate that such grievances were at least one important stimulus. See, for example, Marina Blagojević, 'The Migrations of Serbs from Kosovo during the 1970s and 1980s: Trauma and/or Catharsis' in *The Road to War in Serbia*, op. cit., pp. 212–43. On the Kosovo Serb movement, see Veljko Vujačić, 'Communism and Nationalism in Russia and Serbia', Ph.D. thesis, University of California, Berkeley, CA, 1995, pp. 219–30; Nebojša Vladisavljević, 'Nationalism, Social Movement Theory and the Grass Roots Movement of Kosovo Serbs, 1985–1988', *Europe-Asia Studies*, vol. 54, no. 5, July 2002, pp. 771–90.

[26] This point is well-made by Gojković, op. cit. See also my own 'Les intellectuels serbes et la 'question' du Kosovo, 1981–1987', *Relations internationales*, 89, Spring 1997, pp. 53–70.

[27] A collection of articles and documents surrounding this case can be found in Svetislav Spasojević (ed.), *Slučaj Martinović*, Belgrade 1986. For contrasting Albanian and Serbian perceptions of it, see Julie Mertus, *Kosovo: How Myths and Truths Started a War*, Berkeley, CA, 1999, pp. 95–121.

called for a new investigation. In a subsequent declaration, the
organization also raised the problem of Serbian emigration from
the province, yet still within the framework of calling for the establishment of the rule of law and respect of human rights.[28]

Quickly it became clear, however, that for Serbian intellectuals
the defence of the human rights of Kosovo Serbs was linked to the
issues of Serbia's statehood and 'national' entitlement to Kosovo.
The Serbian-Albanian dispute over Kosovo came to a head in July
1985, when forty Kosovan non-Albanian writers sent out an open
letter alleging they had been victims of 'majorization' (a term designating consistent outvoting of a minority national group), most
recently in the election of an Albanian 'nationalist' as the association's president. Although they had resigned in protest, the organization had continued to function as if nothing had happened.[29] A
few months earlier, the president of Serbia's association, Miodrag
Bulatović, had indicated in a radio interview that he would like for
the republic's three writers' organizations to 'foster closer ties'.[30]
The Belgrade organization's defence of the non-Albanian writers'
'equal rights' in the Writers' Society of Kosovo signalled a refusal to
accept minority status for Serbs in the province and represented an
affirmation that Kosovo was still a part of the Republic of Serbia.
The letter of the forty also provided an occasion for Serbian writers
to place the Kosovo issue on the agenda of the Yugoslav Writers'
Union and to seek 'federal' pressure against the Writers' Society of
Kosovo.

The actions of the Yugoslav Writers' Union, however, did not
bring the Serbs the expected results. The Albanian delegates maintained a defiant stand, refusing to acknowledge any ethnic discrimination in their association and accusing the Writers' Association of
Serbia of meddling in Kosovo's internal affairs. For them, maintaining
their controversial choice of president was symbolic of their assertion of Kosovo's independence from Serbia and of their refusal of
any sort of consociational 'power-sharing' arrangement with minority Serbs in the province. In addition, rather than back the Serbian
demands, the Writers' Union condemned *all* forms of discrimination

---

[28] *Književne novine*, no. 691–2, 1 July 1985, p. 2 and no. 693, 1 Sept. 1985, p. 5.
[29] *Književna reč*, no. 260–1, July 1985, p. 3.
[30] See *NIN*, 20 Jan. 1985.

in the province and merely recommended to the Kosovo society to hold its own 'discussion' about the open letter.[31] At its subsequent meetings, this position of 'equidistance' gave way to more overt support for the Albanian stance by the Slovenian, Croatian and Montenegrin organizations. For them too, the quarrel clearly had political implications beyond the issue of democratic participation in the Kosovo organization's decisionmaking process. In their eyes, Serbian demands regarding Kosovo threatened the 'confederate' status quo in Yugoslavia, as did the Belgrade organization's appeal for 'federal' meddling in the 'internal affairs' of a member institution.[32]

The quarrel was temporarily resolved by the direct involvement of Kosovo's communist leadership, which decided to step in before it could be accused of harbouring nationalism and forced the Kosovo Writers' Society to replace its elected president by an ethnic Serb. A year later, however, when the rotational presidency returned to an Albanian, the conflict merely picked up where it had left off. As the Writers' Association of Serbia embraced the cause of the Kosovo Serbs, it increasingly began to call in its petitions and protest evenings for the reduction of Kosovo's autonomy and painted the human rights situation of the Serbs in such extreme terms that it precluded any compromise on Kosovo's status.[33] Albanian intellectuals, on the other hand, rejected Serbian claims about emigration under pressure, characterizing them as merely an attempt to deny Albanians 'national equality' and ensure Serbian domination in Kosovo. They viewed their own nation as the exclusive victim, subject to Serbian oppression throughout history.[34]

The second main confrontation in the Yugoslav Writers' Union involved Serbian and Slovenian writers and, like the Kosovo issue,

[31] *Književne novine*, no. 693, 1 Sept. 1985, pp. 3–6.

[32] See the statements by Ciril Zlobec, Marija Peakić-Mikuljan and Jevrem Brković, the presidents of the Slovenian, Croatian and Montenegrin associations in *NIN*, 17 Nov. 1985, pp. 33–4.

[33] See, for example, the January 1986 petition of over two hundred Serbian intellectuals, reproduced in Branka Magaš, *The Destruction of Yugoslavia: Tracing the Break-Up 1980–92*, London, 1993, p. 49. For an elaboration of this point, see my *Saviours of the Nation*, op. cit.

[34] For some such positions, see Harillaq Kekezi and Rexhep Hida (eds), *What the Kosovars Say and Demand*, Tirana, 1990, pp. 116–27 and 234–6.

concerned questions of 'national equality' and Yugoslavia's federal arrangement. The conflict initially broke out over the election of the president of the Yugoslav Writers' Union. This organization functioned in the same way as other federal institutions: both its assembly and collective presidency were made up of delegates elected by the associations of the federal units. In return, the latter were supposed to represent all the writers of the 'nation and nationalities' of that republic or province. The sole exception was the Slovenian Writers' Society, which was given an ethno-national character by being allowed to represent all Slovenian-speaking writers regardless of where they lived.[35] Organized according to this 'national key', the leadership of the Union's collective presidency rotated annually in alphabetical order, with a routine election of the president acting as *primus inter pares*. Hence the Slovenian president of the Union, Ciril Zlobec, elected after the Novi Sad Congress, was supposed to be replaced by a member of the Writers' Association of Serbia when his term expired in spring 1986.

In February 1986 the Writers' Association of Serbia decided to nominate the controversial writer Miodrag Bulatović as its candidate for president of the Union. The response from Slovenian writers was like that of the Serbian members of the Writers' Society of Kosovo, which they had refused to support: they saw the proposed candidate as a nationalist and announced they would not accept his election.[36] In this, they managed to get support from the Croatian, Kosovan and Montenegrin associations, gathering the votes necessary to block the election. Similarly to the Kosovan organization which it had criticized a year before, the Writers' Association of Serbia announced, on the other hand, that it would not have its candidate 'dictated' to it and maintained Bulatović's nomination. Without any outside political interference this time, the two sides refused to budge, effectively blocking the Union's functioning for two years. The affair had considerable echo throughout the country and was widely viewed as an 'ominous harbinger of a change in behaviour in important spheres of Yugoslav political life'.[37]

[35] Hence also the difference in name: the Slovenian Writers' Society as opposed to the Writers' Association of Serbia, the Writers' Society of Kosovo, the Writers' Society of Croatia etc.
[36] Janez Menart quoted in *Start*, 5 Apr. 1986, p. 18.
[37] *Književne novine*, no. 706, 15 March 1986, p. 2.

In the meantime, relations between Serbian and Slovenian writers' organizations deteriorated further. The cause of this new quarrel was the Slovenian society's invitations to the writers' organizations of Kosovo and Croatia to present their 'national' literatures in Ljubljana. The problem with these invitations was that they flew in the face of the 'national key' prevalent in all organizations except the Slovenian; the associations represented all writers of their federal units, regardless of their language of creation. The Slovenes' designation of 'national literatures' along linguistic and ethnic rather than civic or regional criteria was thus seen as exclusionary.[38] To the Serbs, the invitation of only Albanian writers from the Writers' Society of Kosovo, despite the protests of the latter's Serbian members, represented a blatant disregard of their struggle to achieve 'equal rights' for the Kosovo society's minority Serbs and a clear taking of a pro-Albanian stand in the dispute over the province.[39]

The Croatian invitation was even more contentious and sparked an immediate and heavy-handed response in Serbia.[40] Whereas in the Albanian case, the Slovenes could argue that they merely wanted to become better acquainted with a literature written in a language not used by the other members of the organization, the Croatian case could not be justified on the same grounds. In fact, some of the Croatian participants of the literary evening expressed their discomfort at the Slovenes' invitation, noting that Croatia, unlike Slovenia, was not an ethnically homogenous republic and that Croatian literature encompassed many distinguished writers who were Serbs.[41] Subsequent attempts to justify the invitations as 'inclusive' (of all Croatian writers regardless of internal borders) and not 'exclusive' (of the republic's Serbs) were not convincing, considering that only writers from the one republic were invited and that the 'confederalist' Slovenes were hardly the ones to try to undermine

---

[38] It should be noted, however, that a previous invitation to the Writers' Association of Macedonia did not spark nearly as much controversy. The reason for this was that the status of Serbs in Macedonia was not nearly as disputed as that of Serbs in Kosovo and Croatia. Albanian literature was, of course, to be represented by the Kosovo society.

[39] *Danas*, 3 Nov. 1987, pp. 42–3.

[40] The Slovenian invitations caused much negative press coverage in Serbia and were referred to as 'ethnically clean'. See *NIN*, 12 March 1988, p. 37.

[41] *Danas*, 29 March 1988, p. 35.

Yugoslavia's republics.[42] The explanation for the Slovenes' behaviour was to be found elsewhere; rather than satisfying purely 'literary' interests or even wanting to deliberately exclude Croatian Serbs, the Slovenian invitation represented primarily an endorsement of the stance that Croatian and Serbian were separate languages, which was being backed by Croatian cultural institutions in the new 'language debate' that had erupted in the republic in the mid-1980s.[43] In December 1988, a Slovenian delegation visited the Writers' Society of Croatia, specifically stating that Slovenia was searching for 'democratic allies' in Yugoslavia.[44]

The complete divergence between the Slovenian and Serbian standpoints on the common state became clear when in February 1987 the Presidency of the League of Communists of Yugoslavia called for a public debate on its draft 'Proposal for Change of the SFRY Constitution'.[45] By spring 1988, the two republican writers' associations ended up producing documents which—although they both endorsed democratic systemic change, the respect of human and civil rights, free elections and the rule of law—were fundamentally irreconcilable on the issue of Yugoslavia's internal arrangement. The Slovenian 'writers' constitution' of April 1988 dropped all pretence at being 'Yugoslav' and focused solely on defining the Republic of Slovenia as 'the state of the Slovenian nation'. Evoking the Slovenes' 'historical right to self-determination, including the right to participation in a union of states or the secession from such a union of states, the right to free decision making about internal political relations and about matters of defence', it stated that

---

[42] This was argued by Predrag Matvejević, *NIN,* 24 Apr. 1988, pp. 40–1.

[43] This new 'language debate' resurfaced when Croatia's leading communist, Stipe Šuvar—well-known 'pro-Yugoslav' and political conservative—tried to change the republic's constitutional provision designating 'Croatian' as the language of public use in Croatia (this was one of the concessions made by the régime in 1974). The Writers' Society of Croatia spearheaded the resistance to this change, emerging victorious when, in August 1989, the Croatian parliament voted to maintain the existing provision. See *Danas,* 3 Nov. 1987, p. 37, and 23 May 1989, pp. 35–7.

[44] Ervin Fric quoted in *Danas,* 13 Dec. 1988, p. 38.

[45] On the federal proposal, see Sabrina P. Ramet, *Nationalism and Federalism in Yugoslavia 1962–1991,* Bloomington, IN, 1992, p. 219 and Susan L. Woodward, *Balkan Tragedy: Chaos and Dissolution after the Cold War,* Washington, DC, 1995, pp. 82–5.

only once this right had been put into practice should the republic enter negotiations to define its future relationship with the rest of Yugoslavia.[46] To Slovenian intellectuals, whose republic encompassed almost all ethnic Slovenes in Yugoslavia and contained no significant minorities, the common South Slav state was clearly dispensable.

The Serbian intellectuals' 'Contribution to the Public Debate on the Constitutional Changes', on the other hand, maintained a 'Yugoslav' veneer, reflecting the fact that for Serbs, the common state still represented the best framework for the solution of their 'national question'. Yet, their proposal was tailored to fit Serbian needs and thus contained an inherent contradiction. On the one hand, it advocated reintegration of the federation to ensure 'the establishment of total national, spiritual and cultural integrity of each Yugoslav people, regardless of republic or province'—which went against the 'confederate' arrangement of the country. On the other, it called for the constitution of the Republic of Serbia as a state, with powers over its whole territory, including the autonomous provinces—implying the maintenance of the same 'confederate' structure, but merely applying it 'equally' to Serbia.[47] Only the maintenance of Yugoslavia enabled the Serbs to claim the ethnically preponderantly Albanian province of Kosovo while concurrently promoting their own national unity, alternating between constitutional and ethno-national arguments according to need. If Yugoslavia was to disintegrate, however, this fundamental contradiction in the Serbian national platform was bound to surface.

Conclusion: the demise of the Yugoslav Writers' Union

By 1988 the intellectuals' debate on Yugoslavia had arrived at a dead end. Uncompromising national claims left no room for agreement on the common state or its organizations. For Slovenes, who represented a small nation even by Yugoslavia's standards, 'equality' implied total national sovereignty and the right to veto any decision they disagreed with, regardless of the majority will in the federation. For Serbs, who were both the most dispersed throughout Yugoslavia

---

[46] 'Predlog slovenačkih pisaca: republički ustav', *Književne novine*, no. 755, 1 June 1988, p. 17.

[47] 'Prilog javnoj raspravi o ustavu', *Književne novine*, no. 751, 1 Apr. 1988, pp. 1–4.

and the only ones whose republic had two autonomous provinces, 'equality' meant both statehood for Serbia and national unity in a reintegrated Yugoslavia. For Albanians, it denoted republican status for Kosovo and independence from Serbia. For Croats, it implied the right to Croatian statehood, a separate language and culture. For too many Yugoslav writers, Yugoslavia no longer represented an ideal worth striving for, outside the satisfaction of their own, narrowly defined, national interests. Considering their total lack of empathy for each other's needs and concerns, it is not surprising that the Yugoslav Writers' Union could not survive.

Ironically, the demise of the federal writers' organization came soon after the stalemate over the Union's president had finally been resolved and Serbia's new nominee, novelist and playwright Slobodan Selenić, was unanimously accepted. Yet already the Congress of the Writers' Union, held to formalize Selenić's election, showed that none of the underlying problems had been resolved. At the congress, the Serbs and Montenegrins in the Writers' Society of Kosovo announced they had resigned from their organization, complaining of constant 'majorization'. They were supported, as usual, by the Writers' Association of Serbia and now also by the new pro-Serbian leadership of the Writers' Association of Montenegro, which broke off relations with the Kosovo association. The Montenegrin organization's former president, Jevrem Brković, who represented the 'Green' or Montenegrin-nationalist tradition, had, in turn, been accepted as an honorary member of the Writers' Society of Croatia, which pitted the Montenegrin and Croatian organizations against each other. The Croatian and Slovenian associations now openly backed the Writers' Society of Kosovo, seeing 'no rational argument' for the Serbs' and Montenegrins' resignation.[48] A few months later, in February 1989, following the mass rally in Ljubljana supporting the Kosovo Albanian resistance to the reduction of the province's autonomy, the Writers' Association of Serbia broke off relations with the Slovenian Writers' Society; in turn, the Kosovo organization broke off with the Serbian.

The final meeting of the presidency of the Yugoslav Writers' Union was a complete fiasco: the writers' societies of Croatia and

[48] Rudi Šeligo quoted in *NIN*, 12 March 1989, p. 38.

Kosovo did not even take part, while the delegates from Serbia, Montenegro and Slovenia argued for hours, unable even to produce a concluding statement. When the president of the Slovenian organization, tried to force a vote on a number of controversial issues, the other delegates simply refused to comply. This time it was the Slovenes' turn to complain of 'majorization' and to announce that they would no longer participate in an organization where they had been victim to Serbian 'ultrahegemonic and destructive action'.[49] Soon a joint letter followed from the Slovenian and Croatian organizations announcing that the Yugoslav Writers' Union no longer existed.[50] For most Serbian writers, the Slovenes' and Croats' exit from the Writers' Union was merely a 'rehearsal of something much more serious'.[51]

As Slobodan Selenić, the Union's last president, noted when he resigned after several months of unsuccessfully trying to get the various sides to even talk to each other, the fate of Writers' Union was inextricably linked to that of Yugoslavia as a state.[52] By this time, the process of 'national homogenization' was well under way in the Yugoslav republics and provinces and the local leaderships had adopted the same uncompromising positions as their intellectual élites. The demise of the Yugoslav Writers' Union thus foreshadowed the fate of Yugoslavia's other federal organizations. Not only had critical intellectuals failed to create a genuine alternative to Yugoslavia's moribund communist system and negotiate a democratic, compromise solution to the country's complex 'national question', but they had actually set a precedent for the disintegration of the common state.

[49] *Danas*, 20 June 1989, p. 43.
[50] *Danas*, 27 June 1989, p. 38.
[51] Slobodan Selenić quoted in *Osmica*, 12 Oct. 1989, in Slobodan Selenić, *Iskorak u stvarnost*, Belgrade, 1995, p. 50.
[52] *NIN*, 17 Nov. 1989, p. 34.

Part V. ALTERNATIVES

THE DEMOCRATIC ALTERNATIVE

Desimir Tošić

How was the Democratic Alternative (DA), a group of exiled Yugo-slav democrats, formed and what was its position *vis-à-vis* national-ism and Yugoslav unity? Before we attempt to find an answer to these questions, it should be borne in mind that émigré communi-ties from Yugoslavia, especially the Serbian and Croatian, were not only anti-Communist but also extremely nationalist. It may be argued that the Yugoslav civil war that took place during the Sec-ond World War had continued verbally, in the diaspora. The DA had not only opposed Tito's Communist régime at home, but also émigré groups abroad. Because of Yugoslavia's specific international position following the break-up with the Soviet Union in 1948—a Communist country outside the Warsaw Pact—and Tito's prestige, the country was receiving, at least while its leader was alive, substan-tial economic and political support from the West. So, ideas and views of the DA were not supported not only by the régime in the country and the nationalist diaspora, but also by Western countries, where members of the group lived.

What were the main ideological differences between the Demo-cratic Alternative and Tito's régime? The DA supported federalism because it believed that it was the best way in which to solve the national question in Yugoslavia. But, it did not agree that the national question had been solved, especially not already during the revolution and liberation struggle of 1941–5, as the Yugoslav com-munists and their supporters in the West claimed. The DA did not underestimate nationalism and it did not think it could simply dis-appear. Its members argued that Yugoslav Communists were in fact using nationalism, both during the war, and after, in order to con-solidate popular support and the authoritarian régime. Yugoslavia was much more a party-state than a state of Serbs, Croats, Slovenes, Macedonians, Montenegrins and Bosnian Muslims. Therefore, once the League of Communists of Yugoslavia collapsed, Yugoslavia was doomed to failure. The DA believed that the national question can only be solved through the democratisation of Yugoslavia and through a more realistic approach to nationalism.[1]

What was the essence of the Yugoslavism of the Democratic Alternative? Firstly, it supporetd a unified Yugoslav state, but rejected the interwar integral Yugoslavism. It believed that federalism was the best way to internally arrange Yugoslavia. The DA recognised the right of each Yugoslav *nation* to self-determination, because each nation had a right to its own state, but that right was extended to a whole *nation*, not to a *republic*. Apart from recognising the existence of strong ethnic, cultural, and economic bonds between the Yugoslav nations, the DA supported the unity of Yugoslavia because it believed—both in 1963, when the debate about a democratic alternative began, and in 1982, when 'The Design for a Democratic Alternative: Final Text' (reproduced in full in this volume) was published—that

[...] to try and establish separate independent states and to do so in a manner aimed to satisfy separate majorities of Serbs, of the Croats, the Slovenes, the Macedonians and of the Bosnian Muslims is likely, in the course of setting frontiers to produce fatal conflicts that would bring into question the interests of each one of them.

The Democratic Alternative clearly did not distinguish between Serbs and Montenegrins, nor did it envisage a separate Montenegrin republic. Its view was that this issue should be decided by the peoples of Serbia and Montenegro. It should also be noted that the DA emphasized that the right to a separate state should only be exercised by those Yugoslav nations which had their own 'national territory'. That meant that although the Bosnian Muslims were recognized as a separate Yugoslav nation, equal to other Yugoslav

---

[1] For a discussion on nations and nationalism organised by the Democratic Alternative see 'Nationality and "The National Question"', *Review of the Study Centre for Jugoslav Affairs*, vol. 2, no. 2, London, 1975, pp. 123–66. The participants in the debate were Vane Ivanović, Stevan K. Pavlowitch, Franjo Sekolec, Ljubo Sirc and Desimir Tošić.

nations, because they had no clearly defined national territory, the possibility of them having the right to a separate state was not considered feasible.

The DA's genuine insistence on democracy and legality distinguished it not only from the former Communist régime, but also from Yugoslavia's successor states and from some international factors which mediated the Yugoslav conflicts of the 1990s. It was clear that all referenda organized in post-Yugoslav republics were more results of manipulation of masses than genuine democratic exercises. The DA throughout its activity emphasized that the decision on the future arrangement of the country must be based on principles of pluralist democracy and real equality. For instance, in the 'The Design for a Democratic Alternative', it envisaged that:

> In the interest of ensuring the equality of Member-States and individual nations the seats of the principal organs and institutions of the Union should be distributed policentrically among member-states and not centralized in the territory of any one Member-State.

Who were these people who attempted, while ignoring the nationalist émigré circles, and without any material or moral support from the West, to establish a dialogue with the Yugoslav régime over the national question in Yugoslavia?

The Democratic Alternative was founded in 1963, when a group of Yugoslav émigré politicians and their younger collaborators met at an estate in Stansted, in Great Britain. They were: Božidar Vlajić, former General Secretary of the interwar Democratic Party (DS) of Ljuba Davidović and Milan Grol, Ilija Jukić, a leading younger member of the pre-war Croatian Peasant Party (HSS) and a deputy Minister of Foreign Affairs of several governments-in-exile between 1941–44, Miha Krek, a leader of the pre-war Slovene People's Party (SLS) and a former government minister; Branko M. Pešelj, another leading younger member of the HSS and a legal expert from George Washington University, who drafted the basis of the 1982 Text. Than, there were the journalist Franjo Sekolec (SLS), Catholic priest Nace Čretnik (SLS), Vladimir Predavec (HSS, son of Josip, the former vice-president of the HSS while Stjepan Radić was the president), Vane Ivanović, a well known Yugoslav sportsman and businessman, Dušan Popović (formerly of National Radical Party—NRS), Miodrag Djordjević, a former army officer, and Desimir Tošić, president of the youth section of the DS in the late 1930s and editor of the monthly *Naša reč*, (published first in Paris and than in London between 1948 and 1990).

The Stansted meeting followed a series of regular informal meetings between Božidar Vlajić, Vane Ivanović and Franjo Sekolec, who were later joined by Desimir Tošić. The *spiritus movens* behind the initial meetings was Vlajić, while Vane Ivanović, half Croat, half Serb, provided both financial support and a 'link' between Serbs and Croats who later took part in the Democratic Alternative. Vladko Maček, who did not officially join the group, nevertheless supported its activities, and gave his blessing to the HSS members, Pešelj and Jukić, who were an integral part of the DA. In the twenty years between the two events—the Stansted meeting and the completion of the Final Text—members of the DA and other democratic-minded Yugoslav émigrés, had a number of meetings and discussions, and the results of some of these were published in Serbo-Croat.[2]

By the time the Final Text was being completed, in the early 1980s, the group was joined by Adil Zulfikarpašić, Teufik Velagić (Bosnian Muslims), Bogoljub Kočović and Nenad Petrović (both Serbs). Its activities were supported by two dissidents from Yugoslavia, Mihajlo Mihajlov and Aleksa Djilas and by Ljubo Sirc, a Slovene Professor of economics at Glasgow University.[3]

The Democratic Alternative was severely criticised both in Yugoslavia and among émigré circles, and was largely ignored in the West. The Yugoslav régime accused the DA of being separatist, because it

---

[2] For more on the activities and history of the Democratic Alternative see the following three books by Vane Ivanović, *LX: Memoirs of a Jugoslav*, London, 1977; *Drugo zvono*, 2 vols, Belgrade, 1998, 2nd edn (or the 1993 Zagreb edition); *Yugoslav Democracy on Hold*, ed. by Petar Ladjević and Gregor MacGregor, Rijeka, 1996. See also two books of interviews with members of the DA: Mirko Galić, *Politika u emigraciji: Demokratska alternativa*, Zagreb, 1990, and Gorazd Suhadolnik, *Ključnih pet: Intervjui Gorazda Suhadolnika sa članovima Demokratske alternative*, Ljubljana, 1990.

[3] Vlajić, Jukić, Krek, Čretnik and Djordjević died before the Final Text was completed.

emphasized the right to self-determination, but only 11 years after the Stansted meeting, the Yugoslav Constitution of 1974 had also recognized this right. The émigré circles, especially the Croats, strongly criticised the DA for its pro-Yugoslav position.

From today's perspective it seems to me, and I hope I am not being immodest, that the Democratic Alternative was the only Yugoslav group which offered a real alternative, both in the 1960s and in the 1980s—an alternative vision of Yugoslavia and Yugoslavism, but also an alternative to the violent disintegration of the common Yugoslav state. Did the people around the DA do enough to propagate their ideas more forcefully? Perhaps not, but it must be borne in mind that the Democratic Alternative was a small group of intellectuals, not supported by anyone, either in the country or abroad. The only organized group to lend it its support was the Serbian émigré organisation *Oslobodjenje*, but its support was not enough, especially as *Oslobodjenje* too was a relatively small organization, whose democratic and pro-Yugoslav views did not receive much support either at home or in diaspora. Yugoslavia is no more today and Yugoslavism is a failed idea. A democratic alternative to the royal dictatorship of first and communist one-party rule of second Yugoslavia was never given a chance. If it had been, perhaps the tragedy of the 1990s could have been avoided.

THE DESIGN FOR A DEMOCRATIC ALTERNATIVE: FINAL TEXT[4]

Preamble

The right to decide on the future organization of whatever form of association of the nations of Yugoslavia, based on the concepts of a pluralistic democracy and true equality amongst them, belongs exclusively to the nations themselves at home. Respect for democratic procedures requires that before any decisions are taken there should take place a thorough and comprehensive debate on the state institutions necessary to secure a democratic order that would satisfy not only the citizen as an individual but

[4] Reproduced from Vane Ivanović, *Yugoslav Democracy on Hold*, op. cit., pp. 117–24. Only minor corrections and alterations in style have been made. All emphasis are in original.

each of the national collectives concerned. That is why, from the very inception of communist dominion over the country, men from Yugoslavia living in western democracies began their debate on a democratic alternative that might successfully challenge the régime in power. To be fruitful, any debate requires discipline and method so that acceptable ideas might be woven into a harmonious whole.

The design here presented is the fruit of many years of debate and labour that followed the inaugural round-table conference on the Stansted Estate, Surrey in England in 1963. Of course, this text has no other aim or ambition beyond sparking public and fair exchanges of views on the problem facing our nations. We trust that in the presenting it we may be seen to have initiated a down to earth, tolerant discussion on issues that will determine the very future of all the nations of Yugoslavia.

Introduction

After more than four decades of unrestricted power communist rule in Yugoslavia has bred a host of disquieting developments in the political, economic and cultural fields. Its attempts to resolve the national conflicts in Yugoslavia are merely superficial. In truth, discord among the nations of Yugoslavia has taken new forms and has spread to other spheres of public life. In many ways contentions have deepened, bringing with them impending dangers for each of the nations of Yugoslavia and all of them together.

With the aggravation of difficulties among the nations and also in the spheres of economics and finance, conflicts have erupted in the higher echelons of the League of Communists. Efforts to reorganize the Party have been undertaken not so much to liberalize the present totalitarian power but rather to preserve it. Under the weight of these trials and worries, communist ranks are seized by anxiety and confusion that cannot remain without serious effect on the stability and resilience of their régime.

In these circumstances it is the duty of men of good will and enlightenment from all the nations of Yugoslavia, at home or in the free-world, who seek a truly democratic solution of their political, social and national problems to devote themselves to the development of a democratic alternative to the present communist régime. Such an alternative must embrace the whole area of Yugoslavia. It must outline, in contrast to the power structure of the ruling dictatorship, the features of a future Union of the nations of Yugoslavia established on democratic and mutually agreed foundations.

Fundamental principles

In accord with the principle that every nation is endowed with the right to its independent national sovereign state, this right also belongs to each of the nations of Yugoslavia. The starting point of any accord among the nations of Yugoslavia is the recognition of the right of each of them to declare, through its freely chosen representatives, whether it wishes to remain in the Yugoslav Union or whether it will demand its own independent state. Should any one of the sovereign nations of Yugoslavia decide to establish its own independent national state, it has, on the principles of national self-determination, every right to create such a state.

Nevertheless, we consider that to try and establish separate independent states and to do so in a manner aimed to satisfy separate majorities of Serbs, of the Croats, the Slovenes, the Macedonians and of the Bosnian Muslims is likely, in the course of setting frontiers to produce fatal conflicts that would bring into question the interests of each one of them. The prime purpose of the design here presented is to bring into harmony the sovereignty of each nation with a Union that would enable and secure a free life and the national identity of each nation.

Application

1. The Union would be an association of five sovereign nations—the Serb, the Croat, the Slovene, the Macedonian and the Bosniak-Muslim[5]—which would establish a Union state composed of five member states: Serbia, Croatia Slovenia, Bosnia-Hercegovina and Macedonia. The question whether Montenegro is to be a separate Member-State or is to be united with Serbia would be decided by the national representatives of Serbia and Montenegro.

2. The primary purpose of the Union would be to preserve the sovereignty of each of the five nations of Yugoslavia; to guarantee the equality of all member states; to reconcile their individual interests in the Union.

3. Member-States would have, by their general character as states, through their right of self-establishment, and by the extent of their competencies, the character of state from the point of view of legal doctrine.

4. The territorial boundaries between Member-States would in general follow the present division of Yugoslavia in Socialist Republics. The boundaries between Serbia and Croatia would be decided by the national representatives of Serbs and Croats, elected to the Constituent Assembly, and guided by the wishes of the Serb and Croat boundary populations.

---

[5] In the original, the authors use term *Bošnjaci-Muslimani*, but in this translation both terms 'Bosnian Muslims' and 'Bosniak-Muslims' (which would be a better translation of the original) are used, so it has been decided not alter the original English text, even if it is inconsistent.

5. The first Constitution of the Union would be decided by a single chamber Constituent Assembly, elected, in accord with a common electoral law, on the same day, by all adult citizens of the Union of both sexes. The electoral system must be founded on the number of citizens of each national entity. The decisions of the Constituent Assembly would be valid if they were voted by the majority of Serb, the majority of Croat, the majority of Slovene, the majority of Macedonian and the majority of Bosnian Muslim national representatives to the Constituent Assembly.

The majority of national representatives of any one of the sovereign nations of Yugoslavia, elected to the Constituent Assembly, would be empowered to decide not to take any further part in constituent procedures and to demand the separation of the nation it represented to the Constituent Assembly.

6. The first Constitution of the Union would provide Union organs and the procedure for constitutional revision as well as for the exercise of the right of national self-determination after the Constitution had come into force. In particular, the Constitution would allow for provisions determining whether, in the procedure for revision, Parliaments of Member-States should take part by way of ratification of any proposed revision.

7. On the basis of their right to self-establishment Member-States would enact their own Constitutions and Laws independently. The Constitution and Laws of Member-States would have to be in harmony with the Constitution and Laws of the Union.

Member-states could not enact constitutional an legal provision which would be contrary to fundamental human rights and rights of the citizen and which would differentiate between citizens of the Union by reason of their sex, nationality, religion, domicile or political affiliation.

Distribution of power

The Union would enjoy only such powers as would be explicitly granted to it by the first Constitution—the first Constitution and subsequent amendments. All other powers would belong to Member-States.

The competence of the Union should include:

1. *The establishment of the Union.* The Constitution, Union Laws, the Executive and Judiciary of the Union, as defined in this design.

2. *Foreign policy and international relations.* Member-States would be entitled to establish within the diplomatic missions of the Union their own cultural, commercial, tourist and emigrant agencies.

3. *National defence with the following limitations.* The competence of the Union would include (*a*) The establishment of guiding principles by way of basic laws; (*b*) the organization, direction and command of special defence units and institutions in war and peace. Apart from these specific functions, national defence in times of peace would be in the competence of Member-States with the Member-States having their own defence budgets. In times of war the entire national defence would fall under the omnipotence of the Union. Member-States would be empowered to seek the co-operation of the Union in the establishment of their own national defences.

4. *Finances of Union.* The revenues of the Union would be directly provided by customs charges and indirectly by contributions from Member-States in accordance with scale to be determined annually by the Parliament of the Union.

5. *In the domain of the civil and criminal law* the Union would enact basic laws with guiding principles, while the elaboration of such laws would fall under the competence of Member-States. In the domain of civil and criminal judicial procedures the Union would have exclusive legislative competence. In accordance with the fundamental principles governing relations between a Union and Member-States, and as has here been stated, all powers not explicitly granted to the Union by the Constitution would belong to Member-States.

6. *Monetary and foreign exchange matters,* with the National Bank as the emissary institution, and Customs, so that the Union would form a single monetary and customs region in accordance with specific agreement amongst Member-States.

7. *Trade.* The Union would establish guiding principles, harmonize trading policies of Member-States, and supervise the applications of the general guiding principles it had drawn up.

8. In the domain of *Transport, Posts, Telegraph, Telephones, Radio and Television,* the Union would enact general legislation, drawing up guiding principles.

9. The Union would be competent for basic laws concerning *Citizenship* whilst the elaboration of such basic laws and the granting of citizenship would fall to Member-States.

10. The Constitution would set out guarantees and procedures so that, in the services of the Union and its institutions, the nations of Yugoslavia and national minorities would each be represented in proportion to the number of their citizens in the Union. (Example: The Ministries of the Union,

National Defence Command, the Constitutional Court, the National Bank, etc).

The Constitution would provide corresponding guarantees in regard to the composition of the Government of the Union and the Head of the State.

Institutions of the Union

1. In the interest of insuring the equality of Member-States and individual nations the seats of the principal organs and institutions of the Union should be distributed policentrically among Member-States and not centralized in the territory of any-one Member-State.

2. The supreme organ of the Union would be the Parliament of the Union consisting of two Houses: The National Assembly and the Council of Members of States. The National Assembly would be elected on the same day, in conformity with a common electoral law, by adult citizens of the Union of both sexes. The electoral system must be founded on the number of citizens of each nation and national minorities in the Union. The Council of States would consist of an equal number of delegates elected for each Member-State by the Parliaments of Member-States.

Each national group in the Parliament of a Member-State would elect for the Council of States such a number of delegates that corresponded to the proportion which each national group in the Parliament bore to the aggregate number of Members of Parliament in the Parliament of the Member-State.

The two Houses of the Parliament of the Union would be equal in power.

Political Laws, such as laws establishing the organization of the Union, laws establishing the relations between the Union and the Member-States, and laws determining the political rights of citizens, primarily the Electoral Law, would be decided upon by a two-thirds majority in both Houses. Legislation of a non-political character would be decided by a simple majority in both Houses.

3. The Constitution of the Union would contain provisions defining the function and powers of the Head of State and the Government of the Union in conformity with the principles of parliamentary government and of full equality of the nations of the Union, by applying the principle of rotation and limits to terms of office.

4. The Constitutional Court of the Union would decide on the constitutionality of the laws and procedures of the executive of the Union and on

the compatibility of the laws and acts of the executives of Member-States with the Constitution and Laws of the Union. The Constitution of the Union would provide organs of the Union competent to supervise the application of the Constitution and its Laws on the part of Member-States. The Constitution would also provide for sanctions in the case of violation of the Constitution and the Laws of the Union by organs of Member-States. The Constitutional Court would furthermore have competence for the protection of human rights of citizens of the Union from violation by institutions whether of the Union or Member-States.

Building principles for the Union and member-states

1. All citizens of the Union would enjoy full national, civil, political and religious liberties and would enjoy equality throughout the territory of the Union without regard to their sex, nationality, religion, domicile or political affiliation. All citizens of the Union would have the right of unhindered movement, residence, employment and political activity throughout of the Union.

2. The trading, social and cultural policies of the Union and Member-States within their competencies, should be founded on the principle of respect for the dignity of the human individual and on principle of respect for the dignity of the human individual and on rationally conceived principles of the welfare state. In the economy all three sectors—the private, the co-operative and the public—should occupy their appropriate places so as to harmonize the interests of individual members of society with the interests of society as a whole. Individual enterprises and central institutions in the public sector should be distributed among individual boroughs, Member-States and the Union in order to achieve harmony of their interests.

3. In particular, the following should be guaranteed; free co-operative association and the establishment of co-operative property, the right of peasant property; free trade union association and the introduction of real participation of producers in enterprise management and income in a manner that would take account of the economy and society as a whole.

4. Freedom of religion and conscience and the freedom of churches, religious organizations and the public expression of their faiths to be guaranteed throughout the territory of the Union. Churches and religious organizations would be separated both from the Union and Member-States and they would at the same time be guaranteed freedom from interference by the authorities of the Union and Member-State in internal religious and church matters.

The churches would be guaranteed freedom of religious teaching.

5. Unlimited freedom and independence of the press and all other media of information.

6. Unlimited freedom of artistic creation, cultural activities, education, science and research, and unlimited freedom of Universities.

We agree on the principles stated in this text and we bind ourselves to support the essential ideas laid out in this text of a design for a Democratic Alternative.

Dr Branko Pešelj, Desimir Tošić, Franjo Sekolec, Vane Ivanović, Adil Zulfikarpašić, Vladimir Predavec, Nenad Petrović, Teufik Velagić, Dr Bogoljub Kočović.

London, 22 February 1982

THE ASSOCIATION FOR YUGOSLAV DEMOCRATIC INITIATIVE[1]

Branko Horvat

Because it will be much discussed later what we are, I shall try to explain briefly what we are not. The public has been misinformed about the proceedings of our first meeting of January [1989]. There have emerged three main 'myths' about our Association, and the aim of these remarks is to counter them.

1. *We are not an alternative movement.* To have an alternative means to have at least two possible solutions. For Yugoslavia there is no alternative to any other solution but radical democratisation.

2. *We are not a new political party,* like the ones that are being formed in Slovenia. Every political party is an organization of the like-minded, whose aim is to take power. We are not interested in power, nor do we all think the same [...] We do not want a uniformed way of thinking and I do not expect all my colleagues to agree with every single word I am saying now. We believe in different opinions. We think that a struggle of opinions is a guarantee of progress.

We do not wish to be a political party, because our aim is more fundamental: [it is] the formation of a movement for a democratic transformation of Yugoslavia. Therefore, we are not interested in power, but in creating conditions in which such a [democratic] transformation would be possible. Naturally, if someone tried to violently prevent the democratisation of the country, we would

---

[1] Published as 'Uvodna riječ' in *Republika*, vol. 1, no. 1, Zagreb, March 1989. The text has been translated and slightly edited by Dejan Djokić.

have to organize ourselves politically, in order to stop the violence. Luckily, the present situation does not merit such an action.

It goes without saying that the Yugoslav society is in a state of deep crisis. The roots of the crisis lay in the long and systematic prevention of the democratic processes in the country. It was the lack of democracy which discredited the self-management, destroyed any initiative and motivation for work and created an almost limitless degree of political irresponsibility. That is why we are organizing the Association [for Yugoslav Democratic Initiative], as an organization of individuals who feel intellectual and moral duty towards their own country.

3. *We are not a militant or*—to use the old jargon—*a revolutionary organization*. We do not wish to bring the régime down by creating chaos, nor by organizing street protests and meetings of solidarity. Instead of destruction and public disorder, we propose reconstruction and rebuilding [of the society] by democratic means. Discontent in Montenegro and even Vojvodina is understandable and I myself wondered how it did not break-out earlier and also in other parts of the country. Because of the lack of democratic institutions, the people have come out on the streets, and are now, as it usually happens, used by political demagogues whose sole interest is power. We campaign for a democratic initiative; we want to prevent future problems by solving them in time and by democratic means.

Democracy means tolerance towards different opinions, dialogue instead of accusations, full acceptance of the will of the majority and effective protection of the rights of the minority. To those who were brought up in the warrior's and epic tradition, such views might appear soft, mild and opportunistic. But they are not. In the long term only such an approach can lead to lasting solutions. Luckily, Yugoslavia's [existence] is no longer under threat, so weapons—both real and metaphorical—can be given up. [The language of] violence and destruction must be replaced by deep principles and persistence. Such a democracy is the key to the Yugoslav problems. That is the basis from which we will argue for a democratic transformation of the Yugoslav federation and each of its constituent parts. It is on that basis that we hope to help the creation of a state of law which will guarantee the civic rights of every Yugoslav.

If I may at the end be allowed a personal remark, only by the country's democratisation will we be able to return to building the authentic socialism, which without the democracy is turning into a terrifying farce.

MANIFESTO FOR THE YUGOSLAV DEMOCRATIC INITIATIVE[2]

Yugoslavia's political, cultural and economic crisis, which has been going on for years now, is reversing the results of the country's earlier achievements and is placing a large number of [Yugoslav] citizens under difficult living conditions. National and social divisions are making impossible the [Yugoslavs'] co-existence today and, especially, in future, while the lack of a democratic government precludes any changes.

1. In such a situation, the Association for Yugoslav Democratic Initiative believes that the most fundamental reason for its establishment is the fact that in present-day Yugoslavia there is no political initiative that is both Yugoslav *and* democratic.

2. In its attempts to introduce a democratic initiative into Yugoslav politics, the Association begins from the following premises:

a. Yugoslavia today is a state which is neither organized democratically nor it has a democratic legitimacy; its current constitutional and legal system does not allow for the public existence and activities of diverse interests and ideas, of individual and different [views], whose public debate could create conditions for solutions satisfactory to the majority and acceptable to everyone.

b. Political decision-making in present-day Yugoslavia is in many respects possible only between previously legitimised national-states, so that the federal system hardly functions and is not based on direct decision-making of its [Yugoslavia's] citizens.

c. Yugoslavia—with its enormous political, economic and cultural difficulties—functions with the help of a political system which has been imposed on the society and especially on the economy, preventing individuals—as subjects—from managing their own

[2] Published as 'Manifest za Jugoslavensku Demokratsku Inicijativu' in *Republika*, vol. 1, no. 1, Zagreb, March 1989. Translated by Dejan Djokić. All emphasis added.

existence and joining with other [individuals] for the purpose of material, spiritual and political improvement on the basis of personal interests.

d. Due to privileges systematically granted to the state–party leaderships, the establishment of the concept of the *democratic nation*, which would unite all citizens regardless, but with respect to, their ethnic, sexual, professional, religious, political, social, cultural, and other differences, is in present–day Yugoslavia impossible.

3. Due to all these reasons, the Association will concentrate its activities in order to enable the following to come about:

a. Yugoslavia turn into a democratic and federal community, that is a community of [its] citizens *and* federal units.

b. The citizen constitutionally becoming the basis of a democratic integration of the [Yugoslav] union, both at the federal level and at the level of federal units, as well as local communities.

c. Yugoslavia being politically governed—as a representative, democratic federal community—by a Yugoslav parliament (with the [two] houses directly representing Yugoslav citizens and federal units).

d. The creation of political, cultural and legal conditions for a legally guaranteed, rather than simply granted by the will of the régime, political pluralism; such political pluralism should bring long-term national benefits, but also, at least in a long run, vis-à-vis Europe.

e. The preservation of legal rights of each employed citizen to influence the management of their companies.

4. In order to achieve these aims, and to strengthen their results for the benefit of future generations, it is assumed that the members of the Association:

a. Have voluntarily joined the Association, in order to contribute to the fulfilment of the above-mentioned aims.

b. Are aware of limitations of seeing Yugoslavia simply through national divisions, because there are important aspects of everyday life of all Yugoslav citizens which can be rationally governed at the level of Yugoslavia as a whole.

c. Have accepted mutual ideological, national, political, religious and other differences as facts which have to be taken into account, so that a solution to problems be sought on democratic principles.

d. Accept that democracy means having the government elected by
a majority, the rights of *all* minorities guaranteed, as well as
undisputable rights of individuals, whose mutual differences are
tolerated.

e. Strongly believe that only by a democratic and public action it is
possible to achieve democratic aims.

MEMBERS OF THE UJDI COUNCIL

Bogdan Bogdanović, Belgrade
Blaženka Despot, Zagreb
Radivoje Lola Djukić, Belgrade
Jug Grizelj, Belgrade
Franjo Grčević, Zagreb
Branko Horvat, Zagreb (PRESIDENT OF THE COUNCIL)
Smiljan Jurin, Zagreb
Milan Kangrga, Zagreb
Lev Kreft, Ljubljana
Andrija Krešić, Belgrade
Muhamedin Kullashi, Priština
Ivan Kuvačić, Zagreb
Skëlzen Maliqi, Priština
Siniša Maričić, Zagreb
Predrag Matvejević, Zagreb
Jovan Mirić, Zagreb
Milan Mirić, Zagreb
Vesna Pešić, Belgrade
Miroslav Pečujlić, Belgrade
Nebojša Popov, Belgrade
Koča Popović, Belgrade
Nada Popović-Perišić, Belgrade
Ivan Prpić, Zagreb
Ljubiša Ristić, Subotica
Laslo Sekelj, Belgrade
Božidar Gajo Sekulić, Sarajevo
Abdulah Sidran, Sarajevo
Mirko Simić, Zemun
Svetlana Slapšak, Belgrade

Karlo Štajner, Zagreb
Rudi Supek, Zagreb
Ljubomir Tadić, Belgrade
Aleksandar Tijanić, Belgrade
Dubravka Ugrešić, Zagreb
Mirjana Ule, Ljubljana
Tibor Varadi, Novi Sad
Laslo Vegel, Novi Sad
Zoran Vidaković, Belgrade
Nikola Visković, Split
Predrag Vranicki, Zagreb
Srdjan Vrcan, Split
Boris Vušković, Split
Ante Zemljar, Zagreb

THE UJDI EXECUTIVE COMMITTEE

Alija Hodžić, Bojan Munjin, Ivo Špigel, Lino Veljak, Mirjana Kasapović, Mladen Lazić, Nenad Zakošek, Petar Ladjević, Srdjan Dvornik, Tomislav Reškovac, Zoran Milović, Žarko Puhovski (PRESIDENT OF THE EXECUTIVE COMMITTEE), Silva Mežnarić, Milorad Pupovac (ALL FROM ZAGREB).

ALBANIANS IN YUGOSLAVIA

A PERSONAL ESSAY

Ramadan Marmullaku

In April 2001 the twentieth anniversary of the turbulent events of 1981 at the University of Prishtina (Priština)[1] was celebrated by the university staff and students as 'the Albanian spring'. I spent several days in Prishtina at that time and did not notice much interest among the Kosova (Kosovo) Albanians for the celebration or for the events of 1981, despite the organizers' best attempts to promote the commemoration. This despite that it may be argued that the political crisis of the second Yugoslavia began with the riots at the Prishtina University on 7 March 1981, leading to the disintegration of Yugoslavia in June 1991.

I spent two weeks in 1981 in the municipality of Klina in Kosova, and with other political activists from the province attended meetings of political organisations in villages and schools, trying to calm down the situation and convince young Albanians that the riots were not in their best interests. The leaders of the demonstrations were university and high school students. The unrest began as a protest against the bad food in the student canteen and was initially led by a student of Bulgarian nationality. Nevertheless, twenty years after those events I am convinced that they were incited and that Albania's intelligence service, the *Sigurimi*, played a role.[2] One cannot eliminate the possibility of involvement of other factors, such as

---

[1] The spelling of place names in this chapter is given in Albanian. However, Serbian spelling is also given in brackets when a place name is first mentioned, unless the two coincide, like in case of Klina or Prizren.

[2] My opinion is based on conversations I had in the period between 1991 and 1997 with a number of Albanian intellectuals and retired functionaries in Albania.

the Yugoslav intelligence service. However, the leading role was played by nationalist students who demanded that Kosova becomes a republic in Yugoslavia.[3] The demonstrators—after being joined by high school pupils from Podujeva (Podujevo), Ferizaj (Uroševac), Gjilanë (Gnjilane), Vushtrn (Vučitrn), Mitrovica e Titos (Titova Mitrovica) and Gjakova (Djakovica) at the end of March and beginning of April—were becoming increasingly militant. On 10 April 1981, when the authorities in Kosova could not control the situation any longer, the president of the Presidency of Kosova, Xhavid Nimani, asked the Yugoslav People's Army (JNA) to intervene. The Army responded to the call swiftly, without waiting for approval from the federal Presidency or indeed from Kosova's provincial Presidency.[4] Admiral Branko Mamula wrote in his memoirs that the army decided to intervene without approval from the Presidency of the Socialist Federal Republic of Yugoslavia (SFRJ):

The movement of the armed forces was noticed and the army informed the provincial leadership and the Presidency of the SFRJ about it. When asked what we were doing and what our intentions were, we answered that we were having military exercises. That was completely unconvincing, since the army was entering into Kosovo from all sides.[5]

Among the slogans by which the demonstrators formulated their demands were 'Kosova–Republic!', 'We are Albanians, not Yugoslavs!' and 'Unification with Albania!'[6] The last two slogans indicate that the demonstrators were under the influence of Marxist-Leninist groups of Kosovar Albanians, which operated in the West, notably in Switzerland and Germany, and called for Kosova's secession from Yugoslavia and its unification with Albania.[7]

---

[3] The organisers of the demonstrations were arrested. They were not interrogated and judged in Kosova as one would expect, but sent to Belgrade and to different jails throughout Serbia (Požarevac, Sremska Mitrovica).

[4] As General Veljko Kadijević, the Yugoslav Minister of Defence in the early 1990s, wrote in his memoirs, 'the Kosovar riots and uprisings of the Albanians always had to be suppressed by military force'. Veljko Kadijević, *Moje vidjenje raspada*, Beograd, 1993, p. 85.

[5] Branko Mamula, *Slučaj Jugoslavija*, Podgorica, 2000, p. 39.

[6] Branko Horvat, *Kosovsko pitanje*, Zagreb, 1988, p. 100.

[7] Several leaders of these groups were assassinated in the 1980s by the Yugoslav secret service.

According to the official information, nine demonstrators and one policeman were killed in the riots at this time. However, the real figure on both sides was higher: there were approximately five times as many victims among the demonstrators, while the number of policemen killed was approximately fifteen.[8]

A few weeks after the Army's intervention the situation calmed down and the institutions and authorities in Kosova began to function. Admiral Mamula writes in his memoirs:

> There were a lot of armed men in Kosova, but not enough for an armed conflict with the JNA...It was very important for us to avoid a massive bloodshed, not to get involved into a war and not to provoke an intervention. We succeeded in this thanks to an early and decisive engagement of the JNA with a clear objective: to prevent war and not provoke it.[9]

Writing about these events twenty years later, I remember as if it was yesterday, a trip by train from Belgrade to Prishtina in September 1981, during which I got engaged in a long conversation with a young Serbian woman who worked in Fushe Kosova (Kosovo Polje), a small town south-west of Prishtina, near the site of the famous battle of 1389. She was returning from a visit to her husband, in Belgrade, where he had moved with their daughter after finding a job there. The woman intended to join them as soon as she too could find a job in Belgrade. When I asked her why were they leaving the province, she explained that it was for several reasons: poor living and working conditions, poor education health care and, cultural life, and pollution, but she also said that they felt the Serbs were being pressurised by the Albanian majority to leave. It was hard to question or doubt those reasons. The dominant concept of development in Yugoslavia, especially in Serbia and Kosova,

---

[8] As I was told by a high-ranking police commander of the Federal Ministry of Interior that on the first day the special police forces entered Prishtina from the Slatina airport five policemen of the special unit were killed from an ambush. He added that four policemen from a special unit were killed in a village near Klina and five in a village near Skenderaj (Srbica). The newspapers wrote about the latter. During the demonstrations of Nov. 1968, there was only one high school student killed, and not by the police, but by a Serb civilian, who shot from his apartment into a crowd of demonstrators passing by. In 1968 Tito sent a tank brigade to Kosova.

[9] Mamula, op. cit., p. 40.

was urbanisation, and people increasingly moved from villages to towns. Equally, the problems between the (Albanian) majority and (Serbian) minority were real. Problems of this kind exist in other societies and in my opinion can only be solved by democratic means and through the legitimate institutions. But was this possible in Yugoslavia, where all the key decisions were made from above by the top Party leadership?

After the events of 1981 the older generation of Albanians became increasingly concerned. They had lived through a war every 15–20 years and they warned younger generations about the possibility of aggravating the conflict, saying that forty years was the longest period peace could last in the Balkans. The majority of the Albanian population in Yugoslavia and in Kosova awaited the disintegration of Yugoslavia with anxiety. Most of them knew that they were worse off than other Yugoslavs, and they were aware of their bitter experiences in Yugoslavia. However, they also knew that they were better off than their compatriots across the border, in Albania, and were generally contented with the overall development and prosperity that they had achieved in Tito's Yugoslavia. In the late 1980s I often heard ordinary Kosova Albanians, especially those living in the countryside, wondering why Milošević was driving them out of Yugoslavia.

Especially in the 1960s and '70s, Albanians in Tito's Yugoslavia experienced an overall national, political, economical and cultural revival and development. They demanded greater national, political and cultural rights in the framework of Yugoslavia and especially for Kosova to become a *de jure* republic, since the 1974 Constitution granted it a *de facto* republican status. This was a natural wish considering that in the early 1980s the population of Kosova was 80 per cent Albanian. Moreover, the Albanians in Kosova, together with those living in Macedonia, Montenegro and southern Serbia, represented the third largest nation in Yugoslavia, after the Serbs and Croats.[10]

Attempts by Serbia's leadership in the 1980s to change the (con)federal Constitution of 1974 were at the core of the disintegration of Yugoslavia. The status of Kosova was a matter of particular concern

---

[10] Branko Horvat argued that the riots and uprising of students that erupted in 1981 in Kosova are typical of nations that are searching for their identity and which are in the phase of being formed as nations. Horvat, op. cit., p. 11.

to Belgrade. The anti-Albanian hysteria and propaganda in the Serbian press, radio and TV throughout the 1980s was followed by measures of repression: the arrest of students, school pupils, and other young people, torture, beatings by the police and the secret service, and dismissal of employees from work and students from schools and faculties at the Prishtina University on the grounds of being morally and politically unsuitable. This policy resulted in the Albanians seeing themselves as unwanted and feeling increasingly alienated in Yugoslavia.

On 23 March 1989 the autonomy of Kosova was suspended, and the national, cultural, political and economic rights of the Albanians in Kosova were abolished. This led to the sequence of events which have brought us to where we are today, more than a decade later: the war, in which tens of thousands died, the exodus of more than half of the Albanian population of Kosova, their return, another exodus—this time of Kosova Serbs and other non-Albanians—and the setting up of the UN interim administration.

How did Albanians see Yugoslavia? Did they consider it to be their state? Did Yugoslavia offer them the chance to feel as free as the other nations in Yugoslavia and on a basis of equal citizenship with them? It is difficult to answer this question with a simple 'yes' or 'no'. As already indicated, during the 1970s the Albanians in Yugoslavia experienced real affirmation. Therefore, the answer for that period would be 'yes', but for other periods it would probably be 'no'. I believe that this question was best answered in the 1980s by the Serb politician and the Second World War General Koča Popović, who famously said that Albanians can become Yugoslavs but not Serbs. Being a Yugoslav in Tito's Yugoslavia was understood by the country's nations, including the Albanians, as being part of a state which provides for the optimal national development of all its nations and nationalities. The Constitution of 1963 abandoned the classical term for 'national minorities', replacing it with 'nationalities', since it was felt that the former was too limited and not in the spirit of building a multiethnic and multicultural society of equal citizens.

On his last visit to the United States in March 1978 Tito was asked by a journalist of NBC news whether he considered it a failure that he could not form a Yugoslav nation. Tito answered that it was definitely not a success that he had not created greater cohesion among the peoples of Yugoslavia.[11] Being Yugoslav was a category by which the nations and nationalities of Yugoslavia defined themselves as citizens of Yugoslavia. Yugoslavism in Tito's Yugoslavia meant above all Yugoslav citizenship, and this was not in contradiction with the particular national identities. However, a number of Yugoslav citizens declared themselves only as 'Yugoslavs', i.e. they regarded themselves as Yugoslavs in an ethnic sense. In Kosova this was less frequently the case, because the Albanians are not South Slavs. Also, the term 'Yugoslav' was abused in the 1950s and '60s by the Yugoslav secret police, the UDBa (later renamed the SDB).

During the debate which followed the adoption of the constitutional amendments in 1968, most Albanian intellectuals demanded that Kosova become a republic. That is why the first student demonstrations erupted in Prishtina on 27 November 1968, when the Yugoslav leadership were attending a ceremony marking the twenty-fifth anniversary of the Second Congress of the Anti-Fascist Council for the National Liberation of Yugoslavia (AVNOJ). Marko Nikezić, Secretary of the Central Committee of the League of Communists of Serbia (CK SKS) and Veli Deva, the Secretary of the Provincial Committee of the League of Communists of Kosova (PK SKK), went to meet Tito to discuss the crisis, and there found General Nikola Ljubičić, the Minister of Defence of Yugoslavia, talking to Tito. Marko Nikezić later told his friends that as a democratic politician seeking a solution to a conflict by political means he was bothered by Tito's over-reliance on the army.[12]

Most Communists in the Kosova region during the interwar period came from among Serb and Montenegrin colonists. They opposed the royal régime and especially its policies in relation to the Albanian minority. The Communist party of Kosova and Metohija was formed in the mid-1930s, as a branch of the Communist Party of

---

[11] The interview on NBC news was published in a shortened version in the *New York Times*, 5–8 March 1978.
[12] My friend, the diplomat Arsa Milatović, who was a close friend of Nikezić's, confirmed to me that Tito, before consulting Nikezić and Veli Deva, met and discussed the situation with Gen. Ljubičić.

Yugoslavia, with the same rights as other provincial Communist parties. Albanians also joined the Communist movement, but to a less extent and only in urban areas.

During the interwar period young Albanians from Kosova went to Albania to get an education in the Albanian language, and most of them later joined the Communists. Among them was Fadil Hoxha, who led the armed resistance movement in Kosova against the Italian and German occupiers. After the Italian occupation of Albania in 1939 and the invasion and partition of Yugoslavia in April 1941, parts of present-day Kosova, Metohija and Macedonia were annexed to Albania. While the population of Albania considered Italy as an occupier, most of the population of Kosova considered the Italians (in 1941–3) and Germans (1943–4, when they established a Quisling government in Kosova) as liberators. This was the result of twenty years of economic, political and national oppression in the first Yugoslavia (1918–41). Even though the Italians were not liberators in any true sense, the situation seemed like liberation compared to the previous one.

The Provincial Committee of the Communist party of Kosova and Metohija (PK KPKM), acting on the instruction of the Central Committee of the Communist Party of Yugoslavia (CK KPJ) sent in the summer of 1941 Miladin Popović, a member of the CK KPJ and Dušan Mugoša, a member of the PK KPKM to Albania. They played the instrumental role in forming a unified Communist Party of Albania.

As the resistance movement grew stronger in both Albania and Yugoslavia, the question about the future of the territories populated by Albanians in Yugoslavia was raised even before the war ended. The Yugoslav Communists stated in their contacts with the Albanian Communists that this issue would not be raised before the end of the war, and only then would the people decide themselves in which country they wanted to live. At the Second Congress of AVNOJ on 29 November 1943, held in the central Bosnian town of Jajce, the basis of a federal Yugoslavia was established. No decisions were made about Kosova, Metohija and Macedonia in order not to upset Albania and Bulgaria, but the Yugoslav Communists had nevertheless promised equality of all the peoples of Yugoslavia, including Albanians and Macedonians.

At its First Congress held between 31 December 1943 and 2 January 1944, the National Liberation Movement of Kosova and Metohija decided to join the two regions to Albania. The minutes of the meeting were sent to the Communist leaderships of Yugoslavia and Albania. Three months later, writing in the name of the CK KPJ, Milovan Djilas sent a letter to the Communist leadership of Kosova, in which he benevolently criticised them for taking this decision. Before the end of the war a delegation of the supreme command of the National Liberation Army of Albania, led by a member of the Communist Party of Albania leadership, Bedri Spahiu, arrived in Vis, an island in the Adriatic sea where Tito had moved his headquarters in the summer of 1944. The Yugoslav side, in their talks with the Albanian delegation, stated for the first time during the war that it did not agree to Kosova and Metohija joining Albania.[13]

Kosova was liberated in the autumn of 1944 by Tito's partisans and two brigades of partisans from Albania. The Kosovar partisans were sent, together with those in the two brigades from Albania, to Vojvodina and Bosnia to fight the withdrawing Axis troops. At the end of 1944 and the beginning of 1945 the Serb and Montenegrin brigades came to Kosova, and there were many acts of revenge against local Albanians for their oppression of Serbs and Montenegrins during the war. This alarmed the Albanian population, and some Albanian fighters mobilised in the partisan brigades came back to Kosova from Vojvodina in early 1945 to join a rebellion against the Yugoslav authorities. The new Yugoslav government proclaimed the martial law over the territory of Kosova and Metohija in February 1945. The Albanian rebellion was quickly put down, and in July 1945 the Second Congress of the National Liberation Movement of Kosova and Metohija was convened in Prizren. The delegates of Kosova and Metohija overruled the decision made at the First Congress, accepting that their territories should be part of Yugoslavia and of Serbia. Some pro-Albanian delegates later became opponents of the Yugoslav state. The session was attended by

---

[13] Personal interview with Boško Šilegović, General of National Liberation Army and Tito's Chief of Military Cabinet after the Second World War in 1972. I worked with Šilegović from 1972–74 at the Central Committee of the League of Communists of Yugoslavia in Belgrade.

representatives of Serbia, Macedonia and Montenegro, who would have asked for the division of Kosova and Metohija, just as it happened *de facto* in the first Yugoslavia, had the Kosovan delegates continued to argue for unification with Albania.

It was mainly thanks to Miladin Popović and Fadil Hoxha that Kosova became an autonomous region within Serbia. According to Veljo Stojnić, who succeeded Popović as the Yugoslav representative to the Albanian supreme command in the summer of 1944, the Yugoslav leaders were not pleased with the cordial relations between Popović and the Albanian leader Enver Hoxha, and especially not with the attitude of the former towards the Kosova issue. Tito and Edvard Kardelj personally gave instructions to Stojnić to reverse the previous policy.[14] Miladin Popović was killed in early 1945, while holding the post of the Secretary of the Regional Committee of the Communist Party of Kosova and Metohija. Ironically he was shot by an Albanian Communist and nationalist Haki Tafa, who opposed Kosova being part of Yugoslavia and not Albania.

During and after the Second World War, the old idea of a Balkan (con)federation was revived in the milieu of socialist movements and communist parties. It would comprise Yugoslavia, Bulgaria, Albania and Greece. The Bulgarian Communist leader, Georgi Dimitrov, who was at the same time the leader of the Communist International in Moscow, was especially engaged in this 'project'. Tito, as the leader of the strongest resistance movement in Europe and the most powerful Communist leader in Europe after Stalin, probably saw himself as the president of a future (con)federation. When Enver Hoxha, the Albanian Communist leader, arrived on his first official visit to Yugoslavia, he discussed with Tito about Albania becoming Yugoslavia's seventh republic. They signed the Agreement of Friendship and Cooperation between the two countries. The agreement had an annex of two secret articles,[15] whereby

---

[14] I had several conversations and interviews with Veljo Stojnić in 1971–2, while researching the Yugoslav-Albanian relations.

[15] Conversation with Josip Djerdja in 1972 in Belgrade. Djerdja was the first Yugoslav Ambassador to Albania in 1945–6. He was from Zadar, Croatia, and had old Albanian roots (he came from the Arbanasi, Catholics from northern Albania, who fled the Ottomans in the sixteenth century). He spoke Albanian and was Tito's and Hoxha's translator during their *tête-à-tête* talks. Djerdja told me about the secret annex in 1972, when I was doing research for my book *Albania and*

the two sides agreed that Kosova and Metohija would be united
with Albania, in an event of Albania joining Yugoslavia or the
Balkan (con)federation.[16]

Albania sided with the Soviet Union after the 1948 Tito–Stalin
split. Although the Yugoslav Albanians effectively supported Tito's
policy towards the Soviet Union, Tirana's official line had aggra-
vated their situation and position in Yugoslavia. There are historical
reasons for their support of Tito, but most importantly, the system
of collectivisation in agriculture, which Yugoslavia began to implement after the example of the Soviet Union, discontented the
Albanians and they hoped that Yugoslavia would soon abandon it.
This system resulted in the taking of land and cattle from peasants
and was very unpopular among the predominantly peasant Kosova
Albanians.

---

the Albanians, London, 1975. As an official of the League of Communists of
Yugoslavia, I could not publish this important information at the time.

The Central Committee of the League of Communists of Yugoslavia decided
in the early 1960s to issue a White Book on its relations with Albania. The task
of going through the archives of all of Tito's residences and finding the secret
annexé to the Agreement on Friendship and Cooperation between Albania and
Yugoslavia was given to Arsa Milatović, former Yugoslav Ambassador to Albania
(1955–8). This decision was made only after Albania broke off diplomatic relations with the Soviet Union in 1961 and joined China in the Sino–Soviet conflict. Milatović did not find the document. Tito had probably destroyed the
secret part of the Agreement after the deterioration of relations between the two
countries in 1948. It is interesting that the annexé cannot be found in the
archives in Tirana either, because Enver Hoxha, who was obsessed by Tito and
Yugoslavia, probably destroyed it too.

[16] Aleksandar Matunović, Tito's personal doctor in the 1970s, quotes Tito as saying: 'Historians often write that Churchill and Stalin prevented the formation of
a Balkan confederation during the war. This is true. However, it is not well
known that I continued to pursue this goal also after the war. There are several
reasons why this goal has not been achieved, but one of the main reasons was
that I did not accept the partition of Yugoslavia. Enver Hoxha wanted to enter
the confederation under the condition that Kosovo and Metohija be joined to
Albania, and the Bulgarians demanded the division of Macedonia. It is Stalin's
fault that the Partisan movement in Greece failed. Those are the true reasons
why there wasn't a Balkan confederation and why I didn't realize my idea.
I think that a confederation of Balkan states is inevitable, sooner or later.'
Matunović, *Enigma Broz: Ko ste Vi druže predsedniče?*, Belgrade, 1997, pp. 208–9.

Up till the 1960s the situation did not improve for Yugoslav Albanians. There had been practically no economic development and investments into the Kosovan economy, because it was feared until the mid-1950s that the Soviet Union would attack Yugoslavia from Albania. In addition, in the early 1950s, the Yugoslav authorities encouraged the Albanians in Kosova and Macedonia to register as Turks and thus facilitate their emigration to Turkey.[17]

During this period the Yugoslav Albanians were *de facto* second-class citizens. They were exposed to the oppression of the authorities, especially the secret police until 1966, when Aleksandar Ranković, the country's vice-president and in charge of internal affairs, was purged. His policies in regard to Kosova were later judged to be inadequate and unjust towards the Albanian minority and had been revised. As already argued, the policy of affirmation of the Albanian nationality in Yugoslavia lasted from 1966 until 1981. After that year, the anti-Albanian feeling, especially in Serbia, increased. Slobodan Milošević's rise to power in the late 1980s was based around the 'Kosova question'. This ultimately led to the collapse of Yugoslavia and tragic civil wars, but it is now well documented and does not need to be recapitulated here.

Epilogue: the future of Kosova

The war in Kosova ended in June 1999, but there is still no lasting peace. The Interim Administration of the United Nations in Kosova (UNMIK) has been set up, and the first phase—the return of Albanian refugees and rebuilding of their destroyed homes—has been largely accomplished. However, it is now the houses of Serbs, Montenegrins and Roma that have been burnt and destroyed by extremist Albanian groups, who oppose the return of non-Albanians to their homeland and aim to create an 'ethnically-pure' Kosova.

The Albanians of Kosova asked for and accepted the international protectorate in order to get rid of an apartheid system and the tyranny of the minority Serb population. However, most Albanians, especially the middle and older generations, do not endorse

---

[17] The Yugoslav leadership agreed to this decision, Tito included, except for the secretary of the Central Committee of the Communist Party of Croatia, Andrija Hebrang, who disagreed to this policy as inhuman.

the violence and killings of Serbs, Montenegrins and Roma.[18] But younger generations, in particular those born in the 1980s in an atmosphere of conflict and confrontation with the Serbian régime, are not so willing to accept a multi-ethnic Kosova. The Serbs, on the other hand, are not prepared to live in an independent Albanian state. The only alternative and the best possible solution would surely be to give Serbs three cantons within the framework of an independent Kosova: the northern part of Mitrovica with Zveqan (Zvečan), Leposaviq (Leposavić) and Zubin Potok; Graçanica (Gračanica) with the surrounding villages; and Shtrpce (Štrpce).

UNMIK holds the major responsibility for the security of all citizens of the province and for the establishment and rule of law along with the development of a market economy. Unfortunately, it has failed to create a peaceful and orderly society. Apart from the anti-Serb violence, another problem is the local mafia (once even connected with the Milošević régime through commerce and trade, mostly in petrol, arms and other illegal actions, in breach of the UN embargo), which has exploited the power vacuum that has followed the end of the war in June 1999. Despite plans for economic development and the reconstruction of schools, hospitals and factories, unemployment is very high and most of the destroyed infrastructure is yet to be rebuilt. If we consider the failures of the international community's economic development plan in Bosnia, it seems that the situation will not be much different in Kosova.

The new police force is being built too slowly, and on the wrong premises; it is incapable of investigating even the simplest criminal acts. At the same time as building a legal system, a mechanism for the protection of Kosova's minorities and ethnic groups should be set up. The Constitutional Framework for Kosova, which was negotiated between Albanian and Serb representatives, under the guidance of the international community and which was approved by the former administrator of Kosova, Hans Haekkrup, is based on both the Constitution of Kosova of 1974 and on Resolution 1244 of the Security Council of the United Nations of 10 June 1999.

[18] I spent six months in Kosova in the OSCE Mission between June and December 2000. During this period, I had many conversations with people of different ages and social structures, both Albanians and Serbs.

Even though the 'Kosova question' is not a question of decolonisation, there are some elements of that in it. But above all it is a national question which was not properly resolved within the framework of Yugoslavia and Yugoslavism, despite the considerable progress that was made in Tito's Yugoslavia. Now, ten years after the break-up of the Yugoslav state, the time has come to untie the Kosova knot and finally solve the Albanian national question in the Balkans. The independence of Kosova is what virtually all Albanians strive for. Establishing good neighbourly relations and cooperation with all neighbours, including Serbia, and open borders, where the circulation of people, goods and ideas would be possible, is the only alternative to the recent policies of separation, fighting and confrontation.

For any future settlement, the wishes of all the peoples of Kosova, including the Serbs, have to be taken into account. The neighbouring countries and the international community should help to find a lasting solution which would make possible coexistence between Albanians and Serbs and others who live or used to live in Kosova. The presence of the international community in the province should be established for a period of at least three to five years, so that the current difficult economic and political situation can be improved and the process of regional cooperation and integration—a priority for the countries of the region and of the international community—can begin. The European Union should also begin the integration of South Eastern Europe into its institutions. Peace, which all peoples of the region want and which they all certainly deserve, must have no alternative.

FUNERAL ORATION FOR YUGOSLAVIA
AN IMAGINARY DIALOGUE WITH
WESTERN FRIENDS

Aleksa Djilas

As the second millennium was drawing to a close, democracy at last prevailed in Serbia. In the previous decade, Milošević's régime had fought wars and repressed the opposition, whose leaders in turn vied with him and with each other in nationalistic rhetoric, puerile political manoeuvring and self-promotion. But in the elections of the autumn and early winter of 2000, the coalition of eighteen democratic parties, which had been formed after much chagrin and many theatricals, wrested control of the Yugoslav federal parliament from Milošević's Socialist Party of Serbia and its allies, and then proceeded to win the majority of seats in the Serbian assembly. Most sensationally, the opposition candidate Vojislav Koštunica defeated Slobodan Milošević and became the President of Yugoslavia—or rather of what was left of the Yugoslav federation of six republics. Yugoslavia had survived one debacle in the twentieth century when the Axis overran it in 1941 and carved it up. At the end of the Second World War the communist-led resistance liberated and restored it. In the early 1990s Slovenia, Croatia, Macedonia and Bosnia and Herzegovina seceded and soon gained international recognition as independent states. So Yugoslavia remained a federation, but with increasingly loose bonds and consisting only of Serbia and diminutive Montenegro.

Visitors to Serbia have long ago noticed—or should I say diagnosed?—an idiosyncrasy common to all sections of Serbian society. This is *inat*—malevolent, vengeful and obstinate defiance. Although through their history *inat* helped the Serbs to resist foreign and

317

domestic tyranny and to persevere in calamitous wars, it was mostly
a malady that fostered immoderation and irrationality and hindered
civilized politics. During the elections of 2000, however, the Serbs
turned their beloved *inat* against themselves and suppressed their
pernicious instinct for political violence. No, no and no, they seemed
to be telling themselves, there must be no killing. So although the
police were not at all gentle, and the demonstrators demolished the
state television and set fire to a wing of the federal parliament, no
one was murdered. It was amazing that the 'Serbian revolution'
unfolded in such a velvety, Czech way. Even inveterate optimists
about Serbian politics like myself did not expect that no blood
would need to be shed for democracy.

While Yugoslavia was disintegrating in the early 1990s, the Serbs,
Croats and Muslims began a civil war in which each group played a
dual role of aggressor and defender, ethnic cleanser and expelled
refugee, torturer and tortured. When the dust of fighting settled, it
became clear that no one had even tried to be a good guy and that
all should feel guilty and ashamed (although, regrettably but not
unexpectedly, very few people actually did). But through brutal
wars in Croatia and Bosnia, permanent crisis in Kosovo and humili-
ating internal political chaos, through economic sanctions and NATO
bombing, the Serbs were growing up. They were learning by experience—a Chinese proverb rightly calls experience a good school
whose fees are too high. Serbian progress was slow and with occasional relapses which made many both inside and outside the country lose hope. But the Serbs eventually came of age politically and
even transformed their noxious brew of *inat*, as if by a magic wand,
into an antidote to violence.

I

In the West a large majority of politicians and diplomats, of journalists, scholars and academics, loudly predicted that Milošević, whom
with characteristic bombast they proclaimed a 'vile tyrant', 'Balkan
butcher' and 'evil incarnate', indeed a new Hitler, Stalin and Pol Pot,
would resort to brutal force to keep himself in power, thereby
plunging the country into a civil war no less bloody than the one
which had been fought in Bosnia and Herzegovina. In many of

these prognostications I could detect gladness, even exhilaration at the prospect of such a cruel and bloody outcome.

Whenever such *Schadenfreude* troubled and grieved me, I could hear a chorus of Western voices rebuking me: Just remember what you Serbs did! You shelled Dubrovnik and laid Vukovar to waste; you surrounded Sarajevo with canons and snipers, and massacred several thousand Muslim men in and around Srebrenica; last but definitely not least, you engaged in the repression and ultimately the expulsion of Kosovo Albanians. You have not apologized and are not forgiven. You must be punished and who is more expert and practised at death and destruction than you yourselves? Have a taste of your own medicine. And have a nice day.

There was, of course, much truth in these accusations. But it was wrong to pass over the villainy of Croats, Bosnian Muslims and Kosovo Albanians with such insouciance. I tried to point this out, but the imaginary Western voices interrupted me: You disregarded our appeals and frustrated our diplomatic initiatives, belittled and mocked our threats, dared to survive under economic sanctions, and needed as much as two and a half months of what for us was very costly bombing to give up Kosovo, a dirty, squalid, worthless piece of real estate no self-respecting agent in the West would ever undertake to sell. For all that, for resisting and challenging us, the West, you Serbs must pay and pay dearly. We—NATO and the European Union,—we, the Western media, non-governmental organizations and think tanks, we, Bill Clinton and Tony Blair, Gerhard Schroeder and Jacques Chirac, we, the State Department and Foreign Office and Auswärtiges Amt and the Quai d'Orsay, we condemn you—for your *chutzpah* (your effrontery is truly shameless) and for your *hubris*, that arrogant pride with which the characters in ancient Greek tragedies annoy the gods (and we are the gods now). Do you not remember how the gods steered King Oedipus to kill his father unknowingly and marry his mother? Well, he got what he deserved, though if we had been there we would simply have bombed him.

The chorus of imaginary Western voices threatened furiously: As far as our Western and European institutions are concerned, you are unclubbable, simply not *salonfähig*. Indeed, the only time we think of you as Europeans is when we characterize your war crimes as a villainy we had not seen in Europe since the Second World War or depict one of your beloved leaders as Europe's most wanted fugitive. You may proudly show us frescoes in your churches and remind us that they are an integral part of European medieval civilization, but we do not think they are worth a second look. You may point out how keenly you follow all the styles in European literature, philosophy and art, but we do not care. You Serbs are an essentially un-European and anti-European people whose chauvinism spits in the face of our Euro-Atlantic multiculturalism, feminism, humanrightism. We saw every day on television what you really are like: wild drunken Balkan macho he-men, unshaven ruffians with broken teeth. (And don't you dare accuse our Western television of bias—it always broadcasts the truth, the whole truth and nothing but the truth.)

You Serbs must suffer and suffer you will. For God's and, more important, NATO's sake you should do penance. Weep and wail and beg for mercy, confess each crime, atone for every sin. Be good and try to be better. Although we Westerners can tell you in advance that you can never become wonderful like us, you may still someday cease being your horrible selves. What could be a more enticing prospect! And for your moral self-flagellation, as far as we are concerned, there is no better whip than a nice, big, bloody civil war.

I had to retort: But, my Western friends, did any nation ever deserve a civil war? Had the Serbs not been punished enough? They were expelled from Croatia, from many parts of Bosnia and Herzegovina (including Sarajevo, much vaunted in the West for its multi-ethnic tolerance) and from the whole of Kosovo, except its most northerly part, making Serbia of the all states of former Yugoslavia the one with the largest number of refugees—800,000 at the last count. These mass expulsions and territorial losses were accompanied by the destruction of Serbian historic monuments, Orthodox churches and monasteries, and collections of art, rare books and historical documents.

The cost of fighting the war and the devastation it brought, the embargo the United Nations imposed on international trade with Yugoslavia, as well as on investment and air traffic, and finally the NATO bombing in the spring of 1999—they all cumulatively devastated Serbia's economy. In 2000 Serbian gross domestic product *per capita* was $820 (by comparison, Haiti's was around $1,000 and Equatorial Guinea's $800), while unemployment in Serbia exceeded 40 per cent. Serbia is entering the twenty-first century as a country in which undernourishment and malnutrition are common, many illnesses are on the increase and environmental protection has seriously declined. Cultural contacts with Europe and other parts of the world, once usual and customary, have all but ceased and the large majority of people neither have enough money nor can get a visa to travel abroad. Tens of thousands of the most educated and talented young people, including many of my personal friends and acquaintances, scattered all over the globe in the 1990s, mostly in the Anglo-Saxon world—from Australia and New Zealand in the east to Canada and the United States in the far North and west. Few are returning.

II

Now Serbia is a democracy and the civil war has been avoided. Or has it? Perhaps the civil war which you, my Western friends, were hoping for has actually taken place. Quite simply, when we Serbs, Croats and Muslims fight against each other we also fight against ourselves. For we, as well as Slovenes, Macedonians and Montenegrins, are in so many respects similar or even indistinguishable. History books, newspaper articles, radio and television programs, and politicians' speeches, both foreign and domestic, have repeated *ad nauseam* in the past decade how and why 'former Yugoslavia' was an artificial and doomed multi-national country. It is imperative, therefore, for me to point out that it had a parallel identity as a uninational country.

I have never met an educated Slovene or Macedonian who did not speak Serbo-Croatian nor have I met one who has had to take courses to learn it. A Dalmatian (barring that lovable black-spotted quadruped) spoke and sang, ate and drank like a Dalmatian, whether he was Catholic or Orthodox, Croat or Serb. The same can be said of Herzegovinians or Slavonians, people of Lika or Bačka, and so on. Indeed, there were many other multi-national regions and almost all had distinct, homogenous and strong identities. In Yugoslavia there were numerous friendships and marriages (including my own parents') which were 'nationally mixed'. And this was how they were classified by sociologists and treated by politicians; those actual friends and spouses themselves experienced them as uninational.

No, you my Western friends do not have to remind me that there had been previous conflicts among the South Slavs and I am well aware that those between the Serbs, Croats and Muslims during the Second World War were rather bloody. At the same time, the South Slavs had many common historical memories and traditions, and crucially, most of the people most of the time lived outside history and inside their villages. They neither embraced nationalistic causes nor brandished weapons to further them, but cooperated with their neighbors of different faith and nationality. Once the history of these a-historical, uncharismatic, decent people is written and we finally hear the voices of the South Slav 'silent majority', we will undoubtedly discover that a kind of proto-Yugoslav identity preceded the actual creation of the country at the end of the First World War.

Communist bureaucrats in Yugoslavia's six republics and two provinces found it in their interest to erect invisible borders around their fiefdoms and Yugoslavia's economy was much less unified than it should have been to assure prosperity and help keep the country together. But there was a flourishing common market in books and movies, in pop songs and sporting idols, in colloquial expressions, jokes and swearing. After the disintegration there is still an illicit one, spontaneous and wonderfully anarchic, much more fun than that over-regulated, bureaucratic pseudo-union which has the impertinence to call itself European although it does not—and probably never will—embrace large parts of Europe. The durability of this post-Yugoslav black market proves that tolerance, or at least curiosity, can be stronger than bigotry and that not all the damage the Yugoslav civil war has caused is irreversible.

So I am hopeful. Of course, we South Slavs will never again live inside a common state—there are too many graves, marked and unmarked; refugees are rarely returning and never forgiving those who forced them out of their homes; ruins will disfigure towns and villages for a long time. It would be conceited to expect that the walls of hatred will come tumbling down at the sound of liberal trumpets playing the tune of reconciliation. But if full-time Yugoslav unity cannot be restored, some part-time version of it may be achieved. The nations of former Yugoslavia still live next to each other—whatever our leaders may desire—and economic, cultural and security factors tell us that we should cooperate. Those of us who identify with the Yugoslav 'idea', who uphold 'Yugoslavism', should use our energies to further such cooperation. And let us not beg our governments to assist us. In the era of privatization, let us rely on private initiative to promote the partial resurrection of Yugoslav unity.

If we agree that in a deeper sense Croatian and Muslim losses at Serbian hands were Serbian losses too, and vice versa, then in the Yugoslav civil war no side could ever have won but could only have lost. The degrees of loss, of course, were different. The Bosnian Muslims lost a greater percentage of their territories and had more casualties than the Serbs, and Serbs more than Croats. But at the same time, we are all (Slovenes, Montenegrins and Macedonians included) at the top of that imaginary scale of Yugoslav suffering, we have all been equally defeated, we are all victims—because we do not have Yugoslavia any more.

III

I can hear you, my Western friends, saying: These are the sentimental musings—*eine Schwärmerei, un monde imaginaire*—of a chronic, hardened, inveterate, impenitent 'Yugonostalgic'. Perhaps you are right, my Western friends, and undoubtedly all nationalists of former Yugoslavia, who actually invented the expression 'Yugonostalgic' to scorn and ridicule us, their critics, would agree with you. But I am not at all embarrassed to admit I still love that country that was murdered savagely and for no reason by its malicious children. Indeed, in the next official population count, I intend to declare myself a Yugoslav. This is what I was in census of 1971, 1981 and 1991; this is what I am in 2001.

We, the despised Yugonostalgics, acknowledge defeat and admit that the unified Yugoslav state will not be recreated; we will still not allow its *damnatio memoriae* to proceed unopposed nor will we ever concede that the slayers of Yugoslavia were right. Yugoslavia was innocent, they were guilty. That much-maligned country did not crush national cultures, nor are they flowering after its demise; it did not enslave us, nor are we free now; no tyranny was overthrown, nor was liberation attained. Anti-Yugoslav nationalists did not perform a heroic deed—they simply committed a heinous matricide. Not one of them distinguished himself either as a political or a military leader, let alone achieved international prominence. Indeed, not one of them ever delivered a moving, inspired speech, or said something wise or witty to be remembered by posterity.

The post-1945 efforts of the Third World countries to achieve freedom from colonialist domination enjoyed the support of many people in all parts of the globe. Progressive intellectuals and the Left in general saw the anti-colonialist struggle as noble even when it was waged with ruthless means, because it transcended the collectivist goal—the establishment of independent sovereign states—and was fought for individual human dignity and self-respect. The citizens of the imperial powers were often on the side of freedom fighters. Let us just remind ourselves that Gandhi was revered in Britain and that the Labour party deserves no less credit than the Congress party for Indian independence.

The enlightened, tolerant and well-intentioned of the world, those advocating international respect for human rights and championing the establishment of liberal democracy in every country, never favored Yugoslavia's disintegration nor did they admire or respect the separatist leaders. Further, the founding in 1918 of the Kingdom of the Serbs, Croats, and Slovenes (Yugoslavia's appellation till 1929) was welcomed by many more people all the world over than was the creation of any state emerging from Yugoslavia's debris in the 1990s. No less significantly, during more than seven decades of Yugoslavia's existence, it enjoyed the support, indeed the enthusiastic support, of world leaders who are considered the good guys, the superstars in the chronicles of the twentieth century—Clemenceau, Masaryk, Roosevelt, Churchill and de Gaulle, Nehru, Kennedy and Brandt, and many others—while the villains, the tyrants like Hitler, Mussolini and Stalin, were almost always its enemies.

Outside their nation the anti-Yugoslav nationalists enjoyed the support only of those who resembled them or had similar problems, prejudices and agendas. So even before the beginning of the civil war quite a number of Roman Catholics, Muslims and Eastern Orthodox of the world took the side of Yugoslav Roman Catholics,

Muslims and Serbian Orthodox respectively. They shed tears and cheered for their co-religionists, collected money and sent weapons. In a similar vein, Germany and Austria did not forget their historic ties to Croatia, nor did Russia and Greece theirs to Serbia. Most predictably of all, Albanians from Albania fought shoulder to shoulder with Albanians in Kosovo against the Serbian police and army, and in the spring of 2001 started fighting with their co-nationals in western Macedonia against the Macedonian forces.

After colonial rule came to an end, people of the newly-liberated countries were full of enthusiasm for national renewal. The young, especially, were ready to make sacrifices for the common good. This period rarely lasted longer than a few years and mostly ended in disappointment as far as the establishment of liberal democracy and the acceleration of economic growth were concerned. Still, it was a proof that the national revolutions were genuine. In the new post-Yugoslav states, faith, hope and readiness to bear a great burden for one's country were rare; only the chauvinistic hatred was abundant. There was a huge increase in theft, fraud, smuggling, financial malversation and Mafia-style 'hits'. Instead of devotion to one's country there prevailed 'that pretended patriotism which so many, in all ages and countries, have made a cloak for self-interest'—as James Boswell explained Samuel Johnson's well-known but puzzling dictum that 'patriotism is the last refuge of a scoundrel'.[1]

So why should I then feel ashamed of my nostalgia for Yugoslavia? On the contrary, all of us 'former Yugoslavs' should be troubled by guilt and remorse because Yugoslavia disintegrated and especially because of the way it happened. Not only was our loss great, but we also deprived the international community of a valuable member. During its whole existence, from the end of the First World War till the end of the Cold War, Yugoslavia was a respected country which had diplomatic relations with almost all states of the world. Rarely feared by its neighbors, it was often busily engaged in promoting reconciliation in the Balkans and, relative to its moderate size and modest economic resources, was a beneficent, constructive factor in European politics. Its spirit of independence and

---

[1] James Boswell, *Life of Johnson*, Oxford University Press, 1980 (first published in 1791), p. 615.

efforts to establish harmony among its different national groups
were an example to many countries.

From the early 1960s onwards Yugoslavia was the leading force
of the Non-Aligned movement, which encompassed many states in
Africa, Asia and Latin America. Not a few political analysts, myself
included, censured the movement.[2] I was not opposed in principle
to its goals, such as ending colonialism, aiding the Third World or
reducing confrontation between the superpowers. But I used to
point out that the Non-Aligned movement had no right to call
itself a 'conscience of mankind' since most of its members, Yugoslavia included, violated human rights and their jails were full of
political prisoners. Further, the movement did not distribute evenly
either its sympathies or its antipathies between the capitalist West
and the communist East: the Non-Aligned often sided with the
Soviet empire and facilitated its encroachments upon the Third
World. This belied the movement's claim that it was morally above
the Cold War, and led one to despair the prospects for democracy in
the non-aligned states. Finally, I used to add that for Yugoslavia
non-alignment was very costly, due to Tito's appetite for grandiose
conferences and his desire to flaunt himself on the world stage.

From my present vantage-point I still think that my critical remarks were valid. In any case, the movement proved ineffective in
preventing or stopping wars between member states and has all but
disappeared from the international scene. And shame on us 'former
Yugoslavs' for not preventing Tito from ruling autocratically inside
the country and for allowing him to indulge his megalomania and
pretentiousness outside it. Yet we can be proud that during the
Cold War with its genuine threat of a nuclear holocaust ours was a
country which urged the United States and the Soviet Union
towards peaceful coexistence, and that in our self-involved, parochial Balkan hearts we found some compassion for the Third
World, for 'the wretched of the earth'.[3]

---

[2] See, for example, Aleksa Djilas, 'Yugoslavia After Nonalignment', *The New Leader*,
6 Apr., 1981, pp. 7–9.
[3] This, of course, is the title of Frantz Fanon's moving, ferocious, inflammatory,
influential, vindication of anti-colonialist violence. *Les Damnés de la terre* was first
published in 1961 with a preface by Jean-Paul Sartre.

IV

So you are shaking your heads, my Western friends, and your voices are rising: Yugoslavia was a dictatorship! How dare you extol and venerate it! Have you forgotten the 'personal régime' of King Alexander, the dandyish, disdainful authoritarianism of his cousin Prince Regent Paul, the unrestricted domination of Tito and the Communist Party? With the generous assistance of you, his subjects, Tito even transmuted himself into an *ersatz* monarch, with a proviso that his bearing and lavishness resembled the Habsburgs rather than Karadjordjevićs. Dictatorship was Yugoslavia's natural form of government. The country could never have been anything else since there was no other way to keep you—Serbs, Croats, the lot—together. Nationalistic conflicts simply could not be alleviated let alone eliminated by democratic means. Since it is all but impossible to communicate anything to you people—as this conversation is amply confirming—there is no alternative but to command and control you. If Yugoslavia had survived the collapse of the Berlin Wall, it would still have remained a dictatorship. Perhaps you Serbs might have invented some new, original form of oppressing others and yourselves. Maybe designed a post-modern surrogate for that once *avant-garde* dominatrix, the League of Communists? We gladly pay tribute to your creativity in such matters. The remodeled Yugoslavia, however, would still not have been a free country.

You misconstrue the words and deeds of Western politicians who supported Yugoslavia. They were not noble idealists, but hard-boiled, even cynical realists. In the inter-war period they endeavored to prop up all the states encircling the wrathful post-Versailles Germany; Yugoslavia was an essential link in that anti-revisionist chain. During the Cold War they of course preferred you outside the Warsaw Pact rather than inside it and gave the ambassadors they sent to Belgrade simple instructions: Support Yugoslav unity, never mind democracy! After the demise of communism, there was no need for *cordons sanitaires* in Europe. Your country appeared to us, the Westerners of today, an anachronism, like a dinosaur or steamboat. Perhaps you are not entirely naive about the motives of the Western leaders of the past. The truth is we could not care less whether or not they were sincere. And so we telephoned our embassies: Support democracy, never mind unity! Yugoslavia's unnaturalness instantly became obvious. Stop mourning the death of something which was never alive anyway and donate your bizarre collection of Yugoslavia's pros and anti-cons to a museum of historical trivia.

Some of the things you are saying, my Western friends, are true, indeed painfully true. But many others are unfair or simplistic or both. Let me counter your categorical answers with hesitant questions. Is it not possible that the pro-Yugoslav Western statesmen were both idealists and realists at the same time? Why cannot one need a country and admire it too? The nationalists had to work hard to destroy Yugoslavia and it bled much before expiring—does this not suggest to you that it was far from lifeless? A special question to Americans: Doesn't the disintegration of Yugoslavia remind you of your own Civil War, but a version in which the Confederacy wins and then proceeds to break up into member states?

Is it really so difficult to conceive of a democratic Yugoslavia in the new Europe? Would it not have been, exactly because of its multi-national composition, a country larger than its size and an example to Europe of how to continue with integration? In what way are the small, poor and democratically deficient states that have taken Yugoslavia's place less artificial and more modern than it was? You accuse me of being a sentimentalist, *Träumer, utopiste,* but why are you so easily deceived? What has happened to your sense of the ridiculous? Can you not see through their rhetoric of human rights, democracy, toleration, 'European values'? How is it that you do not realize that with their presumptuousness and pomposity the post-Yugoslav states are feeble imitations, indeed travesties, of European nineteenth-century nation states?

Between the two world wars, fascism was advancing in Southern Europe, Stalinism in Eastern Europe and Nazism in Central Europe. But the prospect for democracy was also gloomy in many countries outside the direct reach of 'totalitarianism' and even well-established democracies seemed unstable. For example, in Paris during the riots of February 1934 the police killed several dozen people. Of all countries in the immense expanse encircled by Germany, the Soviet Union and Turkey, historians now recognize only Czechoslovakia as having been a democracy. But even Masaryk's republic was seriously flawed: the Czechs predominated overwhelmingly and excluded the Slovaks, Sudeten Germans and Magyars from the political process.

In democracy-crushing, liberty-hating, violence-worshipping inter-war Europe, the dictatorships of the Karadjordjević cousins do not appear as either unusual or unusually evil. And between the proclamation of Yugoslavia on 1 December 1918 and Alexander's *pronunciamento* of 6 January 1929, Yugoslavia was a parliamentary democracy. Of a sort, of course, since our parliament was often restricted, sometimes obstructed, always turbulent. Still, it was alive and kicking and there was no tyranny.

In the nascent kingdom of the quarrelsome South Slavs serious attempts to resolve the national question were indeed rare. Hardly anyone, however, was indifferent. The democratically elected governments, the régimes of Alexander and the Prince Regent Paul, and the opposition (of the Right almost as much as of the Left), the Serbian politicians not much less than non-Serbian—all were worrying, sighing, expressing concern, crying, making jokes, shouting, begging, threatening, commenting, writing, publishing, resolving to do something, deciding to wait a bit, holding meetings, organizing and leading demonstrations or counter-demonstrations, drafting programs, preparing plans. It is entirely possible that had there been no Second World War or had the peace lasted longer, or had *Wehrmacht* somehow bypassed Yugoslavia, the contested kingdom would have peacefully changed into a federation and in this way consolidated itself. But slightly more than two decades of peace were not enough and could not have been enough to resolve issues some of which were centuries old.

No one is more glad than I to agree with you, my Western friends, that Tito's régime was not democratic. But this was because Yugoslav communists were, well, communists; not because they were Yugoslavs. Like their kin in other countries, they decided to put liberty on hold until they created a classless, stateless, conflictless and in general all-bad-things-less society. Paradise would not be reached and, without wishing to give offence, not even NATO could ever reach it. I will conclude, paraphrasing 'Saki' on good cooks, that communists were good dictators, as dictators go; and as dictators go they went. And their peaceful exit was, together with their struggle against fascism, the best thing they ever did.

There is no evidence that Yugoslav communism was harsher than other communist régimes in the world, indeed there is some that it was milder. And it is doubtful, to say the least, that our communism would have been more tolerant and open if somehow there had been no Yugoslavia but only South Slav communist nation-states. It is true that Tito, like the Karadjordjevićs, often used the threat which national confrontations posed, or were alleged to pose, to state unity as a pretext to silence all critics and expel from the party any would-be reformers. But then it is also true that the plurality of nations which under communism found institutional expression in the federal system of six republics and two autonomous provinces was conducive to a degree of political pluralism since it imposed some limits on monolithic state power.

Even now with twenty-twenty hindsight I am not convinced that we Serbs, Croats, the lot (as you, my Western friends, are calling us) could not have agreed on a common program of democratic reforms and freed ourselves from communism much sooner. Indeed, there were some examples of successful cooperation. Tito, a *divide-et-impera* ruler at heart, feared nothing more than the creation of a united Yugoslav opposition—in the party, outside it, in the worst case both—and in particular he feared any Serbo-Croatian agreement. From the standpoint of keeping and augmenting his power he was absolutely right; from the standpoint of Yugoslavia's future tragically wrong.

V

Forgive me for doubting your sincerity, my Western friends, but do you really not care for Yugoslavia? Would you truly not prefer the last decade to have been different? Are you not simply trying to justify your failed policies? I strongly suspect that you wish you could borrow from H.G. Wells his time machine and fly back to the early 1990s so as to do the very opposite of what you did. I am certain you know, although of course you will never admit it, what a terrible mistake it was not to insist that the elections for the federal government in Belgrade be held before the elections for the governments of the republics, and to give such hasty recognition to Slovenia and Croatia, and later also to Bosnia-Herzegovina, as independent sovereign states. Let me add that these blunders were just a warm-up for your feats of cowardice, indecision, confusion, mismanagement, malice, heartlessness and hypocrisy during the Yugoslav civil war. I dare to suggest that as soon as the time machine landed in the past and you disembarked, you would begin pressuring the leading generals of the Yugoslav People's Army to stage a *coup d'état*, disarm all paramilitary formations by force and arrest nationalist leaders. It would not trouble you in the least that Milošević, Tudjman and Izetbegović had won elections and enjoyed the support of the majority of their people. You would find it easy to overlook democracy remembering all the worry and effort and time and, above everything else, money you would have to squander on Yugo-wars.

Germany was united in 1871 and two world wars were a consequence; Yugoslavia fell apart in 1991 and several local wars broke out. Europe and the world did not know how to contain the mighty Reich; they were baffled how to prevent or stop Yugoslavia's successor states from fighting against each other. In short, for the international community living with Germany was very difficult and living without Yugoslavia not at all easy. And after all the calamities and tribulations of the 1990s there is still no end in sight to troubles with post-Yugoslavia. The dawn of the third millennium reveals Bosnia as disunited and unstable as it ever was. Montenegro is split between those who prefer to stay with Serbia and those who crave independence, while minorities, a fifth of the population, distrust the good intentions of the majority, which in turn questions their loyalty. Kosovo is neither democratic nor multi-ethnic—though during the bombing of Serbia in the spring of 1999 the NATO leaders firmly promised they would make it both; the West does not want to govern Kosovo for ever, and cannot grant it independence because this would make the region unstable, yet it knows that the province could never again be incorporated into Serbia. Macedonia is disintegrating Bosnia-style—the western part will be Muslim Albanian and the central-eastern part will be Orthodox Macedonian; the fighting is increasingly bloody and accompanied by ethnic cleansing. All this adds up to a disaster: no less than four post-Yugoslav political entities have a bleak future, while Serbia, Croatia, and even Slovenia suffer from a democratic deficit and an unsatisfactory economy (in the case of Slovenia the economy is

merely mediocre). And you, my Western friends, tell me Yugoslavia was an artificial country.

Whenever I feel nostalgic for Yugoslavia, and I often do, I remember—with nostalgia, of course—that old joke in which a nostalgic says that even nostalgia is not what it used to be. Very witty,
but it actually does not apply to me at all, since my Yugonostalgia is
improving all the time. I yearn for Yugoslavia not only because of
what it was, but even more so for what it might have been. My
Yugoslavism was always a blend. I realized that Yugoslavia was the
most sensible and practical, simply the most anti-destructive, answer
to the difficult South Slav national question, and I was also enthusiastic for a visionary idea which allowed the small South Slav nations
to free themselves through unification from enslavement and margin-
alization. With Yugoslavia we would have been a partner in European politics—not equal to Germany or France, needless to say, but
still a partner. And we would have been on the top of admission lists
of whatever we wanted to be members of—NATO, the European
Union, the lot.

I believed in urban Yugoslavism, not in some semi-mythical
fusion of South Slav peasants with their quaint costumes and out-
landish legends. For me the axis of Yugoslavia was the cooperation
between Belgrade and Zagreb—not only because it put an end to
the most dangerous of all South Slav conflicts, but also because
these were the two largest cities, with the most industry, the greatest
number of cultural institutions and with major universities. Through
them we could exchange ideas and technologies with Europe and
the world on something like an equal basis. And Yugoslavia was
not only a way to make us more stable, peaceful, free, wealthy and
respected, but also more intelligent and cosmopolitan. Let me just
mention that the collapse of Serbian historiography, with only a few
honorable exceptions, into parochial self-pity and chauvinism
would not have happened if Yugoslavia had survived.

Last and least, but not insignificantly, we would have won together
many more medals in the Olympic Games than the sum of medals
we win separately. Yugoslav national teams in football, basketball,
water-polo, handball and volleyball would be much stronger (incidentally, another common trait of the South Slavs is their love of
and proficiency at team sports played with a ball). We would have

avoided the embarrassment of being a former world power in chess, second only to the Soviet Union, which now does not have a single player among the world's 100 best. And our tourist industry would not have collapsed; this meant not only deficiency in foreign currency but fewer contacts with foreigners, preferably young and handsome ones. (If Yugoslavia had a well developed superego, it is only fair that it had a well developed id as well.)

So, my Western friends, now that I have added some laughter to many tears, I take my leave of you. Let us hope the time is not far away when many 'former Yugoslavs' will realize that the civil war we fought was against ourselves and our future. Then we can transform the South Slav peace into something more than the absence of war: open borders for visitors and goods, economic cooperation, cultural exchanges, respect for differences and an end to denial of similarities, common search for historical truth, solidarity and common voice on regional and European issues. In this way we will both build a monument to Yugoslavia and raise it from the dead.

Belgrade, 17 May 2001

NOTES ON CONTRIBUTORS

Mile Bjelajac is Senior Research Fellow at the Institute of Contemporary History of Serbia. He is the author, *inter alia*, of *Vojska Kraljevine Srba, Hrvata i Slovenaca 1918–1921* (The Army of the Kingdom of Serbs, Croats and Slovenes, 1918–1921), Belgrade, 1988, *Vojska Kraljevine SHS/Jugoslavije 1923–1935* (The Army of the Kingdom of SCS/Yusgoslavia), Belgrade, 1994, and *Jugoslovensko iskustvo sa multietničkom armijom 1918–1991* (The Yugoslav Experience with a Multiethnic Army, 1918–1991), Belgrade, 1999.

Xavier Bougarel is a Research Fellow at the Research unit for Turkish and Ottoman studies at the Centre national de la recherche scientifique (CNRS) in Paris. He is the author of *Bosnie. Anatomie d'un conflit* (Paris, 1996), and co-editor, with Nathalie Clayer, of *Le nouvel Islam balkanique. Les musulmans, acteurs du post-communisme (1990–2000)*, Paris, 2000.

Tihomir Cipek is a Lecturer at the Faculty of Political Science, University of Zagreb. In 2001 he was a Humboldt scholar at the University of Goettingen, Germany. Dr Cipek is the author of *Ideja hrvatske države u političkoj misli Stjepana Radića* (The Idea of a Croatian State in the Political Thought of Stjepan Radić), Zagreb, 2001.

Aleksa Djilas is a writer, sociologist and historian living in Belgrade. He studied in Yugoslavia, Austria and England, and has a doctorate in sociology from the London School of Economics. Between 1987 and 1993 he was a Fellow at the Russian Research Center, Harvard University. In the autumn of 2000 he was a Public Policy Scholar at the Woodrow Wilson International Center for Scholars, Washington, DC. Dr Djilas is the author, among other books, of *The Contested Country: Yugoslav Unity and Communist Revolution, 1919–1953*, Cambridge, MA, 3rd edn, 1996. His articles have appeared in *The Spectator, The New York Times, The New Republic,*

Foreign Affairs, Prospect, Commentary, Granta and *Nexus* (Netherlands), and he has also published poems and short stories.

Dejan Djokić is Lecturer in Contemporary History at Birkbeck College, University of London. Between 1998 and 2002 he taught Yugoslav and East European history at the School of Slavonic and East European Studies, University College London, where he is currently completing a doctorate on national politics in interwar Yugoslavia.

Jasna Dragović–Soso is a Swiss National Science Foundation Scholar and Research Fellow at the School of Slavonic and East European Studies, University College London, working on issues of democratisation, nationalism and international intervention in the post–Yugoslav states. She is the author of *'Saviours of the Nation': Serbia's Intellectual Opposition and the Revival of Nationalism*, (London, 2002).

Branko Horvat is Emeritus Professor of Economics, University of Zagreb. Among his many books are *The Political Economy of Socialism*, (New York, 1982), *Kosovsko pitanje* (The Kosovo Question) Zagreb, 1988, *The Theory of Value, Capital and Interest: A New Approach*, Aldershot, 1995 and *The Theory of International Trade: An Alternative Approach*, New York, 1998. Professor Horvat was the President of the Council of the Association for Yugoslav Democratic Initiative and an eminent opponent of nationalist regimes in Croatia and Serbia throughout the 1990s.

Dejan Jović is Lecturer in International Politics at University of Stirling, Scotland. He studied in Zagreb, Ljubljana, Manchester and London, where he received a PhD from the London School of Economics in 1999. In 2000 he was a Jean Monnet Fellow at the European University Institute in Florence. Dr Jović is the author of *Jugoslavija. Država koja je odumrla* (Yugoslavia. A state that withered away), Belgrade and Zagreb, 2002.

John R. Lampe is Chair and Professor of History, University of Maryland, College Park, USA. He is the author of *Yugoslavia as History: Twice there was a country*, Cambridge, 2nd edn, 2000. Among his other publications are *Balkan Economic History, 1550–1950: From Imperial Borderlands to Developing Nations*, Indiana University Press,

1982, co-authored with Marvin R. Jackson; *The Bulgarian Economy in the Twentieth Century*, London, 1986; and *Yugoslav-American Economic Relations*, Durham, NC, 1990, co-authored with Ljubiša S. Adamović and Russell O. Prickett. From 1987 to 1997, Professor Lampe also served as the Director of East European Studies at Woodrow Wilson International Center for Scholars, Washington, DC.

Ramadan Marmullaku is a former career diplomat and ambassador of Yugoslavia to Nigeria (1982–9). He resigned from the Ministry of Foreign Affairs of Yugoslavia in 1989 and has since worked as a human rights activist and free-lance writer in Ljubljana, Slovenia. He is the author of *Albania and the Albanians*, London, 1975.

Andrej Mitrović is Chair and Professor of General Contemporary History, Faculty of Philosophy, University of Belgrade. Among his many books are *Jugoslavija na Konferenciji mira, 1919–1920* (Yugoslavia at the [Paris] Peace Conference, 1919–1920), Belgrade, 1969; *Vreme netrpeljivih. Politička istorija velikih država Evrope, 1919–1939* (The Age of the Intolerant. Political History of the Great European Powers, 1919–1939), Belgrade, 1974, Podgorica, 2nd edn, 1998; *Srbija u Prvom svetskom ratu* (Serbia in the First World War, Belgrade, 1984); *Raspravljanja sa Klio. O istoriji, istorijskoj svesti i istoriografiji* (Discussions with Clio. On History, Historical Consciousness and Historiography), Sarajevo, 1991; and *Propitivanje Klio. Ogledi o teorijskom u istoriografiji* (Questioning Clio. Essays in Theory of History), Belgrade, 1996. In 2001 Professor Mitrović received the Herder Prize.

Aleksandar Pavković is Associate Professor of Politics at Macquarie University, Sydney and an honorary research fellow at the University of Melbourne. Apart from the *Fragmentation of Yugoslavia: Nationalism and War in the Balkans*, London, 2nd edn, 2000, he wrote *Slobodan Jovanović: An Unsentimental Approach to Politics*, New York, 1993, and edited, with Peter Radan, *Serbs and their Leaders in the Twentieth Century*, Aldershot, 1997, and with Halyna Koscharsky and Adam Czarnota, *Nationalism and Postcommunism*, Aldershot, 1995.

Kosta St. Pavlowitch is deputy editor of the *Cyprus Mail* (Nicosia). He is a graduate of the University of Oxford and the Institut d'Etudes Politiques de Paris, where he completed a Diplôme d'études approfondies (DEA), submitting a thesis on the unification of Yugoslavia in 1918.

Stevan K. Pavlowitch is Emeritus Professor of History, University of Southampton. His most recent books are *A History of the Balkans, 1804–1945*, London and New York, 1999, and *Serbia: The History behind the Name*, London and New York, 2002.

Hugh Poulton is a Researcher on Southeast Europe for Amnesty International. He is the author of *The Balkans: Minorities and States in Conflict*, London, 2nd edn, 1993; *Who Are the Macedonians?* London, 2nd edn, 2000; *Top Hat, Grey Wolf and Crescent: Turkish Nationalism and the Turkish Republic* (London, 1997); and co-editor, with Suha Taji-Farouki, of *Muslim Identity and the Balkan State*, London, 1997.

Radmila Radić is Senior Research Fellow at the Institute of Contemporary History of Serbia. She is the author, among other works, of *Verom protiv vere. Država i verske zajednice u Srbiji 1945–1953* (With Faith against Faith. The State and Religious Communities in Serbia), Belgrade, 1995, *Hilandar u državnoj politici Kraljevine Srbije i Jugoslavije 1896–1970* (The Hilandar in the state politics of the Kingdom of Serbia and Yugoslavia), Belgrade, 1998, and *Drzzava i verske zajednice 1945–1970* (The State and Religious Communities), 2 vols, Belgrade, 2002.

Dennison Rusinow is retired as Adjunct UCIS Professor in East European Studies from the University of Pittsburgh. His numerous publications on Yugoslavia include *The Yugoslav Experiment, 1948–1974* (London, 1977), which he edited, *Yugoslavia: A Fractured Federalism* (Washington, DC, 1988), and 'The Yugoslav Peoples', in Peter Sugar (ed.), *Eastern European Nationalism in the Twentieth Century* (Washington, DC, 1995). Professor Rusinow reported on Yugoslavia for the American Universities Field Staff from 1963 to 1988.

Desimir Tošić is a writer and political commentator living in Belgrade. He is the vice-president of the Democratic Centre (DC) party and a former president of the European Movement in Serbia. In the late 1930s he led the student section of the Democratic Party of Ljuba Davidović and Milan Grol. After spending most of the war in German prison camps, he stayed abroad, where he edited the *Naša reč* (Our Word) monthly, first in Paris, than in London. Tošić

338 *Notes on Contributors*

was one of the founders of the new Democratic Party in 1990 and its vice-president until 1996, when he joined the DC. Between 1992 and 1996 he was a deputy in the Yugoslav Parliament. Tošić is the author, among other books, of *Stvarnost protiv zabluda. Srpsko nacionalno pitanje* (Reality versus myths. The Serbian national question), Belgrade, 1997; *Snaga i nemoć. Naš komunizam 1945–1990* (Power and Powerlessness. Our Communism, 1945–1990), Belgrade, 1998 and *O ljudima* (On People), Belgrade, 2000.

Ljubinka Trgovčević is Professor of Contemporary History at the Faculty of Political Science, University of Belgrade. Previously, she was a Senior Research Fellow at the Historical Institute, Serbian Academy of Arts and Sciences. Professor Trgovčević is the author of *Naučnici Srbije i stvaranje jugoslovenske države, 1914–1920* (Serbian Intelectuals and the Creation of the Yugoslav State, 1914–1920), Belgrade, 2nd edn, 1987, and *Istorija Srpske književne zadruge, 1892–1992* (History of the Serbian Literary Society, 1892–1992), Belgrade, 1992.

Mitja Velikonja is a Lecturer at the Faculty of Social Sciences, University of Ljubljana. He is the author of *Religious Separation and Political Intolerance in Bosnia-Herzegovina* (Texas A&M University Press, 2003), *Bosanski religijski mozaiki. Religije in nacionalne mitologije v zgodovini Bosne in Hercegovine* (Bosnian Religious Mosaics. Religions and National Mythologies in the History of Bosnia-Herzegovina) Ljubljana, 1998, and *Masade duha. Razpotja sodobnih mitologij* (Masadas of the Mind. Crossroads of Contemporary Mythologies), Ljubljana, 1996.

Andrew B. Wachtel is Bertha and Max Dressler Professor in the Humanities at Northwestern University, where he is also Chair of the Department of Slavic Languages and Literatures, Director of the Program in Comparative Literary Studies, and Director of the Consortium for Southeast European Studies. His most recent books are *Making a Nation, Breaking a Nation: Literature and Cultural Politics in Yugoslavia*, Stanford, CA, 1998, and *Petrushka: Sources and Contexts*, Chicago, 1998. Professor Wachtel is also the editor of Northwestern University Press's acclaimed series 'Writings from an Unbound Europe', which publishes contemporary poetry and prose from Central and Eastern Europe.

INDEX

339

291, 309–10, 311n, 313, 327; in
the 1920 elections: 89; and the
national question: 66, 76–7, 79, 80,
106, 142–3, 252–3; and Serbs: 66–7,
82; and Croats: 80, 81; and
Slovenes: 91, 94; and Bosnian Muslims: 105–06, 107n; and the status
of Kosovo: 311–12; and Macedonians: 117; rivalry with Bulgarian
Communists over Macedonia: 119;
and Albanian Communists: 163;
Yugoslavism of: 157–81; returns to
Marxist roots: 165; and religious
institutions: 204–05; organises resistance in the Second World War:
218; and the Army: 219; loss of
legitimacy of: 96; 8th Congress of:
172; 10th Congress of: 175; 14th
Congress of: 97; *see also* Tito
League of Prizren, 125
Leibnitz, 44
Lenard, Leopold, 231
Lenin, Vladimir Ilich Ulyanov, 262
Leposavić (Leposaviq), 315
Lika, 321
London: 44, 55, 64, 91, 125, 141, 160,
232, 289, 297; Treaty of: 21, 26, 49,
53–4
Ljubičić, Gen. Nikola, 309
Ljubljana, 16, 35, 38, 86, 88–92, 95,
96n, 97, 173n, 186, 226, 272, 281,
284, 302–3
'Ljubljana Points', 88
Lueger, Karl, 76

MAAK (Movement for All-
Macedonian Action), 124
Macedonia and Macedonians: 7, 17,
24n, 31, 35, 41, 49–50, 59, 62, 79–
80, 103n, 112, 126–7, 136, 142n,
157, 160, 184, 186–8, 223n, 230,
281n, 287, 292–3, 307, 310, 312,
313n, 314, 317, 321, 323, 325, 331;
identity of: 115–16; and Balkan
wars and the First World War: 116–
17; in 'first' Yugoslavia: 117–9; in

the Second World War: 119–20; in
'second' Yugoslavia: 120–5;
becomes a republic: 66, 121; recognised as a nation: 121–2; language
of: 121; and Yugoslavism: 123–4;
nationalism of: 124–5; Albanians in:
7, 118, 123n, 314, 331; and disintegration of Yugoslavia: 123–5
Macedonian Orthodox Church, 122,
205–6.
Maček, Vladko: 199, 203; *Sporazum*
and *banovina* of Croatia: 64, 78, 153;
and the Ustašas: 78; received by
King Alexander: 146; initially wel-
comes Alexander's dictatorship: 148;
views of Yugoslavism and the Croat
question: 152n, 153; and United
Opposition: 154–5; and the Con-
cordat crisis: 202; *see also* Cvetković-
Maček Agreement (*Sporazum*)
Magyars, *see* Hungary and Hungarians
madrasa (Muslim religious school), 106
Mahnič, Bishop Anton, 87
Majar-Ziljski, Matija, 85
Maliqi, Skëlzen, 302
Mamula, Admiral Branko, 220, 305–6
Marburg (Maribor), 43
Maričić, Siniša, 302
Marković, Ante: 176n; and the Alli-
ance of the Reformist Forces of
Yugoslavia (SRSJ): 100, 110; and
economic reforms: 193.
Marković, Božidar (Boža), 233–4
Marković, Dragoslav (Draža), 167n
Marković, Lazar, 234
Marković, Mihailo, 257n
Marseilles, 136
Martinović, Djordje, 277
Marx, Karl, 161, 165
Marxism: 108, 132n, 143n, 157–61,
165, 171, 176, 178, 257n, 305; and
the state: 158–9, 161; and the
nation: 159–61
Masaryk, Thomas, 324, 328
Matica Hrvatska, 79, 81, 226
Matica Ilirska, 4n

352   *Index*

Serbian Royal Academy (SKA), 226, 234

Seton-Watson, R. W., 142, 229–30
Šeper, Archbishop Franjo, 206
Shtrpce, *see* Štrpce
Shukria, Ali, 179n
Šibenik, 37, 230n
Sidran, Abdulah, 302
Sigurimi (Albanian secret police), 304
Šilegović, Gen. Boško, 311n
Silvi, Gen. Karlo, 214
Šimić, Antun, 240
Simić, Mirko
Simović, Gen. Dušan, 215n
Sirc, Ljubo, 287n, 289
Šišić, Ferdo, 151n
Skenderaj, *see* Srbica
Skenderbeg, 127n
Skenderbeg SS division, 127
Skerlić, Jovan, 224–5, 227
Skopje, 116, 120, 124, 186
Skupština (Serbian and Yugoslav Parliament or National Assembly): 29, 33, 44, 47, 137, 144–5, 146n, 154, 254, 317; *see also* Constituent Assembly (of the Kingdom of Serbs, Croats and Slovenes)
Slapšak, Svetlana, 302
Slavonia, 24, 38, 43, 59
Slijepčević, Pero, 228
Slovak (newspaper), 202n
Slovaks, 329
Slovenia and the Slovenes: 5–7, 13–20, 23–6, 28–33, 34n, 43–4, 46, 49, 60–1, 73–4, 80, 111–12, 120, 124–5, 130, 138, 153, 157, 169n, 170, 182, 196, 199, 200, 206–7, 210–12, 214–16, 219–20, 222, 225–31, 233, 235–6, 239–41, 245–6, 260–2, 269–70, 287, 292–3, 298, 317, 321, 323, 330–1; and 'United Slovenia': 84; and Austro-Slavism: 85; in the First World War: 33–7, 47–9, 52; in 'first' Yugoslavia: 46, 59, 63, 78, 87–90, 141–3, 149–50, 154–5, 186–8, 198,

214; in the Second World War: 90–2, 217n; in 'second' Yugoslavia: 67–8, 79, 83, 93–7, 111, 160, 162, 165n, 170, 174n, 180, 190, 207, 219, 273–6, 279–85; and Yugoslavism: 15–6, 25–6, 72, 84–7, 89, 94, 199, 222–30, 233, 236; declared Yugoslavs in: 123n; and alternative movements: 95; achieves independence: 95–7; and war in: 265; contemporary nationalism of: 98; and EU and NATO: 98; and 'Yugonostalgia': 99
(Slovene) Liberals: 85, 88–9, 91n
Slovene People's Party (SLS; a.k.a. the Clericals), 48, 85–6, 88–9, 91, 103–4n, 145, 154n, 288; *see also* Korošec, Anton
(Slovene) Social-Democrats, 85–6, 89
Slovenian Writers' Society, 273–5, 280–1, 284
Slovenski jug (journal), 22
Smodlaka, Josip, 46n, 226
Smuts, Jan Christiaan, 49–50
Social-Democratic Party of Croatia-Slavonia, 15, 25
Socialist Party of Serbia (SPS), 68–9, 257n, 317
Socialist Party of Yugoslavia, 216
Sofia, 51, 119–20, 227–8
Soviet Union (USSR), 160, 164, 166–7, 178, 183, 252, 286, 313–14, 326, 328, 333
Spahiu, Bedri, 311
Spaho, *reis-ul-ulema* Fehim, 201, 204
Spaho, Mehmed, 88, 104n, 200, 201; *see also* Yugoslav Muslim Organization (JMO)
Špigel, Ivo, 303
Špiljak, Mika, 167n
Split, 30n, 35, 39, 49, 192, 230n, 247, 303
Sporazum, see Cvetković-Maček Agreement
Srbica (Skenderaj), 306n

Index 353

Srem (Srijem), 43, 59
Srpska Književna zadruga (journal), 226
Srpski književni glasnik (Serbian Literary Review), 225
Štajner, Karlo, 303
Stalin, Joseph, 121, 129, 161–5, 168, 184, 328
Stalinism, Stalinists: 162, 164, 167–8, 184, 328; see also Tito-Stalin split
Stambolić, Ivan, 167n, 174n
Stambolić, Petar, 167n
Stanković, Borislav (Bora), 227
Stanojević, Stanoje, 232
Stansted, 288–9, 291
Starčević, Ante, 14, 20, 21, 73
Starčević, Mile, 15
State Department, 319
State of Slovenes, Croats and Serbs, 36, 40, 61, 87
Stepinac, Archbishop Alojzije, 203, 205
Štip, 118
Stojadinović, Milan: 88, 103n, 118, 153, 154n, 187–8; and the Concordat crisis: 201–2
Stojanović, Ljubomir, 234
Stojnić, Veljo, 312
štokavian (štokavski) dialect, 19–20, 239
Stokes, Gale, 19
Strossmayer, Bishop Josip Juraj, 13, 14, 17, 18, 22–3, 72–3, 197, 210, 247
Štrpce (Shtrpce), 315
Styria (Štajerska), 15, 58
Šubašić, Ivan, 152n
Subotica, 44, 302
Supek, Rudi, 303
Supilo, Frano, 224
Suppan, Arnold, 14
Šušterčič, Ivan, 48
Šušterčič, Admiral Vjekoslav, 48
Šuvar, Stipe, 162, 167n, 282n
Švabe (Swabians), 211
Switzerland, 54, 233, 305
Szeged, 43

Tadić, Ljubomir, 303
Tafa, Haki, 312
Tartalja, Ivo, 226
Tepavac, Mirko, 171n
Tetovo, 118
Thrace, 58
TIGR (Trieste, Istria, Gorizia, Rijeka), nationalist Yugoslav organisation operating in Italy between the world wars, 87–8n
Tijanić, Aleksandar, 303
Timişoara, 44
Timok (river), 229
Tisza, Count Istvàn, 35
Tito, Josip Broz: 7, 77–82, 92, 94, 98, 119, 157, 168, 182–3, 189–90, 241n, 257n, 274, 286, 308–09, 313, 316, 326–7, 329–30; and Serbs: 65–9; and Montenegrins: 65, 126n; and Croats: 78; death of: 82, 252, 272; seen as a 'positive historical figure' in present-day Slovenia: 99n; and Macedonians: 118, 120–1; and Kosovo Albanians: 128–9, 306n, 307, 309, 311–12, 314n; purging of Ranković: 129 (see also Ranković); parallels with King Alexander: 137n (see also Karadjordjević); Yugoslavism of: 158–67, 171–2; declares himself as a Croat: 172; and the crisis of the late 1960s-early 1970s: 173, 271; accepts Kardelj's concept of Yugoslavia: 174–6; defended by Milošević: 180; and Yugoslav economy: 192–4; and the Army: 173, 208, 309; and the 1974 Constitution: 254; see also League of Communists of Yugoslavia (SKJ)
Tito-Stalin split, 121, 129, 189–90, 269, 313
Titograd, see Podgorica
Tommaseo, Nikola, 226
Tomić, Jovan, 232
Topalović, Živko, 216
Toplica, 47